Opening Up the University

Higher Education in Critical Perspective: Practices and Policies

Series editors:
Susan Wright, Aarhus University
Penny Welch, Wolverhampton University

Students and academics, along with university managements, national governments and international organisations are contesting the purpose and practice of 'higher education' around the globe. For many the future is purported to lie in a 'global knowledge economy' in which universities and other higher education institutions are suppliers of the two crucial raw materials: knowledge and graduates. This series critically reflects on this new constellation and on how academics and students find ways to explore new forms of learning and teaching, participate creatively in the organization of their own institutions and engage with policy arguments about the national and international purpose of universities.

Volume 1
Learning Under Neoliberalism:
Ethnographies of Governance in Higher Education
Edited by Susan Brin Hyatt, Boone W. Shear and Susan Wright

Volume 2
Creating a New Public University and Reviving Democracy:
Action Research in Higher Education
Morten Levin and Davydd J. Greenwood

Volume 3
Death of the Public University? Uncertain Futures
for Higher Education in the Knowledge Economy
Edited by Susan Wright and Cris Shore

Volume 4
The Experience of Neoliberal Education
Edited by Bonnie Urciuoli

Volume 5
Opening Up the University: Teaching and Learning with Refugees
Edited by Céline Cantat, Ian M. Cook and Prem Kumar Rajaram

Opening Up the University
Teaching and Learning with Refugees

◆◆◆

Edited by

Céline Cantat, Ian M. Cook and Prem Kumar Rajaram

berghahn
NEW YORK • OXFORD
www.berghahnbooks.com

First published in 2022 by
Berghahn Books
www.berghahnbooks.com

© 2022, 2024 Céline Cantat, Ian M. Cook and Prem Kumar Rajaram
First paperback edition published in 2024

All rights reserved. Except for the quotation of short passages for the purposes of criticism and review, no part of this book may be reproduced in any form or by any means, electronic or mechanical, including photocopying, recording, or any information storage and retrieval system now known or to be invented, without written permission of the publisher.

Library of Congress Cataloging-in-Publication Data

Names: Cantat, Céline, editor. | Cook, Ian M, editor. | Rajaram, Prem Kumar, editor.
Title: Opening Up the University: Teaching and Learning with Refugees / Edited by Céline Cantat, Ian M. Cook and Prem Kumar Rajaram.
Description: New York : Berghahn Books, 2022. | Series: Higher Education in Central Perspective: Practices and Policies; Volume 5 | Includes bibliographical references and index.
Identifiers: LCCN 2021039726 (print) | LCCN 2021039727 (ebook) | ISBN 9781800733114 (hardback) | ISBN 9781800733138 (open access ebook)
Subjects: LCSH: Refugees—Education, Higher. | School improvement programs. | Higher education and state. | Education, Higher—Aims and objectives.
Classification: LCC LC3727 .O64 2022 (print) | LCC LC3727 (ebook) | DDC 371.826/914—dc23/eng/20211012
LC record available at https://lccn.loc.gov/2021039726
LC ebook record available at https://lccn.loc.gov/2021039727

British Library Cataloguing in Publication Data

A catalogue record for this book is available from the British Library

ISBN 978-1-80073-311-4 hardback
ISBN 978-1-80539-326-9 paperback
ISBN 978-1-80073-312-1 epub
ISBN 978-1-80073-313-8 web pdf

https://doi.org/10.3167/9781800733114

The electronic open access publication of *Opening Up the University: Teaching and Learning with Refugees* has been made available under a CC BY-NC-ND 4.0 license as a part of the Berghahn Open Migration and Development Studies initiative.

This work is published subject to a Creative Commons Attribution Noncommercial No Derivatives 4.0 License. The terms of the license can be found at http://creativecommons.org/licenses/by-nc-nd/4.0/. For uses beyond those covered in the license contact Berghahn Books.

*For all of those who have collectively shaped
the Open Learning Initiatives (OLIves)*

Contents

List of Illustrations   x

Acknowledgements   xi

Introduction. Opening Up the University   1
   Céline Cantat, Ian M. Cook and Prem Kumar Rajaram

PART I. ACADEMIC DISPLACEMENTS

Chapter 1. The Refugee Outsider and the Active European Citizen: European Migration and Higher Education Policies and the Production of Belonging and Non-Belonging   31
   Prem Kumar Rajaram

Chapter 2. The Double Bind of Academic Freedom: Reflections from the United Kingdom and Venezuela   51
   Mariya P. Ivancheva

Chapter 3. Rethinking Universities: A Reflection on the University's Role in Fostering Refugees' Inclusion   69
   Rosa Di Stefano and Benedetta Cassani

Chapter 4. The Authoritarian Turn against Academics in Turkey: Can Scholars Still Show Solidarity to Vulnerabilised Groups?   78
   Leyla Safta-Zecheria

Chapter 5. The Politics of University Access and Refugee Higher Education Programmes: Can the Contemporary University Be Opened?   89
   Céline Cantat

PART II. RE-LEARNING TEACHING

Chapter 6. 'Can We Think about How to Improve the World?' Designing Curricula with Refugee Students 111
Mwenza Blell, Josie McLellan, Richard Pettigrew and Tom Sperlinger

Chapter 7. Experts by Experience: The Scope and Limits of Collaborative Pedagogy with Marginalised Asylum Seekers 123
Rubina Jasani, Jack López, Yamusu Nyang, Angie D., Dudu Mango, Rudo Mwoyoweshumba and Shamim Afhsan

Chapter 8. What Happens to a Story? En/countering Imaginative Humanitarian Ethnography in the Classroom 138
Erin Goheen Glanville

Chapter 9. Digital Literacy for Refugees in the United Kingdom 156
Israel Princewill Esenowo

Chapter 10. Insider Views on English Language Pathway Programmes to Australian Universities 164
Victoria Wilson, Homeira Babaei, Merna Dolmai and Suhail Sawa

Chapter 11. Enacting Inclusion and Citizenship through Pedagogical Staff Development 178
Luisa Bunescu

Chapter 12. Focus Pulled to Hungary: Case Study of the OLIve Participatory Video Workshop 192
Klára Trencsényi and Jeremy Braverman

PART III. DEBORDERING THE UNIVERSITY

Chapter 13. Fuck Prestige 209
Ian M. Cook

Chapter 14. Reimagining Language in Higher Education: Engaging with the Linguistic Experiences of Students with Refugee and Asylum Seeker Backgrounds 220
Rachel Burke

Chapter 15. Our Voice 240
   Kutaiba Al Hussein and Akileo Mangeni

Chapter 16. 'Where Are the Refugees?': The Paradox of Asylum in Everyday Institutional Life in the Modern Academy and the Space-Time Banalities of Exception 247
   Kolar Aparna, Olivier Thomas Kramsch and Oumar Kande

Chapter 17. The Importance of the Locality in Opening Universities to Refugee Students 260
   Ester Gallo, Barbara Poggio and Paola Bodio

Chapter 18. Strategies against Everyday Bordering in Universities: The Open Learning Initiatives 275
   Aura Lounasmaa, Erica Masserano, Michelle Harewood and Jessica Oddy

Afterword. Privilege, Plurality, Paradox, Prefiguration: The Challenges of 'Opening Up' 293
   John Clarke

Index 307

Illustrations

Figure 7.1. Training and workshops: the women attended training in the formal setting of university classrooms and creative workshops at the project building. We reflected on working in both settings.   129

Figure 7.2. Transferrable skills: the group experimented with visual methodologies, learning skills in film, photography and zine making.   131

Figure 7.3. Analysis workshops: group analysis of interview and observation data was critical to the peer ethnographic evaluation approach.   132

Figure 7.4. Zine making: Creativity and art making as method flowed more freely when we held workshops in a community setting.   133

Figure 11.1. Example of stimulus material.   184

Figure 12.1. Stills from participants' films, Budapest, 2016. Open Learning Initiative.   197

Figure 12.2. Participants' homework, Budapest, 2017. Open Learning Initiative.   199

Figure 12.3. Role play and shooting exercise, Budapest, 2017. Open Learning Initiative.   201

Acknowledgements

This book is the result of conversations – mostly real, sometimes imagined – with friends, scholars, practitioners and students invested in opening up universities. It is also the result of engagements with people and positions that we disagree with; those contentions have helped shape the ideas in this book. We acknowledge all of them, but here we would like to particularly acknowledge those who have supported, motivated and worked in the writing and production of this volume.

We, the editors, have tried to ensure that this book is collectively wrought, and we would like to thank all the authors for the inspirational work that they have put into making this book what it is.

Kanchi Ganatra was our editorial assistant, and we thank her for her proofreading, manuscript production and patience. We would further like to thank Zainab Shumail for her background research and Cristina-Simona Bangau for her contributions to early discussions about the shape of the volume.

Particular thanks are also due to the participants of the conference 'Publics, Pedagogies and Politics: Refugees and Higher Education in the 21st Century' held at Central European University in Budapest, March 2019. Thanks also go to Marius Jakstas for his initial work on assembling the proceedings.

We would also like to acknowledge our debt as editors of this volume towards all of those who were involved in creating and running OLIve programmes in Budapest and elsewhere, as teachers, staff and volunteers. We thank you for offering conversations, support and inspiring examples of dedicated pedagogic and political work.

The production of the book was assisted with funds from the European Union under the Horizon 2020 Programme, project MigSol, Grant Agreement no. 751866, headed by Celine Cantat. The initial conference was additionally co-funded by the Erasmus+ Social Inclusion project Refugee Education Initiatives, Grant Agreement no. 604544-SOC-IN.

Finally, and perhaps most importantly, we would like to acknowledge the students with whom we have worked and learned. Universities are strange places. They are, in many ways, becoming places in which we feel increasingly uncomfortable working. Original and critical knowledge and learning does not exclusively belong to universities, however, especially not to those who seek to commodify, control and calm it. Against this, learning together with those students whom we were lucky enough to meet through our work has opened up the university for us in myriad ways. We hope that by assembling this book universities can be opened for others too.

INTRODUCTION
Opening Up the University

CÉLINE CANTAT, IAN M. COOK AND PREM KUMAR RAJARAM

◆◆◆

This edited volume reflects on university access for students who have experienced displacement, what the varied responses of higher education to displaced learners can teach us about the boundaries of academic institutions, and how struggles over access for these students may lead to new openings.

In this Introduction, we offer a frame in which to think about the university in relation to the issue of access to higher education for displaced students. We prefer to use the term 'displaced students' or 'students who have experienced displacement' rather than 'refugee' or 'refugee students', as refugee is a legal term, and people are more than their legal status. When we use the term 'refugee', we recognise that it describes a lived political experience that does not require state authorisation. In what follows, we will argue that the university is a site in which the historically contingent relationship between knowledge, higher education and publics materialises and that, in its current form in Europe and elsewhere, this relationship has led to a narrowing of the university. It is narrowed by Eurocentric epistemologies and pedagogies that ignore imperial colonial histories and patriarchal occlusions; narrowed by an increasingly marketised understanding of higher education as a 'sector of the economy'; and narrowed by its focus on the individualised careers of teachers and students. As such, when thinking about the inclusion of current and future students who have experienced displacement, we need an expansive definition of 'university access' that calls for a different politics around admission. We need to understand access as part of a wider drive towards equity, which entails meaningful inclusion, representation and participation in classrooms, at decision-making levels within institutions and society at large. On the basis of the chapters in this volume and our own experiences of trying to create access to university with and for displaced students, we put forward three proposals which we believe may have wider transformative potential for opening up the university: the insistence on education programmes for learners (not humanitarian programmes for 'refugees'); an allowance for disruptive education (not the cultivation of safe learning); and a defunding of university management (opposing the trend spearheaded by anglophone higher education systems to overpay top administrators and thus reclaim money for teaching and learning[1]).

University access and exclusion are experienced, challenged and reworked across at least three different scales: (1) in the classroom; (2) in programmes and institutions; and (3) at the level of the wider social formation. These three scales are not discrete, but interrelated. We find thinking with these scales an analytically useful way to focus on different processes and types of questions, both in this introductory chapter and the ones that follow, as we advance the claim that struggles around the inclusion and exclusion of students who have experienced displacement are important for understanding the contemporary university.

Unfortunately, in recent years, providing access to higher education for displaced students has often been understood as a response to the proclaimed 'crisis' of refugee arrivals in Europe, leading to the conclusion that they have distinct problems requiring separate solutions. National and supranational policy changes and recommendations were introduced as part of government agendas to advance particular notions of 'refugee integration'. Casting 'refugees' as a problem requiring 'integration' legitimises education programmes as interventions aimed at addressing a condition of 'otherness', and remedying this condition by helping 'the refugee' adapt to an extant and unchanged 'Europe' (Rajaram, this volume). As such, governmental actions and sometimes non-state initiatives (such as independent programmes for access to higher education) are susceptible to reproducing certain notions of what 'refugee students' need. Moreover, the crisis-response dialectic is one that, for the most part, fails to challenge deeply embedded exclusionary structures as it operates within short-term horizons.

Education as a 'crisis response' or 'tool for integration' further ignores past and present struggles over access to university. Minority students, including students from racialised groups and students with disabilities alongside women and students from working-class backgrounds, have historically been marginalised from and in universities. Students labelled as 'asylum seekers' or 'refugees' tend also to be subjected to forms of marginalisation based on race, status, class and other factors. Obstacles to entering higher education are sometimes particular to the experiences and situations of displaced students (e.g. a lack of understanding over missing or incomplete paperwork), but they can also be similar to those encountered by other marginalised social groups (e.g. being made to feel as if they do not belong). In this sense, barriers faced by displaced students reflect both the way in which particular statuses such as 'asylum seeker' and 'refugee' are perceived and operationalised within a specific context, and the broader and intersectional social hierarchies – to do with class, race, religion and gender, among others – within which universities function.

Against this, we do not wish to put forward an alternative prescriptive approach to education for displaced learners. Rather, opening up the university for us entails cultivating an openness to complex and messy social realities, challenging how these are filtered to close off the university, allying with struggles outside the university that challenge its boundaries, and finding the time and space to co-learn and co-create in classrooms, in universities and in society at large.

Some of these inclinations can be found in the grassroots initiatives that have been developed in order to further access to higher education for students who have experienced displacement. These were often brought about through the combined efforts of university academics, students and staff, and may reproduce or challenge crisis discourses. These initiatives have also been varied in their approach: they have developed different vocabularies and repertoires to discuss the reasons, motives and objectives of their work; taken formal, informal, alternative and mainstream forms; have been both buoyed and rebuffed by different politics, pedagogies and policies; and have been variously institutionalised or formalised. The initiatives have also, importantly, developed a wide range of reflections on what providing higher education to displaced students means and implies for the university at large, and questioned whether 'refugee education' differs from efforts to include other marginalised social groups. Many have also raised the urgent question of what 'opening up' the university means at a time when powerful structural dynamics change the university locally and globally in ways that often lead to further closure.

In this volume, we put in conversation actors involved in the question of access to higher education for displaced students and those engaged in rethinking the university. This is an attempt at initiating a cross-cutting conversation among groups working on the question of access to higher education for displaced students (policy, activist, learner and academic worlds) who are not in regular and sustained dialogue with each other. For instance, refugee access to higher education is often not thought in relation to pedagogic development, including reform of curricula and teaching, or, for example, in relation to university administrative and governance structures. We are keen to examine collectively what thinking higher education from such a perspective teaches us about the institution of the university as a whole, its complex and intersectional dynamics of inclusion and exclusion, as well as the limitations and shortcomings of its pedagogic practices.

As editors, our drive to initiate this collection comes from a desire to reflect collectively on our experiences as teachers and administrators in education programmes for displaced people in a hostile national, and at times institutional environment. We have been involved in establishing and running the Open Learning Initiative (OLIve) at Central European University (CEU) in Budapest, which started in 2016 and focuses on opening access to higher education for refugees and asylum seekers. In 2018, all OLIve activities were suspended by the university after the Hungarian government passed legislation that appeared to fiscally penalise organisations seen to be helping refugees. The programme's part-time weekend courses have since reopened as a separate private entity, while OLIve faculty restarted the full-time university preparatory programme at Bard College Berlin.

Throughout our work we have been lucky to have active, engaged and critically minded students who continually remind us of the social and pedagogical contexts that both create and restrict opportunity and within which we operate. However, because of the fraught and conflictual circumstances in which our education work operated, we have had little chance to reflect on what we do, or to learn from others who run similar (yet surprisingly different) initiatives. With this in mind, we organised the conference 'Publics, Pedagogies and Policies: Refugees and Higher Education in the 21st Century' in Budapest in March 2019. We did this with a view to inspire and question other groups and individuals who are considering creating their own interventions; to speak to policy makers, scholars and university administrators on specific points relating to the access and success of displaced students in higher education; and to suggest concrete avenues for further action within and beyond existing academic structures. We have worked hard to ensure that the voices of learners who have experienced displacement are given prominence alongside the contributions from scholars and practitioners. For the most part, the focus of this book, and this introduction, is Europe, though some chapters and our discussion take us to the USA and Australia. Despite the geographical focus, we strive to locate our discussion in relation to broader global socio-political contexts in relation to which higher education is framed.

In what follows, we describe the contexts for the book, for the broader issue of opening up the university and for understanding issues that displaced people face when trying to access higher education. We begin by laying out the argument that universities are part of broader social contexts and that their admissions policies and pedagogic practices are reflections of social, political and economic power. We make the case that observing who gets into universities at any given time and place teaches us a lot about the dominant social and political architecture: it tells us what types of people and subjectivities are valued and perceptible and which are not. We argue that for universities to be transformative spaces, there needs to be an impetus to look beyond its imposed boundaries, and to connect our work to mobilisations against other forms of exclusion and marginalisation (from education and from social, political and economic participation) and to struggles to put forward new constellations of the relationship between knowledge, learning and publics. We end with three proposals intended to suggest ways of pushing the boundaries of the university and engaging with these broader social dynamics and struggles, and thereby encouraging transformative openings in the university.

University Borders

The question of whether universities are open or closed has limited analytical, pedagogical and political purchase. The focus should be on the university's borders, that is, the way entry to higher education is governed so that it is open and welcoming to some, imposes an obligation to adapt on more than a few, and outrightly excludes others. These borders apply not only to who is accepted to university, but also what types of knowledge production and curricula are made canonical, what types are tolerated, and what types are entirely dismissed. We see the effects of bordering practices in how value and meaning (positive and negative) are cast on students, knowledge and institutional rules.

In the sense that we refer to it here, opening up the university is a means of calling into question how higher education has been institutionalised in ways that serve larger projects of political and economic power and how this leads to the exclusion or marginalisation of certain populations from the university through pedagogic practices and institutional structures that reinforce and solidify historically contingent expressions of the relationship between knowledge production and publics.

What we teach and learn, how we teach and are taught, and whom we teach and are taught by are questions of moral economy; they reflect how things are valued and for whose interests (Thompson 1968). This leads us to ask: what types of education programmes are legitimate in the modern university? And, as a consequence, what learners and types of learning are imaginable (or not) in a university setting? While there are differences across geographies, how universities teach, what they teach and whom they teach are matters of political, economic and cultural concern.

Two interrelated hegemonic projects – the nation-state and capitalism – have exerted considerable influence over the shaping of contemporary higher education. With the rise of the nation-state and its welfare regimes, and socialist state projects in western and eastern Europe, particularly in the period following the end of the Second World War, there emerged a belief that higher education should be accessible to larger numbers. Higher education was recast as a public good that benefits both the individual and society, with the state responsible for expanding access to the broadest spectrum of students, including those from under-represented groups. The university and the state had an entwined nation-building purpose, with the university 'set at the apex of institutions defining national identity' (Kwiek 2005: 331). This 'nationalisation' of higher education (Neave 2001; Kwiek 2005) was reflected in the development of centralised patterns of validation and the nationalisation of scholars through, for example, the introduction of civil servant status for academics in some countries, hence contributing 'to impress firmly upon the consciousness of academia its role as an emanation of the national wisdom and genius, creativity and interest' (Neave 2001: 30).

Since at least the 1980s, this project has intersected with transformations of capitalism. Under conditions of neoliberalism, the onset of financial deregulation across global markets, the denationalisation of both fixed and financial capital, and the close relationship of the governing class with the economic elite have led to a marketisation of state-building. Market thinking and logics have expanded beyond the strictly economic sphere to inform how public and non-capitalist sectors are organised and managed (Clarke and Newman 2012; Newman and Clarke 2009). The focus is increasingly on mobilising social agents that fit within the ideological and political project of neoliberalism. This interrelation has, in turn, reshaped ideas of the university in ways that institutionalise ideas about economic arrangements, including methods of value extraction and the autonomy of the market (Harvey 2016). The articulation of capitalist and nation- or state-building projects is strongest when the interests of each serve the other and there is sufficient control over the representation of this relationship (in what is taught in schools and universities, for example).

Neoliberal capitalism values specific character traits – individual resilience, responsibility and adaptability (Joseph 2013). This has made education institutions important as cultivators of the right type of subjects, while reproducing an intellectual agenda supportive of the neoliberal political-capitalist project. This can be clearly seen in the narrow conception of education as part of an individual life project, something that makes it very difficult to translate individual concerns into public ones (Giroux 2016), because when university education is seen as part of an individual life career project the purpose of the university narrows (Simionca 2012). Individualised and privatised pressures to succeed can come to dominate issues that might properly be of public concern. The extent and causes of this vary, but the broader lesson to be taken is that attempts to regulate the university – in this case to gear it to assist in the development of market-oriented individual life projects – may be seen as modes of controlling, organising, ordering and orienting the relationship of a 'public' to structures of rule.

Politics of Access

The regulation of access to the university – who is allowed and expected in higher education – thus reflects broader socio-political shifts and ideas of the relation between authorities and publics (Cantat, this volume). Across time, different governing rationales have shaped the politics of university access (Clancy and Goastellec 2007). Before what we have referred to above as the 'nationalisation' of higher education in Europe, only members of dominant social groups were able to access universities (in most of western Europe this meant white, urban, upper-class men, while in other contexts such as the colonies it meant children of local elites). Student selection has thus long reflected which socio-political subjects are valued not only by universities but also by broader social systems, as well as the needs of rulers for administering their territories and governing their populations.

In this sense, developments over the last century have tended to enlarge and massify access in ways that have allowed the inclusion of a more diverse student body into the walls of the university. Social groups previously excluded from higher education, such as women and racialised students, are now supposed to be able to access higher education on the basis of academic merit; formal barriers to entry have officially been abolished. Yet the existence of social inequalities that impact on the extent to which students may access dominant knowledge, resources and norms before entering university is not taken into account. The issue of how different social groups build different *habitus* that result in variegated social and cultural capitals, and how this determines their perceived *merit* and thus their opportunities for higher education, is often overlooked (Bourdieu 1977). Additionally, internal restructuring of higher education systems has reproduced inequality through various mechanisms, such as the development of a private education sector available only to the wealthiest social layers or institutional stratification where elite universities continue to recruit students from the most privileged social backgrounds (Cantat, this volume). The increasingly dominant neoliberal academic culture – whereby all tasks and outputs are increasingly quantified and assessed through auditing and ranking in order to classify institutions and academics in relation to one another – further accentuates this situation (Cook, this volume).

Because they are seen as spaces fostering meritocracy, contemporary universities are important ways of cultivating consent to dominant arrangements of the political and the economic, including the exclusions and marginalisations those involve. The key slogan is that those who deserve to will get in. At its most convincing, this discourse can focus attention on the procedure, the entry assessment and the individual, meritorious acquisition of credentials and qualifications that allow entry. This means that less attention may be paid to the way in which qualification acquisition is skewed against many, as well as to the way in which the collection of qualifications reinforces and authorises specific political and economic arrangements. It is in this sense that the university is an instrument of governance: education fosters life trajectories that seem to serve the economic and political interests of a ruling class (Freire 1970; hooks 1994). Instruments of governance are not of course simply repressive: the massification of the university has meant access to these 'life trajectories' (market-oriented or otherwise) for many individuals, including segments of the working classes at universities in Europe.

Questions of access and inclusion are, of course, especially relevant for displaced students. The aforementioned process of massification has meant that, to varying extents and under diverging conditions, formal access to some type of higher education is now available for (almost) all social groups in most of Europe. However, this is not the case for many potential students who have received or are seeking asylum. Displaced people constitute one of the few social groups that can find access to higher education blocked on the basis of their administrative status. Concretely, asylum-seeking and refugee students' access is determined in large part by national configurations and traditions: within the European Union, the possibility of studying for people holding different forms of documentation differs from one country to another. As Rosa Di Stefano and Benedetta Cassani detail in their chapter:

> The incorporation of refugees and asylum seekers into higher education is approached at different degrees across Europe and only a few countries have adopted specific strrategies at national or regional level to facilitate refugee access into universities . . . As a result, in many cases support to refugees has been left to the action of individual institutions.

Beyond access policies at the national, federal or institutional levels, assessing the effective possibility for displaced students to enter university requires examining how these policies intersect with migration frameworks and welfare provision in different places of residence (Sontag 2019). For instance, in Germany, asylum seekers must reside within a particular Land to which they are assigned upon arrival, which reduces opportunity for university study. In France, many newly recognised refugees receive the RSA (*revenu de solidarité active*), which provides a (minimal) revenue for unemployed or underemployed people. Yet students are officially not eligible for the RSA, meaning that registering at university would effectively deprive prospective students with refugee status of their main and often only source of income.

Therefore, in the case of displaced students, the issue of formal access intersects not only with the racialised, gendered and classed social hierarchies that structure societies in their new countries of residence, but also with migration law and welfare systems. This often leads to these students facing situations that are not easily comprehended by the administrative structures and bureaucracies of higher education institutions, which can result in their de facto exclusion from university, even in cases where formal access would be possible. Admission procedures can thus become insurmountable obstacles for people in administrative and legal situations that do not fit within the understanding of institutions. Besides, as the literature on street-level bureaucrats has amply demonstrated regarding asylum procedures (Graham 2002; Lipsky 2010; Bhatia 2020), refugees tend to be more vulnerable to arbitrary and discretionary practices on the part of individual administrators: such practices may work towards performing exclusion or supporting inclusion, depending on the particular person in charge of a university application (Wilson, Babaei, Dolmai and Sawa, this volume; Cantat, this volume). As we have noted, inclusion can depend on the subjective interplay and encounter between representatives of structural power and displaced people. It is largely in response to such situations that many of the initiatives described in this book arose as grassroots efforts within university structures aiming to address the specific difficulties faced by displaced students.

The Purposes of Higher Education

Opening up the university in a more radical sense therefore requires moving beyond individualising approaches and rethinking the relations between knowledge, higher education and publics. One key way to approach these relations is to call into question and expand the purposes of higher education. For us, to open up the university is to reflect on the democratic possibilities that rethinking the purposes of the university can bring. This means parsing out 'the university' into its components and reconsidering the articulations of the moral to the political and the economic (Thompson 1968; Clarke and Newman 2012). Opening up the university in the sense that we understand it here is a project of radical democracy centred on the understanding that the control of knowledge production and learning in universities is fundamental to the durability and dominance of political and economic architectures (Kmak and Björklund 2021).

In an expansive understanding of opening up the university, inclusion goes beyond formal access to the university: it is also about the possibility for those within the university to be represented through the knowledges that are taught and valued, to participate through classroom practices that cultivate horizontality and embrace differences, and to be included via reflexive approaches that contest the exclusionary dynamics that persist within the university. This requires us to acknowledge the tension between the idea of the university as a space of learning and knowledge-making whose boundaries are not pre-set and the capacity of the state and market to make higher education a constitutive part of hegemonic projects. The pressure to translate dominant hegemonic moral economies (Thompson 1968 into the site of the university operates at multiple levels: it feeds into and from wider processes of social formation, forms institutional structures and shapes classroom experiences.

At the scale of the wider social formation, closures emanate from the exclusion or marginalisation of the social presence of subaltern groups. These groups have been institutionally misrepresented or made outrightly invisible in the curation of social reality. Consequently, they have been overlooked in the articulation of legitimate knowledge and in the moral economy of social, political and economic institutions and arrangements. Put another way, the experiences of large groups of people have been devalued or disregarded in ways that allow a particular situated knowledge to be presented as universal. This rendition of social reality on the basis of dominant knowledge produces epistemological hierarchies whereby relations of power (and the positions of privilege that ensue) are naturalised. This critique is not new; it has been made by a number of feminist, Marxist and postcolonial scholars. The derogation or delegitimation of other ways of knowing and other experiences is the building block of an instrumentalising and universalising mode of knowing, which is 'European' to postcolonial scholars, bourgeois to Marxist thinking, and patriarchal or phallocentric to feminist theory (Dussel 1993; Tuhiwai Smith 1999; McClintock 1995). Despite these longstanding critiques, it is remarkable how occlusions continue to come to light.

Addressing this requires moving away from the obvious binary – the excluded versus the included – and towards an account of the intersectional and multidimensional nature of power and its repressions. Intersectional feminist theory has pointed to the ways in which marginalisation and repression occur in multiple ways, with class, gender and race intertwining (Crenshaw 1991). Other social features such as religious belief, sexual orientation or perceived physical ability, for instance, also play a role. The capacity of dominant forms of power to parse out the multidimensionality of the oppression on which it relies and concede gains to specific groups on the basis of their race, gender or class is an important means of maintaining control. In the university, the consequence is the validation of curricula within which a number of people do not see their experiences or find a basis for articulating their knowledge, or, if it is referenced, it is often through a tokenistic nod or the incorporation of classes on feminist or postcolonial thinking within a wider syllabus that reinforces the canon. All this produces higher education institutions that regulate access through the demand that people – including postcolonial migrants displaced by imperial violence, and from whom knowledge, artefacts, objects and more have been appropriated – adapt to dominant ways of thinking and knowing and of academic practice.

Struggles against such large-scale forces may seem daunting or, for some, not best-addressed through thinking at the scale of the institution. When it comes to challenging such closures, such as with the call for 'decolonising the university' (Bhambra, Gebrial and Nişancıoğlu 2018), we want to emphasise that the university is but one site in which this form of repressive power and knowledge plays out, and probably not even the most important. As such, the university is not necessarily a privileged place for anti-imperialist practices, for intersectional interventions into the production of power or the production and dissemination of decolonial knowledges (hooks 1994; Freire 1970). Furthermore, it is important to highlight how the increased individualisation and marketisation of higher education leads to valuing (including in a monetary sense) Western higher education over other forms of knowledge.

Expensive programmes are actively marketed at students from outside Europe with the promise of elite advancement. However, perhaps the most telling consequence is that what underpins and legitimises these knowledge claims – a belief that mastery of this way of thinking will lead to attainable progress and a capacity to know and understand social and natural reality in ever greater depth – is concealed. One result is a goal- or destination-oriented learning and education system that propels the student forward: education is judged by this endpoint rather than the means towards that goal (and the violences and silencing that are a part of the process) (Azoulay 2019). Overall, this contributes to a university system that appears daunting for many groups, including many displaced people. The sense of comfort and certainty in their aims and purposes, and of the inherent superiority of their knowledge claims, has led to Western universities naturalising entry criteria, curricula and pedagogic practices that either obstruct access or make it dependent on the adequate performance, or mimicry, of pre-existing norms and beliefs about knowledge.

To push back against this at the level of the institution or programme is to strive to create a different form of learning environment, one with less certainty about what it will do to students and where it will take them. Ingold (2018), drawing heavily on John Dewey (1916), argues that education should not be instilling knowledge (a 'stilling in') but rather an intellectual discovery (a 'leading out'), similar to Freire's (1970) argument against an education system where students passively 'bank-in' received knowledge. Beginning from the point that we are all different (through experience, education or otherwise), Ingold calls for an education based on communication, where teachers and students alike attempt to find the possibility of an accord by working with and through difference. On an institutional level, this flies against the dominant forms of programme design we see in most European universities in which codified sets of knowledge are to be acquired. This links back to the intersectional and postcolonial critique which points to how dominant knowledge denies the legitimacy of other ways of knowing (Lorde 1984). This confines 'alternative' forms of knowing to 'informal' spaces, ultimately enforcing boundaries around the university, and preventing its engagement with other struggles around the relation of learning, knowledge and publics.

On a classroom level, this necessitates that students and teachers are open to changing their views and understandings as they engage in communication and, consequently, such a learning can be a transformative experience for all. Fundamentally, and thinking explicitly about displaced learners, this means a radical acceptance of difference. However, 'difference' is often appropriated by universities through a rhetoric of 'multiculturalism', occluding the histories of conflict and animosity through which 'difference' and hierarchies of knowledge have arisen and privileging the most visible markers of difference (e.g. race or ethnicity). As such, transforming classrooms into communicative spaces requires an awareness of social hierarchies that bleed into the university and the classroom and that can clamp down on expression, often of those who speak differently and who reference subaltern histories, identities, cultures or ways of knowing (Freire 1970; hooks 1994). Individuals are not isolated actors but are the subjects of global and local histories of conflict and antagonism that have institutionalised material opportunity and discursive authority for some and subjugation for others. Democratic education, education for democracy, would then be centred on an awareness of the historical constitution of inequality and how individuals represent broader populations who occupy different positions in a social formation.

And yet, even as we hold these desires for difference-embracing universities close to our hearts when we design programmes with and for displaced learners, we are reminded of why, for many, education is an instrument to remake one's life in a new and often hostile country. We can discuss radical, critical social theory until we are blue in the face, but it does not help those labelled 'refugees' to find a better job in the short term, to feel self-worth in the vulnerable years following arrival in a new country, or to feel as if their horizons have opened up. This is, in part, a question of time – of slow-moving academics and academic structures, and the urgent immediacy of students' desire to learn, and sometimes to use that learning instrumentally. This does not entail a rejection of a desire for transformation, but rather means that wider projects of fostering inclusion and difference must run concurrently with the expressed needs of those students enrolled, or with the potential to enrol, in education programmes. To some extent, we must live with the tensions and contradictions this produces.

Making Openings Transformative

Our quest to foster transformative openings in the university is based on an understanding of how universities and higher education are part of broader social dynamics. We thus strive to move away from the bourgeois, patriarchal and imperial-tinged self-representation of the university as an isolated and expansive centre of knowledge production. Rather, we acknowledge the social imbrication of the university and assert that its transformation must be allied to the struggle against other practices of power, inequality and injustice in society. People in universities have often been reticent in forming transformative alliances beyond the institution, but we assert that it is folly to pursue transformative change solely from 'inside' the university; indeed, there is no 'inside' within the university in splendid isolation from an 'outside'. Borders between inside and outside are akin to a Moebius strip: processes, relations and connections interweave and cross-connect between 'inside' and 'outside' in ways that make dichotomies analytically, socially and politically problematic (Bigo and Walker 2007).

We welcome practical proposals that universities along with regional, national and supra-national higher education areas could implement to better allow students who have experienced displacement to access universities in an equitable way. These include help with processing paperwork (especially around admissions), better coordination with local social service agencies, flexible solutions to accreditation hurdles (e.g. around transfer of credits from previous study), an understanding of the need for help with living costs (Fourier et al. 2017; Streitwieser and Unangst 2018), proactively reaching out to such groups with information about any non-traditional entry routes, offering specialised advice and guidance for these potential students, and creating taster or bridging courses for displaced learners (Hannah 1999).

However, moving beyond these suggestions, we argue that opening up the university is about questioning the narrowing of the purpose of higher education to the pursuit of individualised and privatised life projects. It is about considering the diversity of publics whose access to the production of learning and knowledge can transform democratic relations. What would things look like if the university were to step away from its role as an instrument of governance, a conduit to manufacture consent of 'a public' to hegemonic projects of state and capital? How may we encourage the university in the sense defended by Giroux (2016), as a site crucial in producing a public space of dissension and critique vital for democracy? With this in mind, we offer three proposals, fleshed out below, that could lead to a transformative opening up of the university.

Proposal one: reconceptualise initiatives for displaced learners so they are seen not as humanitarian programmes by (or even for!) universities, but rather as educational, intellectual initiatives built on foundations of solidarity and respect. *Create education programmes for learners!*

Proposal two: create difference-embracing learning environments within which those who have experienced displacement do not feel the need to integrate, be grateful or perform the 'good refugee', but rather classrooms and institutions from within which learners can challenge, destabilise and disrupt the academic status quo. *Allow for disruptive education!*

Proposal three: recognise that programmes for displaced learners have real material costs that must be secured for longer than a typical project cycle and that most university managers, while multiplying themselves and their salaries, are unwilling or unable to fund transformative academic programmes. *Defund the university management!*

Create Education Programmes for Learners

We need academic programmes for humans, and not humanitarian programmes for universities. It would be unfair to suggest that some within universities only create 'refugee programmes' to feel good about themselves or to promote an institution. While certainly this might be the case – and indeed we came across such attitudes in our experience of helping run programmes for displaced learners – such extremes are part of a much deeper-rooted sense of helping the needy foreign other, especially in European cultures and pointing to the imperial and colonial nature of benevolent help (Gilbert and Tiffin 2008; Malkki 1996). It is also a way of domesticating difference, bringing 'diversity' into the university in ways that shear it of its broader social and political contexts (hooks 1994). Education programmes for learners in our sense place emphasis on the social worlds of would-be students, bringing these into the classroom, and placing them in conversation and in opposition to restrictive and destination-driven education systems.

Erin Goheen Glanville's chapter in this volume can provide us with a useful starting point to rethink the stories we ask or do not ask of displaced learners and, related to this, the stories universities like to tell about themselves. The dominant ways of demanding stories of displaced learners, we argue, are ways of containing social contexts and controlling potential disruption. Thinking about how to teach the 'refugee story' as it appears in literature, Glanville rails against an imaginative 'humanitarian ethnography', in which the readers behave as anthropologists uncovering the 'refugee experience' or 'refugee culture' and quickly search for solutions to the problems faced by refugees. She argues:

> Many students arrive in a classroom already primed to commit humanitarian ethnography against stories. In addition to overriding the lifeworld of the story, this can be an alienating and diminishing experience for students with correlative experiences. Reading refugee stories as imaginative humanitarian ethnography layers the complexity of global politics, onto a personal sense of responsibility to strangers, onto the emotional impact of reading about violence, onto assumptions about human rights and equality, onto a growing knowledge of migration in unmanageable scope. Discussions then about what should be done can turn to despair and short circuit more nuanced analysis.

Telling one's story does not end with the asylum process; it becomes an ingrained and readable part of the person to be deployed as they negotiate and justify access in society. The well-meaning charity worker, humanitarian volunteer or caring teacher who asks for a story does not, of course, ask for a story in the same way as an officer deciding on the fate of an asylum claim, but the stories are nevertheless often asked for and dutifully performed. As one student who was enrolled in two different OLIve programmes in Budapest put it, 'I know one type of white person and another type of white person and what story I need to give to this one and which one to that one'.

In their introduction to *Mistrusting Refugees* (1995: 1), Daniel and Knudsen write: 'from its inception the experience of a refugee puts trust on trial. The refugee mistrusts and is mistrusted'. The authors argue that trust is a 'habitus', a culturally constituted social world. People are displaced because one social world becomes un-constituted, and the process of understanding and entering into another – differently constituted – social world is difficult, not least because displaced people can be reduced to people who tell stories about themselves, to be validated by those in positions of power. This is not to suggest that the experiences of people who have experienced displacement should not be taken into account in university programmes. We suggest, though, that rather than focusing on desperate stories, programmes should be aware of social contexts common to displaced people. Programmes might include trauma-related counselling, or classes on understanding often impenetrable higher education systems. One particular pertinent area is digital literacy because, as Israel Princewill Esenowo argues in this volume, 'while digital exclusion is a broad problem affecting different social groups, displaced learners are confronted with particular forms of digital exclusion, rooted in global and local inequalities in access to and use of digital technology'.

Importantly, these issues – and many others that might arise – relate to the special educational or bureaucratic needs of learners due to particular constellations of marginalities, which may or may not relate to the learners having experienced displacement (they may also relate to gendered, classed or other marginalities); they do not require educators to have the full details of hardships and turmoil experienced either in the students' home countries or on their journeys. Other stories, stories that university management and communications teams often feel the need to tell, are those relating how they 'helped refugees' and, in these instances, programmes or initiatives can shift from being 'for the refugees' to being for the institution. It is, of course, often a game those running programmes for displaced learners have to play: keep the university administration happy enough by allowing them to proudly display their civic credentials, but maintain the integrity of programmes and initiatives as places of education not humanitarianism.

One potential way of overcoming pulls towards paternalistic othering is to build relationships of solidarity (Cantat, this volume). For a start, this involves recognising that many people – to greater or lesser degrees depending on a multitude of circumstances – may find themselves or their families in variously vulnerable, marginalised or excluded positions vis-à-vis education. We must also accept that solidarity may create uncomfortable and unforeseen circumstances that need to be worked through, and thus may take more time and effort than top-down 'gifts' of education to 'the needy'. However, as Leyla Safta-Zecheria reminds us in her chapter in this volume, finding the opportunity for solidarity is increasingly complex as academic freedom comes under attack from regimes who see higher education as a threat to their authority (as we witness in Hungary, Turkey, India and elsewhere). This increases the vulnerability of academics, and while this potentially increases the scope for politicisation and thus solidarity, it also curtails their ability to act both inside and outside the classroom.

Allow for Disruptive Education

We need to shake the image of the 'good refugee' with her meek, mild and grateful presence from the minds of those running, approving or planning to set up 'refugee education' programmes or initiatives. This paternalistic view of displaced learners not only removes the dignity of actual or potential students, but it also intellectually limits the growth of learners as it can pre-define what they should learn and what they should do with that knowledge.

Moreover, as Kolar Aparna, Olivier Kramsch and Oumar Kande note in their chapter in this volume, it is as the *subject* of research, holders of authentic experience to be mined by the non-migrant researcher, that displaced people are visible in universities, not as students or scholars (see also Wilson, Babaei, Dolmai and Sawa, this volume). As they argue, 'this desire to see the Other at arm's length while operating within institutions that deny relations of knowledge production on an equal footing produces a partial inclusion (i.e. we want to see you and hear you as different and therefore cannot accept you as Us (those who study you))'.

There are, however, ways in which universities can create learning environments open to difference. This is vital if we are to consider not only whose right to be in the classroom, university or country is recognised, but also whose critique is valued, and, building on this, who can turn specific and local critiques into more general critiques of their education environment and society. For example, as Klára Trencsényi and Jeremy Braverman (this volume) argue from their experience running a participatory filmmaking course in Hungary, not only can such courses offer the chance to learn a creative skill, but also 'lay the foundation for a documentary film that would challenge the majority Hungarian (and European) society's view on refugees . . . [becoming potentially] conscious producers of their own image in the mainstream media'.

Dangerous learners armed with critical thinking skills are constrained by the injunction to express themselves in specific ways. As Victoria Wilson, Homeira Babaei, Merna Dolmai and Suhail Sawa argue in this volume, language plays a role 'as a means to exercise agency, participate in society, and to build meaningful careers that meet their aspirations and abilities' and yet many state-run and private programmes fail to teach anything more than basic communication, with students' voices left unheard (see also Baker and Dantas 2018). One way in which universities could reduce the importance of this barrier and help realise the potential of their learners would be to develop flexible approaches to learning with and through the diversity of students' skills, experience, knowledge and potential. Rachel Burke (this volume), in making the case for recognising and responding to linguistic strengths of students who have experienced displacement, suggests that such a 'reimagining of linguistic practices' within higher education provides an opportunity to 'transform "mainstream" instructional practices in higher education . . . [because] genuinely engaging with the specific yet wide-ranging language/literacy resources of students with refugee and asylum seeker experiences provides an opportunity to better acknowledge and value all diverse linguistic repertoires. . .'.

What would it mean to open up the university and classroom in a way in which the end point is unclear and in which the teacher and students together explore and learn and grow as they move in and through topics, methods, research and ideas? Rubina Jasani, Jack López, Yamusu Nyang, Angie D., Dudu Mango, Rudo Mwoyoweshumba and Shamim Afhsan detail in their chapter a project they realised built on both 'self-advocacy activism' and 'pedagogy of peer ethnographic practice'. By allowing the agenda to be driven by the participants/students and not the academics (and thus the dominant narratives within their discipline), the two anthropologists in the project found the process to be 'chaotic' in a way that was not unlike the students' lives, but pushed themselves to let go of academic perfectionism and unpack the surprises that came their way. They argue that, 'through embracing the immediacy of the present in the classroom we see how teaching and learning are both constantly taking place and under revision. This immediacy and exchange of world knowledge in the few hours a month we had to work together forces an intense practice of critical thinking unconstrained by academic norms'. Such a move also destabilises hierarchies of expertise. It requires validation of knowledge and expertise gained outside the university.

In a similar vein, Mwenza Blell, Josie McLellan, Richard Pettigrew and Tom Sperlinger explore in their chapter the designing of curricula with (rather than for) 'refugee students'. This means recognising the knowledge of such students, including those knowledges developed through their experiences of mobility and survival, rather than starting from the position of recognising what the students are 'lacking' and thus must be taught. While such student-centred freedom might be possible in courses and programmes that take place outside the formal constraints of the university – as it allows pedagogical, financial and structural freedom – it becomes much more difficult to institute on a wider level. Indeed, they ask, 'How can institutions create capacity to respond to the intersections of race, gender and class, which are often experienced at their most acute by students themselves (or those unable to become students)? How can they enable, rather than constraining, their teaching staff who have the "will" to undertake such work?'. This is a core concern of this volume: how might universities become open to the complex social worlds outside?

Luisa Bunescu argues in this volume that teachers should be given both the opportunities and incentives to learn about how they understand the classroom, the learning environment and their role within it. More specifically, in relation to students with refugee or asylum seeker backgrounds, she suggests this means a rethinking of 'inclusion' and 'citizenship' beyond their formal senses, so that teachers understand how inclusion and citizenship are enacted, enclosed and reflected upon in an educational setting.

However, universities do not, for the most part, allow for expensive, non-prestige-granting, labour-intensive programmes to function in ways that live up to their promise. As Ian M. Cook argues in this volume, universities and individual scholars are trapped within performative and quantifiable displays of prestige, with programmes for displaced learners struggling to assert value. Bluntly put, within the logic of countable prestige, why should institutions or scholars 'waste' their time on programmes for learners who have experienced displacement when that work does not translate into something usable for tenure promotions, job applications or university rankings?

Defund the Management

In some Western/Global North institutions, especially in the anglophone sphere, university management has become an increasingly elite collection of individuals, paid such high amounts that their salaries are often the focus of student protest or newspaper headlines. While this is not necessarily the case (yet) in many European public higher education systems, the tendency is nonetheless becoming evident in different national contexts, for example with the expansion of private provision and the spread of neoliberal management practices. The growth of an administrative and essentially non-productive class occupying elite and highly paid positions is not unique to the university and speaks to wider trends in the global economy oriented towards the service sector and the consequent cultivation and the (over) valuation of skills and rationalities to do with management and administration (Graeber 2018a). Depressingly, as Ginsberg (2011) notes, these newly emerging managers have little experience as faculty, and see the expansion of their administrative power and control as key to wresting control of the university away from scholars. As Shore and Wright (2017: 8) argue, 'today, rather than being treated as core members of a professional community, academics are constantly being told by managers and senior administrators what "the university" expects of them, as if they were somehow peripheral or subordinate to "the university"'. The impact of this is felt differently depending on positionality within the university. OLIve at CEU, where the three of us have worked, relies principally on the work of short-term and precariously contracted staff to direct education programmes and supervise students, while only those seen as 'valuable assets' by the university management (i.e. those with a permanent or tenure track contract) were regularly invited to strategic university-level discussions about the programme or the university. Making faculty 'assets' is also problematic in another sense: teachers (and students) become 'assets' (valued capital) only if the university operates in a market-oriented fashion, assessing and instrumentalising the value of its held capital (see Cook, this volume).

University administration seems to take on an end in itself: a powerful class has instituted itself across universities and bears resemblance to an elite takeover of a complex socially embedded institution for its own enrichment. Certainly, with the amount spent on administration in universities, often disproportionate to anything else in the budget, the impression is of a university existing not to further learning and education (much less transform these) but to legitimise bullshit jobs (Graeber 2018b). Budget decisions are made by this administrative class by and large, and the consequence is that there is a tendency for funds to be spent on narrow initiatives (or on large salaries) meaningful to a class of administrators (who often come from the corporate world). Those that are not read as inherently important, such as specialised programmes for displaced learners, as well as precarious staff members within the institution, struggle and fight on a regular basis not just for funding but also for visibility. More generally, system-wide development and initiatives are often disavowed in favour of top-heavy growth.

At a bare minimum, university leaders should be able to uphold academic freedom in its most simply understood liberal formation – freedom from state interference or outside political pressure. However, as Aura Lounasmaa, Erica Masserano, Michelle Harewood and Jessica Oddy argue in this volume, in the UK context, university leadership has consistently failed to shield students from the hostile anti-migrant political environment. In the UK, university staff must report on international students, as the state wants to ensure students really are studying at the university and not 'abusing' their visa. The authors note that 'the same university may be policing the immigration status of its students and staff and providing support for those caught in the immigration system. . .'. In Hungary, anti-migration legislation in 2018 resulted in CEU leadership choosing to close its refugee education programme and a refugee-related research project, as they were scared that a new tax on organisations being seen to help migrants would be applied (meanwhile nearly all civil society organisations who would also fall under the law continued their operations and are yet to pay any tax at all).

Running a university is political work. As Ester Gallo, Barbara Poggio and Paola Bodio argue (this volume), the politics of a particular university's locality is of central importance when it comes to setting up and running programmes for displaced learners because 'universities do not operate in a vacuum but have been integral to the history, socio-economic development and cultural outlook of local urban environments . . . [thus] the opening of universities to displaced students constitutes a process that goes beyond the physical and intangible borders of academic institutions to reflect their broader embeddedness'.

If, as is often the case, university leaderships fail to protect students and staff from even these very clear breaches of academic freedom, how might they respond to more insidious and harder-to-counteract enclosures on freedom, such as those from market forces? As Mariya P. Ivancheva argues in this volume, the marketisation of higher education in the UK has confined freedoms related to teaching, research and service. She writes that 'academics become less free in their pursuit of knowledge, tied by requirements of fundraising and publication peer-reviews that disadvantage "controversial", "daring" or even interdisciplinary ideas and research. Research and teaching are pitted against each other while done by two reserve armies: researchers "lucky" to have publications under the publish-or-perish ideal; and teaching-only faculty invisible and fearful of losing even their insecure low wages. Research, teaching and service are put to serve businesses and prioritise profit to scholarship'. In marketised systems where everything is collated and measured through ever deepening circles of competition (between individuals and between institutions), running programmes for displaced learners becomes increasingly difficult for staff as their labour in these programmes is not 'worth' enough according to the matrices set up by state bodies and enforced by university leadership. A concrete example of how university management fails refugee education programmes by blocking teacher continuity is given by Mwenza Blell in her co-authored piece in this volume. She reflects on how she was only allowed to teach within an education programme for displaced learners because she faced a period of underemployment. Once her hours increased, her line manager refused to allow her to continue in the programme, even when she volunteered to do it in her own time.

Education programmes for vulnerable communities do cost money, and there is little use in pretending they do not (Danny, Santina and Grossman 2008). As such, we must further fight the costing of access programmes when the cheaper option of online teaching is growing apace across higher education, in part (but only in part) due to the pandemic (Ivancheva 2020). Research has shown how online courses for displaced learners face significant challenges, including low completion rates, questioning online education as a 'solution' for 'refugee students' (Halkic and Arnold 2019). Another facet of increased marketisation of higher education is the cycles of grant writing and funding applications that render many different academic practices precarious, and often access programmes are no different. Against this, we argue management should adopt longer-term perspectives for refugee education programmes that use evidence-based approaches when evaluating and developing initiatives (Streitwieser et al. 2019).

The problem for university leadership when they, on the one hand, treat pioneering access programmes as secondary and thus liable to be costed against other priorities and, on the other hand, are paid extortionate salaries, is that it is possible to work out how many education programmes an institution could run for the cost of one rector or vice-chancellor. Or, if we take the market logic to its stupefying extreme (as, for instance, the UK higher education sector does year on year), then we could imagine how many programmes we could run for displaced learners if we hired a rector only half as good as the one we have.

Opening Up This Book

Opening up the university is not a matter of cutting new doors in an abstract edifice. Rather, it is to understand the historical-cultural contexts that account for the emergence of a specific relationship between learning, knowledge and publics at a specific time and place and to work on reinvigorating such relationships in the face of dominant projects. The 'university' is the point of analysis that arises from this relationship and one that guides this collection of chapters.

Opening up the university is also a process. 'Opening' is distinct from 'openness', which is a static moral category that ignores the attempted closures pushed through actors working within the paradigms of hegemonic projects and the histories and politics of attempted openings, false openings and empty gestures. It is vital to challenge claims of openness by liberal institutions that engage in a series of closures through processes of marketisation, patronising humanitarianism, elitism, exceptionalism, and self-aggrandising claims about their role in society. It is our hope that this volume does this through both concrete case studies and wide reflexive pieces.

Opening up the university is also to focus on the tensions between the university as a space of learning and public engagement and the cultivation of higher education as a project of the state and market seeking to entrench their authority and mythos and reproduce functionaries. By thinking through this constellation from the perspective of students who experienced displacement and too often fall in the gaps of higher education systems, the chapters, taken together, speak both to the specificities of refugees' access to the university and make broader points about the embeddedness of the university in socio-political contexts that shape and regulate entry and content.

This is done, across three parts. Part I, Academic Displacements, sets some of the key contexts within which programmes or initiatives for displaced students take place: policy landscapes, struggles for academic freedom, attempts at solidarity. Part II, Re-learning Teaching, hones in on how working with and for students who have experienced displacement pushes educators and associated bodies to rethink their pedagogical practice in new and often exciting ways. Finally, Part III, Debordering the University, explores the limits of the contemporary university and the linkages made beyond it. Some of the chapters focus more on the wider social formation (1, 2, 4, 10, 17, 18), some more on the institutions of higher education (3, 5, 11, 13, 14, 15, 16) and some more on the classroom (6, 7, 8, 9, 12), but together we think they provide an important starting point for an ongoing struggle to open up the university and foster the access and success of displaced learners.

We refuse any claim to completeness and aim instead to foster conversation and critical debate. In reading these chapters together, we hope it will engender thoughts of what it might mean to co-create a university that does not know its future; to build a university that welcomes the dangerous, unmanageable and learner-centric intellectual and educational promise contained within such a non-destination-orientated approach to higher education; and to be part of a university unafraid of what lies beyond its borders.

◆

Céline Cantat holds a PhD in Refugee Studies from the Centre for Research on Migration, Refugees and Belonging at the University of East London and is currently a Research Fellow at Sciences Po Paris. Previously, Céline worked at the CEU in Budapest where she conducted project MIGSOL: Migration Solidarity and Acts of Citizenship along the Balkan Route and worked as teacher and academic director for CEU's OLIve programmes. Her research interests include migration solidarity, globalisation and migration, racism and exclusion in Europe, state formation and dynamics of mass displacement.

Ian M. Cook (Central European University, Budapest) is an anthropologist who works on urban change, environmental (in)justice, podcasting and opening up the university.

Prem Kumar Rajaram is Professor of Sociology and Social Anthropology at Central European University and head of the OLIve unit at the same university. He works on issues to do with race, capitalism and displacement in historical and contemporary perspective.

Note

1. In many national contexts, university management are not disproportionately paid. However, we believe this is an increasingly global trend linked to the neoliberalisation of higher education.

References

Alatas, S.F. 2003. 'Academic Dependency and the Global Division of Labour in the Social Sciences', *Current Sociology* 51(6): 599–613.
Azoulay, A.A. 2019. *Potential History: Unlearning Imperialism*. London: Verso.
Baker, S., and J. Dantas. 2018. 'Universities Need to Do More to Support Refugee Students', *The Conversation*, 29 May. https://theconversation.com/universities-need-to-do-more-to-support-refugee-students-97185.
Ball, S.J. 2012. 'Performativity, Commodification and Commitment: An I-Spy Guide to the Neoliberal University', *British Journal of Educational Studies* 60(1): 17–28.

Bhambra, G.K., D. Gebrial and K. Nişancıoğlu. 2018. 'Introduction: Decolonising the University?', in G.K. Bhambra, D. Gebrial and K. Nişancıoğlu (eds), *Decolonising the University*. London: Pluto Press.

Bhatia, M. 2020. 'The Permission to Be Cruel: Street-Level Bureaucrats and Harms against People Seeking Asylum', *Critical Criminology* 28(1): 277–92.

Bigo, D., and R.B.J. Walker. 2007. 'Political Sociology and the Problem of the International', *Millennium: Journal of International Studies* 35(3): 725–39.

Bourdieu, P. 1977. *Outline of a Theory of Practice*. Cambridge: Cambridge University Press.

Bresser-Pereira, L.C. 2018. *Rentier-Finance Capitalism*. Sao Paolo School of Economics, Working Paper 477. https://bibliotecadigital.fgv.br/dspace/bitstream/handle/10438/23922/TD%20477-Luiz%20Carlos%20Bresser%20Pereira.pdf?sequence=1&isAllowed=y.

Christophers, B. 2019. 'The Problem of Rent', *Critical Historical Studies* 6(2): 303–23.

Christophers, B. 2020. 'The PPE Debacle Shows What Britain Is Built On: Rentier Capitalism', *The Guardian*, 12 August.

Clancy, P., and G. Goastellec. 2007. 'Exploring Access and Equity in Higher Education: Policy and Performance in a Comparative Perspective', *Higher Education Quarterly* 61(2): 136–54.

Clarke, J., and J. Newman. 2012. 'The Alchemy of Austerity', *Critical Social Policy* 32(3): 299–319.

Crea, T.M. 2016. 'Refugee Higher Education: Contextual Challenges and Implications for Program Design, Delivery, and Accompaniment', *International Journal of Educational Development* 46: 12–22.

Crea, T.M., and M. McFarland. 2015. 'Higher Education for Refugees: Lessons from a 4-Year Pilot Project', *International Review of Education* 61 235–45.

Crenshaw, K. 1991. 'Mapping the Margins: Intersectionality, Identity Politics, and Violence against Women of Color', *Stanford Law Review* 43(6): 1241–99.

Daniel, E.V., and J. Chr. Knudsen. 1995. 'Introduction', in E.V. Daniel and J. Chr. Knudsen (eds), *Mistrusting Refugees*. Berkeley: University of California Press.

Danny, B.-M., B. Santina and M. Grossman. 2008. 'Refugee Access and Participation in Tertiary Education and Training'. Institute for Community, Ethnicity and Policy Alternatives (ICEPA), Victoria University.

Dewey, J. 1916. *Democracy and Education: An Introduction to the Philosophy of Education*. New York: Macmillan.

Dussel, E. 1993. 'Eurocentrism and Modernity (Introduction to the Frankfurt Lectures)', *Boundary 2* 20(3): 65–76.

Fourier, K., J. Kracht, K. Latsch, U. Heublein and C. Schneider. 2017. 'The Integration of Refugees at German Higher Education Institutions: Findings from Higher Education Programmes for Refugees'. Deutscher Akademischer Austauschdienst, DAAD.

Freire, P. 1970. *Pedagogy of the Oppressed*. London: Continuum.

Gilbert, H., and C. Tiffin. 2008. 'Introduction: What's Wrong with Benevolence?', in H. Gilbert and C. Tiffin (es), *Burden or Benefit? Imperial Benevolence and Its Legacies*. Bloomington: Indiana University Press.

Ginsberg. B. 2011. *The Fall of the Faculty: The Rise of the All-Administrative University and Why It Matters*. New York: Oxford University Press.

Giroux, H.A. 2016. 'Writing the Public Good Back into Education: Reclaiming the Role of the Public Intellectual', in J.R. Di Leo and P. Hitchcock (eds), *The New Public Intellectual*. New York: Palgrave Macmillan.

Graeber, D. 2018a. *Bullshit Jobs: A Theory*. New York: Simon & Schuster.

Graeber, D. 2018b. 'Are You in a BS Job? In Academe You're Hardly Alone', *The Chronicle of Higher Education*, 5 August.

Graham, M. 2002. 'Emotional Bureaucracies: Emotions Civil Servants, and Immigrants in the Swedish Welfare State', *Ethos* 30(3): 199–226.

Halkic, B., and P. Arnold. 2019. 'Refugees and Online Education: Student Perspectives on Need and Support in the Context of (Online) Higher Education', *Learning, Media and Technology* 44(3): 345–64. https://doi.org/10.1080/17439884.2019.1640739.

Hannah, J. 1999. 'Refugee Students at College and University: Improving Access and Support', *International Review of Education* 45(2): 153–66.

Harvey, D. 2016. 'Neoliberalism Is a Political Project', *Jacobin*, 23 July. https://www.jacobinmag.com/2016/07/david-harvey-neoliberalism-capitalism-labor-crisis-resistance/.

hooks, bell. 1994. *Teaching to Transgress: Education as the Practice of Freedom*. New York: Routledge.

Ingold, T. 2018. *Anthropology and/as Education*. New York: Routledge.

Ivancheva, M.P. 2020. 'A Perfect Storm', Rosa Luxemburg Stiftung, Post-Brexit Europe blog, 21 May. https://www.brexitblog-rosalux.eu/2020/05/21/a-perfect-storm-uk-universities-covid-19-and-the-edtech-peril/?fbclid=IwAR17NZRWi27VzT6m1Y1B7OiSQhCG4zK1jcYLpOp2TZ-Q6qcawFTy83SbwzY.

Joseph, J. 2013. 'Resilience as Embedded Neoliberalism: a Governmentality Approach', *Resilience* 1(1): 38–52.

Journal of Blacks in Higher Education (JBHE). n.d. 'Key Events in Black Higher Education'. https://www.jbhe.com/chronology/#:~:text=1870%3A%20John%20Mercer%20Langston%2C%20who,though%20he%20does%20not%20graduate.

Kmak, M., and H. Björklund. 2021. *Refugee Scholarship and Refugee Knowledges of Europe*. London: Routledge.

Kwiek, M. 2005. 'The University and the State in a Global Age: Renegotiating the Traditional Social Contract?', *European Educational Research Journal* 4(4): 324–41.

Lipsky, M. 2010. *Street-Level Bureaucracy: Dilemmas of the Individual in Public Service*. New York: Russell Sage Foundation.

Lorde, A. 1984. 'Poetry Is Not a Luxury', in A. Lorde, *Sister Outsider: Essays and Speeches*. Berkeley, CA: Crossing Press.

Malkki, L. 1996. 'Refugees, Humanitarianism, and Dehistoricization', *Cultural Anthropology* 11(3): 377–404.

McClintock, A. 1995. *Imperial Leather: Race, Gender, and Sexuality in the Colonial Contest*. New York: Routledge.

McLaren, P. 2006. *Rage + Hope: Interviews with Peter Mclaren on War, Imperialism and Critical Pedagogy*. New York: Peter Lang.

Morrice, L. 2009. 'Journeys into Higher Education: The Case of Refugees in the UK', *Teaching in Higher Education* 14(6): 661–67.

Naidoo, L. 2015. 'Educating Refugee-Background Students in Australian Schools and Universities', *Intercultural Education* 26(3): 210–17.

Neave, G. 2001. 'The European Dimension in Higher Education: An Excursion into the Modern Use of Historical Analogues', in J. Huisman, P. Maassen and G. Neave (eds), *Higher Education and the Nation-State*. Oxford: Pergamon.

Newman, J., and J. Clarke. 2009. *Publics, Politics and Power: Remaking the Public in Public Services*. London: Sage Publishing.

Shore, C., and S. Wright. 2019. 'Introduction: Privatising the Public University: Key Trends, Countertrends and Alternatives', in S. Wright and C. Shore (eds), *Death of the Public University? Uncertain Futures for Higher Education in the Knowledge Economy*. New York: Berghahn.

Simionca, A. 2012. 'Critical Engagements with and within Capitalism: Romania's Middle Managers after Socialism', PhD thesis submitted to Central European University. http://www.etd.ceu.hu/simionca_anca.

Smit, R. 2012. 'Towards a Clearer Understanding of Student Disadvantage in Higher Education: Problematising Deficit Thinking'. *Higher Education Research & Development* 31(3): 369–80.

Sontag, K. 2019. 'Refugee Students' Access to Three European Universities: An Ethnographic Study', *Social Inclusion* 7(1): 71–79.

Streitwieser, B., and L. Unangst. 2018. 'Access for Refugees into Higher Education: Paving Pathways to Integration', *International Higher Education* 95 (Fall): 16–18. https://doi.org/DOI: http://dx.doi.org/10.6017/ihe.2018.95.10687.

Streitwieser, B., B. Loo, M. Ohorodnik and J. Jeong. 2019. 'Access for Refugees into Higher Education: A Review of Interventions in North America and Europe', *Journal of Studies in International Education* 23(4): 473–96. https://doi.org/10.1177/1028315318813201.

Thompson, E.P. 1968. *The Making of the English Working Class*. London: Vintage Books.

Tuhiwai Smith, L. 1999. *Decolonizing Methodologies: Research and Indigenous Peoples*. London: Zed Books.

PART I
ACADEMIC DISPLACEMENTS
◆◆◆

CHAPTER 1

The Refugee Outsider and the Active European Citizen
European Migration and Higher Education Policies and the Production of Belonging and Non-Belonging

PREM KUMAR RAJARAM

❖❖❖

Thinking about access to higher education for refugees[1] allows us to examine the relationship between two policy figures often taken to be worlds apart: the refugee as outsider, subject to policies of exclusion or of very slow incremental integration, and the European 'active citizen' learning civic competencies to represent and foster European values (Mascherani et al. 2009; European Commission 2017). The separation of these actually deeply interconnected figures is enabled by the narrative simplification of the complex cultural and social formations 'Europe' and 'Europeanness'. Whittled down by culturalist and populist rhetoric, 'Europe' and 'Europeanness' become stylised representations of complex historically contingent realities that generate and normalise policies based around insider/outsider distinctions (Hall 1996; Newman and Clarke 2009). I will show that a culturalist rhetoric about Europeanness and European values underpins European active citizenship and that it is constituted by demarcating what it is not: groups that cannot be expected to embody Europeanness and European values, including the refugee/migrant. The increasing dominance of a culturalist rhetoric about European belonging shows the centrality of racism and racialisations to the constitution of Europe (it is telling that alongside refugees and migrants, Muslim and Roma Europeans are groups subject to questioning about their belonging to Europe).

While there are many fields in which the mutual constitution (and illusion of separation) of active citizen and refugee/migrant is illustrated, I will focus on European higher education. Higher education in Europe is a privileged site for the cultivation of active citizens by enabling the acquisition of 'civic competencies' (Hoskins and Crick 2010; Biesta 2009) through curricula and through mobility across Europe. Higher education has a central role to play in cultivating a European public sphere. What has been called a 'European way of life' (European Parliament 2020) is fostered by active citizens and by the exclusion or marginalisation of migrants. Active citizens learn appropriate civics in university and in study-mobility programmes like Erasmus, with the focus in civics education being how to teach effective participation within an order, and not how to transform that order (Biesta 2009). For refugees, higher education is, by contrast, intended to be a tool of 'integration' into national social and cultural formations.

In this chapter, I will show that the European public sphere centres on a stylised cultural object, 'Europeanness' or 'Europe'; the backdrop to the European public sphere is a value-based ahistorical rendition of the complex social formation 'Europe'. This produces a system of representations (Hall 1996) which cultivates ways of seeing politics and society in terms that reinforce the ahistorical and restrictive values signified by 'Europe'. The active citizen is a product of this system of representations, participating in and reinforcing the institutions and structures that stem from 'Europe' (and thus legitimising the whole arrangement). So too is the 'refugee' in Europe a product of this system: the European public sphere legitimises the participation of those who can feasibly be trusted to perform European values, and produces the refugee as its constitute 'outsider' who cannot be so trusted. The insider/outsider structure of the European polity enables a culturalisation of the 'refugee' as outsider, lacking in the values necessary to be trusted to participate. Higher education participates by being a key site for teaching civic competencies and enabling the mobile sociality of citizen-students; and by being used as a tool for the gradual integration of the refugee in Europe into national social and cultural formations (refugee access to the European polity is another matter altogether).

While European citizen-students are encouraged to be mobile without consideration of cost or borders – taken as a natural right that comes from being a citizen of an area of freedom and mobility – refugee students meet difficult obstacles. Mobility enables citizen-students' participation in the European public sphere, creating an imagined geography of smooth and unfettered mobility that becomes important in framing political subjectivity. The space of freedom and mobility is fetishised, a no-disadvantage opportunity for social and economic gain, and the violent and marginalising border instruments that enable this space are invisibilised. The outcome is that important political questions of how to live and in solidarity with whom are ignored in a politics premised on participating in pre-given institutions and structures said to embody 'European values' (Biesta 2009). Reducing citizen politics to participation in pre-given structures is an act of depoliticisation; it is an attempt at foreclosing transformative political action while ensuring the reproduction of the status quo, and the interests it serves and the inequalities it fosters.

The mobility of European students is premised on a biopolitical processing that distinguishes on the basis of the citizen/non-citizen dichotomy and, implicitly, on assessment of cultural belonging. There are cases of course where an individual or group's European citizenship does not appear commensurate with 'European culture': Roma European citizens for example are subject to forms of mobility control. Like Roma, refugees, lacking European values, cannot take part in the mobility of European students; for them, higher education is to do with integration. Citizen-students, by contrast, participate in the naturalised and depoliticised space of freedom and mobility, magically rent of the bordering mechanisms and violence that enable it. The outcome for refugees is further marginalisation; for European citizens it is the limiting of spaces for transformative politics.

To flesh out this argument about the interconnections between active citizens and refugees, this chapter proceeds in three sections. The first studies how policies to do with governing refugees come to be inflected by culturalist readings of belonging, and how their framing of issues naturalises certain responses. The second section elaborates on points in the Introduction about the culturalisation of a European public sphere and the depoliticisation of active citizens, and then studies how European refugee and migration policies emerging in this context repeat and normalise culturalist tropes about insiders and outsiders and 'European values'. The third section studies how European higher education policy and policy prescriptions cultivate depoliticised active citizens, normalising a sense of Europe as a space of shared values from which refugees must be restricted. With reference to Erasmus study programmes for citizens and refugees, I further flesh out the core argument of this chapter: that the refugee outsider and the depoliticised active European citizen are two sides of the same coin and that they are both crucial to the maintenance of a project of domination in Europe.

Governing Refugees as Outsiders

States tend to treat refugees as a distinct aspect of government, separated out from other spheres and requiring management through specific policies (Sassen 2000). Anthropologists of policy suggest that we should study the connections between framing issues and problems and the naturalisation of policies that address these (Wedel et al. 2005). European policies of fostering active citizenship and controlling migrant mobility both stem from the emotive stylised cultural object, 'Europe' and 'Europeanness'.

Newman and Clarke (2009) study the ways in which stylised cultural objects lay the basis for policies. Policies can be tinged with nationalist tropes ('Britishness' in Newman and Clarke's example), generating patterns of politics and social reproduction in their terms. These policies cultivate and produce subjectivities that are both in affinity with and in opposition to these cultural objects: in Europe, policies cultivate identities in affinity with 'Europe' (the active citizen) and in opposition to it (the migrant).

With citizens, and indeed often the European Parliament, distracted by culturalist identity games or socialising and celebrating 'Europe', technical and expert views gain precedence and undertake governance in their stead. The fact that migrants and refugees are subject to technical and pseudo-scientific surveillance to compile knowledge about human mobility and then followed up by a regulative and administrative procedure, which takes for granted migrants' non-belonging as political subjects in Europe, is a good example of the interrelations of a value-based politics, the culturalisation of the public sphere, and the rule of experts in Europe.

Policies are based on representations of complex social reality, making it meaningful in one rendition and not in others (Mitchell 2002). The technique is based on empiricism mediated with scientific abstractions, leading to local knowledge about actually existing relations being displaced (Cullather 2007) or derogated. This 'local knowledge' points to the lived reality of people, for example to the practices of transnational solidarity and new forms of community, and evasions of the state and its governing, that are part and parcel of refugee reality (Cantat 2016). These representations, when it comes to policies designed to govern displaced people, perform and produce the 'outsiderness' of refugees. Refugees are to be caught in an encompassing relationship with state authority, and the broader interests and ideologies served by these representations are concealed. The ironic centrality of refugee (and other) outsiders to the political, social, economic and cultural 'inside' is also hidden.

States typically have the responsibility for governing migration and devising policy. In Europe, there is common policing of the external border through the agency Frontex, directives on 'asylum reception' and 'processing' and common policies designed to foster 'burden sharing' of asylum claims. Additionally, the existence of the European Union maintains a 'Europeanising' framework on migration policy, providing a supra-level juridical framework which can influence how migration and refugee policies are implemented. Europe also provides a 'value guide', a bricolage of reference points and 'European values' that can guide migration policy. The bricolage is contested as much as it is revered, as which 'European values' should guide migration policy is argued over, particularly in recent times by the right and far right.

The idea of 'European values' arose as a way of cultivating ideological buy-in to the project of European union. Like other political projects, the durability of the EU project requires large-scale public buy-in, typically achievable through a sense of common value, purpose, culture and identity: in effect, establishing an idea of common cultural sensibility, backed up by institutions, the media and public discourse, to manipulate submission to the European project and make its relations of rule opaque. From the 1970s on, the Europeanising project deployed symbols about a geographically delimited history and culture that circumscribed 'Europe' and cultivated a value-based discourse about Europe based on commonality (Cantat 2016). Central to imaginations of 'Europe' is a form of magical thinking where citizens are taken to embody similar cultural values. The actual outcome is, of course, a disciplinary or pastoral process when 'culture' and 'citizenship' are not commensurate (in the case, for example, of racialised European citizens). The social formation of 'Europe', a historically emergent economic, social and political articulation, is taken as a stylised cultural object fostering an emotive and ahistorical connection to the value of its cultural, political and economic polity. The active citizen is a product of this imagined geography, an outcome of the system of representation that provides a specific and restricted definition of politics and political action (Hall 1996). It is not particularly difficult to see the limits of this representation, an indication perhaps that its hegemony is far from complete. For example, asking simply if actions by European citizens to help migrants in the Mediterranean reach safety would count as acts of active citizenship (the EU's responses to such actions suggest they would not) allows us to see the fetishisation of an ahistorical sense of borders and political solidarity underpinning Europe.

European policies designed to police the mobility of refugees, including border-processing and integration policies, work from and in reference to the system of representations that emanate from 'Europe' and

'Europeanness' as stylised cultural objects. These policies normalise a way of operating towards refugees in ways that attempt to conceal the ahistorical rendition of the social and political formation 'Europe' that is at its core. In the next section I explore key policies to do with processing migrants at the border, making an argument that they have this culturalist trope at their centre, and that the result is a multiplication of borders based on the insider/outside trope and its encroachment onto the lives of refugees who have moved 'inside' Europe, for example when they seek access to higher education.

The Cultural Tropes of European Refugee and Migration Policies

A number of mainstream (a euphemism for right-wing) scholars bemoan the lack of policy cohesion on migration, refugees and asylum seeking in Europe.[2] For these scholars, this is particularly evident in the aftermath of what they call the 2015 'refugee crisis' where, in their reading, some member states obstructed the development of common solutions. This led, they say, to a breakdown in cohesion and solidarity between EU member states because national politics got in the way of cooperation. These accounts often note that all this constitutes a threat to 'European values' (e.g. Mos 2020).

This is noteworthy, first of all, because of the displacement of violence that occurs: 'crisis' is what happens to imagined geographies and abstract values rather than to displaced peoples. The second important issue is that blaming 'national politics' and, by extension, nation states not adequately respectful of 'European values' misses an important point. 'European values' were actual justifications employed by those states whose policies towards displaced people were seen as obstructive to European solidarity and cohesion (Cantat 2016), in particular the Hungarian government's appeal to a 'Christian' Europe requiring protection from 'Muslim' migrants. This amounts to a challenge from within the EU to the cultural coherence necessary for the maintenance of its hegemony.

Yılmaz (2012) argues that since about the 1980s, far right political parties and groups in Europe have gained influence in the public debate about migration, linking it to questions of cultural identity. The culturalisation of identity goes hand in hand with the weakening of class solidarity as a basis for politics, eroding workers' rights and real wages (Kelsh and Hill 2006) and precipitated by complex changes in Europe and North America centring on legitimising a culture of competition and entrepreneurship in place of community or class politics and protections. Indeed, much of the right-wing discourse is as misogynist as it is racist, intertwining notions of family, religion, culture and ethnicity to imagine European 'culture'. Similarly, while culturalisation casts displaced people (and Muslims, and Roma and any number of outsiders to 'Europe') as external others whose entry to and belonging in Europe must be strictly regulated, the broader consequence is the culturalisation of the public sphere (Tonkens and Duyvendak 2016). This culturalisation leads to fundamental questions about belonging and solidarity in public space being resolved under the banner of large statements about who is discernible as culturally 'European' and who is not (Junuzi 2019). As noted earlier, a consequence of a public sphere hemmed in by 'European values' is the marginalisation of refugees and migrants in the public sphere except as outsiders to be excluded or warily integrated. This applies to other European 'outsiders'; the culturally tinged public sphere privileges identity or culture-based expressions of agency but crowds out those identities or values that are said to not speak to or be not compliant with 'European' values.

Moving on to studying policy directed at refugees and migrants cast as outsiders, I note three characteristics of these policies: (1) making displaced people amenable to specific types of governance through forms of knowledge production focusing on surveillance and data collection; (2) the prevalence of a risk assessment framework in policy designed to govern refugee mobility; and (3) the prevalence of technical administration in the actual work of governing migrants. One consequence of these three characteristics of policy is the multiplication of the border (Mezzadra and Neilson 2013). These policies materially mark 'refugees', institutionalising their outsiderness in documentation that they carry with them, in biometric data collection, and a host of other bureaucratic procedures. The European border stretches beyond Europe to holding centres in North Africa and elsewhere and is carried on the bodies of migrants as outsiders subject to risk assessment and technical management long after actual processing of right to entry, including when it comes to access to higher education. I look at policy at three 'stages' of displaced peoples' mobility as they head towards Europe (while noting that the term 'stages' with its ideas of progression needs to be qualified because of the way the border shifts and multiplies impacting on temporal and spatial progression): policies designed to understand and repel mobility to Europe; policies designed to ensure coherence in the asylum procedure at the formal border; and policies of integration, specifically here policies governing access to higher education. There are limits to this study. I do not look in detail at the implementation of policies, including the responses and resistance by displaced peoples, and I do not have scope to focus on the full breadth of policies governing migrants and refugees in Europe.

Understanding and Repelling Human Mobility: Frontex's Surveillance and Risk Assessment Strategy

Mitchell (2002) has argued that policy activity typically relies on empirical data acquisition to make complex social reality knowable as a problem of public policy. Releasing annual *Risk Analysis* digests, Frontex, the European border policing agency, borrows risk assessment methodologies (for example those to do with public health) in which the EU is well established as a risk regulator (Frontex 2020). Regine Paul notes that the risk analysis paradigm and method 'normalises migration and border crossings as scientifically assessable risks similar to health risks' (Paul 2017: 692). Frontex's science-by-association normalises assumptions about the adverse impacts of border crossings, closing space for political discussion about the borders of Europe and the types of community and politics that are privileged.

Frontex's risk analysis framework is based on a knowledge practice that makes migration a knowable phenomenon, amenable to specific types of intervention (Scheel, Ruppert and Ustek-Spilda 2019). It builds on empirical methods designed to make the mobility of displaced people visible and which bear close resemblance to colonial modes of rendering 'natives' comprehensible and visible but still exotically other (Rajaram 2017). Data is inseparable from 'migration' itself. Policy makers have no direct engagement with the human experiences of displacement and dangerous mobility to Europe; these are mediated through numbers and visual representations that lead to the abstraction called 'migration'. Even if its outcome is abstract, data collection itself is material and embodies violence of all sorts. Pollozek and Passoth (2019) studied data collection on Moria camp in 2018, taking note of how power inequalities between data collectors, including from Frontex, and people living in the camp were effective in ensuring the creation of a data infrastructure intended to regulate and surveil the mobility of migrants across Europe. Frontex's data-driven risk assessment strategy normalises a deterrence-based approach. Csernatoni (2018) notes that these measures have had limited effectiveness in deterring mobility but have become normalised and entrenched, backed up by research spending by the EU on data-driven securitising measures and normalising a 'military bias' in border management. The military bias is premised on the idea that such mobility is criminal, justifying a proxy war against people on the move (Hintjens and Bilgic 2018). In addition to deterrence at sea, the EU has set up holding camps in Libya, brokered a deal with Turkey to hold migrants at bay, and enabled deportation to countries that are far from safe. States of exception are rife, whether in the Mediterranean or at the EU's land borders, cultivating violence by border guards against people on the move (Isakjee et al. 2020). Data collection is not only distant, but also corporeal, with biometrics used to trace people on the move in Europe, enabling returns and restrictions on mobility.

Quite explicitly underpinning all this is Europe's zone of free mobility for citizens. Frontex exists to ensure the coherence and sustainability of the Schengen zone.[3] The abstraction of human mobility behind datasets (Scheel, Ruppert and Ustek-Spilda 2019), itself possible because of the culturalist othering of migrants, presents migration as a military issue, only to be dealt with by experts and only on the basis of abstracted data. Properly political questions about who Europeans may live with, what its borders are and what sorts of action constitute ethical or moral responses to displaced people have been placed at a remove. With Frontex and EU policies of data-driven militarisation, European citizens have ceded these political questions to expert management.

Processing People on the Move: (Re)Producing Anxiety

In addition to border cooperation, another example of policy cooperation when it comes to managing migration is the Asylum Procedures Directive (APD). The APD is notable for four features: (1) it makes no provision for making asylum claims to an EU state from outside the EU; (2) it allows for the detention of asylum seekers; (3) it fixates on identifying 'abusive' claims; and (4) it establishes a procedural and not a legal approach to assessing claims with little possibility of recourse to courts. No free legal assistance is provided to the asylum seeker (Schittenhelm 2018).

The APD is part of a nascent and much-argued-over Common European Asylum System (CEAS) and intends to provide directives to ensure that asylum assessments are undertaken in much the same way across EU member states. The APD explicitly directs the containment of asylum seekers 'outside' the territorial jurisdiction of the country, leading to the establishment of legal fictions where camps and holding zones at the border are territorially 'outside'. Harmonisation of asylum directives are the subject of much more anxiety than other harmonisation procedures in the EU: there is by comparison a much more detailed account of what to do, particularly in exceptional cases. The anxiety is rooted in the idea that some states may be 'softer' than others in granting asylum: it is not the rejections that the member states are concerned with, it is the fact that not all asylum claimants can be turned away.

The APD is a legal procedure designed to deal with the abstraction called 'migration' that Frontex and its datasets provide and only after the first response strategy of repelling boats has failed. Again, there are interesting overtones with colonial policies. Whereas Frontex data gathering and risk assessment are ways of knowing at a distance, the administrative procedures at the border are more nuanced categorisations of humans so that they fit within the governance strategies of states, while at the same time maintaining a sense of anxiety about the difference of the other. In effect, it is a coming together of bureaucratic processes and culturalist ideology. Like all asylum processing, what goes on at the borders of the EU is the creation of legal fictions: complex social reality is made into legally defined notions of 'persecution' (or not, as the case may be).

The spectre of the European area of freedom and mobility and its preferred subject, the culturally recognisable European citizen, arises yet again. The Directive of the European Parliament setting up this takes note:

> A common policy on asylum, including a Common European Asylum System, is a constituent part of the European Union's objective of establishing progressively an area of freedom, security and justice open to those who, forced by circumstances, legitimately seek protection in the Union. (European Parliament 2011)

One of the ways in which the EU legitimates itself (and justifies hierarchical and capitalist relations of rule) is with recourse to the 'long peace' that union has supposedly effected (Cantat 2016). Jennifer Mitzen (2018: 394) argues that 'peace' in Europe has been achieved by 'rendering cooperation apolitical by focusing on functional ties' between member states. I would add also emphasising socialisation as a means of fostering connections between European citizens. Mitzen adds also that the conflictual European past is 'othered'.

European zones of peace and security are maintained by the delegitimation of political disagreement and by modes of stigmatisation, surveillance and securitisation at its border (Mitzen 2018). The suspicious asylum processing directive focuses energy on distinguishing the abusive asylum seeker; an entire political and economic system is based on the identification, reproduction and management of anxiety. This anxiety is fundamental. Without it, the ontological treasure that is the EU citizen could not exist. Anxiety is reproduced, its production and management are as much a part of displaced peoples in Europe as surveillance and securitisation, and – as I will show – it continues to pop up in integration practices and policies in Europe.

With regard to higher education access, it continues to reverberate because of a fear that migrants may attend university unlawfully, or their admission will bring down educational standards. However, as I will explore in the next section, the key anxiety is caused by the way in which European policies on higher education centre on the development of active civic citizenship, in which there is no place for the refugee.

Active Citizenship, Higher Education and the Governance of Refugees as Students in Europe

In the preceding section, I have suggested that at the first two 'stages' of mobility (keeping in mind, again, that the term 'stages' is problematic) policies are framed by the abstractions of data, by a commitment to risk assessment and by the cultivation of anxiety. I have argued that the refugee as outsider is the mirror image of the depoliticised European citizen. This depoliticisation takes a number of forms, including the translation of political agency into 'socialisation', the delegitimating of political disagreement especially around borders and belonging, with the consequence that properly political or ethical questions are ceded to administrators or experts, and the growth of functional forms of connections in Europe in place of political and social relations. In this section, I look at higher education policy at the European scale as a key engine of this depoliticisation, and I look at the way in which those strategies of management at the so-called external borders of the EU are repeated 'inside' when the refugee as student is encountered.

Citizenship is normally associated with national or sub-national levels, where engagement with politics and participation in civic life appear more straightforward. At the European level, citizenship was expressed in relation to economic issues to do with employment across borders, the impacts of a single currency and so on. European socio-cultural citizenship lagged behind, creating an anxiety, by the early 2000s, about the extent to which citizens of member states also see themselves as 'European citizens and identify with and actively support the European Union as a unit of democratic governance' (Biesta 2009: 147).

In response, in the early 2000s the EU turned attention towards the idea of active citizenship, defined as participation in civic life. Active citizenship came to be associated with the acquisition of 'civic competencies', participation in pre-established fora for social activity (particularly European civil society) and connected to European policy measures in creating areas of lifelong learning and mobility for researchers and students. Biesta (2009: 150) argues that the idea of the active citizen is fostered by a 'neoliberal' political and economic agenda. The active citizen scurries to fill holes left by the withdrawal of state funding in key areas, while developing civic competencies intended to maintain order rather than give real and potentially transformative political education. All in all, the concept of active citizenship is a useful way of normalising capitalist accumulation under the guise of value-oriented citizenship. It is in Europe, more than elsewhere perhaps, that the fostering of active citizenship has taken root in higher education systems, and this is because of a systematic strategy by the EU to do so (European Commission 2012).

Active citizens are well informed and depoliticised. Higher education, in particular through the Erasmus mobility schemes, has become a key area for socialisation and, consequently, acquisition of 'European values'. Higher education begets active citizenship, and the question is typically posed like this: what should we teach in order to contribute to European citizenship (as opposed to more fundamental questions like how can we teach so that our students may understand how political orders have come to be normalised?) (Biesta 2009)? Curricular change in Europe is not directed from above but is influenced by the Union's 'soft power', evident in its capacity to connect participation in the labour market with the exercise of European values. A central aspect of higher education in Europe is the development of knowledge and values-based competencies, not simply jobs for a market but jobs for a market that enables the development of political, economic and ethical values (European Commission 2019).

Active citizenship is a means of ensuring social cohesion; it is functionalist, Biesta says (2009), and it has a community orientation, favouring quiet civic participation in existing institutions rather than transformative political action, with large question marks about whether disruptive expressions of civic participation (like working with migrant rescue boats in the Mediterranean) actually fit the vision of citizenship being articulated. The idea of active citizenship very much presumes service to and reproduction of an existing order but it also, Biesta continues, has an individualising trait. The active citizen, in the singular, is to be empowered; the practice of individualising acts as a deterrent to community-based action and indeed to developing community resources that might enable active collective political action (and social change). Finally, according to Biesta, active citizenship understands democracy as consensus, as opposed to disagreement or conflict, and the active citizen takes a close interest in preserving that consensus. Biesta notes that the consequence of this is the normalisation of the boundaries of political community, and the institutions and people they include or exclude. It is important that this exclusion (and inclusion) is values-based and not politics-based. The active citizen works within and seeks to preserve a social order that is desirable because it enables active citizenship. This is a closed circle that reinforces itself. Participation is premised on active citizenship, and a type of active citizenship that reinforces the borders of the political community. If the borders of society are not political but values-based, then it militates against debate about how to expand borders and include others (Biesta 2009).

For refugees, higher education is a tool of 'integration', rather than active citizenship. Following the large-scale movement of people to Europe in 2015 ('the refugee crisis'), the European Commission set up measures to foster the 'integration' of those who passed through asylum processing, with access to work and employment taking priority. It is notable that the focus of these measures is 'third country nationals', avoiding, as Dvir, Morris and Yemini (2018) note, a distinction between those who have come to Europe by more peaceful means and those who have fled conflict, evaded the EU's militarised deterrence and come through traumatic asylum processing often in holding or detention centres. In doing so, according to Dvir et al., 'thus the discourse around their integration is limited to the practical concerns of citizenship (as the right to work or study) and not around the political or moral means' (2018: 213). This modality of integration neatly puts aside discussion of 'Europe's values' and leaves in abeyance the question of whether migrants and refugees are to be 'active citizens'.

The 'integration' of refugees and migrants in relation to higher education has two stages: enabling access to higher education, and the acquisition of European values through integration into university and society. But there are blocks to the realisation of the second goal and active citizenship does not come directly to refugees. Most obviously, participation in civic society and in the European public sphere is limited because of restrictions on refugee mobility (when travelling to other European countries for higher education, refugees are treated as third country nationals; they need a visa and have a limited right to work).

However, the acquisition of European values remains a goal of integration, the European Commission write:

> This dynamic two-way process on integration means not only expecting third-country nationals to embrace EU fundamental values and learn the host language but also offering them meaningful opportunities to participate in the economy and society of the Member State where they settle. (European Commission 2016: 5; cited by Dvir, Morris and Yemini 2018: 214)

It is unclear how this is a two-way process. Indeed, the sheer number of speeches, statements, directives and policy stances outlining the scope and implementation of 'integration' betrays an anxiety about migrants who must be expected to 'embrace EU fundamental values'. Following a review of Erasmus+ documents and funding schemes for university students in Europe, Dvir et al. note that funding for programmes to help refugees enter into or succeed in higher education focuses on the benefit that such integration may bring to member states. The focus is local and national, rather than European, and there is a stark difference between Erasmus+ programmes for EU citizens (and third country Schengen-visa-holding education migrants) and refugees. The former types of programme highlight mobility and the cultivation of European identity through active citizenship. Education programmes for refugees, on the other hand, identify integration as the main goal and argue its economic benefits to member states.

The focus of Erasmus programmes specifically designed for migrants and refugees is largely intended to assist acquisition of host country language and to understand the norms and requirements of European higher education systems. Such programmes are often backed up with a stated anxiety about the consequences for integration and not doing so. This is the case in the Erasmus+ Social Inclusion through Education, Training and Youth programme, which funded education programmes for displaced people that my fellow editors of this volume and I, together with other staff and faculty, developed at Central European University in 2016. In the section on providing programmes for 'newly arrived migrants', the call for proposals states:

> Education, training and youth policies have a key role to play in fostering social inclusion, mutual understanding and respect among young people and communities. This is particularly true given the growing diversity of European societies, which can bring opportunities but, in combination with the impact of the last economic and financial crisis, can also bring significant challenges for social cohesion.

> Education and training systems need to ensure equal access to high-quality education, in particular by reaching out to the most disadvantaged and integrating people with diverse backgrounds, including newly arrived migrants, into the learning environment, thereby fostering upwards social convergence.
>
> Young people are increasingly excluded from social and civic life and some are at risk of disengagement, marginalisation and even violent radicalisation.
>
> Associated with increased migration flows, recent studies have revealed growing tensions between different cultures and communities, including in educational settings, and involving intolerant attitudes and behaviours, bullying and violence.
>
> The tragic terrorist attacks which occurred in Europe in 2015 reminded us of the importance of safeguarding the fundamental values stipulated in Art. 2 of the Treaty on the European Union. (Education, Audiovisual and Culture Executive Agency [EACEA] 2016: 4)

The text of this call is typical of what Dvir et al. have noted. There is first a focus on inclusion and diversity before revealing an anxiety about the need to integrate the euphemistically termed 'newly arrived migrants', while explicitly and jarringly referencing a fear of violent 'radicalisation' and 'terrorist attacks'. Running together radicalisation, intolerance, bullying, differences in cultures and a wholly decontextualised mention of terrorist attacks places them in the same register. There is no attempt to say there is a causal connection between migration and terrorism; its mention is strange and seems out of place in the structure of the text but leaves the subject in the imagination of educators and grassroots workers, a power of suggestion that associates education for migrants with terrorism.

In our application we avoided speaking to these anxieties and fears, and wrote critically about 'integration', and the fact that this is possible does show that recipients of funds are able to come up with more critically minded programmes. The main indicators of progress are statistical indicators – numbers of people entered into higher education after the programme and so on. While entry to higher education here is seen by Erasmus+ as a means of alleviating 'violent radicalisation' or fostering 'integration' (and presumably preventing 'terrorism'), it does not preclude other aspects of education.

Dvir et al. argue that these programmes emphasise 'integration' of migrants and do not aim to foster anything like 'active citizenship' for them. The Erasmus+ call referred to above has as one of its objectives 'preventing violent radicalisation and promoting democratic values, fundamental rights, intercultural understanding and active citizenship' (EACEA 2016: 6), but it becomes clear that by active citizenship they mean the work of EU citizen youth volunteers engaged in migration programmes (integrating migrants is an act of active citizenship). In not providing a pathway towards 'active citizenship' participation at the European scale, refugees are effectively blocked from participating in the European public sphere, such as it is (Dvir, Morris and Yemini 2018).

There are, as mentioned, limits to my analysis here: people receiving funding are able to play with the conditions associated with grants and use politically creative pedagogies, within the limits of a need to demonstrate 'integration'. There is little that we as educators can do about the restrictions on mobility for displaced peoples in the European sphere. Indeed, the education programmes for displaced people at Central European University encountered difficulties when attempting to enrol students from elsewhere in Europe. This is because host countries resisted refugee students moving to other countries for education. Once again, there are differences in the implementation: some students did find a way to avoid their host country's 'integration contracts' and attend education programmes in Budapest. But these were incidental and dependent on individual capital and networks. The community imagined and performed by active EU citizens is closed, obstructing the entry of people who cannot be trusted to understand and enact European values. Dvir, Morris and Yemini (2018: 217) say that the EU 'unintentionally' leaves refugees in purgatory. It is more accurate to say that in the EU's political imagination there is no space for refugees to participate in the public sphere.

The flip side to all this is that the non-challenge to the political borders of EU community (for they are indeed actually *political* borders) leads to a form of depoliticisation. The consequence is a culturalist account of the public sphere, with an emphasis on 'EU fundamental values'. These values are under question in Europe, but not because a 'value'-based account of the political is depoliticising and excluding, or because they should be replaced with a more political and historically accurate account of how and why 'values' emerge. The internal European critique about its 'values' arises because some EU citizens and member states say these do not represent 'European values' at all, being overly liberal or overly western European in their fundaments. This feels like a dominating voice in Europe at the moment, with the rise of the far right into mainstream politics, but it would be important to remember the leftist critique of 'European values' which questions its ahistorical and truncated, racist and imperialist notions of community and solidarity.

But it is the far right's critique of the EU and European values that must be dealt with. Once the shock of the far right Hungarian government's hate speech towards migrants and accompanying brutal deterrence receded after 2015, EU institutions increasingly saw Hungary as a vanguard and that their sense of a Europe needing protection from migrants was actually quite agreeable, at least in parts. The challenge to what constitutes EU values led by the European right has led to the reinforcement of values-based politics. This is evident in European Commission President Ursula von der Leyen's plans for an office to 'protect the European way of life', changed soon enough to 'promoting the European way of life', with its two key areas being, yet again, education to foster active citizens and value-driven skills, and protecting the continent from migrants with a rhetoric about an ahistorical set of values, 'the European way of life', explicit and prominent (European Parliament 2020).

Conclusion

In this chapter, I have looked at two policy figures central to the constitution of the European public sphere and an imagined European community: the refugee as outsider and the active EU citizen. I have suggested that both these figures operate in relation to a stylised cultural object, 'Europe' or 'Europeanness', that fosters a system of representations that normalise ahistorical readings of community, belonging and solidarity and their borders. A restrictive culturalism can be found at the hidden centre of European governance of both its citizens and its refugee others. Refugees are inherent outsiders; their mobility must be controlled, and they become the subject of an anxiety-ridden integration programme. On the other hand, European citizens are taught to be 'active citizens', busily participating in the European public sphere while ignoring its violent bordering mechanisms. The inequalities and elite interests that are enabled by bordering are ignored, and properly political questions about how we live and with whom are left to the rule of experts.

In the EU, higher education is central both to the making of active citizens and to the integration of migrants. These apparently different policy figures are interconnected to bleed into each other. Tropes of anxiety and of the fundamental non-belongingness of migrants to a European community are central to the boundaries of community and citizenship. Rather than progressive movement towards the mythical European space of mobility and freedom, refugees continue to encounter more of the same distrust, fear and cynical politicking with their lives.

◆

Prem Kumar Rajaram is Professor of Sociology and Social Anthropology at Central European University and Head of the OLIve unit at the same university. He works on issues to do with race, capitalism and displacement in historical and contemporary perspective.

Notes

1. The term 'refugee' is a legal fiction that restricts protection to those seen to have been subject to specific types of persecution; it is a term of governance and not one that conforms to the reality of 'refugee' mobilities. I will use the term 'refugee' or 'asylum seeker' to indicate this process of government, and I will use the term 'migrants' to indicate mobilities to Europe, qualifying it as needed to show 'illegalised' mobilities.
2. For example, Garcia-Zamor speaks straightforwardly of 'refugee invasion' in the journal *Public Organization Review* (2017) and repeats the claim in a book on the *Ethical Dilemmas of Migration* (2018).
3. From Frontex's website: 'When the "Schengen area" – a territory in which the free movement of persons – entered into force in 1995, checks at the internal borders were abolished and a single external border was created . . . In order to keep a balance between freedom and security, participating Member States agreed to introduce additional measures focusing on cooperation and coordination of the work of the police and judicial authorities. Because organized crime networks do not respect borders, this cooperation became key to safeguarding internal security'. https://frontex.europa.eu/about-frontex/origin-tasks/ (accessed 16 September 2020).

References

Biesta, G. 2009. 'What Kind of Citizenship for European Higher Education? Beyond the Competent Active Citizen', *European Educational Research Journal* 8(2): 146–58.
Cantat, C. 2016. 'The Ideology of Europeanism and Europe's Migrant Other', *International Socialism* 152. http://isj.org.uk/the-ideology-of-europeanism-and-europes-migrant-other/ (accessed 25 September 2020).
Csernatoni, R. 2018. 'Constructing the EU's High-Tech Borders: FRONTEX and Dual-Use Drones for Border Management', *European Security* 27(2): 175–200.
Cullather, N. 2007. 'The Foreign Policy of the Calorie', *The American Historical Review* 112(2): 337–364.

Dvir, Y., P. Morris and M. Yemini. 2018. 'What Kind of Citizenship for Whom? The "Refugee Crisis" and the European Union's Conceptions of Citizenship', *Globalisation, Societies and Education* 17(2): 208–19.

Education, Audiovisual and Culture Executive Agency (EACEA). 2016. *Call for Proposals EACEA No 05/2016 Key Action 3: Support for Policy Reform: Social Inclusion through Education, Training and Youth*. https://euroalert.net/call/3319/call-for-proposals-erasmus-key-action-3-support-for-policy-reform-social-inclusion-through-education-training-and-youth (accessed 11 October 2021).

European Commission. 2012. *Citizenship Education in Europe*. https://ec.europa.eu/citizenship/pdf/citizenship_education_in_europe_en.pdf (accessed 23 September 2020).

European Commission. 2016. *Action Plan on the Integration of Third Country Nationals*. Luxembourg: EU.

European Commission. 2017. *The European Passport to Active Citizenship*. https://www.eesc.europa.eu/eptac/en/ (accessed 19 September 2020).

European Commission. 2019. *Key Competencies for Lifelong Learning*. https://op.europa.eu/en/publication-detail/-/publication/297a33c8-a1f3-11e9-9d01-01aa75ed71a1 (accessed 25 September 2020).

European Parliament. 2011. *Directive 2011/95/EU of the European Parliament and of the Council of 13 December 2011*. https://eur-lex.europa.eu/LexUriServ/LexUriServ.do?uri=CELEX:32011L0095:EN:HTML (accessed 25 September 2020).

European Parliament. 2020. *Legislative Train Schedule: Promoting our European Way of Life*. https://www.europarl.europa.eu/legislative-train/theme-promoting-our-european-way-of-life/fiche (accessed 25 September 2020).

Fekete, L. 2009. *A Suitable Enemy: Racism, Migration and Islamophobia in Europe*. London: Pluto Press.

Frontex. 2020. *Risk Analysis for 2020*. https://frontex.europa.eu/assets/Publications/Risk_Analysis/Risk_Analysis/Annual_Risk_Analysis_2020.pdf (accessed 23 September 2020).

Garcia-Zamor, J.C. 2017. 'The Global Wave of Refugees and Migrants: Complex Challenges for European Policy Makers', *Public Organization Review* 17: 581–94.

Garcia-Zamor, J.C. 2018. *Ethical Dilemmas of Migration: Moral Challenges for Policy Makers*. Springer.

Hall, S. 1996. 'New Ethnicities', in D. Morley and K.-H. Chen (eds), *Stuart Hall: Dialogues in Cultural Studies*. London: Routlege.

Hintjens, H., and A. Bilgic. 2019. 'The EU's Proxy War on Refugees', *State Crime* 8(1): 80–103, 157–58.

Hoskins, B., and R.D. Crick. 2010. 'Competences for Learning to Learn and Active Citizenship: Different Currencies or Two Sides of the Same Coin?', *European Journal of Education* 45(1): 121–37.

Isakjee, A., T. Davies, J. Obradovic-Wochnik and K. Augustova. 2020. 'Liberal Violence and the Racial Borders of the European Union', *Antipode* 52(6): 1751–73. https://onlinelibrary.wiley.com/doi/full/10.1111/anti.12670 (accessed 23 September 2020).

Junuzi, V. 2019. 'Refugee Crisis or Identity Crisis: Deconstructing the European Refugee Narrative', *Journal of Identity and Migration Studies* 13(2): 117–47.
Kelsh, D., and D. Hill. 2006. 'The Culturalization of Class and the Occluding of Class Consciousness: The Knowledge Industry in/of Education', *Journal for Critical Education Policy Studies* 4(1): 1–47.
Mascherani, M., et al. 2009. *The Characterization of Active Citizenship in Europe*. Brussels: European Commission.
Mezzadra, S., and B. Neilson. 2013. *Border as Method, or the Multiplication of Labour*. Durham, NC: Duke University Press.
Mitchell, T. 2002. *Rule of Experts: Egypt, Technopolitics, Modernity*. Berkeley: University of California Press.
Mitzen, J. 2018. 'Anxious Community: EU as (In)Security Community', *European Security* 27(3): 393–413.
Mos, M. 2020. 'Ambiguity and Interpretive Politics in the Crisis of European Values: Evidence from Hungary', *East European Politics* 36(2): 267–87.
Newman, J., and J. Clarke. 2009. *Publics, Politics and Power: Remaking the Public in Public Services*. London: Sage.
Paul, R. 2017. 'Harmonisation by Risk Analysis? Frontex and the Risk-Based Governance of European Border Control', *Journal of European Integration* 39(6): 689–706.
Pollozek, S., and J.H. Passoth. 2019. 'Infrastructuring European Migration and Border Control: The Logistics of Registration and Identification at Moria Hotspot', *EPD: Society and Space* 37(4): 606–24.
Rajaram, P.K. 2017. *Ruling the Margins: Colonial Power and Administrative Rule in the Past and Present*. New York: Routledge.
Sassen, S. 2000. 'Regulating Immigration in a Global Age: A New Policy Landscape', *Annals of the American Academy of Political Science* 570 (July): 65–77.
Scheel, S., R. Ruppert and F. Ustek-Spilda. 2019. 'Enacting Migration through Data Practices', *EPD: Society and Space* 37(4): 579–88.
Schittenhelm, K. 2018. 'Implementing and Rethinking the European Union's Asylum Legislation: The Asylum Procedures Directive', *International Migration* 57(1): 229–44.
Tonkens, E., and J.W. Duyvendak. 2016. 'Introduction: The Culturalization of Citizenship', in J.W. Duyvendak, P. Geschiere and E. Tonkens (eds), *The Culturalization of Citizenship: Belonging and Polarization in a Globalizing World*. London: Palgrave Macmillan.
Wedel, J.R., C. Shore, G. Feldman and S. Lathrop. 2005. 'Toward an Anthropology of Public Policy', *Annals of the American Academy of Political Science* 600 (July): 30–51.
Yılmaz, F. 2012. 'Right-Wing Hegemony and Immigration: How the Populist Far-Right Achieved Hegemony through the Immigration Debate in Europe', *Current Sociology* 60(3): 368–81.

CHAPTER 2

The Double Bind of Academic Freedom
Reflections from the United Kingdom and Venezuela

MARIYA P. IVANCHEVA

❖❖❖

Over the last years, the concept of academic freedom has received renewed attention. Fighting for autonomy from state bureaucracies, academics have tried to reclaim this asset of the academic profession. However, there is a certain blind spot in the discussion. Academic freedom has predominantly been portrayed as absent in peripheral countries with illiberal regimes. Such narratives follow the 1980s liberal democratisation formula: a state capture by an illiberal regime blocks the free flow of capital and frustrates competition. The systemic solution, termination of state regulation by full embrace of liberal democratic values, including free flow of capital (Gagyi and Ivancheva 2019), is seen as a silver bullet solution to the problem of academic freedom. In this framework, the 1989–91 regime changes in Eastern Europe and the Soviet Union were celebrated for, among other reasons, the return of academic freedom as yet another freedom from state coercion (Altbach 2001). With the triumph of the liberal democratic West against the autocratic socialist East, celebrated with the 'end of history' (Fukuyama 1993) and There Is No Alternative (TINA) narratives, the legitimate concern about any type of freedom focused stubbornly on coercions by the 'big state' and side-lined any discussion of the coercion of the market (Harvey 2005). Accordingly, the literature on academic freedom has continually neglected key challenges to academic freedom in capitalist democracies, or the predicaments of democratic socialist regimes confronted with a liberal concept of academic freedom.

Building on my work on the Venezuelan higher education reform under late President Hugo Chávez (e.g. Ivancheva 2013, 2017a, 2017b) and my more recent research on the UK higher education system (Ivancheva 2020), this chapter problematises the liberal concept of academic freedom. Discussing the market intrusion into universities with broader implications for academic freedom in both core and peripheral contexts of the global field of higher education (Marginson 2008; Ivancheva and Syndicus 2019), I show how ambiguous concepts such as academic freedom can be subverted and used against their transformative reading. In the case of academic freedom, while certain instances of state intervention under so-called 'illiberal regimes' are undeniable and need urgent action, the insistence on freedom from the state conceals bigger enclosures on university autonomy from state-enabled market forces, performed within liberal and illiberal regimes alike. It is also being used to hinder positive state intervention when progressive governments emerge.

The chapter complicates the concept of academic freedom in two ways. On the one hand, I speak of cases in advanced capitalist democracies where, under the rhetoric of academic freedom, state intervention that redistributes to and hugely benefits private companies, curtails workers' rights and securities. The increased control of public higher education by market forces is expressed in enclosures that connect academic freedom to core areas of university activity: research, teaching and service (Swartz et al. 2019). On the other hand, in democratic socialist countries like Venezuela under Chávez, aiming to subvert such devastating trends, a concept of academic freedom was used by conservative opposition forces to entrench themselves in traditional universities and defy redistribution and social justice (Ivancheva 2017a). I show how, in both cases, the 'occupation' of the concept of academic freedom reflects broader structures of power, facilitates the reproduction of hierarchies, and – in the case of Venezuela despite the equitable institutional design – can inhibit the process of widening access to marginalised groups.

Academic Freedom: Conceptual Notes

The meanings of what constituted academic freedom have changed in different historical epochs and geographical areas with their specific university models. Originally, in late medieval universities across Europe, it signified the relative freedom from secular or religious authorities for faculty and students alike (Altbach 2001). It was reinforced in the nineteenth-century Humboldtian university model of *Lehrfreiheit* and *Lernfreiheit* – two concepts which stood, respectively, for teaching and learning freedom within the confines of scholarly discipline (Altbach 2001: 206). Such freedom did not protect the academic community from broader social and political issues; it did not extend beyond the university gates, and did not mean any special protection for dissenting faculty or students (Altbach 2001: 206–207). Under the Napoleonic university model, developed in the same era and dedicated to civil service education, universities were central institutions to train and thus reproduce the elites presiding over the nation-state (Sam and Van der Sijde 2014). Academics were seen as public or clerical servants accountable to the secular or religious power rather than to science. State or clerical authorities had indiscriminate rights to intervene in university operations (Enders, de Boer and Weyer 2013; Lynch and Ivancheva 2015).

It was in the Americas at the end of the nineteenth century that the individual and guild privileges and the public service aspect of the university institution were combined in an extended definition of academic freedom (Einaudi 1963). Under the insistence of the public relevance of scientific knowledge, and the service function of higher education, the university community was seen as responsive to broader issues in society (Einaudi 1963). Protections of the academic community in public life beyond the ivory tower were seen as vital (Altbach 2001). In the US this meant research faculty were entitled to special protections of freedom of public speech and writing on all topics. Throughout Latin America, under the influence of the Cordoba Reform in Argentina from 1918, this protection went a step further (Altbach 2001). In Cordoba, and later through student discontent and public reforms across the continent, progressive students and academics demanded protection of the financial, legal and political autonomy of universities and even protection from police forces entering their campuses. This reform introduced some of the key principles of public higher education in Latin America: free access, democratic co-governance, transparent recruitment, and applied academic knowledge through outreach (*extensión*) (Tünnermann 2008; Ivancheva 2013, 2017a).

Thus, the concept remained stretched between distant, and even somewhat controversial definitions. At one end stands a narrow definition of individual or institutional freedom premised on an adherence to the scientific or disciplinary ideal. At the other extreme, academic freedom has had strong institutional connotations that require not only students and faculty, but also university institutions to be accountable to the public, by serving official authorities or by openly confronting powers-that-be (Altbach 2001; Traianou 2015). These definitions now find hybrid manifestations in different contexts. The broader concept is central in places where academic communities are involved in struggles for national liberation or against authoritarian dictatorships (Altbach 2001). The narrower one is professed in contexts where the academic community is not seen as a politically relevant actor, but its right of free speech is regarded as unquestionable (Lynch and Ivancheva 2015).

The broader definition of academic freedom lost traction with the collapse of the socialist bloc in 1989 (Altbach 2001). Since then, academic freedom has mostly been absent or only featured in a limited sense in policy documents. In a rare appearance in the international arena, UNESCO defined academic freedom as academics' 'right, without constriction by prescribed doctrine', to freedom of teaching, discussion, research, publication, and uncensored critical speaking of the institution or system in which they work (UNESCO 1997). Institutional autonomy was, then, a guarantee of the rights of 'teaching personnel' to function to 'the proper fulfilment' of the teaching personnel's and institutions' duties (UNESCO 1997). In national documents, such as the UK Education Reform Act 1988, Section 202 (2), academic freedom was 'the freedom [academics have] within the law to question and test received wisdom and to put forward new ideas and controversial or unpopular opinions without placing themselves in jeopardy of losing their jobs or privileges they may have at their institutions'.

Such individually focused conceptualisations of academic freedom nowadays growingly surface in debates within academia and in public in relation to new illiberal governments' measures against liberal academics and universities (Ignatieff and Roch 2018). Individual institutions' and academics' right to be independent from any regulation, paradoxically, is also defended by the opposite conservative camp as they defend the right of misogynist, racist and other controversial opinions to be platformed at university campuses (see e.g. Simpson and Kaufmann 2019). While the latter discussion mostly takes place in advanced capitalist democracies, the former happens in the postcolonial or post-socialist space and in (semi-)peripheral economies where universities play a political role and academic communities express liberal democratic ideals (Lyer 2019). Yet both discussions omit the question of what project of statehood or public interest is represented in specific regulatory initiatives. Both also hail academic freedom as a privilege granted to universities and their faculty, without requirement that they serve a positively transformative social project (Lynch and Ivancheva 2015).

In light of this, a new wave of discussion of academic freedom has emerged in recent years, one that challenges both the broad and narrow definitions of academic freedom (Moreno 2008; Lynch and Ivancheva 2015; Traianou 2015; O'Keefe 2016; Ivancheva 2017a). While agreeing that freedom should be granted to academics and students, authors express concerns about the way in which discussions of academic freedom elude the question of marketisation of university education. And while UNESCO (1997) insisted that academics, like all other citizens, are expected to 'enhance the observance in society of the cultural, economic, social, civil and political rights of all peoples', these authors have questioned how exactly the university institution serves the public. The question remains: under which circumstances should universities claim academic freedom, and under which could such freedom be challenged? This discussion first emerged around the question of campus freedom of speech and no-platforming, where freedom should not be given to those who harm the most vulnerable (O'Keefe 2016); and then around the question of how marketisation challenges academic freedom in advanced capitalist democracies (Lynch and Ivancheva 2015). It has also transpired that in certain contexts, academic freedom is used to prevent reform in universities that serves the public (Ivancheva 2017a). Two cases illustrate these points.

Case Study I. The UK: Enters the Market

Beyond the collegiate universities like Oxford and Cambridge, famous for blue-sky research conducted in scholastic isolation and dedicated small-group teaching for the chosen few, the UK has developed one of the most inclusive public university systems. As early as the mid-nineteenth century, a number of medical, science and engineering colleges were awarded royal charters and became secular universities, known as 'red brick colleges'. Thereafter, university gates gradually opened not only to men from wealthy families, but also to women (Dearnley 2018), members of the colonial elites (Pietsch 2013) and, gradually, to students from working-class and ethnic minority backgrounds (Carpentier 2018). Massification accelerated after WWII with the foundation of new universities and colleges of advanced technology, which were eventually granted university status. With the Further and Higher Education Act in 1992, the binary system was abolished: all former polytechnics, numerous colleges of higher and further education and a handful of newly established universities received the status of universities, now known as 'post-1992 institutions' (Carpentier 2018). All these now amount to more than 160 public degree-granting institutions of higher learning, and are accountable for the steep rise of student intake of UK and foreign students (Carpentier 2018). The push for massification was paralleled with efforts towards 'research excellence' assessed through global and national university evaluation.

These produced a powerful image of a public university system in a capitalist democracy, offering universal access, education excellence and academic freedom alike.

Yet has academic freedom really been performing up to the same standards as such triumphant narratives suggest? How has academic freedom been affected by what scholars and commentators in the UK have declared over the last decade, namely a public higher education under attack (Bailey and Freeman 2011; Docherty 2015), suffering a 'toxic' or 'Zombie' turn (Smyth 2017; Murphy 2017) or even a tragic end (Wright and Shore 2017; Eagleton 2015)? To answer these questions, we need to take into account the different aspects of the introduction of a market logic into every aspect of higher education in the country through a number of historical shifts over the last half a century.

The oil crises of 1973 and 1979 prompted a recession that resulted in a period characterised by cuts in university funding as part of broader public sector austerity (Traianou 2015). Using its structural position, the central government carried out public sector reforms in ways impossible in federal states like Germany or the USA (Brandist 2017: 585). Under the motto of TINA, this was used as the ideological justification to introduce the new public management doctrine, which allowed successive UK governments to reposition higher education as a public service in need of cost-cutting and 'streamlining', while also indicative of the growth of the national economy (Carpentier 2018). To foster competition between institutions, policies involved the end of the block grant to universities, the introduction and gradual rise of student fees, performance management through metrics, installing competition as an organising principle of research, and the takeover of core functions of the university by private corporations and outsourced services (Komljenovic and Robertson 2016; Lynch and Ivancheva 2015). Power was centralised into a management structure more fit to run a business enterprise than a public service (Traianou 2015: 43). This affected the core functions of universities – research, teaching and service – in complex ways, challenging the myth of academic freedom.

In terms of research, academic freedom has been impacted by the dissolution of the block grant to public universities. The decoupling of research from the core budget (now generated from student fees) has meant universities no longer have research budgets, but scholars have to cyclically compete for them from external funders. Research council funding is increasingly tied to priority topics, rather than academics' own research priorities (Traianou 2015: 42). Priority is placed on natural and life sciences as opposed to social sciences, arts and humanities, which remain subject to increasingly Euro-centric, developmentalist, neocolonial frameworks (Lynch and Ivancheva 2015). Academics are discouraged from 'straying away' from established disciplinary dogmas as competition between universities, departments and individuals is measured through funding-based, discipline-bounded audit of outputs (Brandist 2017: 586). This commercialisation of research, aimed at unleashing freedom and creativity, has instead produced new academic enclosures. Obtaining research funding requires enormous human and financial resource investment in incessant grant applications with a minuscule chance of success, usually privileging a handful of historically advantaged universities (Anonymous Academic 2014) as well as historically advantaged social groups or classes. 'Research excellence' is measured by individual or institutional performance in the Research Excellence Framework (REF) or world rankings.

The effects especially of REF – a cyclical peer review process, making research funding subject to performance of 'world class excellence' – compromise academic freedom (Wells 2012). Research collaboration and interdisciplinarity are effectively discouraged through discipline-specific reviews (Wells 2012). To score higher, universities headhunt VIP academics while turning those not on an accelerated academic track into second-class citizens; these are usually women and academics from black and minority ethnic (BAME) backgrounds (Megoran and Mason 2020). The proliferation of casualised contracts ensures that despite growing workloads, permanent faculty receive more time for grant applications and publications (Megoran and Mason 2020: 19). In 2017–18, 67 per cent of researchers and 49 per cent of teaching 'only' staff in the university sector were employed on fixed-term contracts. Together with seventy thousand 'atypical' contract staff, they form a reserve army of academics doing a significant part of teaching and research across UK universities (Megoran and Mason 2020: 6). Restrictive eligibility criteria make only permanent faculty eligible for grant applications. They are incentivised to take credit for work developed by researchers on low-paid fixed-term contracts, deepening the hierarchical culture of patronage (Mahalyfy 2014; Megoran and Mason 2020: 19–21).

In terms of teaching, when student fees became the core source of university budgets in the early 2010s, a number of significant infringements on individual and institutional academic freedom took place. The introduction of student fees meant accumulation of huge debt which new generations have to pay throughout their working life. Capped at £9,000 for Bachelors' studies for home students, student fees exceed £20,000 per year for non-EU nationals attending some Masters' programmes

(Hillman 2018). Loan programmes, covering subsistence, require debt repayment for graduates employed above the living minimum wage of £21,000 per year, setting university priorities to courses with a direct link to employability, jeopardising less career-focused programmes (Metcalfe 2020). Teaching is now measured by its 'value-for-money' benefit rather than its contribution to student empowerment (Tomlinson 2018). The 'digital turn' requires the use of learning management systems, software and other technologies monitoring teaching, and increasing academics' workload. Often bought via monopoly purchases from ed-tech corporations (Metcalfe 2006), technologies limit faculty decision-making and freedom over teaching, while allowing for the appropriation of teaching materials as intellectual property of universities (Galpin 2018). Universities also bend under pressure from foreign governments, such as China's, whose UK embassy 'expressed concern' about academic strikes and cracked down on Hong Kong support among students (Cavendish 2019). The UK government also obliged staff to monitor students as 'PREVENT duty', under the Counter Terrorism and Security Act (Simpson and Kaufmann 2019).

As national and global rankings rate research, teaching itself has become increasingly devalued in staff promotion and evaluation, and is increasingly done by casualised faculty (Ivancheva, Lynch and Keating 2019). Under working conditions that have become more and more insecure, the latter also have to deal with students suffering anxiety due to debt, insecure futures and consumer orientation (Bunce, Baird and Jones 2017). Yet, while students experience a mental health epidemic (Shackle 2019), services and face-to-face time with faculty are barely available (Goddard 2019), unless care is volunteered by faculty members undergoing their own mental health crisis (Morrish 2019). And yet the new Teaching Excellence Framework (TEF) 'awards' top-performing universities nothing but the right to increase student fees (Hale and Viña 2016). Meanwhile, the 'student experience' mantra legitimates that universities invest part of the £44 billion sector-wide surplus (Bennett 2018) into on- and offline facilities (Adams 2019). While student debt has risen to £121 billion (CBDU 2018), new private dorms often run by offshore companies with over £2.5 billion total annual profit (Adams 2019) offer students residency at exorbitant prices (Osborne and Barr 2018). Public-private partnerships with online programme management companies (OPMs) develop online degrees and short courses with over 50 per cent profit for OPMs (Hill 2018). Often taught by precarious or outsourced staff, such courses target online students not using residential facilities (Lieberman 2017). Student data is sold to marketing firms but kept behind payroll for researchers (McKie 2020; Matthews 2019).

In service, changes in research and teaching have produced similarly acute contradictions. Deriving from critique of the lack of practical application of academic knowledge, within the market framework the pressure to conduct research applicable by 'external' users (Traianou 2015: 42) means that practical utility and impact have to be known during the grant application, that is, before research is conducted. Academics need to prove they work with various – often commercially minded – 'stakeholders' (Knowles and Burrows 2014). As a commercialisation benchmark, however, 'impact' often means scientific production averse to academic freedom. Medical trials in capitalist democracies like the US have long been serving the tobacco and sugar industries (Bero 2019). Social scientists increasingly also cooperate with tech giants, for example Google funding research on ethics of Artificial Intelligence (Williams 2019), or Uber co-authoring articles concealing the problematic sides of the gig economy (Horan 2019). Research contracts often include clauses giving the funder the final say on whether the research can be published and jeopardising especially early career researchers' work when such contracts are controlled by their line managers (Bero 2019).

Tied to the narrative of freedom, the narratives of data and resource openness have also been compromised. Articulated initially as vital to research transparency, data openness stemmed from a necessity to protect research participants, and research as replicable and publicly transparent. Resource openness addressed a global and historical asymmetry of knowledge produced and accessed by core countries, even when it was conducted about and with participants and scholars from the periphery (Ivancheva and Syndicus 2019). Yet new standards of processing personal data render research challenging for scholars, dangerous for vulnerable participants, and protective of repressive states and corporations (Yuill 2018; Peter and Strazzari 2016). An institutional and international push to break monopolies of publishing companies, which charge universities to access their own production, has raised awareness about how the surplus from academic labour benefits businesses and commercial publishers. Yet only scholars working at wealthy universities on grants can publish 'gold' Open Access articles, privileged in the UK competition for excellence (Tennant et al. 2016). Against the design and desire of movements for open data and resources, these now stratify scholars, endanger vulnerable participants, and sponsor for-profit publishers.

Case Study II. Venezuela: Exits the Market?

While the case of UK public higher education raises serious concerns about the curtailing of academic freedom under the logic of the market, this logic works even in places where it is identified, critiqued and acted against by progressive governments. The case of Venezuela under late President Hugo Chávez is noteworthy. Having come to power in 1998 and suffered a backlash from the educated middle class in Venezuela, by 2003 Chávez had set a programme to massify higher education in the country. Until then, higher education was predominantly public but also with a quite 'elite' and thus limited profile. It was also split between a few research-intensive, mostly 'autonomous' institutions and 'experimental' universities with a more teaching-focused vocational training profile (Ivancheva 2013).

Against this negative background, after the attempted coup d'état in 2002 and the petrol strike, which showed that the knowledge elite in the country was in large numbers averse to reforms challenging their privilege, Chávez received support from a group of progressive academics. The latter saw universities as a vantage point of transformation (Ivancheva 2017b). Under their design and leadership (Ivancheva 2017a), the new Bolivarian institutions of higher learning opened free access to all who wished to study; education was based on the premise of academic quality through challenging the marketisation of research, teaching and service alike (Ivancheva 2013).

In terms of teaching, the new Bolivarian University of Venezuela (UBV) and its decentralised classrooms (*aldeas universitarias*) across the country offered equitable education for all. They used critical pedagogy and decolonial thought to address severe social inequalities and the elitist culture of the classist and racist higher education system (Ivancheva 2013). In terms of research, UBV prioritised applied research where science had to serve society and address social ills. This happened through an alternative vision of the university-educated individual: a community organiser as responsible for social change. In service terms, UBV came back to the Cordoba reform's premise of work with communities (*extensión*) for practical application of knowledge in order to achieve redistribution and social justice, and participation (Ivancheva 2017a). Within this framework, higher education in Venezuela followed a rationale of success and quality that did not fit the metrics universally accepted within the global field of higher education (Ivancheva 2013).

Yet, paradoxically, exactly in this scenario, the ideal of academic freedom was used to circumvent this project and make it impossible to live up to its progressive design. Fought through many bloody struggles by liberal and left political factions since the early twentieth century, academic freedom has been a long-lasting ideal for Venezuelan university communities (Tünnerman 2008). As such, it became subject to one of the first reforms of the liberal government after a popular revolt that toppled the dictatorship of Marcos Perez Jiménez in 1958. Yet subsequent governments after 1958 did not decriminalise the Venezuelan Communist Party (PCV), which fought against the dictatorship together with them. Academic autonomy was used by the underground left to protect its activity on university campuses where governments had no right to intervene (Ivancheva 2017a). Liberal 'democratic' governments, however, still intervened in key episodes of academic contention, especially during the University Renovation (1969–70), a sustained student protest wave demanding curricular and structural reform of the university. Such governments, regardless of whether they were from the Christian Democratic (COPEI) or Social Democratic (AD) part of the political spectrum, also found cunning ways to circumvent academic freedom. With the 1971 Law of Higher Education, autonomy was cemented for a small number of old public universities, but all new 'experimental' universities were deprived of autonomy, with management and curricula appointed by the government (Moreno 2008; Ivancheva 2017a).

At the few autonomous university campuses still functioning as oases of free speech and gathering, academic freedom remained a strategic asset in the struggle against the police state and the anti-neoliberal discontent in the 1980s and 1990s (Ivancheva 2017a; Moreno 2008). Yet universities have been increasingly subject to commercialisation and to becoming ever more exclusive with the introduction of graduate studies fees and entry exams (Lopez and Hernandez 2001). With the rise to power of Hugo Chávez, progressive academics tried to use the campus of the autonomous Central University of Venezuela (UCV) to wage a battle to make public universities more inclusive, but academic autonomy was used against them (Ivancheva 2017a; Moreno 2008).

In 2001, during a sustained occupation of UCV, progressives under the name 'Movement for Academic Transformation' (MTU) demanded reform of the university. However, guided by the principle of non-intervention in campuses under the ideal of academic freedom and institutional autonomy, the government of Hugo Chávez did not support the 2001 occupation (Ivancheva 2017a). A year later, UCV and other autonomous universities under increasingly conservative leadership failed to condemn the attempted coup d'état against the democratically elected President Chávez (Ivancheva 2017b). In 2003, a general strike in the petrol sector blocked the country; almost twenty thousand workers in the state petrol industry walked out, causing huge disruptions in everyday life (Vessuri, Canino and Sánchez-Rose 2005). It became clear that if the government could not enter universities to reform them, they had to create new universities.

Established in 2003 by left-wing intellectuals and former student activists, the Bolivarian University of Venezuela (UBV) became the vanguard institution of this reform. In order to provide schooling for over half a million poor Venezuelans, UBV employed thousands of university graduates new to the academic profession. However, those entrenched at traditional universities and state agencies, academics, university leaders and policy makers hostile to the Bolivarian government denied accreditation to UBV's programmes (Ivancheva 2017b). This caused traditional universities to remain dominant in the field of knowledge production and their students retained privileged access to graduate programmes and job market placements (Ivancheva 2017b). In contrast, UBV students – often adult learners and women, first-generation higher education scholars – remained at a disadvantage in the educational and job market. Their credentials were not officially certified, so they received little to no recognition or economic return for their education.

Inscribed within a global field of higher education dominated by rankings and performance metrics (Marginson 2008), and a national policy landscape in which UBV could only be accredited by official bodies dominated by representatives of established elite institutions, UBV faculty had to face a double-edged sword. Despite their huge teaching loads with a complex student population, they needed to gain postgraduate degrees to facilitate the accreditation of UBV's programmes, so that UBV students would be able to participate in the traditional job market. In this regard, it became clear that the government's decision not to intervene in support of the 2001 MTU occupation of UCV or in state accreditation agencies on the basis of the old ideal of academic freedom was a dangerous risk. Read through a liberal lens, academic freedom, once an ideal of the left used to promote political activity for transformative social change, was now used to defend the liberal *status quo* subverting the UBV project.

Conclusions

Academic freedom is under threat not only when political powers suspend democracy, but also when state and institutional-level decisions are dictated by the logic of the market. In the UK, one of the oldest democracies of this world, scholars and students face ever increasing restrictions on '[their] ability to choose research topics . . . teaching subjects . . . organise their own time, and . . . choose the networks and communities in which they located themselves' (Megoran and Mason 2020: 18). Academics become less and less free in their pursuit of knowledge, tied down by the requirements of fundraising and publication peer reviews that disadvantage 'controversial', 'daring' or even interdisciplinary ideas and research. Research and teaching are pitted against each other while done by two reserve armies: researchers 'lucky' to have publications under the publish-or-perish ideal; and teaching-only faculty invisible and fearful of losing even their insecure low wages. Research, teaching and service are put second to serving businesses and prioritising profit as opposed to scholarship.

Thus, even if academic freedom is taken with its narrower definition of non-infringement by the political state apparatus into individual academic conduct, there is much reason for concern. If we do not have an understanding of the institutional and systemic importance of 'academic freedom' – a term that safeguards public universities as spaces of social change contributing to the public good – there is no basis for critique if a leading public university system increasingly serves the market (Traianou 2015: 39). With such understanding, the Venezuelan case demonstrates the limitations of the concept of academic freedom when it is used to perpetuate the market logic in higher education, bestowing individual or guild privileges on a tiny elite against a project that benefits the many, not the few.

The role of the state in this process merits a larger discussion that is beyond the scope of the current chapter. Suffice to say that cases like the UK show how many governments too willingly facilitate the market's entry into the higher education system through the front door, subjecting research to fundraising competition, teaching to student fees revenue, and service to profit for private companies. Cases like Venezuela show that unless progressive governments take regulatory control over universities, qualifications recognition systems and job markets, reform is difficult to advance. As long as scholarly debates focus on the narrative of academic freedom only as freedom from authoritarian states, the market assault on it in liberal democracies will remain unchallenged.

In this framework, it is especially important to remember when working with asylum-seeking students and faculty that condemning regimes in sending peripheral countries that destine them to migrate often happens in parallel to a dangerous romanticisation of the liberal democratic institutions and states in receiving core countries. Such a stance is problematic given the key role of capitalist democracies in war and economic warfare against peripheral and formerly colonial territories, but also vis-à-vis the lack of discussion of the (barely existing) prospects of migrant scholars for a stable position beyond short-term 'refugee' or 'scholars at risk' grants (Vatansever 2020). Such selective omission legitimates the economic and military intervention by core countries, while overlooking the market-caused infringements on rights and freedoms in the former. It also overlooks the continuous precarity and economic coercion that migrants (and academic migrants) face in receiving countries as a more disadvantaged sub-group within their own profession. A liberal concept of freedom (and of academic freedom as its sub-species) can be used as a disciplining tool against non-conforming states, and – at times – against university reforms challenging free-market capitalism.

◆

Mariya P. Ivancheva (University of Strathclyde) is an anthropologist and sociologist of higher education and labour. Her academic work and research-driven advocacy focus on the casualisation and digitalisation of academic labour, the re/production of intersectional inequalities at universities and in labour markets, and on the role of academic communities in processes of social change, especially transitions to/from socialism.

References

Adams, R. 2019. 'Spiralling Rents Consume Increasing Portion of Student Loans', *Guardian*, 11 December. https://www.theguardian.com/education/2019/dec/11/spiralling-rents-consume-increasing-portion-of-student-loans.

Altbach, P.G. 2001. 'Academic Freedom: International Realities and Challenges', *Higher Education* 41(1/2): 205–19. https://doi.org/10.1023/A:1026791518365.

Anonymous Academic. 2014. 'European Research Funding: It's Like Robin Hood in Reverse', *Guardian*, 7 November. https://www.theguardian.com/higher-education-network/2014/nov/07/european-research-funding-horizon-2020.

Bailey, M., and D. Freedman. 2011. *The Assault on Universities: A Manifesto for Resistance*. London: Pluto Press.

Bennet, R. 2018. 'Universities Are Hoarding £44bn in Reserves – but the Cost of a Student Loan Will Rise', *Times*, 27 April. https://www.thetimes.co.uk/article/universities-sit-on-44bn-after-tuition-fee-increase-03ngzv8q2.

Bero, L. 2019. 'When Big Companies Fund Academic Research, the Truth Often Comes Last', The Conversation, 2 October. http://theconversation.com/when-big-companies-fund-academic-research-the-truth-often-comes-last-119164.

Brandist, C. 2017. 'The Perestroika of Academic Labour: The Neoliberal Transformation of Higher Education and the Resurrection of the "Command Economy"', *Ephemera: Theory and Politics in Organization* 17(3): 583–608.

Bunce, L., A. Baird and S.E. Jones. 2017. 'The Student-as-Consumer Approach in Higher Education and Its Effects on Academic Performance', *Studies in Higher Education* 42(11): 1958–78. https://doi.org/10.1080/03075079.2015.1127908.

Carpentier, V. 2018. 'Expansion and Differentiation in Higher Education: The Historical Trajectories of the UK, the USA and France', Centre for Global Education, Working Paper 33. https://www.researchcghe.org/publications/working-paper/expansion-and-differentiation-in-higher-education-the-historical-trajectories-of-the-uk-the-usa-and-france/.

Cavendish, C. 2019. 'British Universities Must Stand Up to Chinese Pressure', *Financial Times*, 8 November. https://www.ft.com/content/df27ad90-017d-11ea-b7bc-f3fa4e77dd47.

CDBU (Council of the Defence of British Universities). 2016. 'The Higher Education and Research Bill: What's Changing?' CDBU. http://cdbu.org.uk/the-higher-education-and-research-bill.

Dearnley, E. 2018. 'The First Women to Attend a UK University and Their Remarkable Story', i: The Essential Briefing, 13 September. https://inews.co.uk/news/long-reads/university-london-first-british-women-female-students-graduates-507725.

Docherty, T. 2015. *Universities at War*. London: Sage.

Eagleton, T. 2015. 'The Slow Death of the University', *The Chronicle of Higher Education*, 6 April. https://www.chronicle.com/article/The-Slow-Death-of-the/228991.

Einaudi, L. 1963. 'University Autonomy and Academic Freedom in Latin America', *Law and Contemporary Problems* 28(3): 636–46.

Enders, J., H. de Boer and E. Weyer. 2013. 'Regulatory Autonomy and Performance: The Reform of Higher Education Re-visited', *Higher Education* 65(1): 5–23. https://doi.org/10.1007/s10734-012-9578-4.

Fukuyama, F. 1993. *The End of History and the Last Man*. London: Penguin Books Limited.

Gagyi, A., and M. Ivancheva. 2019. 'The Reinvention of "Civil Society": Transnational Conceptions of Development in East-Central Europe', in N. McCrea and F. Finnegan (eds), *Funding, Power and Community Development*. Policy Press, pp. 55–68.

Galpin, C. 2018. 'Video Must Not Kill the Female Stars of Academic Debate', *Times Higher Education*, 8 November. https://www.timeshighereducation.com/opinion/video-must-not-kill-female-stars-academic-debate.

Goddard, E. 2019. 'Universities Must Confront the Student Mental Health Crisis', *Vice*, 8 October. https://www.vice.com/en_in/article/ywabdy/student-mental-health-expert-advice-universities.

Hale T., and G. Viña. 2016. 'University Challenge: The Race for Money, Students and Status', *Financial Times*, 26 June. https://www.ft.com/content/c662168a-38c5-11e6-a780-b48ed7b6126f.

Harvey, D. 2005. *A Brief History of Neoliberalism*. Oxford University Press.

Hill, P. 2018. 'Online Program Management: Spring 2018 View of the Market Landscape', e-Literate, 2 April. https://eliterate.us/online-program-management-market-landscape-s2018/.

Hillman, N. 2018. 'Differential tuition fees: Horses for courses?' *HEPI*. https://www.hepi.ac.uk/wp-content/uploads/2018/02/HEPI-Differential-tuition-fees-Horses-for-courses-Report-104_FINAL.pdf.

Horan, H. 2019. 'Uber's "Academic Research" Program: How to Use Famous Economists to Spread Corporate Narratives', ProMarket, 5 December. https://promarket.org/ubers-academic-research-program-how-to-use-famous-economists-to-spread-corporate-narratives/.

Ignatieff, M., and S. Roch (eds). 2018. *Academic Freedom: The Global Challenge*. Central European University Press.

Ivancheva, M. 2013. 'The Bolivarian University of Venezuela: A Radical Alternative in the Global Field of Higher Education?', *Learning and Teaching* 6(1): 3–25. https://doi.org/10.3167/latiss.2013.060102.

Ivancheva, M.P. 2017a. 'The Discreet Charm of University Autonomy: Conflicting Legacies in the Venezuelan Student Movements', *Bulletin of Latin American Research* 36(2): 177–91. https://doi.org/10.1111/blar.12472.

Ivancheva, M.P. 2017b. 'Between Permanent Revolution and Permanent Liminality: Continuity and Rupture in the Bolivarian Government's Higher Education Reform', *Latin American Perspectives* 44(1): 251–66. https://doi.org/10.1177/0094582X16666021.

Ivancheva, M.P. 2020. 'The Casualization, Digitalization, and Outsourcing of Academic Labour: A Wake-up Call for Trade Unions', Focaal Blog, 20 March. http://www.focaalblog.com/2020/03/20/mariya-ivancheva-the-casualization-digitalization-and-outsourcing-of-academic-labour-a-wake-up-call-for-trade-unions/.

Ivancheva, M., K. Lynch and K. Keating. 2019. 'Precarity, Gender and Care in the Neoliberal Academy', *Gender, Work & Organization* 26(4): 448–62. https://doi.org/10.1111/gwao.12350.

Ivancheva, M., and I. Syndicus. 2019. 'Introduction', *Learning and Teaching* 12(1): 1–16. https://doi.org/10.3167/latiss.2019.120101.

Knowles, C., and R. Burrows. 2014. 'The Impact of Impact', *Etnografica* 18(2): 237–54. https://doi.org/10.4000/etnografica.3652.

Komljenovic, J., and S.L. Robertson. 2016. 'The Dynamics of 'Market-Making' in Higher Education', *Journal of Education Policy* 31(5): 622–636.

Lieberman, M. 2017. 'OPMs: Fee for Service is Growing, But Revenue-Share Models Dominate', *Inside Higher Education*, 25 October. https://www.insidehighered.com/digital-learning/article/2017/10/25/opms-fee-service-growing-revenue-share-models-dominate.

Lopez, R., and C.A. Hernandez. 2001. 'Movimientos estudiantiles y crisis del sistema político en Venezuela: 1987–1988', *Espacio Abierto* 10(4): 631–66.

Lyer, K.R. 2019. 'Academic Freedom: Repressive Government Measures Taken against Universities in More Than 60 Countries', The Conversation, 30 October. http://theconversation.com/academic-freedom-repressive-government-measures-taken-against-universities-in-more-than-60-countries-118412.

Lynch, K., and M. Ivancheva. 2015. 'Academic Freedom and the Commercialisation of Universities: A Critical Ethical Analysis', *Ethics in Science and Environmental Politics* 15(1): 1–15. https://doi.org/10.3354/esep00160.

Marginson, S. 2008. 'Global Field and Global Imagining: Bourdieu and Worldwide Higher Education', *British Journal of Sociology of Education* 29(3): 303–15. https://doi.org/10.1080/01425690801966386.

Mihalyfy, D.F. 2014. 'Higher Education's Aristocrats', *Jacobin*, 27 September. https://www.jacobinmag.com/2014/09/higher-educations-aristocrats.

Matthews, D. 2019. 'Researchers Concerned as Tech Giants Choke off Access to Data', *Times Higher Education*, 23 October. https://www.timeshighereducation.com/news/researchers-concerned-tech-giants-choke-access-data.

McKie, A. 2020. 'Do Edtech Apps Keep Student Data Safe?', *Times Higher Education*, 14 January. https://www.timeshighereducation.com/news/do-edtech-apps-keep-student-data-safe.

Megoran, N., and O. Mason. 2020. 'Second Class Academic Citizens: The Dehumanising Effects of Casualisation in Higher Education', University and College Union, January. https://www.ucu.org.uk/media/10681/second_class_academic_citizens/pdf/secondclassacademiccitizens.

Metcalfe, A.S. 2006. 'The Corporate Partners of Higher Education Associations: A Social Network Analysis', *Industry & Innovation* 13(4): 459–79. https://doi.org/10.1080/13662710601032846.

Metcalfe, W. 2020. 'University of Sunderland to Stop Teaching History, Politics and Languages', Chronicle Live, 23 January. https://www.chroniclelive.co.uk/news/university-sunderland-closes-history-department-17616249.

Moreno, A. 2008. 'Historia sociopolitica de la universidad y autonomia en Venezuela: Rostros y mascaras', *Educere* 12(41): 351–77.

Morrish, L. 2019. 'Pressure Vessels: The Epidemic of Poor Mental Health among Higher Education Staff', HEPI, 23 May. https://www.hepi.ac.uk/2019/05/23/pressure-vessels-the-epidemic-of-poor-mental-health-among-higher-education-staff/.

Murphy, S. 2017. *Zombie University: Thinking under Control*. Repeater.

O'Keefe, T. 2016. 'Making Feminist Sense of No-Platforming', *Feminist Review* 113(1): 85–92. https://doi.org/10.1057/fr.2016.7.

Osborne H., and C. Barr. 2018. 'Revealed: The Developers Cashing in on Privatisation of Student Housing', *Guardian*, 27 May. https://www.theguardian.com/education/2018/may/27/revealed-developers-cashing-in-privatisation-uk-student-housing.

Peter, M., and F. Strazzari. 2016. 'Securitisation of Research: Fieldwork under New Restrictions in Darfur and Mali', *Third World Quarterly* 38(7): 1531–50. https://doi.org/10.1080/01436597.2016.1256766.

Pietsch, T. 2013. *Empire of Scholars: Universities, Networks and the British Academic World, 1850–1939*. Manchester University Press.

Sam, C., and P. van der Sijde. 2014. 'Understanding the Concept of the Entrepreneurial University from the Perspective of Higher Education Models', *Higher Education* 68(6): 891–908. https://doi.org/10.1007/s10734-014-9750-0.

Shackle, S. 2019. '"The Way Universities Are Run Is Making Us Ill": Inside the

Student Mental Health Crisis', *Guardian*, 27 September. https://www.theguardian.com/society/2019/sep/27/anxiety-mental-breakdowns-depression-uk-students.

Simpson, T., and E. Kaufmann. 2019. 'Academic Freedom in the UK', Policy Exchange, 11 November. https://policyexchange.org.uk/publication/academic-freedom-in-the-uk/.

Smyth, J. 2017. *Toxic University: Zombie Leadership, Academic Rock Stars and Neoliberal Ideology*. Palgrave Macmillan.

Swartz, R., M. Ivancheva, L. Czerniewicz and N.P. Morris. 2019. 'Between a Rock and a Hard Place: Dilemmas Regarding the Purpose of Public Universities in South Africa', *Higher Education* 77(4): 567–83. https://doi.org/10.1007/s10734-018-0291-9.

Tennant, J.P., F. Waldner, D.C. Jacques, P. Masuzzo, L.B. Collister and C.H.J. Hartgerink. 2016. 'The Academic, Economic and Societal Impacts of Open Access: An Evidence-Based Review', *F1000Research* 5: 632. https://doi.org/10.12688/f1000research.8460.3.

Tomlinson, M. 2018. 'Conceptions of the Value of Higher Education in a Measured Market', *Higher Education* 75(4): 711–727. https://doi.org/10.1007/s10734-017-0165-6.

Traianou, A. 2015. 'The Erosion of Academic Freedom in UK Higher Education', *Ethics in Science and Environmental Politics* 15(1): 39–47. https://doi.org/10.3354/esep00157.

Tünnermann, C. 2008. *Noventa años de la reforma universitaria de Córdoba (1918–2008)*, 1st ed. CLACSO.

UNESCO. 1997. 'Recommendation Concerning the Status of Higher-Education Teaching Personnel'. UNESCO. https://unesdoc.unesco.org/ark:/48223/pf0000113234.page=2.

Vatansever, A. 2020. *At the Margins of Academia: Exile, Precariousness, and Subjectivity*. Brill.

Vessuri, H., M.V. Canino and I. Sánchez-Rose. 2005. 'La base de conocimiento de la industria petrolera en Venezuela y la dinámica de lo público-privado', *Redes* 11(22): 20–49.

Wells, P. 2012. 'The REF Will Strangle Our Vibrant Academic Community', LSE Impact Blog, 23 January. https://blogs.lse.ac.uk/impactofsocialsciences/2012/01/23/ref-will-strangle-academia/.

Williams, O. 2019. 'How Big Tech Funds the Debate on AI Ethics', *New Statesman*, 6 June. https://www.newstatesman.com/science-tech/technology/2019/06/how-big-tech-funds-debate-ai-ethics.

Wright, S., and C. Shore (eds). 2017. *Death of the Public University? Uncertain Futures for Higher Education in the Knowledge Economy*. New York: Berghahn Books.

Yuill, C. 2018. 'Is Anthropology Legal?' *Anthropology in Action* 25(2): 36–41. https://doi.org/10.3167/aia.2018.250205.

CHAPTER 3
Rethinking Universities
A Reflection on the University's Role in Fostering Refugees' Inclusion

ROSA DI STEFANO AND BENEDETTA CASSANI

◆◆◆

Refugees' Participation in Higher Education: Limits and Obstacles

Starting from the evidence shown by the InHERE project,[1] this chapter reflects on the role of higher education in fostering inclusive societies and the way in which universities have managed to adopt tailored initiatives to facilitate refugees' participation in the European university system. Despite the fact that international studies have identified the role of education as crucial for the inclusion of refugees, their access to higher education is still hindered by several obstacles (UNHCR 2019a). Moreover, a common strategy to support universities in setting up an accessible and inclusive university system is currently missing. The analysis carried out by the InHERE project on initiatives implemented in Europe for refugee students has not only demonstrated the ability of EU universities to act autonomously in response to emerging issues, but it has also shown some limits. Within this context, this chapter aims to provide an opportunity for reflection on the strategies that universities can put in place to further strengthen their support for the inclusion of refugees.

In the Strategy for Refugee Inclusion 2030, the United Nations High Commissioner for Refugees set the ambitious goal of 15 per cent of refugees participating in higher education over the next ten years (UNHCR 2019b). The higher education system has been identified as having a key role in achieving the successful incorporation of refugees into the host country (Dryden-Peterson and Giles 2012) and in ensuring that the entire community can experience an inclusive economic growth in refugee-hosting areas (in line with the 2030 Agenda for Sustainable Development). Nevertheless, the rate of refugee participation in tertiary-level education is still significantly lower than global averages: only 3 per cent of the world's refugee population has access to university, compared to a global picture of 37 per cent of people in 2018 (UNCHR 2019b). As pointed out by UNESCO's 'Global Education Monitoring Report 2019', the chances for refugees to access tertiary education are hindered by several obstacles: lack of documentation (particularly school certificates), linguistic barriers (little or no knowledge of the language of instruction), insufficient financial resources (to cover university fees as well as other education-related costs such as textbooks) are among the most common (UNESCO 2018). Such obstacles are strictly related to the displacement condition of refugees, who are often forced to flee their country with no preparation. This has several consequences: they may not be able to choose their final destination and they may settle in a country where they have no knowledge of the local language, making it difficult for them to access information on education opportunities and enrolment requirements, or to have the language level required to enrol in a university course; and they may leave behind documents proving their former education experiences (documents that might not be possible to retrieve once settled in another country), limiting the possibility to obtain recognition of their qualifications and apply to a higher education institution (Bajwa et al. 2017).

A recent survey[2] conducted in seventy European universities also points to four main systemic barriers faced by refugee students: (1) information barriers; (2) non-recognition of former educational paths; (3) linguistic barriers; and (4) financial barriers (Soberon, Reuter and Chibuzor 2017). Information on higher education opportunities for refugees is often reported to be unclear or confusing for prospective refugee students. One reason for this is that refugees may not be familiar with the educational systems of their host country and may need more thorough information than that provided on institutional websites and leaflets. The non-recognition of former educational paths is another issue that affects both refugees who lack or have left behind their educational certificates and those who can provide documentary proof of their qualifications; in both cases, the procedure for recognition is lengthy and may result in delayed access to higher education or in repeating studies (UNHCR 2013). Concerning the linguistic barrier, lack of proficiency in the language of instruction not only affects students' performance and success (Bajwa et al. 2017), but may also represent a barrier to inclusion in the educational system in the first place (UNESCO 2018). This is because enrolment procedures in European Higher Education

Initiatives (HEIs) tend to have high language requirements, in some cases involving two languages. Finally, the fact that refugees may not be able to count on financial support from their families and may not meet the requirements to access national scholarships is yet another obstacle (Soberon, Reuter and Chibuzor 2017).

Even though refugees who have finished secondary school almost universally express the desire to attend university (Dryden-Peterson and Giles 2012), they may ultimately decide to abandon their aspirations as a result of such obstacles. According to the Institute of International Education (IIE), around 450,000 Syrian refugees are of university age and about 100,000 are eligible to enter university, but only a few have been able to enrol in an HEI in their host country (UNESCO 2018). The danger of 'missing out' an entire generation of potential university students is exacerbated by what has been defined as a 'lock-in' effect: after five or six years working in unskilled jobs, it is almost impossible to take up further education (UNHCR 2013), with potentially major consequences for the process of inclusion in the host country as well as for the rebuilding efforts and future prosperity of their home country (UNHCR 2019a). It is also important to note that over 50 per cent of asylum seekers in Europe are aged between eighteen and thirty-four, which is the age range identified with tertiary education (European Commission/EACEA/Eurydice 2019). The need to act quickly to ensure the inclusion of refugees in higher education has been reaffirmed in the 'Action Plan on the Integration of Third Country Nationals' (June 2016), a plan in which the European Commission urges member states to guarantee the timely recognition of refugees' academic qualifications and to provide language integration programmes as soon as possible (European Commission 2016).

Universities' Initiatives to Foster Inclusion

Despite the recommendations of the European Commission, many member states are still lagging behind in regard to the implementation of measures aimed at facilitating academic inclusion of refugees. As pointed out by a recent Eurydice Report (European Commission/EACEA/Eurydice 2019), the incorporation of refugees and asylum seekers into higher education is approached at different degrees across Europe, and only a few countries have adopted specific strategies at national or regional level to facilitate refugee access to universities. Moreover, even among those countries that have adopted national policies, there are substantial differences concerning the levels and scope of such policies (European Commission/EACEA/Eurydice 2019). As a result, in many cases support to refugees has been left to the action of individual institutions, which have tried to fill the gap of missing national and European policies by putting in place new procedures and services to support the inclusion of refugees.

Based on initiatives collected through European University Association's (EUA) Refugees Welcome Map Campaign, the InHERE project carried out an analysis of such actions, which have been put in place unilaterally by European universities in their attempts to make their institutions more accessible to refugee students. Several good practices have been showcased in the InHERE Catalogue[3] that could be used as an example to inspire other universities. Helping refugee students to access and understand information concerning their academic opportunities and requirements is essential to facilitate their access. The Harokopio University of Athens has launched an initiative called Study in Greece (SiG), which aims to provide comprehensive instructions and support to third-country nationals wishing to enrol in Greek universities. The initiative has since grown and SiG is now set up as a non-profit, non-governmental organisation, serving as an official gateway for information related to studying in Greece; a special section is dedicated to services for refugees and their integration into the education system. Websites such as the one provided by the SiG initative[4] are certainly an important and far-reaching means of communication. However, information should also be distributed through more traditional means that allow two-way communication and tailored support. Through the Supporting Immigrants in Higher Education in Finland (SIMHE) project, the University of Jyväskylä hosts an info-desk where refugees can seek information and personal guidance on suitable higher education and career paths, as well as support with recognition of prior learning. Heedful of the fact that refugee centres are spread all around the country and often far from academic institutions, the Artic University of Norway (UiT) has set up an interesting strategy to reach out to potential refugee students. They organise 'information campaigns' through which they travel to refugee centres and deliver half-day information sessions.

Setting up fast-track procedures for the recognition of previous learning and qualifications, either with or in the absence of documentation, is another crucial aspect for the inclusion of refugees in higher education. Despite the provisions set in article VII of the Lisbon Recognition Convention, most European countries are still not fully complying with its application (European Commission/EACEA/Eurydice 2019). European HEIs have therefore tried to fill this gap, either by putting in place new procedures or strengthening existing ones. For example, the University of Bari set up a procedure that goes beyond the recognition of formal education permitted by Italian regulations. Through the Centre for Lifelong Learning (CAP), it is performing the recognition of non-formal and informal learning and its translation into credits towards a university programme. At Ghent University, refugee researchers can have access to doctoral training and be integrated into a research group even though they do not own legal diplomas from their previous studies, as normally required in Belgium.

Paying attention to the fact that having a good command of the language of instruction is one of the main aspects that determine the access and future success of students in a university programme, many HEIs have created 'ad hoc' language courses for refugees. In Hungary, the Central European University has launched a Weekend Programme and a University Preparatory Programme for refugees, offering (among other activities) English and academic English classes. Similarly, the Université Paris 1 Panthéon-Sorbonne offers a twelve-week intensive language training course for refugees as well as access to the 'learning French online' platform through the computer room of the Language Department. A different approach to language training has been adopted by University West. It allows asylum seekers to realise internships in different university sectors (faculties, library, administration office), covering various tasks (IT support, teacher assistant or administrative duties), so they can practise Swedish while they become familiarised with the university system and its functioning.

To foster refugee inclusion in higher education, it is essential to make university an economically viable option. Yet funding for institutions to support refugees as well as direct funding for refugee students is still very limited, and several universities in Europe are resorting to their core budget to offer scholarships or fee waivers to refugee students. To broaden the scope of the financial support provided, some universities have combined different sources of funding. The University of Porto, for example, is offering scholarships that also include accommodation, food, transportation and language training, on account of its collaboration with a Portuguese non-profit organisation. The university has allocated a special budget to cover the costs of academic fees and language programme, while students' subsistence is covered by the Global Platform for Syrian Students.

An Overarching Strategy for More Inclusive Universities

The analysis developed through the InHERE project has revealed the capacity of the academic community to act in response to emerging issues and to act autonomously, despite the limited support at national and governmental levels. It is interesting to note that the entire university community (students, academics and administrative staff) have mobilised and engaged in providing a response to the challenges described above. However, it must be said that only rarely has a single university been able to tackle all of them at once. The fragmentation of the university response to the needs of and challenges faced by refugee students stresses the necessity to develop a more integrated approach, that would allow the university to go beyond the single emergency.

Aware of these criticalities, the InHERE project has developed a set of recommendations to inspire universities' future actions.[5] In particular, the recommendations, which were presented in Brussels in September 2018, have indicated a number of key elements to make the university system more accessible. These include: improving access to information through the provision of comprehensive information and advisory services; increasing the funding for universities to support refugees; enhancing the harmonisation of procedures; supporting the employability and the overall incorporation of refugees into societies. To ensure sustainability and continuity of actions, the recommendations stress the importance of including initiatives for refugees in a broader overarching strategy, as part of universities' social responsibility under their Third Mission, as this would enable the different departments and stakeholders of institutions to collaborate in providing the best possible support to refugee students and scholars.

In Italy, the recommendations have been incorporated in an initiative promoted among Italian HE institutions by UNHCR to create a 'Manifesto of Universities' to foster the access of refugees to higher education and research, and to encourage their social inclusion and active participation in academic life. As mentioned in the Manifesto itself, through its adoption universities contribute to realising their Third Mission, by favouring the valorisation and the use of knowledge for the social, cultural and economic development of society (UNHCR 2019c). Several universities have embraced the Manifesto, which represents an important example of synergy between European projects and national initiatives, in view not of duplicating actions but rather multiplying their overall effects and impact. Through its implementation, the Manifesto led to the establishment of a permanent task force at Sapienza

University that, in collaboration with UNHCR and other stakeholders, aims at sharing good practices and promoting common initiatives with other Italian universities.

The recommendations also inspired a new project called 'UNI(di)VERSITY, Socially responsible university for inclusive societies in the era of migration' that wishes to contribute to the European debate on the development of an integrated approach to the issue of migrant and refugee inclusion in HE. The project, funded by the European Commission, builds upon the results of InHERE with the aim to support HEIs to integrate initiatives addressed to refugees and migrants in a broader approach to diversity. To this end, UNI(di)VERSITY will analyse some of the most relevant social responsibilities and diversity approaches adopted by European HEIs, design instruments to integrate issues related to migration holistically and develop a methodology for socially responsible universities in the era of migration.[6]

Much remains to be done for universities to fully embrace an exhaustive approach that goes beyond single initiatives and builds inclusive HEIs and societies. The results of InHERE projects and the subsequent initiatives put in place show the need for a common path that leads towards the institutionalisation of a systemic approach, integrated in the universities' Third Mission. Today, such an approach may identify refugees and migrants as the main actors, but it can open the way to include a wider pool of beneficiaries, keeping in mind that internationalisation, diversity and inclusion are part of the enrichment of society and that 'the student body within higher education should reflect the diversity of Europe's population' (European Commission 2017).

◆

Rosa Di Stefano obtained a double major in Political Science and International Relations from the University of Toronto (2010) and later specialised in development studies and project cycle management at the Institute for Advanced Study of Pavia-IUSS. She worked in Ecuador in the field of international cooperation for various NGOs and she joined Sapienza International Office as European Projects Officer in 2015. She has been actively contributing to projects and initiatives dedicated to the social inclusion of migrants and refugees (InHERE, Higher Education Supporting Refugees in Europe; Manifesto of Inclusive University-UNHCR; UNI(di)VERSITY).

Benedetta Cassani graduated in Economics and obtained a PhD in Economic Geography. Before joining Sapienza IRO Office, she carried out research activities in collaboration with several institutions (Council of Europe, Sapienza

University, UNESCO Chair) focusing on migration and development issues. Since 2011, she has been working at Sapienza University International Office providing support to the submission and management of European projects mainly in the area of social sciences and humanities. She is actively involved in several projects dedicated to the social inclusion of migrants and refugees such as InHERE, Higher Education Supporting Refugees in Europe; Manifesto of Inclusive University-UNHCR; and UNI(di)VERSITY.

Notes

1. InHERE is co-funded with support from the Erasmus+ programme of the European Union during the period September 2016 to September 2018. The project has been implemented by UNIMED (coordinator), Sapienza University, University of Barcelona, Campus France, EUA and UNHCR (associate partner). More information can be found at www.inhereproject.eu.
2. The survey has been realised in the framework of the Erasmus+ S.U.C.R.E. project: http://sucre.auth.gr/.
3. InHERE's Good Practice Catalogue is available at https://www.inhereproject.eu/outputs/good-pratice-catalogue.
4. The SiG website is available at http://studyingreece.edu.gr/.
5. InHERE's recommendations are available at https://www.inhereproject.eu/outputs/recommendations.
6. The results of the project will be publicly available by the end of 2022 at www.unidiversity.eu.

References

Bajwa, J.K., S. Couto, S. Kidd, R. Markoulakis, M. Abai and K. McKenzie. 2017. 'Refugees, Higher Education, and Informational Barriers', *Refuge: Canada's Journal on Refugees* 33(2): 56–65. doi:10.7202/1043063ar.

Dryden-Peterson, S., and W. Giles. 2012. 'Higher Education for Refugees', *Refuge: Canada's Journal on Refugees* 27(2): 3–9. https://refuge.journals.yorku.ca/index.php/refuge/article/view/34717.

European Commission. 2016. 'Action Plan on the Integration of Third Country Nationals', EU COM (2016) 377 final.

European Commission. 2017. 'A Renewed EU Agenda for Higher Education', COM (2017) 247 final.

European Commission/EACEA/Eurydice. 2019. 'Integrating Asylum Seekers and Refugees into Higher Education in Europe: National Policies and Measures', Eurydice Report. Luxembourg: Publications Office of the European Union.

Eurostat. 2017. 'Asylum and First Time Asylum Applicants by Citizenship, Age and Sex: Annual Aggregated Data'. http://appsso.eurostat.ec.europa.eu/nui/show.do?dataset=migr_asyappctza&lang=en.

Soberon, M.A., L. Reuter and A. Chibuzor. 2017. 'Accessing Higher Education in Europe: Challenges for Refugee Students and Strategies to Overcome Them'.

University of Cologne. https://www.portal.uni-koeln.de/sites/international/aaa/92/92pdf/GlobalSouth_pdf/92pdf_SUCRE_Publication2017.pdf

UNESCO. 2018. 'Global Education Monitoring Report 2019: Migration, Displacement and Education – Building Bridges, Not Walls'. Paris: UNESCO.

UNHCR. 2013. 'A New Beginning: Refugee Integration in Europe', September 2013. https://www.refworld.org/docid/522980604.html.

UNHCR. 2018. 'Global Compact on Refugees'. New York: United Nations. https://www.unhcr.org/gcr/GCR_English.pdf.

UNHCR. 2019a. 'Stepping Up: Refugee Education in Crisis, 2019'. New York: United Nations. https://www.unhcr.org/steppingup/wp-content/uploads/sites/76/2019/09/Education-Report-2019-Final-web-9.pdf.

UNHCR. 2019b. 'Refugee Education 2030: A Strategy for Refugee Inclusion, 2019'. New York: United Nations. https://www.unhcr.org/publications/education/5d651da88d7/education-2030-strategy-refugee-education.html.

UNHCR. 2019c. 'Manifesto dell'Università inclusiva. Favorire l'accesso dei rifugiati all'istruzione universitaria e alla ricerca e promuovere l'integrazione sociale e la partecipazione attiva alla vita accademica'. New York: United Nations. https://www.unhcr.org/it/wp-content/uploads/sites/97/2020/09/Manifesto-dellUniversita-inclusiva_UNHCR.pdf.

CHAPTER 4
The Authoritarian Turn against Academics in Turkey
Can Scholars Still Show Solidarity to Vulnerabilised Groups?

LEYLA SAFTA-ZECHERIA

── ◆◆◆

In January 2016 a group of academics published a petition criticising the human rights infringements against civilian populations in the Kurdish provinces of Turkey (Barış için akademisyenler [BAK] 2016). The launch of the petition ignited a massive backlash from multiple sources ranging from local communities to government decrees impeding the signatories' employment and travel abroad. In a very different context, in 2017 and 2018, the Hungarian parliament passed a bill impeding the possibility of legal functioning of Central European University in Budapest, the institutional home of university access programmes for the Roma minority, as well as refugee students. Soon after, another bill that criminalised helping asylum seekers in Hungary was passed. During the same time span, gender studies programmes came under attack in Hungary, as in other places around the world. Although these situations are markedly different, I argue that they are part of a transformation of the academic profession that is under way to different degrees (almost) everywhere in the world.

In a nutshell, my argument is that academic solidarity with vulnerabilised groups has come to be penalised by authoritarian governments through criminalisation and precarisation of academics (and students). This, in turn, has given rise to public campaigns to defend higher education promoting academic freedom, and has led to practices of transnational precarious mobility of academics and institutions and to spaces of solidarity and democratic knowledge production outside the formal structures of the academe (universities and research institutes). This situation has reshaped academic spaces, contributing to increased pressure (economically, socially and legally) on academics who are in solidarity with non-majoritarian, marginalised groups, and especially those academics who already were in precarious positions (such as early career, non-permanent researchers, etc.). In the context of institutions unable or unwilling to support those members who displayed solidarity, some of these practices are moved outside of the realm of the university. That is, solidarity practices and meaningful collective knowledge production have been forcibly pushed outside of universities and research institutes. In this, the present chapter relates to the theme of academic displacement explored in this section of the book in two ways. On the one hand, in the wake of the petition crisis in Turkey, academics who showed solidarity with vulnerabilised groups from a precarious position were displaced and pushed to the fringes of the hypermobile transnational academic labour market. This perspective helps to shed light on the intricacies of academic displacement as a phenomenon affecting not only students, but also faculty and researchers. On the other hand, and part of the same transformation, spaces for collectively meaningful knowledge production have also been displaced from within to outside of the formal structures of the academe.

In the upcoming chapter, I will first explore one such situation in more detail: the petition crisis in Turkey. Significant parallels exist to developments in other higher education settings worldwide, most notably in Hungary, but I will only reference these in passing to allow for a more focused account. I will embed my analysis in the transnational, as well as local dynamics set in motion by the 2016/17 turn towards authoritarian pressures on academics. Finally, I will relate the recent developments to theoretical debates about the limits of academic freedom and collective, meaningful knowledge production.

The Petition Crisis in Turkey and Its Transnational Ramifications

On 11 January 2016, a group of academics published a petition entitled 'Bu Suça Ortak Olmayacağız/We Will Not Be a Party to This Crime!' (BAK 2016). This appeal is often referred to as the Peace Petition, criticising the human rights infringements in the Kurdish provinces of Turkey. These infringements had come about after consecutive states of emergencies were decreed in these provinces, as well as violent clashes leading to the deaths of over three hundred civilians and the displacement of 355,000 citizens of the Turkish Republic (Odman 2018). The petition sought to intervene in this process and was initially signed online by more than one thousand people. This was followed shortly by the harassment and prosecution of the signatories, leading to an almost doubling of the number of signatories (Odman 2018).

Almost five hundred signatories lost their positions through firing, forced early retirement or refusal to extend contracts. In addition, disciplinary investigations were opened by universities against the signatories (see Odman 2018; BAK Solidarity Group 2019). Moreover, signatories were taken into preventive detention, and the academics who had read out the petition publicly were detained for forty-four days (Odman 2018) as exemplary punishment. On an everyday basis, local lynching campaigns were started against signatories (Ilengiz 2016), and signatories were prevented from entering their university workplaces; their pictures were printed in local newspapers or on social media pages, while some were named as alleged 'supporters of the PKK' (BAK Solidarity Group 2019) and confined to their houses or publicly humiliated (Odman 2018). After the failed *coup d'état* in July 2016, signatories were also dismissed by statutory decrees and their passports taken away, meaning that they could no longer leave the country (Odman 2018), *de facto* forcing them into immobility.

Since September 2017, the criminalisation process has also involved regular trips to the Istanbul Çağlayan Justice Palace for the first round of petition signatories (1128) as defendants in trials for terrorist propaganda[1] (Odman 2018). As of 2 September 2020,[2] ninety-one trials were still ongoing. The trials are considered to lead to the acquittal of all signatories (until 2 September 2020, 622 of the 822 trialled signatories had been acquitted), since with a near tie vote on 26 July 2019, the General Assembly of the Constitutional Court ruled that the petition fell within the limits of the freedom of expression and that thus the conviction for propagandising for a terrorist organisation on the basis of having signed the petition is a rights violation.[3] While the ruling of the Constitutional Court offers a welcome resolution to the legal prosecution of the signatories, it does not indicate an end to the other forms of prosecution that the signatories faced, prompting BAK academics' demands to be reinstated.[4]

The individual negative consequences of the petition crisis were unevenly distributed along class and status lines, primarily affecting early career researchers (doctoral students from provincial universities migrating to more prominent universities in academically well-developed cities, academics based at universities in conservative rural areas, etc.), whereas signatories based at transnationally relevant high-status universities in metropolitan centres were spared disciplinary inquiries by the universities (Odman 2018). While lists of names attached to statutory decrees (after the attempted *coup d'état* in July 2016) were necessary to dismiss those academics who had secure public servant positions at public universities, non-permanent limited contract academics were the first victims of dismissals (Odman 2018).

As Elif Birced (Birced and Kocak 2019) convincingly argues, in the petition crisis the government became an agent in the precarisation of scholars. In this sense, the authoritarian backlash against academics that followed the signing of the 'Bu Suça Ortak Olmayacağız / We Will Not Be a Party to This Crime!' petition (BAK 2016) re-articulated the neoliberal precarisation of critical scholars who chose to make their solidarity with the victims of war visible. In this sense, the story of Mehmet Fatih Traş (see Özkirimli 2017) provides biographical evidence. A recent PhD graduate, Traş could not secure an academic position due to the professional marginalisation of signatories. After attempting to move to a number of different cities and universities in Turkey and abroad, he took his own life (Özkirimli 2017).

The opposition to the dismissals and prosecutions has mainly been organised around the demands for academic freedom and freedom of expression, which in the end yielded precious fruit through the Constitutional Court's ruling, reading the Peace Petition as an act within the boundaries of freedom of expression of academics. Yet, as Ilengiz (2016) convincingly argues, the discourse of freedom of expression and its transnational corollary of academic freedom also further shifted the boundaries of solidarity by limiting the boundaries of political inclusion, while at the same time re-articulating Orientalist visions of the West versus East and working to make the ongoing violence in the Kurdish regions less visible (Ilengiz 2016).

Such responses have been institutionalised in the forms of academic fellowship programmes, such as the Germany-based Academy in Exile.[5] This type of programme offers a welcome continuation of academic life for persecuted academics, outside of Turkish state borders, provided they can obtain a visa/passport. Yet they are necessarily selective, reinforcing neoliberal standards of performance, alongside a newly created category of vulnerability standards. Moreover, these programmes are, per definition, limited in time (generally up to two years; CARA in Britain also offers three-year fellowships), whereas the political reality of academic persecution in Turkey does not have a foreseeable end. These positions foreground the 'at risk' status of the scholars, placing them outside of the regular academic labour market of the host countries and obscuring their position on the margins of the global academic market (Vatansever 2020: 3f, 53f). Once faced with the end of fellowships, these transnational scholars will yet again be faced with a precarious position as immigrant, cheap, flexible labour in the international academic market (Tören and Kutun 2018), becoming part of the 'floating' academic reserve army detached from institutional environments, as well as having to move between countries (Vatansever 2020: 48f). Changing this situation would imply solidarity struggles for changing working conditions within academia worldwide (Tören and Kutun 2018). These struggles need to be built on transnational or global networks of solidarity that on the grounds of the precariousness of academics in exile cannot be initiated by them alone (see Vatansever 2020: 128–29).

This form of academic displacement is grounded in being forced into transnational mobility in the international academic job market. Precarious as it may be, academic displacement is also a form of privilege, since through the cancellation of their passports or the rejection of visa applications a series of BAK academics (including Mehmet Fatih Traş) were forced into immobility. At the same time, those forced into immobility had little or no prospect of access to stable employment and income in Turkey.

Promising forms of resistance have also emerged as solidarity academies have appeared in several Turkish cities (Kocaeli, Mersin, Eskişehir, Ankara and others), explicitly looking to establish new loci for collectively, socially and politically relevant academic research and teaching (Bakırezer, Demirer and Yeşilyurt 2018; Özcer 2018; Odman 2018; Aktaş, Nilsson and Borell 2019). What these initiatives share is a drive to overcome hierarchical relationships and create alternative pedagogical models (Özcer 2018), as well as an educational model that is a feasible alternative to the market-driven university models (Bakırezer, Demirer and Yeşilyurt 2018). These experimental spaces have gradually come to institutionalise themselves, taking different forms, organising discussion platforms, several semester-long seminars and summer schools (Odman 2018). Moreover, since March 2017, there have been coordination meetings among the solidarity academies dealing with such topics as alternative pedagogies (Odman 2018).

Yet these spaces also risk institutionalising forms of precarity, informality and lack of access to formal certification and associated status privileges, because the financing and credentialisation of such initiatives is still part of the struggle (see Bakırezer, Demirer and Yeşilyurt 2018).

Transformation of the Limits of Academic Freedom

Mainstream readings of academic freedom understand freedom in terms of academic autonomy to conduct research, whether it is socially meaningful or not, and irrespective of its relevance for broader social actors (see de Sousa Santos 2010). Nevertheless, even before 2016/17, the debate surrounding academic freedom included a relatively marginal, yet very important discussion on the limits of academic freedom within the neoliberalisation of universities worldwide (see Ivancheva 2015), the limitations imposed on specific positionalities within the neoliberal university, such as those of women and other vulnerable and caring academic subjects (see e.g. Davies et al. 2005; Grummell, Devine and Lynch 2009; Lynch and Ivancheva 2015), those of non-tenured academic staff (Stergiou and Somarakis 2016), and those imposed on epistemologies in search of equality (Brown 2011; Bendix-Petersen and Davies 2010; Lynch, Crean and Moran 2010). Of those epistemological limitations, from today's perspective, the most significant appears to have been the impossibility to undertake research on subjects of collective interest and create new avenues for collectively meaningful research (Lynch and Ivancheva 2015).

This epistemological limitation, which was previously incorporated in the logic of how universities and academic institutions operated, took on a different form in the wake of the turn discussed here. The drivers of these limitations were no longer circumscribed to the academic milieu; governments became actively involved in curtailing the spaces for academic freedom and solidarity. Thus, possibilities for meaningful knowledge production in relation to and in solidarity with specific vulnerabilised groups (civilian victims of violence in the Kurdish provinces in Turkey, in the case discussed here) by academics became limited. At the same time, as visible above, previously academics were marginalised on the grounds of positions they inhabited and from which they produced knowledge, most significantly those of vulnerable and caring individuals (see e.g. Davies et al. 2005; Grummell, Devine and Lynch 2009; Lynch and Ivancheva 2015). The turn seems to have accentuated and extended this development by bringing about the marginalisation, criminalisation and precarisation not only of specific positionalities, but also of the solidarity publicly manifested by academics with vulnerabilised positionalities outside of academia.

This process of curtailing spaces for solidarity intersected negatively with another process, namely the precarisation of the academic profession. The precarity of the academic profession, characterised by a decades-long steep decrease in tenured positions (Stergiou and Somarakis 2016) and increased pressure on junior scholars to put up with flexible low-paid contracts and recurrent transnational migration (Ivancheva 2015), created a generation of academics that due to low income and job instability appear to have taken the higher education route into more precarious employment rather than out of it (see Kendzior 2014). This transformation has had its negative effects, yet it has also narrowed the distance between marginal populations and the academics who research them (Ivancheva 2015). Academic freedom thus no longer operated to ensure a privileged stance as far removed from those of marginalised groups, though it remained a position of relative privilege. In this sense, the neoliberal transformations of the academic field imposed limits on academic freedom well before 2016/17 and set the ground for this transformation to unequally affect those academics who were already precarious.

Read in this key, the 2016/17 increase in authoritarian pressures on academics and academic institutions has exacerbated a state of affairs that was ongoing. A new generation of academics, who had already lost the privileges of the past generation, also suffered more intensely if engaged in acts of solidarity with vulnerabilised groups. Thus, as we have seen in Turkey, full professors at transnationally recognised academic institutions, as well as public servants, were more protected in the face of the government's backlash, as opposed to graduate students or recent PhD graduates.

Conclusion and Outlook: Collectively Meaningful Knowledge Production and Academic Solidarity with Vulnerabilised Groups after the 2016/17 Turn

As de Sousa Santos (2010) notes, universities have long been affected by a crisis of legitimacy that springs from the contradiction of the university's ethical and knowledge imperatives. On the one hand, the university is expected to produce specialised, hierarchical knowledge, and must thus restrict access to its spaces and the credentials and competences it produces and certifies. On the other hand, there is a demand that the university become a more democratic space of equal opportunity that can contribute to the production of socially meaningful knowledge.

Therefore, a struggle emerges around academic freedom and academic solidarity as differing stances regarding the ethical and knowledge imperatives directed at the university. The production of knowledge that is collectively meaningful, and knowledge production from marginalised perspectives, were always contested processes within universities associated with institutional and economic precarity, where the guarantees of individually conceptualised academic freedom claims would reach their limits (Lynch and Ivancheva 2015). If understood as researcher autonomy, academic freedom can act as a barrier to the production of collectively meaningful knowledge. The autonomous researcher is free in the pursuit of knowledge and therefore free not to think about the social consequences of the knowledge he/she produces. On the other hand, in this struggle to produce collectively meaningful knowledges from within the university, the partnerships between vulnerabilised social groups and researchers have played a particularly important role. These partnerships rely on academic solidarity with vulnerabilised groups and can be read as a stepping stone to a counter-hegemonic globalising project of redefining the democratic nature of universities (in de Sousa Santos's terms, 2010).

Around the academic year 2016/17, the struggle *against* collectively meaningful knowledge production took on a new form, especially in Turkey, but also in Hungary (see Dönmez and Duman 2020) and elsewhere. The direct response of academics and their allies to the pressures of the authoritarian turn was to demand academic freedom in reference mainly to the first understanding of the term. Yet the transformation also operated to discredit collectively meaningful knowledge production in the academe in solidarity with vulnerabilised groups. This understanding of academic freedom has been addressed less visibly. Nevertheless, this shift also has a global dimension and can be seen, for example, in the move to try and ban gender and other forms of political education in different countries across the world (most recently in Romania [Monitor Civicus 2020]) and in the public attacks against anti-racist and decolonial scholars (most notably recently in France [Ram 2020]).

At the same time, the turn of 2016/17 has brought about new forms of struggle *for* collectively meaningful knowledge production. These struggles can be seen in the creation and extension of transnational support networks for academics at risk, as well as in the creation of spaces for meaningful knowledge production outside of universities. Nevertheless, these spaces and the positionalities from which they are constructed are precarious and contested. They contribute to deepening the cleavages within and outside academia, while, nevertheless, constituting an opportunity to overcome what Wendy Brown has called the 'danger of extinction' of social sciences and humanities (mainly), caused by the growing importance of marketable research and research metrics in the neoliberal university on the one hand, and the impossibility of articulating publicly relevant knowledge that contributes to the democratisation of society within these metrics, on the other (Brown 2011).

Leyla Safta-Zecheria is a postdoctoral research assistant in the Educational Sciences Department at the West University of Timișoara (Romania). She is trained as a pedagogist and an anthropologist and holds a PhD in Political Science from Central European University, Budapest. Her research interests are in the study of inequality, as it intersects with education, disability and memory studies.

Notes

1. An English summary of the indictment, which is common to all individual court cases opened against BAK academics, can be found at https://barisici nakademisyenler.net/node/431 (accessed 28 December 2019).
2. The Academics for Peace platform provides a continuously updated information platform on the trials of Academics for Peace, available at https://docs.google.com/spreadsheets/u/1/d/e/2PACX-1vT05GTWUQMDot1iPfMsie JsWLGBorbNlJyLP5IdtvJVEcKRw8C8qMxFXPighYZkz7pf2ENP2bXZ3DMo/pubhtml?gid = 1873917137&chrome = false&widget = false (accessed 2 September 2020). The data presented in the chapter were updated on 2 September 2020.
3. See https://www.frontlinedefenders.org/en/case/judicial-harassment-academics-peace (accessed 28 December 2019).
4. See https://barisicinakademisyenler.net/node/1727 (accessed 28 December 2019).
5. This programme was set up to support scholars from Turkey facing persecution and is currently being extended to support scholars at risk of persecution in other countries as well. See https://www.academy-in-exile.eu (accessed 28 December 2019).

References

Aktaş, V., M. Nilsson and K. Borell. 2019. 'Social Scientists Under Threat: Resistance and Self-Censorship in Turkish Academia', *British Journal of Educational Studies* 67(2): 169–86.

Bakırezer, G., D.K. Demirer and A. Yeşilyurt. 2018. 'In Pursuit of an Alternative Academy: The Case of Kocaeli Academy for Solidarity (Non-Peer-Reviewed Reflection Article)', *tripleC: Communication, Capitalism & Critique. Open Access Journal for a Global Sustainable Information Society* 16(1): 234–40.

Barış için akademisyenler (BAK). 2016. 'We Will Not Be a Party to This Crime!' Petition text available at https://barisicinakademisyenler.net/node/63 (accessed 28 December 2019).
Barış için akademisyenler (BAK) Solidarity Group. 2019. 'Academics for Peace: Report by Solidarity Group', 4 December. https://barisicinakademisyenler.net/sites/default/files/Bakreporteng041219.pdf (accessed 26 September 2021).
Bendix-Petersen, E., and B. Davies. 2010. 'In/Difference in the Neoliberalised University', *Learning and Teaching* (3)2: 92–109.
Berg, L.D., E.H. Huijbens and H.G. Larsen. 2016. 'Producing Anxiety in the Neoliberal University', *The Canadian Geographer/le géographe canadien* 60(2): 168–80.
Birced, E., and M. Kocak. 2019. 'Neoliberal Reconstruction of Academia: Gendered Experiences of Precarization', CEU Podcast, 6 December. https://podcasts.ceu.edu/content/neoliberal-reconstruction-academia-gendered-experiences-precarization (accessed 9 January 2020).
Brown, W. 2011. 'Neoliberalized Knowledge', *History of the Present* 1(1): 113–29.
Davies, B., J. Browne, S. Gannon, E. Honan and M. Somerville. 2005. 'Embodied Women at Work in Neoliberal Times and Places', *Gender, Work & Organization* 12(4): 343–62.
de Sousa Santos, B. 2010. 'The University in the Twenty-First Century: Toward a Democratic and Emancipatory University Reform', in M.W. Apple, S.J. Ball and L.A. Gandin (eds), *The Routledge International Handbook of the Sociology of Education*. London: Routledge, pp. 274–82.
Dönmez, P.E., and A. Duman. 2020. 'Marketisation of Academia and Authoritarian Governments: The Cases of Hungary and Turkey in Critical Perspective', *Critical Sociology*, https://doi.org/10.1177/0896920520976780.
Engeli, I. 2019. 'Gender and Sexuality Research in the Age of Populism: Lessons for Political Science', *European Political Science* 19: 226–35.
Grummell, B., D. Devine and K. Lynch. 2009. 'The Care-less Manager: Gender, Care and New Managerialism in Higher Education', *Gender and Education* 21(2): 191–208.
Ilengiz, Ç. 2016. 'Bizim Büyük Ifadesizliğimiz', *Birikim*, 4 March. https://www.birikimdergisi.com/guncel-yazilar/7543/bizim-buyuk-ifadesizligimiz?fbclid=IwAR38mxG3BQVEVHStvzEKB-hH1qsZ_r9P1lBp-yVaZn4X3EpBJqm-QIBvuPk#.XhcVNi2B1QI (accessed 9 January 2020).
Ivancheva, M.P. 2015. 'The Age of Precarity and the New Challenges to the Academic Profession', *Studia Universitatis Babes-Bolyai-Studia Europaea* 60(1): 39–48.
Kendzior, S. 2014. 'Professors Making 10000 a Year? Academia Is Becoming a Profession Only the Elite Can Afford', AlterNet, 11 November. https://www.alternet.org/2014/11/professors-making-10000-year-academia-becoming-profession-only-elite-can-afford-0/ (accessed 28 December 2019).
Lynch, K., M. Crean and M. Moran. 2010. 'Equality and Social Justice: The University as a Site of Struggle', in M.W. Apple, S.J. Ball and L.A. Gandin (eds), *The Routledge International Handbook of the Sociology of Education*. London: Routledge.

Lynch, K., and M. Ivancheva. 2015. 'Academic Freedom and the Commercialisation of Universities: A Critical Ethical Analysis', *Ethics in Science and Environmental Politics* 15(1): 71–85.

Monitor Civicus. 2020. 'Press Freedom a Grave Concern during the Pandemic: Attempts to Ban Gender Studies in Education', 31 July. https://monitor.civicus.org/updates/2020/07/31/press-freedom-grave-concern-during-pandemic-attempts-ban-gender-studies-education/ (accessed 4 August 2020).

Odman, A. 2018. 'Akademiker*innen für den Frieden und die soziale Geographie der "Neuen Akademie" in der Türkei', in I. Ataç, M. Fanizadeh and V. Ağar (eds), *Nach dem Putsch: 16 Anmerkungen zur 'neuen' Türkei*. Berlin: madelbaum verlag.

Open Society Justice Initiative. 2018. 'Legal Analysis of Hungary's Anti-NGO Bill', 5 July. https://www.justiceinitiative.org/publications/legal-analysis-hungarys-anti-ngo-bill (accessed 9 January 2020).

Özcer, Ö. 2018. 'In Turkey, Dismissed Academics Nurture Knowledge Off Campus', Index on Censorship, 14 December. https://www.indexoncensorship.org/2018/12/in-turkey-dismissed-academics-nurture-knowledge-off-campus/ (accessed 28 December 2019).

Özkirimli, U. 2017. 'How to Liquidate a People? Academic Freedom in Turkey and Beyond', *Globalizations* 14(6): 851–56.

Petersen, E.B., and B. Davies. 2010. 'In/Difference in the Neoliberalised University', *Learning and Teaching* 3(2): 92–109.

Petö, A., and M. Kocak. 2019. 'Academic Freedom in "Polypore States": Solidarity Linkages between Turkey and Hungary', CEU Podcast, 19 June. https://podcasts.ceu.edu/content/academic-freedom-polypore-states-solidarity-linkages-between-turkey-and-hungary%20 (accessed 4 February 2021).

Ram, S. 2020. '"Islamo-Leftism": Macron Ramps Up Attacks on Muslims and the Left in France', Counterfire, 19 November. https://www.counterfire.org/articles/opinion/21846-islamo-leftism-macron-ramps-up-attacks-on-muslims-and-the-left-in-france (accessed 4 February 2021).

Stergiou, K.I., and S. Somarakis. 2016. 'Academic Freedom and Tenure: Introduction', *Ethics in Science and Environmental Politics* 15(1): 1–5.

Tören, T., and M. Kutun. 2018. 'Peace Academics from Turkey: Solidarity until the Peace Comes', *Global Labour Journal* 9(1): 103–12.

Vatansever, A. 2020. *At the Margins of Academia: Exile, Precariousness, and Subjectivity*. Leiden: Brill.

CHAPTER 5

The Politics of University Access and Refugee Higher Education Programmes
Can the Contemporary University Be Opened?

CÉLINE CANTAT

◆◆◆

Opening Up the University to Displaced Students?

In recent years, a number of access or bridge programmes aimed at students who have experienced displacement have been established in Europe. While often anchored in the problematic and exceptionalising discourse of a 'migration crisis', such programmes also attempt to respond to a number of unfavourable circumstances faced by displaced students. In addition to financial support, they usually consist of a set of interventions aimed at developing students' linguistic and academic skills, helping them identify their discipline and academic programme of interest and providing support with applications for degrees and funding. As illustrated in this volume, these programmes have taken many forms and mobilised different pedagogies, philosophies and ethos of inclusion and participation. They are also embedded in different types of higher education institutions and systems, which leads to a range of arrangements, objectives and relations to the broader structures of the university.

An important aspect of these programmes is that they are usually concerned not only with the 'moment' of entry (formal acceptance into a university programme) but also with the hierarchies and inequalities in processes of learning, teaching, socialising and knowledge production in the space of the university – which may or may not be explicitly recognised as related to factors of race, class, gender, sexuality, religion and positionality more broadly. In this sense, they could be thought of as sites from which new struggles around closures and openings in and at the margins of the university are being conceptualised and enacted. Yet multiple discussions and formal interviews with colleagues and students involved in related initiatives, as well as my own experience as instructor and academic coordinator in CEU's OLIve programmes, indicate that those are located in a space of tensions and perhaps contradictions. Being geared towards the facilitation of entry into existing structures, they heavily focus on preparing and equipping students in order for them to fit into the norms of behaviours (e.g. how to interact, speak, raise questions and carry one's self in the university) and knowledge (e.g. what is legitimate theory and what rather is seen as merely particular or anecdotical; what forms and epistemologies may conceptual knowledge adopt and so on). Besides, though often exhibited by university administrators on their websites and recruitment booklets, access programmes for displaced students constantly face institutional obstacles and disempowering dynamics inside universities, relegating them to the margins of institutions.

This has, of course, an impact on students themselves; in many cases, as they leave the relatively sheltered units preparing them for degree programmes, they are confronted with university structures and behaviours that have remained unchanged and broadly exclusionary. They might feel intimidated and underrated, like they do not belong or like their specific background and experience are less valued than those of mainstream students from dominant social groups (Aparna et al., this volume; Al Hussein and Mangeni, this volume). In other words, while those working and studying within them may dream of reforming the university, various structural and institutional limits mean that the possibilities for access programmes to propel transformative dynamics and social change remain questionable.

In this chapter, I take interest in two main points: the understandings of access and inclusion that such programmes put forward, and whether a more comprehensive conceptualisation of access can become a starting point to push forward progressive openings of the university and its boundaries. In the first part, I explore the politics of access to higher education in a historical perspective in order to illustrate its connections to (raced, classed, gendered, religion- and sexuality-based) valuations that exist outside the university and to the reproduction of the dominant social order. In the second part, I examine how such politics of access have also been contested and appropriated through a range of struggles focused on challenging the boundaries and contours of higher education institutions and systems, and reflect on some of the issues met by such mobilisations against the historical organisation of the university. With this background in mind, in the third part, I critically reflect on the tensions that come with the institutionalisation of access programmes for displaced learners based on my own experiences and discussions with students and colleagues.

I use empirical examples from three access programmes I engaged or worked with, one in a public, non-elite university in the suburbs of Paris, one in a private and elite American-Hungarian university in Budapest, and one in a public, elite institution in central Paris. While I was a volunteer and subsequently a paid staff member in the Budapest-based programme for several years, my relationship to the two access programmes in France was more distant. In one case, I was mostly connected to the students through my involvement in Syria- and migration-related activism. In the other case, I was employed as a researcher in the university where the programme was being run, and I approached the institution with the intention of working together. Based on these experiences, I examine how transformative processes that aim at progressively reforming the university intersect with and confront deep-seated logics of competition and elitism (Cook, this volume) as well as with other types of transformations that push forward closures, in particular the growing dismantlement of ideas of the universities as a public good and state attacks against critical knowledge (Ivancheva, this volume; Safta-Zecheria, this volume). Ultimately, based on the examples of these programmes, the chapter illustrates the embeddedness of higher education's structures and contents in the historical evolution of the university as an establishment for the reproduction of classed, gendered, racialised social relations and argues that attempts at radically opening the university must constantly push forwards understandings of inclusion that feature both effective access and equal participation within the walls of the university.

Historicising the Politics of University Access and Knowledge Production

Since the opening of the first universities, the issue of who can access them and under which circumstances has been a central concern of actors both internal and external to the university. The politics of access across space and time reflect and are embedded in changing social structures and dominant understandings of who constitutes politically legitimate and socially valued groups in different contexts. In this sense, historicising access demands scrutinising the connection between changing paradigms of in/exclusion in higher education, and broad historical shifts that reconfigure political structures and their relation to different publics. Student selection reflects which socio-political subjects are valued, not solely by educational institutions, but by the broader system and social hierarchies within which these institutions exist. This selection also reflects the needs of rulers for administrating their territories, governing their population and for differentially associating social groups with specific characteristics. As we will see below through a series of examples, universities have also been subjected to conflicting ideologies and, at various points in time, their control has represented an important battlefield for opposing actors, for instance religious authorities versus state sovereignty. Observing who can and who does access university therefore tells us a lot about any particular social and political architecture.

Here, I draw largely on Clancy and Goastèllec's comparative study of university access (2007), which identifies three key organising rationales of access policy over time: inherited merit, equality of rights and equality of opportunity. The authors present these rationales as successive over time, while it rather seems to me that these different logics may also coexist, targeting differently various social groups and taking changing shapes across the (European) education landscape, based on different local traditions and histories of the university. All in all, this section historicises and contextualises university access in order to demonstrate how access connects to broader politics of social organisation and valuation. This background is thus necessary for providing further guidance on the question of how displaced people are currently engaged with in higher education institutions.

The first broad organising principle identified by Clancy and Goastellec is that of 'inherited merit', which governed access in the medieval and so-called early modern university. While students were selected academically, they nonetheless had to belong to specific social groups and categories in order to be considered in the first place. In western Europe, university access was opened almost exclusively to males from upper-class backgrounds living in urban areas. Merit-based selection was thus practised, but included only students belonging to the dominant groups in society. Since the specific features of privileged groups vary across social organisations, historical periods and geographical contexts, the social identity of those gaining access to universities was contingent on particular configurations. Yet the reproduction of social and economic elites, and associated hierarchies, was a key function and organising factor of the early university.

Beyond the socio-economic background of potential students, a range of other factors also determined who could enter sites of higher learning. As demonstrated by Goastellec (2019) in her history of women's access to the university, those factors were determined through the confrontation between different forms of authorities and ideologies. Goastellec shows how, between the fourth and seventh centuries, women from the local elites across western Europe had been able to access learning and education, in particular by entering (in fact sometimes establishing) double monasteries: monastic communities made up of both men and women within which learning was central. The author then shows how the gradual assertion of papal authority meant that, by the time the first universities were opened in this part of the world, in the twelfth and thirteenth centuries, a 'world without women' had been imposed. Double monasteries had been forbidden already in the eighth and ninth centuries and if, for some time, distance from royal and religious powers had allowed local aristocracies to perpetuate social arrangements involving women, the consolidation of central authorities eventually made this impossible. Therefore, with few exceptions, from their opening until the nineteenth century, universities and faculties in western Europe excluded women.

Outside Europe, many of the early 'modern' universities were similarly opened to serve the children of dominant groups. In South Africa, the first colleges were built to educate the children of British migrants while, in Indonesia, the first faculties were created by the Dutch in order to provide access to children from both the colonial and the local elite that cooperated with the colonisers (Clancy and Goastellec 2007). In their review of the educational policies of Spain and the English in Mexico and India, respectively, González and Hsu (2014) show that in colonies in which the native population outnumbered European colonisers, and where colonisation thus crucially relied on native cooperation, the education of native elites was seen as an integral part of imperial enterprise.

One of the primary roles of the university has indeed been to produce individuals able to administer the state and contribute to its economy. In such colonial contexts, this was premised on a narrative that saw educating natives as necessary in order to make them understand the new political, moral and economic landscape of colonialism. Importantly, this also foreclosed the possibility of native knowledges, seen as inadequate for dealing with 'modernity'. Higher education was thus closely connected to the civilising and proselyte dimensions of imperial endeavours. For instance, in India, several universities such as the University of Calcutta, the University of Bombay and the University of Madras (opened in 1857), and the University of the Punjab (1882) and the University of Allahabad (1887), were set up following a recommendation from the President of the Board of Control of the East India Company (EIC), in order to 'enhance the moral character of Indians and thus supply EIC with civil servants who can be trusted'.[1] The relation between access and knowledge production was thus at the heart of the politics of inclusion within higher education, while these early examples of internationalised higher education endeavours also highlight the close relationship between the state and capital at play in the establishment of higher learning institutions.

In contrast, in the context of settler colonialism, González and Hsu (2014) show that in countries such as the USA, where white settlers displaced the native populations and carried out the work of the colonies themselves (or by importing labour through slavery), the first colleges were catering exclusively to the offspring of the white Anglo-Saxon Protestant community. It is also interesting to observe how, at the individual level, participation in higher education could be seen as a means or an attempt to subvert dominant regimes of citizenship. In his study of indigenous elites in colonial Mexico, for instance, Villella notes that holding a university degree 'indicated something more than mere education' for members of the local elite: it was a quality that 'transcended ethnicity' (2012: 12) and a means to circumvent colonial hierarchies based on racial stratification. In this sense, university education can be both a result of and a tool towards the acquisition of broader participation rights. Yet politics of knowledge production and participation remained embedded in larger social and political norms to the extent that status acquired through learning would often run up against embedded racisms that obstructed equity, and foreclosed certain modes of knowing and seeing the world.

One important exception in settler colonial contexts were historically Black colleges and universities in the USA, institutions of higher education established primarily in the years after the American Civil War and before the Civil Rights Act of 1964, often with the support of religious missionary organisations, and with the intention of serving the African American community. At the time, especially in the segregated south, the majority of higher education institutions were white and completely excluded African Americans or used quotas to limit their admission. These colleges thus offered the only higher education opportunity for Black students, and they were often characterised by the engagement of Black teachers for whom imparting knowledge and skills to Black youth was seen as a political statement (hooks 1994). Related to our topic here, an important episode concerns the fact that those historically Black institutions were among the only ones to hire Jewish refugee academics (both men and women!) fleeing Nazi Germany and who had arrived in the USA in the 1930s (Jewell 2002; see also Edgcomb 1993), thereby setting an early tradition of sanctuary academia.

Inscribing Access in Rights: Mass Education and the Limits of Formal Inclusion

The second broad organising principle of access policy identified by Clancy and Goastellec is the norm of 'equality of rights'. Broadly speaking, this rationale emerged with the rise of the nation-state and consolidated as part of the welfare state project – meaning, in western Europe, particularly in the period following the end of the Second World War. It is based on the belief that higher education should be accessible to larger numbers and be inclusive of individuals regardless of their social origin. It is seen as a public good that benefits both the individual and society: the state is seen as responsible for expanding access to the broadest spectrum of students, including those from under-represented groups. This, of course, was in no way an exclusively western European process. For instance, during the same period, in eastern Europe, nationalisation coupled with communism also promised to guarantee equal access to education in ways that can be seen as more extensive and encouraged multiple academic and student exchanges with the global south and non-aligned countries, thereby effectively opening up the university to different groups. This idea of the university as a public good draws on its gradual opening over the course of the nineteenth century, in the context of the solidification of the (capitalist) nation-state and of the emergence of a series of nation-building institutions. The university is considered as having a role to play in the construction of a sense of national belonging and loyalty. As noted by Kwiek (2005: 331), 'with the rise of the nation-state, the university was set at the apex of institutions defining national identity'. The university therefore functions in close association with state power, and its role in relation to the public sphere is mediated by the dominant political project of the nation-state. In this context, the issues of the responsibilities of the institution and the boundaries of the student body are resolved by their insertion within the broader project of the nation-state. The 'nationalisation' of higher education (Neave 2001; Kwiek 2005) was also connected to the nationalisation of scholars: the introduction of civil servant status for academics hence contributed 'to impress firmly upon the consciousness of academia its role as an emanation of the national wisdom and genius, creativity and interest' (Neave 2001: 30).

This nationalisation was also reflected in the development of centralised procedures and patterns of validation and certification of academic competencies and education. These differ from country to country and reflect varying ways in which knowledge is valued and assessed.

In western Europe, this set the context for a massification of access in the period following the Second World War. While the process was also shaped by economic motives and demographic needs (e.g. the production of particular types of labour), it should be understood in relation to a specific moment of capitalism marked by the rise of the welfare state and particular ideas of its responsibilities. The idea of the university as a public good opened up space for more radical political and ideological agendas concerned with social inclusion and equality. Those translated into calls for more equity, including by requesting that university systems and students/employees better reflect the diversity of societies. Those calls were also framed as a matter of democratic legitimacy for the state.

It is in part such arguments that were mobilised in struggles to secure women's participation in higher education. As of the 1870s, an increasing number of systems around the world started granting women the right to study, graduate and teach. At later stages, the norm of equality of rights – and struggles to achieve it – were also invoked to remove formal barriers to other social groups that had been preventing access to university on the basis of race, ethnicity or religion. It is important to highlight the conflictual and combative aspects of the opening up of the university. For instance, in the USA, it was not until 1954 and the *McLaurin v. Oklahoma State Regents* decision by the United States Supreme Court case that racial segregation in state-supported graduate education was prohibited so that Black students could formally access all public higher education institutions. This decision followed a series of legal struggles started two decades earlier by African American scholars and activists who helped plaintiffs bring lawsuits against segregated school systems in the name of equal rights.

However, equality of rights as an organising principle around access places an unexamined notion of merit as the sole factor of student selection. In theory, there is now equality of access because formal barriers on the basis of gender, race and class have been officially removed. However, 'merit' is defined in relation to students' ability to acquire certain (dominant) norms, knowledges and resources, and is understood as an individual process. The notion is also premised on specific moral values and particular ideas of success, which people have to work towards in order to be seen as having merited their inclusion into university systems. The existence of social hierarchies that define what constitutes desirable knowledge, skills and norms away from underprivileged groups, and the persistence of social inequalities which in turn shape how much students may access such competencies, are not taken into account. Ideas of merit are in fact premised on certain representations of normalcy and desirable outcomes that reflect the experience and features of particular (privileged) socio-economic groups. In other words, if left unexamined, the notion of merit ends up privileging those students who already have access to enhanced social, economic and cultural capital. Therefore, meritocracy often ends up reproducing dominant social hierarchies while concealing the deeply unequal basis on which access politics operate. In other words, certain notions of merit that in fact favour more privileged groups are one of the points of crystallisation of the tensions and conflicts between the structures of higher education and attempts to open up its boundaries.

Moreover, in a context of increased participation, inequalities in higher education also took on a different form as discriminatory ideas of merit became networked into unequal education systems. In particular, diversification and hierarchisation along disciplinary, institutional and sectoral lines has meant that there is a growing degree of stratification within higher education systems. In France, for instance, the public university system exists in parallel to a highly competitive system of *classes préparatoires* and *grandes écoles*, which to this day is recruiting students among the most privileged social strata in order to train them for upper-level positions in the public and private sectors. These hierarchies exist both between and within the higher education institutions and academic disciplines (Donmez 2020). Therefore, even though access was formally democratised, inequality in relation to higher education became reconfigured in terms of the type of education access granted to different individuals and social groups. Inequality is thus reproduced through various mechanisms, which also include the development of a private sector only available to the wealthiest social layers or institutional stratification where elite universities continue to recruit students from the most privileged social backgrounds. Over the last two decades, these processes have been further encouraged through the intensification of competition within academia, premised on a culture of academic auditing and ranking where all tasks and outputs are increasingly quantified and assessed, with the view of classifying institutions and academics in relation to one another (Cook, this volume). Again, this shows that the politics of access do not solely revolve around the issue of admission, but also involve a range of nuances and dynamics pertaining to the kind of education and knowledge students can engage with, and their possibility to shape and define those. In other words, thinking through these issues shows the embeddedness of structures that make the project of opening up the university extremely difficult.

In *Teaching to Transgress,* bell hooks (1994) proposes a disturbing account of desegregation. She recalls the combative and caring spirit of the segregated high school she attended, where Black teachers imparted a sense of pride into their students. In contrast, she remembers her shock when she entered a desegregated, highly racist and white higher education institution, where she felt like an intruder and where teachers treated her as someone to be adjusted (hooks 1994). This less celebratory account of desegregation powerfully interrogates the limits of the university as an institution, its embeddedness in structures of domination, and the way in which classrooms can become sites for the reproduction and reassertion of social (racial, gendered, class. . .) hierarchies. It illustrates how these structures lead to the normalisation of certain types of pedagogies that can be exclusionary and geared towards reproducing certain hierarchies.

Beyond Formal Access: Rethinking Inclusion, Equality and Equity

In this context, Clancy and Goastellec identify a third governing rationale of university access, that was pushed forward by various groups at the internal or external margins of university in order to respond to and rectify some of the shortcomings of formal equality. According to the authors, the principle of 'equity' emerges from the recognition that formal opportunity of rights does not suffice to prevent social inequalities being reproduced within the university. Therefore, it emerges from a critical assessment of the notions of merit as used in mainstream meritocratic discourses, which calls for interventions aimed at redressing existing inequalities in order to effectively widen access to students from more marginalised groups. This has been done, for instance, through a redefinition of merit that accounts for students' positions in social structures, contextualises school results obtained prior to seeking university entry, and focuses on students' potential and expected benefits from higher education, rather than merely their projected individual ability to obtain a high-class degree (Clancy and Goastellec 2007). In turn, these considerations have led some institutions to design alternative admission paths or to implement access programmes.

These strategies of widening access have been, in many cases, mobilised by prestigious institutions, traditionally tasked with the training of national elites, in order to widen their student body, often following an understanding of the role of prestigious universities as cultivators of individual talents, regardless of background. However, although there is a growing consensus around the need for such affirmative actions, national traditions of elite formation, structures and modes of recruitment in public higher education systems, and dominant understandings of social inequalities, contribute to determining to a great extent the shape, extent, structure and availability of such interventions across contexts.

While they may be extremely important and beneficial at the individual level, generally speaking, these strategies do not fundamentally challenge broader structures, nor do they question in deeper ways how universities participate in reproducing inequalities through filtering access in certain ways, and through their knowledge positions and pedagogies. Rather, they are often intended to bring people into the structures of power while downplaying or limiting their capacity to change those structures.

This short and non-comprehensive overview has attempted to show that university access is crucially embedded in larger processes that prop up the structures of higher education by connecting it to the reproduction of a dominant social order and normalising its inequalities. Notions such as that of merit used in a naturalising way (e.g. people either have or do not have skills and talents at the individual level that allow them to succeed at school and university, and these are seen as disconnected from material conditions) are in turn put at the service of an exclusionary vision of higher education. I have also attempted to illustrate some of the tensions and potential contradictions that may emerge from struggles around enlarging access and opening up the university. I now turn to reflecting on the access programmes I have experienced in order to reflect on the possibilities and limits they come across as they try to navigate this dense field of possibilities and limitations.

Can Access Programmes to Higher Education Open Up the University?

I now draw more directly on my own experiences as teacher and academic coordinator in access programmes for displaced students in Budapest, and as an individual whose research, academic and activist work centres on migrants' and education rights. Through these experiences and interests, I have developed overall knowledge of the workings of access programmes for displaced students in different European contexts. On the basis of my professional and political activities, and of my broader research into such programmes, I present below reflections on three preparatory programmes. These reflections do not have any pretension to exhaustivity. Rather, they point to a number of tensions and possibilities which I have identified as of importance when thinking about and working around higher education and displacement. My relationship to and involvement in these three programmes vary: in one case, I was involved indirectly in a programme as it involved people I work with in the general field of migrants' rights and migration-related activism; in another case, I worked in shaping, developing and running a full-time preparatory programme; and, in a third case, I was tasked with investigating the details of an existing programme with a view to incorporating them into a consortium focused on providing access to university for refugees. The insights I develop below aim to help us examine the way in which such programmes interact, challenge or at times reproduce the complex dynamics and politics around access I have attempted to describe above.

These insights do not pretend to provide a definitive answer to the question of whether the university may or may not be 'opened up' through the inclusion of socially marginalised students – and those who experienced displacement in particular. Besides the fact that inclusion can be tokenistic or differentiated, as mentioned, it also seems to me that such openings always remain unfinished and continuous processes. As structures, relations and contents that exist in evolving socio-political contexts, universities are always in motion as they are shaped by a range of broader developments. In recent decades, for instance, what has been called the neoliberal project and characterised by a situated yet connected series of dismantlement and privatisation of public services has had a key influence on the structures, role, content and working conditions in universities. What I attempt to do, rather, through a series of vignettes based on access programmes I have encountered, is to sketch out some of the issues and possibilities that emerge as we set out to run programmes enlarging university access for displaced students, and see how these impact on the question of the opening up of higher education in a broad sense.

The first 'refugee access programme' I was involved in was launched in France in early 2016. It was primarily offering language classes, in a public university located in the northeast suburbs of Paris. The stated aim was that, once students reach a good command of the language, they would be able to join study tracks at the university (for a critique of certain approaches to language learning, see Burke, this volume). The limited financial means were somewhat counterbalanced by enthusiastic instructors and a combative identity based in the local working-class and migration-related history. Being open to those displaced and dispossessed by global processes and local structures was seen as an integral part of the identity of this left-leaning, critical institution, with roots in student protests and experimental pedagogies.[2] Moreover, the history of exile characterising this part of the Parisian suburbs was evoked as providing a particularly fertile ground for the initiative, whereby mutual understanding between local and displaced students was seen as more instinctive than it would have been in other institutions.[3] Prospective students in the programme also shared this impression, and explained how they appreciated 'not feeling like absolute outsiders here' and, as put by a Syrian friend, 'kind of not sticking out'.[4]

My presence was connected to my involvement in migration solidarity circles and my close relationships with several of the people who had been selected as students. In later conversations, the framework put forward by students to explain their ease was one of intersectionality, whereby the working-class feeling and the presence of Black and Arab students provided a frame for identification and belonging for many. This testifies to the situated and political nature of access, as an experience at the intersection of structural and interpersonal relations and shaped by a number of hierarchies. However, students in the access programme still felt that they had to account for their university interactions in terms that other students, albeit from working-class or migration-related backgrounds, did not. Their narrative insisted on shades of belonging, on questions around the legitimacy of their presence, and on a relation that remained premised on forms of hospitality rather than rights.

I left France a few weeks after the programme first started. By then, a series of strikes and occupations had begun in opposition to a proposed reform of the French labour code, and students of the university had mobilised in support of the social movement. Many of the students from the language programme had joined in the protests and several reported that this common political experience broke down further barriers and produced new grounds for identification. What is perhaps important to highlight, then, is that in contexts where the university retains a public and political role as a space of mobilisation, different transformative horizons sometimes can become imaginable.

Ultimately, the students' experiences of the programme were shaped by the intersection of two converse understandings not solely of university but also of the state, its institutions, and its relation to a broader public. On the one hand, the commitment to a free, public higher education system, which should be accessible to all and function as a means for social change, produced an inclusive environment, where students interacted with peers from a range of backgrounds and felt 'not like outsiders'. While the concrete realisation of equity still met challenges, the feeling that there was a principled dedication to offer equal opportunities was reported by many students in discussions. On the other hand, the unfolding of the programme encountered a social movement that emerged in response to attempts at further neoliberalising the French labour market, through a law that is part of a wide set of measures trying to reshape the French state and its public responsibilities and roles. In this sense, the programme and its students were affected by the exclusionary tendencies that come with the broader neoliberal project of successive French governments, premised on a reduction of public budgets and a shrinking of university resources, which make the effective possibility of inclusion and equity ever slimmer. In sum, this first programme is a striking illustration of the difficulty of setting a genuine social agenda for higher education under conditions of neoliberalism.

I came to explore this issue from a different angle later that same year. In the spring of 2016, I started teaching an academic skills class as a volunteer instructor in the OLIve weekend programme. I had recently moved to Budapest and started working at CEU, a private university established in 1991 with the mission of 'building open and democratic societies' through providing fully funded academic training to the region's youth. By the time I joined, CEU was undergoing intensive transformations, including a process of internationalisation but also a questioning of its 'social' model in favour of a more heavily fee-paying system. These ongoing dynamics were further exacerbated by political attacks against the institution on the part of the Hungarian authorities.

I became involved as the programme was entering its second term, and welcoming new students among its cohort. On the opening day of the new session, some of the academics and administrators involved in creating and running the programme greeted the students, old and new, and insisted on the sense of community, friendship and mutual learning that had characterised the first term of the programme and that they hoped would continue in this new session. OLIve also started in a grassroots manner through the mobilisation of members of the university during their time off and in a volunteer fashion, but was taking place in a private, privileged, English-speaking institution in Budapest. Its politics were less rooted in an intersectional approach to the common positionalities of would-be students and members of the university; it nonetheless insisted on notions of participation, comradeship and equality.

Ten months later, we launched another access programme (a full-time version of the original course), for which I was appointed as a salaried academic coordinator, and which had received funding from the European Commission and the Open Society Foundation. In this position, I had frequent (direct or mediated) interactions with the university's administration and was to an extent dependent on their understanding of our work. What became clear through multiple episodes during which the scope and goals of our programme were being discussed was that, for senior managers, the focus was not on refugee education as a political commitment to further equality, but rather on the programme allowing the 'brightest' to fulfil their own individual talents through their inclusion within the ranks of this prestigious institution (Cook, this volume). This exceptionalising speech was setting the students aside from, and above, other displaced people and using their admission as the benchmark of their social worth and their positions in hierarchies.

On several occasions, I was also puzzled to hear CEU's senior management referring solely to the two, male and tenured, members of staff who became directors (respectively of one of the programmes and of the newly established unit hosting them). The way the directors were turned into the people 'in charge' concealed the collective effort by members of the university, activists and students themselves who created, shaped, fundraised and ran these programmes. It also hid the uneven distribution of labour within the programmes and the double marginalisation experienced by some of its staff – by being peripheral to the key departments and centres of the institution as a whole, and by being kept in a state of precarity and unstable employment. Thereby, the complex story of mutual work, tensions and disagreements that had led to the programmes being established and run was replaced with a narrative of visionary (masculine) minds conjuring a vision from above. I also frequently felt awkward about having myself moved from being a volunteer teacher to a paid employee (on a part-time, short-term contract) officially tasked (among other things) with 'supervising' the hourly-paid instructors who provided students with teaching, mentoring and support.

This illustrates the way in which the process of institutionalisation – which had seemed valuable as we hoped it would bring stability and durability to our activities and thus to our students – came with embedding our initiative within the moral economy and hierarchies of this quickly changing private university. In other words, we were faced with the fact that only certain students were recognised as legitimate subjects, certain forms of labour were valued, and particular notions of merit, success and prestige prevailed. While, as members of the programme, we remained critical of this approach, we also found ourselves engaging with it, for instance by allowing certain institutional representations of our programme that worked towards promoting our institution as a space of social justice and inclusion, even though the narrative reduced those concepts to the cultivation of individual skills, in this case the adjustment of 'refugees' to their new environment. The gap between our experience largely shaped by marginalisation and precarity – as a university unit and its workers and students – and the representations of our work was reminiscent of Sara Ahmed's analysis of the difference between institutions' symbolic commitments to diversity and the experience of those who embody this diversity within institutions (Ahmed 2012).

Although many of us interrogated our pedagogical approach and discussed our drive to develop more alternative, decolonial and/or feminist modes of learning, teaching and producing knowledge, our institutional status and the goal of promoting our students' inclusion in the institution created many restrictions and obstacles in that regard. Most importantly, perhaps, while one of our original aims was to indeed open up the university and to promote inclusion based on equity – by rethinking our curriculums, pushing reforms to administrative structures and addressing the discriminatory if not racist stigmas still present in the university – we found ourselves spending most of our energies on trying to conform to existing systems in order to secure study places for our students. When, a couple of years later, our programmes were suspended (see Introduction, this volume; Trencsényi and Braverman, this volume), we realised once more how little we had achieved in terms of 'opening up the university'. In a private university that was experiencing intensive transformative dynamics, taking it away from a mission of providing fully funded education, we remained a surplus and marginal programme, easily disposable and certainly not seen as fully belonging to the university. Our students could be sacrificed in the name of a (racialised, gendered and class-based) idea of the 'greater good' that, it transpired, excluded them.[5]

The third programme I came into contact with was run at another French – prestigious and elite – institution which I joined on a postdoctoral contract after leaving Hungary. I only had marginal interactions with the programme and its students, and these reflections are based on observation and my involvement in a series of short discussions with the institution's management, as well as with some of the programme's coordinators and teachers. This education programme for refugees had been established primarily following an impulse by concerned members of the student community and then subsequently institutionalised. Partly because of the prestige of the institution in the French higher education landscape, I had previously heard about the initiative and been exposed to some of the official communication around the institution welcoming refugee students within its walls. The adopted model was, however, following a rather different rationale than those underpinning the two other programmes I had been involved in. For instance, when the teaching activities started, the university offered to lend some of its facilities to a separate NGO so that they could run the programme in their building and benefit from their institutional label. While a number of professors have since become involved, the institutional involvement remains limited so that, all in all, the programme exists in a more tangential relation to the broader structure, sharing a space but not necessarily partaking in the same circumstances.

Importantly in this regard, the programmes were not conceived as bridges or access paths to the institution. Rather, classes were seen as an opportunity for students to share in the privileges of an elite university, before continuing their academic life or picking up a career elsewhere. They were temporary guests, welcomed under certain circumstances for a defined period, but not seen as potential equal members of the community. In relation to the typology of access proposed above, this programme seems to rely on yet another path, where a form of differential inclusion is on offer. Rather than educational courses aiming at and based on equity, it is premised on the (necessarily arbitrary) appreciation of the individual circumstances and difficulties of students, seen primarily as 'refugees'.

This indeed resembles a humanitarian gesture, where the right to education is eclipsed by forms of exceptionalism and benevolence that produce uneven and unequal sets of opportunities. Ultimately, and without questioning the commitment to the students animating the programme's instructors, the structural form taken by this programme reflects the extreme challenges that such initiatives may face in the increasingly privatised and neoliberalised landscape of European higher education. It shows that, in spite of attempts at opening up the university, students often face forms of institutional glass ceiling.

All in all, these three programmes follow different shapes, modalities and ethics and exist in different types of institutions – both public and private, elite and more accessible. While broadly identifiable as access programmes, the questions of access for whom and to what are responded to in largely different ways. The budget and resources also vary greatly, leading to differentiate configurations and outcomes. However, they also shared similar features, such as their reliance on short-term funding and precariously employed or voluntary teaching labour; their marginal position within the university's structures even where official discourses present them as central; and the complex sets of relation that their students entertain with the broader community, characterised by various degrees of inclusion but always framed as raising the question of 'belonging'.

These experiences say something about the historical institutionalisation of the university in relation to the capitalist nation-state and its class, racial and gendered hierarchies, and the way this has propped up powerful structures of marginalisation. They also illustrate that inclusion is about much more than formal access and that we need to think beyond the 'moment' of entry – which, for many prospective university students and employees, is always much more than a mere moment – in order to accumulate the necessary capital, resources, networks and formal documents required for effective admission. Inclusion is thus an ongoing process that is both shaped structurally and experienced subjectively, through interpersonal relations with members and representatives of the institution, specific learning experiences and pedagogical practices, and the politics of knowledge production, among others. As explained in the Introduction and Afterword to this volume, in the case of displaced students, the issue of formal access intersects not only with the racialised, gendered and class-based social hierarchies that structure societies in their new countries of residence, but also with migration law and welfare systems, with implications in terms of the administrative 'readability' of students' situations and of their connected dependency on the good-will of specific bureaucrats.

Conclusion

By historicising issues of access to university, this chapter has attempted to provide an angle of reflection on the relation between higher education and inequalities. In particular, it has set out to show that higher education institutions have historically intended the reproduction of an elite or the production of individuals seen as capable to work towards the maintenance of certain structures. While there have been important struggles around such boundaries, which have managed to widen access to higher education for social groups previously marginalised or forbidden attendance, this has not been enough to radically transform and open up the university.

In particular, the very structures that sustain higher education systems and their connections to dominant socio-political projects mean that certain ways of teaching, working and organising have been naturalised. This process narrows down and limits what is seen as constituting education, knowledge, social change and transformation within the university. It has also created norms and hierarchies. When access programmes that aim at pushing against such systems enter the university and become institutionalised within it, they come across not only the formal boundaries preventing access to displaced students on administrative or financial grounds, they also face the way in which certain moral economies have become normalised and certain values have been institutionalised in ways that impede deeper changes. While there is no definite answer to how those pressures may be navigated and fought against, a recognition of the complex set of politics that frame the issue of access, and how it relates to structures, knowledges and modes of being within the university, seems to be the unavoidable starting point from which to keep rethinking and expanding our praxis collectively.

◆

Céline Cantat holds a PhD in Refugee Studies from the Centre for Research on Migration, Refugees and Belonging at the University of East London and is currently a Research Fellow at Sciences Po Paris. Previously, Céline worked at the CEU in Budapest where she conducted project MIGSOL: Migration Solidarity and Acts of Citizenship along the Balkan Route and worked as teacher and academic director for CEU's OLIve programmes. Her research interests include migration solidarity, globalisation and migration, racism and exclusion in Europe, state formation and dynamics of mass displacement.

Notes

1. Wood's Despatch of 1854, available at https://archive.org/stream/dli.csl.5554/5554_djvu.txt (accessed 22 November 2021).
2. Discussions with a range of people present on the programme's opening day, 7 March 2016.

3. Observations based on attending the opening day of the programme (7 March 2016), and on conversations with organisers, volunteers, teachers and prospective students.
4. Discussions with students on opening day and on subsequent occasions.
5. Other critical disciplines were also put under extreme pressure. For instance, official accreditation for gender studies programmes was revoked by the authorities. In many ways, these attacks belong to a larger project of the government to erase any form of diversity both in higher education and beyond.

References

Ahmed, S. 2012. *On Being Included: Racism and Diversity in Institutional Life*. Durham, NC: Duke University Press.

Bhatia, M. 2020. 'The Permission to Be Cruel: Street-Level Bureaucrats and Harms against People Seeking Asylum'. *Critical Criminology* 28(1): 277–92.

Clancy, P., and G. Goastellec. 2007. 'Exploring Access and Equity in Higher Education: Policy and Performance in a Comparative Perspective', *Higher Education Quarterly* 61(2): 136–54.

Donmez, P. 2020. 'Educational Enquiry Reflective Report'. Unpublished.

Edgcomb, G.S. 1993. *From Swastika to Jim Crow: Refugee Scholars at Black Colleges*. Malabar, FL: Krieger.

Goastellec, G. 2019. 'L'accès à l'Université enjeu de l'organisation sociale', *SociologieS*, Dossiers: Repenser les comparaisons internationales: enjeux épistémologiques et méthodologiques. http://journals.openedition.org/sociologies/12152.

González, C., and F. Hsu. 2014. 'Education and Empire: Colonial Universities in Mexico, India and the United States', Research and Occasional Papers Series, University of California at Berkeley, Center for Studies in Higher Education 7(14).

Graham, M. 2002. 'Emotional Bureaucracies: Emotions Civil Servants, and Immigrants in the Swedish Welfare State', *Ethos* 30(3): 199–226.

hooks, b. 1994. *Teaching to Transgress: Education as the Practice of Freedom*. Routledge.

Jewell, J.O. 2002. 'To Set an Example: The Tradition of Diversity at Historically Black Colleges and Universities', *Urban Education* 37(1): 7–21.

Kwiek, M. 2005. 'The University and the State in a Global Age: Renegotiating the Traditional Social Contract?', *European Educational Research Journal* 4(4): 324–41.

Lipsky, M. 2010. *Street-Level Bureaucracy: Dilemmas of the Individual in Public Service*. New York: Russell Sage Foundation.

Neave, G. 2001. 'The European Dimension in Higher Education: An Excursion into the Modern Use of Historical Analogues', in J. Huisman, P. Maassen and G. Neave (eds), *Higher Education and the Nation-State*. Oxford: Pergamon.

Villella, P.B. 2012. 'Indian Lords, Hispanic Gentlemen: The Salazars of Colonial Tlaxcala', *The Americas* 69(1): 1–36.

PART II
RE-LEARNING TEACHING

CHAPTER 6
'Can We Think about How to Improve the World?'
Designing Curricula with Refugee Students

MWENZA BLELL, JOSIE MCLELLAN, RICHARD PETTIGREW AND TOM SPERLINGER

In an aside in *Death of a Discipline*, a book about the 'death' of comparative literary studies, Gayatri Chakravorty Spivak describes sitting in with incoming undergraduates at the City University of New York (CUNY), 87 per cent of whom were in 'so-called remedial' English classes (Spivak 2003: 11–12):

> There are Haitians and West Africans in those CUNY remedial classes whose imaginations are crossing and being crossed by a double aporia – the cusp of two imperialisms. I have learned something from listening to their talk about and in Creole/French/so-called pidgin and English-as-a-second-language crossing-into-first – the chosen tongue. I have silently compared their imaginative flexibility, so remarkably and necessarily much stronger, because constantly in use for social survival and mobility, than that of the Columbia undergraduate, held up by the life-support system of a commercializing anglophone culture that trivializes the humanities.

Spivak notes how sitting in with these students revealed to her 'the institutional incapacity to cope with the crossroads of race, gender and class – even when the teacher has the best will in the world'.

This chapter arises from our experiences of listening to students in a context outside the formal structures of the university. We describe a case study of a taster course with two refugee charities in Bristol, in which responsiveness to the students was not a point of departure or classroom technique or feedback mechanism, but the starting point for the curriculum that was pursued. Through this, we consider the value to higher education institutions of recognising the knowledge that refugee and migrant students bring with them, including those skills they have developed for 'social survival and mobility', rather than treating them as having a 'deficit' that needs to be made up in 'remedial' lessons. In particular, we consider how this might become the work of apparently elite institutions, like Columbia, which are normally closed to such students. This case study thus raises similar questions to those posed by Spivak. How can institutions create capacity to respond to the intersections of race, gender and class, which are often experienced at their most acute by students themselves (or those unable to become students)? How can they enable, rather than constraining, their teaching staff who have the 'will' to undertake such work? Like the other chapters in this book, it provides evidence of the transformative and disruptive potential of stepping outside the usual constraints and structures of university life, and the ways in which we might move towards a more equitable admissions process.

Context

Since 2013, the University of Bristol has offered a year-long Foundation programme in the arts and humanities, which provides a route into undergraduate study for students without any prior qualifications. The Foundation is a year-long course that students take before they start on a degree programme. It provides a combination of study skills and thematic content-based units, one of them a liberal arts-style module called 'What Does It Mean to Be Human?', which is designed to introduce students to the range of academic subjects they might study during their degree. If a student completes the programme successfully, they can progress onto an undergraduate degree at Bristol or apply to study elsewhere.

As part of the recruitment activity for the Foundation programme, the university offers taster courses every year. These are designed collaboratively with local community organisations, including those that support refugees, asylum seekers and wider migrant communities as well as organisations working with single parents, those in recovery from addiction, organisations for women involved in the criminal justice system and others. The Foundation programme is relatively small scale, recruiting thirty students per year, and from that around twenty typically progress to a degree. From 2019, it was expanded to incorporate a social sciences pathway, and increased its intake to fifty students, rising to sixty-five in 2020, when Economics and Finance pathways were also added.[1]

When the programme was initially designed, the taster courses were introduced primarily as a way to recruit students to the programme who may not have thought that university study was something they wanted to pursue; or who wanted to pursue it, but felt that the financial risks and the investment of time were too substantial; or who wanted to study, but felt the University of Bristol would not admit them or that they would feel excluded were they to study there. Early tasters were run in partnership with organisations that support single parents, a charity supporting adults experiencing chaotic circumstances (including those in recovery from addiction) and a youth education charity, with a number of students applying successfully to the Foundation programme and positive feedback from others about the wider benefits of the taster in itself.

As the Foundation programme developed, it became clear that these tasters, co-designed in equal partnership with the community organisations that hosted them and the potential students they would recruit, provided a very creative pedagogical space in which ways of teaching and facilitating learning could be expanded and diversified well beyond the conventional methods typical of UK higher education. The tasters have remained valuable as a way to reach students who aren't already at the point of knowing they would like to apply to university: each year, we receive a substantial batch of applications from students who have learned of the course through this route. But they have become something else as well. They became a catalyst for rethinking and transforming the university itself by enabling all those involved to think about what purpose the university serves, how the expertise a university curates should be made available to a range of communities, and how education can be led by learners themselves. This was particularly true in the taster course run by Mwenza Blell in collaboration with Bristol Refugee Rights and Refugee Women of Bristol. In this chapter we combine Mwenza's perspective on what it was like to run this course, with the reflections of Josie, Richard and Tom, who, as former programme directors of the Foundation programme, developed a range of taster courses, and guided the transition of students into university study.

Case Study by Mwenza Blell

Two organisations, Bristol Refugee Rights and Refugee Women of Bristol, collaborated with the University of Bristol Foundation team to arrange a set of taster sessions about anthropology which were held between

April and June 2015 in the Malcolm X Centre in St Pauls, a neighbourhood famous beyond Bristol for its longstanding Afro-Caribbean population, its Carnival and its 1980 uprising (Slater and Anderson 2012).

Bristol Refugee Rights (BRR) had access to an old projector and a mobile pull-down screen so I prepared and brought slides on my laptop for each session. I assigned no advance readings, expected nothing to be done by the attendees outside of class time, did not expect that the same people would necessarily attend each week, and, although there was childcare made available downstairs, made it clear I was happy with the presence of children. (Participants on the course were able to make use of the creche run by Bristol Refugee Rights each Wednesday afternoon.) I'm an anthropologist but the course, which was built into BRR's existing programme of 'supplementary' courses, was advertised under the name 'Understanding Different Cultures', which avoided the use of a little-known, potentially fearsome and unnecessary word like anthropology. A Bristol Refugee Rights staff member provided essential support for the sessions by targeting people whose spoken English was strong enough to make participation feasible and inviting them to the sessions as well as sending text message reminders each week. BRR, then, provided essential infrastructure and support for participants, without which the taster would not have been possible. The attendees varied in their facility with English but all were able to share thoughts in the classroom.

At the first session, the people attending asked if they would receive a certificate because they liked the idea of getting proof of their participation at the end. Josie McLellan, who was then one of the programme directors, arranged for there to be University of Bristol certificates given at the last session and she handed these out herself. Although we made these certificates look as 'official' as possible, including the university and BRR logos, and printing them on good quality card, the sessions were not officially accredited by the university. If we had decided to pursue accreditation for the course, this would immediately have changed the format and content (since, for example, learning aims would need to have been specified in advance) and would have raised the likelihood that a fee would need to be attached, even if it could then be waived, since all accredited programmes within universities now carry a student fee. In other words, it would have been much harder to get started in anything like a spontaneous spirit or one that was responsive to who turned up. Fifteen people attended at least one of the sessions and six people attended four or more of the six sessions. Those who had attended four or more sessions were offered a certificate. The sessions were once a week for two hours in the early afternoon just after a very well-attended hot lunch for asylum seekers and new refugees at the centre, but finishing in time to accommodate collecting children from school. Tea, coffee and biscuits were available in each session during a short break about halfway through. It added to the happy and relaxed feeling in each session to have something to eat and drink together, and I noticed the contrast with teaching in the university, where students often bring their own cups of coffee. Having a break together to get drinks is different, less individual, and perhaps it helps to further break down hierarchies.

Content

In the past when carrying out non-university-credit courses 'in the community', I chose to organise the teaching in such a way that I taught only what the students asked to learn more about and wanted the chance to discuss. The first time I used this approach was in a free and unaccredited English Communication Skills class that I offered as a volunteer in an organisation serving women newly arrived in the UK from South Asia. I knew we would only have a few sessions together so I wanted them to be as useful as possible. We were able to communicate in South Asian dialects and basic English so I simply asked them where they most needed better communication skills so we could focus on the vocabulary relevant to those situations, rather than more generic content they could learn in longer formal English courses once they had settled in. As a result, we practised things like communicating with doctors and nurses about health problems, since language interpreters were rarely provided in those situations. I wanted to do something similar with these taster sessions and Josie was very supportive of the idea.

As an anthropologist, my research practice is ideally to encourage people to talk about things that interest them. The idea of imposing topics that feel irrelevant to people's lives is something which feels unpleasant to me. Perhaps because teaching 'in the community' is more explicitly for the benefit of the people attending, it seems arrogant to think I would know what would benefit them. I believe that the way I've benefited from higher education is that it has given me tools to understand myself, my experiences and the world around me. The reason 'tool' is a useful metaphor is that tools tend to be specific to tasks. I didn't know what tools the people attending my sessions would need because I didn't know what tasks they wanted to tackle. I also don't think it makes sense to ask 'what do you want?' as a one-off question in this situation since it can be too open-ended. I know from carrying out interviews that asking too broad a question can wreck an otherwise pleasant interaction. It might also be the case that you feel it's risky to admit there are things you don't yet know – you might fear losing face. Once trust has been built, this kind of honesty is more possible. For these reasons, it made most sense to me to approach the curriculum as an ongoing dialogue.

For the first session, I prepared slides explaining my own personal and academic background, introducing anthropology as a discipline, as well as some slides about food and culture, since I thought that was an easy entry point into a whole range of areas: historical, political, economic and so forth. At the start of the session, I introduced myself and asked the students to introduce themselves. I didn't ask for any information about their legal status or expect them to disclose where they were from. I also didn't ask about prior educational attainment. In the section of the lecture about food, I talked about a range of topics in the anthropology of food and eating (domestication of plants, globalisation, food sovereignty etc.) and also invited them to talk about any links between food and identity in their own cultures. The session was lively and generated a lot of great discussion.

At the end of that first session, I explained that I wanted the students to decide what we would focus on, but that our conversations were not to be limited to a single topic on the day. I said I would prepare some slides and activities on topics they chose and that we didn't have to decide on five topics today, we could revisit the choice of topics each week to decide what we would discuss the following week. The students chose to have a full session about food the following week, seemingly excited by the many topics food opened up. The second food session was equally lively and ended up addressing British social norms around food and how anthropology can help us understand the context that we are in as immigrants to the UK. It was striking that the students had noticed, with not inconsiderable hurt feelings, that British people seemed unwilling and unprepared to share food in most settings and reluctant to invite them for a home cooked meal. One attendee explained how in his country eating in public was radically different: when going to restaurants, people arrive and sit with those already eating, rather than separately, and share their food, ordering more to be brought to the shared table. There was relieved laughter as I acknowledged what a big cultural difference there was between that and eating in public in the UK. I explained how habits of highly individualised food consumption are established from very young ages in the UK and how other practices can make people feel uncomfortable, and that there is research showing that even in the case of special occasions and loved ones visiting from far away, white British people tend not to want to cook food at home to share, instead often preferring to be served individual meals in restaurants (Bush et al. 1998). It felt like I could acknowledge that their observations about eating differences were valid and help to heal feelings of personal rejection by assisting the students to understand that these were acknowledged phenomena and explaining the observations from British people's perspective.

In another session, the discussion unexpectedly ended up being about internet propaganda about Asian countries, and one student from an African country in particular expressed a great desire to learn more about Asia so we agreed to have a session about cultures in Asia. Since anthropology is a subject with an explicitly global reach and there has been work done on every continent, it was possible for me to take on the topic. Such a geographical scope, however, meant the lecture was more of a 'broad strokes' introduction to the diversity of societies in Asia, but the students seemed to really enjoy the session – perhaps because none of the students were from East Asia and their prior education might not have covered this area in significant depth, despite its size.

When we were choosing topics for the last two sessions, the discussions began to build on one another in a very clear way. For the penultimate session, the students asked to focus on understanding poverty from an anthropological perspective. The space was now filled with mutual respect and trust that we had built together and students were able to raise important questions such as why their own countries were poor and had virtually no manufacturing capacities, while others were rich or seemed to be developing. One student brought the discussion around to trying to understand why the US so often bombed other countries, including their own, and seemed reluctant to offer basic aid or adequate reconstruction assistance. We all contributed to these discussions in a sincere way and I was able to draw upon my academic knowledge to offer the students explanations of various scholarly debates and conversations about these topics for them to think with. They then asked for the last session to address the topic of political organisation, asking how to organise societies so they could think about how to improve the world. In many ways, I am still very moved by this request and the fact I was able to offer something in response to it. I am unsure of how to fully describe this experience but I can say that it felt like a validation of the approach I took; the approach of treating people I met in classrooms as thoughtful, intellectually-able beings and letting them direct the course in order to learn and discuss the topics that they felt were important to them.

In the final session, Josie explained and answered questions about the Foundation programme's options for further engagement with the university. During the same session, the students agreed to come with me to the university campus for a visit and a tour. None of the students had ever been to the university before, even those who had lived in the UK for many years, and even despite the University of Bristol's main site being quite central within the city, easily accessible by public transport. I interpreted this willingness to come with me as concrete evidence of the trust we had built together, especially since the students had expressed negative feelings towards the university during the early sessions. The university has a reputation within the city for being elitist and racist. I engaged in an open conversation at the end of one of the first sessions about the university's racist reputation, with two women who told me about their experiences of rejection and stories of their friends and friends' children being rejected despite high marks. I discussed with them my own reservations about working within the higher education sector in the UK, especially in an elite institution, and I found it interesting (and, of course, a relief) that they were supportive of my presence in it, saying that it was important to have Black people working in the university. During the visit to the university site, students were provided with short presentations about university admissions and financing and had the chance to ask questions based on their personal circumstances.[2]

Taster Sessions: What Are We Tasting?

I have mixed feelings about the idea that these sessions were a taste of UK higher education. They were, in some clear ways, a pathway for the students to make contact with UK higher education. As in, I am an academic working in the UK and there was a formal way into the university through me and my colleagues organising the Foundation programme. But, in another way, it could be thought of as misleading. I am a Black immigrant and respectful towards and knowledgeable about life in parts of the world from which the students hailed. Most people teaching at the University of Bristol and in comparable Russell Group institutions, however, are not. (The Russell Group is a self-selecting group of twenty-four 'elite' institutions in the UK.)

In addition to this, most of my colleagues do not even aspire to use the teaching methods described above and yet, in my view, it was the best teaching I've ever done. It was the best in the sense that I felt it was actually achieving the true purpose intended, something which my university teaching is aimed at but tends to fall short because of the rigidity of both the students and the system, which requires syllabi and formal examination. This always keeps the possibility of failure open, leading to attendant embarrassment. Before going to university, I saw a video that showed staff and students taking on projects that were initiated to meet the needs of the community, using their expertise, skills and equipment to address problems. One project in the video involved creating a device out of milk crates to help people with disabilities to swim. I realise now that this was aspirational or a form of outreach, but at the time I believed that responding primarily to challenges like this is what lecturers and students do. It would be great if universities were more relaxed and informal in their approach, functioning outside the rigid structures dictated by syllabi and testing. This teaching felt much more like that.

Perhaps even more problematic than this, there is a deeply entrenched hierarchy of asymmetrical power relations that keeps the existing system in place. These issues were absent within the space of our classroom in the Malcolm X Centre. I didn't expect the students to memorise or even accept the ideas or perspective I was offering, I had no interest in assessing them, there was hardly anything of value I could withhold from them, and I did not reserve most of the class time for my own speaking, there was discussion throughout.

It is also worth mentioning that I ran these sessions during a period of underemployment by the University of Bristol, allowing me to take on the project (for which I was paid on a casual contract), something that would otherwise have been impossible because of managerial control of my time and (as I was told) the department's workload model. Later when the opportunity to run another set of sessions for refugees arose, I was on a full-time teaching contract and, even though I offered to do it without extra pay in addition to my other teaching and administrative work, my line manager refused to allow it. They said that it could cause problems in future if the department was expected to provide additional teaching to other programmes. This seemed a strange way of thinking about me (as something they provide) and the situation (as though I was interchangeable with any other member of staff). However, it brings into focus the question of how academics' time is controlled by a model of management in which refugee education initiatives are not sufficiently valuable to gain support. This incident also highlights the ways in which these hierarchical structures might block opportunities for staff to carry out appropriate forms of engagement with refugees. It speaks to the fact that the foundation year is unusual in another way, in being interdisciplinary and staffed by permanent and sessional academics from a range of disciplines. This sometimes makes it hard for individual departments to conceptualise a refugee education programme within the rigid structures (and financial pressures) of a teaching plan. The UK HE sector, particularly the Russell Group institutions, tends to be remarkably rigid in its expectations and processes, and inaccessible to the people outside its historical target group:

- childless, white British, middle-to-upper class, privately-educated 18–19-year-olds;
- those without non-academic work or caring responsibilities as this would interfere with a weekly expectation of reading, coursework preparation or revision of 10+ hours in order to keep up;
- those who are able to attend full time and sit 2–3-hour-long handwritten examinations.

The UK's Open University (OU) and Birkbeck College in London famously operate very differently but, unlike in the US, these open models have certainly not translated into more open ways of working across the sector – and, where they did, many of those gains have been undone by a funding system since the turn of the millennium – something that has mitigated against part-time and mature students. There are two-thirds fewer part-time students in English higher education since 2010. Birkbeck and the OU themselves have been forced into drastic changes as a consequence: Birkbeck now offers a large number of full-time programmes for the first time. Portals into the UK HE sector have been periodically constructed in the form of Foundation programmes but these often operate in similar ways. The Foundation at Bristol offered a very interesting set of pathways to bridge the gap between normal ways of living and working and university student life. The tasters were the first step towards building this bridge, with no compulsion to follow the path beyond any particular step. I wish the rest of my university teaching could be more like the taster sessions.

Conclusions

It is worth noting that none of the students on this taster went on to further study via the Foundation route. Many of them were already qualified to degree level, others had interests that lay beyond the Arts and Humanities, and some did not qualify for student funding. The Foundation team has subsequently built on this experience with further tasters with BRR and developed a relationship with other organisations that support migrant communities, including Bristol Best Tuition (BBT), an organisation that provides a Somali supplementary school to school-age children in the city on Saturdays. The university has offered both content-led tasters and (subsequently) courses in academic English with BBT and the progression rates are encouraging: six students joined the Foundation programme in 2019. Yet we have also tried to keep a balance between tasters where the route on to further study is a key outcome, and space for those who find the tasters useful in and of themselves. In future work, we hope to consider student voices and experiences from the previous tasters.[3]

These tasters are a very different model of teaching to the one we are used to in UK universities. The taster course has no formalised curriculum, no set texts, no assessment, no accreditation, no attendance requirements and no fees. It also, as the case study makes clear, has fewer of the hierarchies of class, race and nationality that characterise UK higher education. It is widely acknowledged that these social and educational structures do much to exclude less-privileged groups, or to discriminate between them within the system, as Spivak's comparison of CUNY and Colombia also reveals. The taster allowed us to – temporarily – remove these structures, giving us a glimpse of what a university that was student-centred and had some of the capacities that Spivak imagined might look like. And this might also thus liberate the teaching staff involved in such programmes. In my experience, taking away some of the pedagogical, financial and structural constraints created a space that felt far freer and more creative than university classrooms normally tend to. It is also striking that the students' interests led them so quickly to the question of how to make things better, something that was both practical and utopian. We might say that a course that was designed as a 'taster' of higher education for those outside the university can also act as a taster of what higher education might be like if it were organised differently.

Mwenza Blell is a Health Data Research UK Rutherford Fellow, a Newcastle University Academic Track Fellow, and a Grant Researcher at Tampere University. Her research draws from ethnography to examine intransigent and often invisible structures of injustice.

Josie McLellan is a historian at the University of Bristol, and co-author of *Who Are Universities For?* (Bristol University Press, 2018) with Tom Sperlinger and Richard Pettigrew.

Richard Pettigrew teaches in the Department of Philosophy at the University of Bristol. Together with Josie McLellan and Tom Sperlinger, he created the Foundation Year in Arts and Humanities and co-authored *Who Are Universities For?* for Bristol University Press (2018).

Tom Sperlinger teaches in the English Department at the University of Bristol and is author of *Romeo and Juliet in Palestine* (Zero Books, 2015) and co-author of *Who Are Universities For?* (Bristol University Press, 2018).

Notes

1. For a fuller account of the Foundation programme, see McLellan, Pettigrew and Sperlinger (2016); Sperlinger, McLellan and Pettigrew (2018).
2. For wider context on race in higher education in the UK, see Ahmed (2012) and Dale-Rivas (2019).
3. For an example of student perspectives on the tasters, see 'Life Long Learning', an article in which students from a BBT taster are interviewed, in *Up Our Street*, a community-led magazine in Bristol (Summer 2019), p. 17.

References

Ahmed, S. 2012. *On Being Included: Racism and Diversity in Institutional Life*. Durham, NC: Duke University Press.
Bush, H., R. Williams, H. Bradby, A. Anderson and M. Lean. 1998. 'Family Hospitality and Ethnic Tradition among South Asian, Italian and General Population Women in the West of Scotland', *Sociology of Health & Illness* 20(3): 351–80.
Dale-Rivas, H. (ed.). 2019. *The White Elephant in the Room: Ideas for Reducing Racial Inequalities in Higher Education*. Oxford: Higher Education Policy Institute.
McLellan, J., R. Pettigrew and T. Sperlinger. 2016. 'Remaking the Elite University: An Experiment in Widening Participation in the UK', *Power and Education* 8(1): 54–72.
Slater, T., and N. Anderson. 2012. 'The Reputational Ghetto: Territorial Stigmatisation in St Pauls, Bristol', *Transactions of the Institute of British Geographers* 37(4): 530–46.
Sperlinger, T., J. McLellan, and R. Pettigrew. 2018. *Who Are Universities For? Re-making Higher Education*. Bristol: Bristol University Press.
Spivak, G.C. 2003. *Death of a Discipline*. New York: Columbia University Press.

CHAPTER 7
Experts by Experience
The Scope and Limits of Collaborative Pedagogy
with Marginalised Asylum Seekers

*RUBINA JASANI, JACK LÓPEZ, YAMUSU NYANG, ANGIE D.,
DUDU MANGO, RUDO MWOYOWESHUMBA AND SHAMIM AFHSAN*

═══ ◆◆◆

> For women, the need and desire to nurture each other is not pathological but redemptive, and it is within that knowledge that our real power is discovered.
> —Audre Lorde, 1984

On a December evening in 2018 our group sat together in a seminar room at the University of Manchester waiting for friends and family to arrive. We distracted ourselves by picking at the food prepared and brought along by members of the group. We commented on how each one of us looked in our posh clothes. The feeling in the room was a mixture of excitement, apprehension and a touch of tension. The women were excited to showcase how far we had come with the research project and to have their families attend the graduation. There was apprehension about how the event would unfold. Who would attend? Would it go according to plan? We were tense as our work was out for public scrutiny and our colleagues were going to be in the audience. On the day, our tension was heightened by the fact that our Chief Guest had not arrived till 6:55 p.m. and we were meant to be starting at 7:00 p.m. and we had an audience of almost seventy people that we wanted to impress. This evening was the culmination of two years of engagement and knowledge exchange between members of the activist group Women Asylum Seekers Together (WAST) and anthropologists Rubina Jasani and Jack López. A cross-section of organisations that WAST works with along with the trustees of the organisation and key workers were present in the audience.

The ceremony was an emotionally charged event with a powerful speech by WAST founder Farhat Khan, who described a personal timeline of events that began with years of neglect and domestic abuse in Pakistan, from which she fled to the UK with her children to seek asylum. Her own narrative of the challenges and rejection she had faced while seeking sanctuary in the UK resonated deeply with the women, family and friends in the audience. Her account moved the audience and the women and there were many tears. Each one of the ten women graduating that evening had faced forced displacement, rejection, homelessness and animosity from the Home Office and remained to that day under the imposed condition 'No Recourse to Public Funds' (NRPF).[1] Aside from excluding people from employment, benefits, social housing and secondary health care services, the NRPF (combined with a rejected asylum application) creates major barriers for adults to access education and training, and as such gradually strips these individuals of their social and intellectual worth. On the odd occasion that women do enter the educational environment, they do so as an object of study rather than individuals with specific expertise and knowledge to offer.

In this chapter we retell our experience of organising and running collaborative research training with women from WAST. This programme was conceptualised by the two anthropologists to challenge the idea of 'giving voice' in anthropology and using peer ethnography as a method to train asylum-seeking women to tell their own stories. This entailed designing a research training programme and training them in basic research skills. This programme was delivered by the anthropologists with support from two other feminist academics from the university. An independent consultant was hired for our first session, who helped us in laying down intentions from both sides and helping us think through the smaller details of the programme. Ten research training sessions were delivered, with a follow-up practice session on interviewing and transcription skills. Skills in research governance were also provided. The Peer Ethnographic Evaluation Approach (PEER) is an innovative method derived from the anthropology of health approach to fieldwork (see Price and Hawkins 2002; Elmusharaf et al. 2017). The method is based on the principle that peer researchers already have an established relationship of trust and understanding with the people they interview. The peer researchers collect data (interviews, observations, pre-existing interpretations) among their own social networks, and this is collectively analysed to explore issues prevalent to the peer researchers' community.

We use text and image to reflect on how we took a combined pedagogy of peer ethnographic practice and self-advocacy activism to *open up* the university as a site of action learning. Our intention was twofold: to interrupt the exclusionary and hierarchical space of the university and begin a project in which the agenda would be directed by the participants as opposed to the dominant narratives within the discipline. Inspired by the empowerment pedagogies of Paulo Freire, bell hooks, Audre Lorde, the activism of groups like WAST, Southall Black Sisters, Right to Remain and anti-racist activist scholars (see Johnson et al. 2018; Bhopal 2018), our aim was to take a leap of faith into a space of a more honest academic co-production. Our (López and Jasani) only standpoint at the outset was that collectively we were experts in ourselves and we had much to learn from each other. The process was messy and often chaotic from the outset, often mirroring the lives of the women who participated in the project. As academics we had to learn to unlearn our pursuit of perfection, be ready for constant surprises and help each other unpack those surprises in our debriefing sessions with the aim to move the project further.

The following paragraphs reflect on our pedagogic practice and the challenges and compromises that the group faced in the first eighteen months of the project. Our approach to research as activism mirrors the WAST philosophy of the activism of coming together. We take this approach into the creation of our outputs, whether written or multi-media. Though Jasani and López have organised the words and paragraphs that make up this chapter, the content is derived from the collective work of the group who took on the task of making this chapter happen (Jasani, López, Nyang, D., Mango, Mwoyoweshumba and Afhsan). The ideas, reflections, observations and comments come from the seven people who came together one warm, stuffy day to structure and discuss the contents. It seems ironic that on the day we worked together to create this chapter we were in a first-floor classroom in the Samuel Alexander building of the School of Arts and Languages, an early twentieth-century building with an impressive white Roman facade, a prime spot for graduation photos. Our classroom window looked over a lawn area where families and students were gathering to celebrate their newly awarded degrees. As described in the opening paragraph, we did hold our own graduation ceremony, but we were unable to mark the occasion with gowns and public recognition, something that the group had felt missing. Such actions are a reminder of the limitations of academic activism within institutions where we are often restrained by the established rules of *how things should be done*. A similar accusation can be made of authorship and writing as something restricted to words typed on paper. When we write our seven names as co-authors, we are moving beyond tokenism to fully acknowledge that the labour involved in knowledge production was undertaken by all of us and these words would not exist without that collective labour.

Peer Ethnographic Practice with Socially Abandoned Populations

People with rejected asylum applications remain in limbo, homeless and without recourse, trapped in what medical anthropologist Joal Biehl (2013) terms 'zones of social abandonment', where neither legal authorities nor welfare or medical institutions directly intervene.[2] Biehl refers to these zones as the space of social death, where those who have no place in the social world, yet who are living, are left until they die. Marrow and Lurhmann (2012: 495) extended the concept further to describe a space that is 'absolute and universal, beyond culture and society, a bleak existential otherness'. Not all adults seeking asylum in the UK are provided with accommodation. This depends on whether they have dependants, whether they are in between appeals and whether or not they are known to the Home Office (undocumented, trafficked or escaping removal). There is no recorded data of what happens to refused asylum applicants in the UK who are not deported or detained by the state. Our own research shows that many women sleep on floors and sofas within their asylum community network, though they drift in and out of homelessness. Directed into these transient migrant zones by the state (via rejection or appeal status), 'individuals are sure to become unknowables with no human rights and with no one accountable for their condition' (Biehl 2013: 4). Black women and women of colour (and minority genders) who make up just under half of the known asylum-seeking population (Walsh 2019) are made more vulnerable as 'increasing numbers of people who are not part of mapped populations' (Biehl 2013: 4). The most significant issue for our project was to interrupt this daily experience of racialised abandonment and in doing so challenge institutional structures. We did that by opening up the university, a site where their subjectivity was a part of academic interrogation, but their bodies could never make it into institutional settings with the aim of gaining skills of the very process that creates their subjectivity in the first place.

Asylum-seeking and refugee women are often the subject of research or classroom analysis but they are rarely the protagonists in the conversation. Moreover, UK higher education institutions tend to make invisible overt questions of race within their new social diversity and widening participation agendas (Bhopal 2018). Though questions of gender, class and disability arise from the ever-increasing institutional strategies, race is a factor that comes to the forefront whenever diversity and widening participation are linked. Bringing women stripped of their scholarly identity and citizenship into the university, we hoped to shine a light on the types of knowledge silenced through the exclusion and oppression of specific communities. As feminists committed to intersectionality, we understand social reality as multi-dimensional, lived identities as intertwined and systems of oppression as meshed and mutually constitutive. We followed epistemic and political recognition of different ways of knowing and living and changed social relations via coalitional dynamics rather than notions of sameness underlying liberal notions of equality. Intersectionality calls for epistemological and political transformation and makes space for alternative notions of subjectivity, agency and equality (May 2013).

As first-generation scholars and anthropologists, we are committed to the idea that ethnography as pedagogy serves as an important tool for engaging with people new to applied participatory research. With little time to give the group a strong grounding in the ethnographic approach, we needed a practical classroom method to teach as we went along. In our context, because the peer researchers were associated with WAST for varying periods of time and the organisation was user led, there was empathy for what they had been through and a belief that they would all get through this together. Every milestone was celebrated at the weekly drop-ins and every downfall was sensitively dealt with, which meant that there was trust between the women and hence the assumption was that the interviewing process would become easier. This is not to say that there were no hierarchies of class and race within the group, but the fact that they were all asylum seekers meant that they had some recognition that they were all in it together. In post-interview reflections, the women spoke about the differences they felt in being in the 'outsider' position. The group was aware this may happen as it was covered in the initial training sessions. Positionality and power dynamics are often reported as a negative in auto-ethnography or anthropology 'at home' texts. In the case of the WAST researchers, the group reported the positive feeling of being shifted out of their role of WAST member to researcher. Comparing the interview transcripts of Jasani, López and Afhsan also demonstrated an openness (in those of Afhsan) that would not necessarily take place with a true outsider.

Over the duration of the project the peer researchers in effect become key informants by virtue of their recognised status. We adapted this method for use in the classroom as a way to guide the initial training workshops with a group of twenty women. It gave us a way to introduce ethnographic research practice to the group without pre-defining the agenda of the research. Before reaching the stage of data collection, we were attempting to create a democratic community of learning with the group that drew from their strengths and knowledge as individuals. In this way we took an ethnographic approach to teaching the group using what we learnt from them and our own reflections at each stage to plan the following workshop.

We were concerned not with pre-supposing the research questions but with observing and listening in workshops to identify the core issues touched upon by the group. Devising a structure of workshops to meet the needs of a research project, while creating an open transformative space to assess knowledge and ideas, to be led by the group but also to take the lead when appropriate. Over months we played with structure, delivery, timescales and materials to see what worked best. As democratic educators we took for granted that anyone who 'knows how to read and write has the tools needed to access higher learning even if that learning cannot and does not take place in a university setting' (hooks 2003: 42). Yet part of this commitment to democratic learning is acknowledging that the conditions for empowerment require other forms of support and environmental understanding if a learning community is to have any measure of success. We had to learn to be reactive to tensions in the group, chaotic and precarious lives, our own lack of focus (due to other teaching and institutional commitments), constant revision of our intentions as a group and how we explained this to the institution housing our project and bodies that were to eventually fund us.

In formalised education and learning there is a focus on the past (what is known) and an obsession with the future (knowledge judged on its ability to predict or be applied to an imaginary timeline). 'Most of us teach and are taught that it is only the future that really matters' (hooks 2003: 167). But what happens when you perceive the future to be unknown in a way completely beyond your control? When you understand that lulling yourself into thinking about the future only makes the precarious present unbearable? The lives of women in the group were and are given to the here and now, a present in a process of perpetual renewal and at risk. Through embracing the immediacy of the present in the classroom we see how teaching and learning are both constantly taking place and under revision. This immediacy and exchange of world knowledge in the few hours a month we had to work together forces an intense practice of critical thinking unconstrained by academic norms. In the following section we invite the reader(s) of this chapter to explore the words and images of the group as we reflected on the activities that led us to our first instance of empirical data collection – a study on self-advocacy and the impact of activism on precarious individuals by being a member of WAST. The 'artefacts' below arose from a collective writing workshop used to plan this chapter. The words below offer a description in the group's own words of the educational process, including what the different spaces and activities meant to us at the time. Our use of unedited outputs within our co-authorship embraces the group's commitment to experimentation and documentation of learning in action.

Creating a Community of Learning

After spending around four months getting to know women in WAST's own environment, consisting of attending meetings at their office base

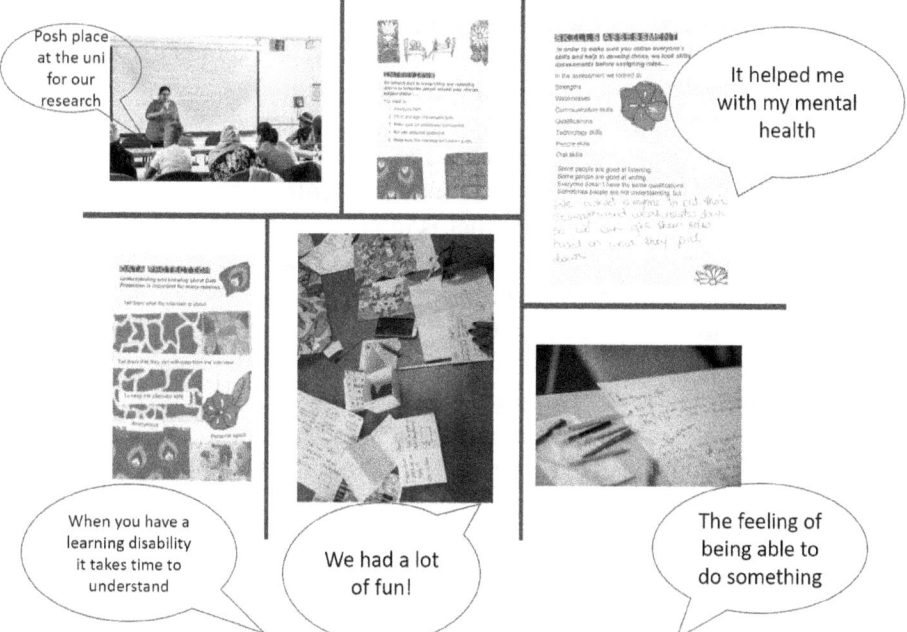

Figure 7.1. Training and workshops: the women attended training in the formal setting of university classrooms and creative workshops at the project building. We reflected on working in both settings. Photos by the authors.

and calling into weekly drop-in sessions, we felt ready to recruit potential community researchers. We held a series of workshops at the university teaching the fundamentals of social research, including ethics, design, qualitative field methods, transcription and analysis. The workshops were initially attended by twenty women, but this quickly reduced to a committed group of ten. We decided from the outset to use the university campus to give the group a sense of place and purpose in their work. Our intention was to create a learning space that felt comfortable yet official.

Many of the women had visited classes that we taught on degrees in Humanitarian Conflict Response and Global Health and were familiar with university spaces. But almost all of them were experiencing university as a learning space for the first time in the UK (some of them were trained teachers and had held NGO jobs in their countries). We realised within the first few sessions that we could not plan sessions and run them, coordinate the logistics and do our job as ethnographers in this space. Once we had conducted a few sessions, we invited colleagues working within the university to teach. We observed that our peer ethnographers were more attentive when external facilitators were in the room. This freed us up for participant observation, understanding the space, the people and the learning dynamic better. The group constituted of African, South Asian and Eastern European women who ranged between twenty-two and fifty-five years of age. There were interesting racial, caste, cultural and community dynamics at play in the classroom settings that were reflected in the WAST drop-ins on Fridays. What brings WAST women together is their experience of forced migration and inhabiting 'zones of abandonment' in the city. Understanding the class, race, community and caste dynamic was extremely important for quelling unrest in the classroom and understanding the difference between entitlement to knowledge and space. We also observed that to keep the interest of the group and for them to connect with the learning, long breaks in between sessions were not a good thing. This was hard on the academic diary as we were constantly fire-fighting between the two different worlds of learning and teaching that we were straddling. We also had to unlearn using academic jargon and instead use language that was clear and simple.

Collaborative Methodology

Based on our group discussions and observations from the workshops we gradually formulated a research design and pilot project to test out

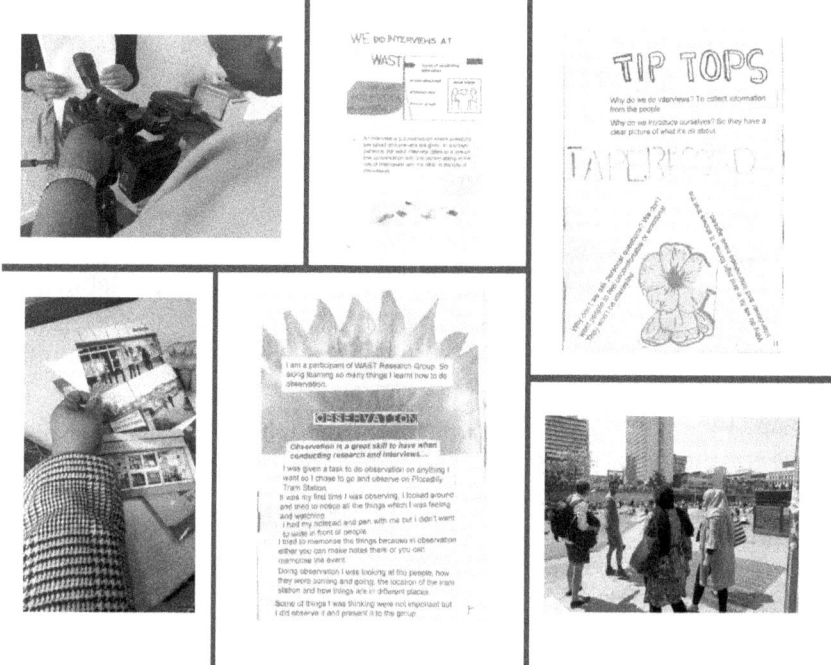

Figure 7.2. Transferrable skills: the group experimented with visual methodologies, learning skills in film, photography and zine making. Photos by the authors.

our data collection skills. We were aware from the information that was often shared among the group that our first attempt at recording data and interviewing had to stay true to the core social research principle of 'do no harm'. We wanted to explore unknown aspects of the lives of WAST members, but we also had identified early on that it was important to avoid framing our participants as victims of circumstance. Over time we were able to compromise on issues and topics that the group thought were important to study, such as mental health, children, resilience and access to support. The group wanted to focus on the strengths of people in their community who were thriving despite being abandoned by the system. We settled on the research question 'What does WAST mean to you?' and the research objective of exploring how a transient population can organise, campaign and support each other while living under the threat of deportation or abandonment. From here we needed to test out the appropriateness of classic qualitative methods and see if they were flexible enough to capture moments in the lives of people whose circumstances shift from one day to the next.

While formal research training took place in university classrooms, data collection took place at the WAST drop-ins, a weekly support and self-help group that takes place in a city centre Methodist church. It is a hectic and animated environment that can be attended by up to eighty women and their children. In this space women exchange information and ideas, organise support for each other and campaigns, eat food, sing and dance. The wall of sound that meets you upon entering the large room, the coming and going, the exchange of clothing, food, spontaneous music and women self-segregating in groups defined by nationality makes it all seem, to an outsider, like utter chaos. Yet, in between the noise and movement there is organisation and community action, a place where women can relax and, for some, feel safe for perhaps the only time in that day. Although the drop-in was a familiar space for the researchers, embodying the 'researcher' role within this space was not easy as some of them struggled with the formal role of explaining information sheets, getting consent and then speaking to the women about their lives 'objectively'. Peer researchers found meetings and participant observation at the drop-in incredibly hard, find-

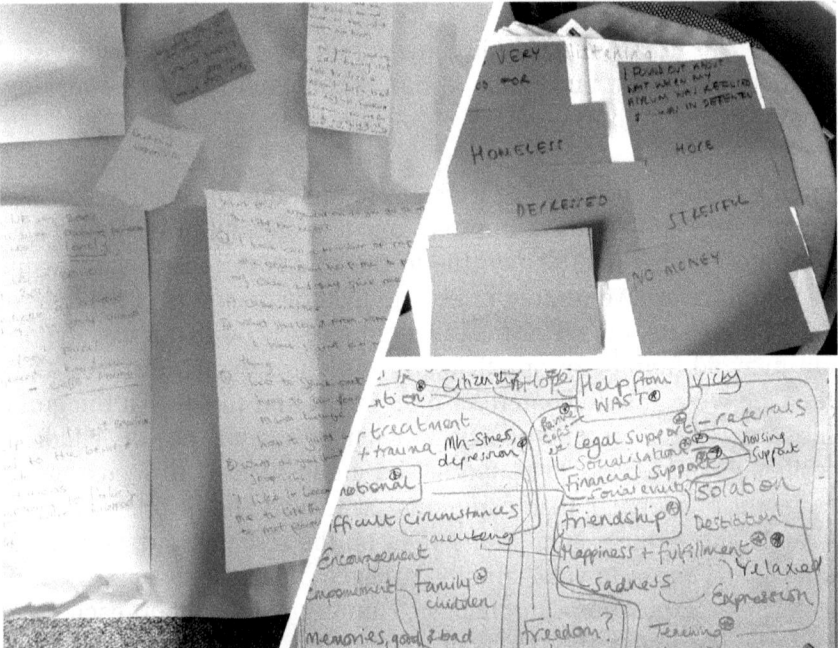

Figure 7.3. Analysis workshops: group analysis of interview and observation data was critical to the peer ethnographic evaluation approach. Photos by the authors.

ing it too difficult to concentrate with the noise, struggling with small children and numerous other distractions. Because they were so implicated within the asylum process, they found it challenging to separate their own experiences from those of other women. We attempted to get around this through listening to tapes and individual feedback sessions that we organised with each of the researchers. We also moved back into the university and the classroom structure to complete transcription work and to attempt collaborative analysis. Trying to translate our thoughts and observations into 'findings' became a major stumbling block and exposed the impractical nature of reducing the incoherent mess of daily life to some 'key points' for learning.

We decided to experiment with different ways to think about understanding what we were learning as a group. The classroom environment began to feel like a hindrance to creativity in this sense and we swapped once more to the community environment to see what would happen if we reflected upon our learning through the art of zine making. The zine workshops were held at the WAST office, where the aim was to chronicle their journey of learning to do research, and were facilitated by an external artist. The space was familiar, informal and

Figure 7.4. Zine making: creativity and art making as method flowed more freely when we held workshops in a community setting. Photos by the authors.

the task at hand creative. While they enjoyed the creative process, we found it difficult to sustain their enthusiasm and wondered if the engagement would have been different if these sessions were conducted at the university. In these spaces, we also wondered if we were turning into yet another NGO that they were engaged with in the city. Asylum seekers were engaged in various activities with a few organisations within the city, some of whom provided practical support and others engaged with them creatively. Most organisations reimbursed bus fares and provided a warm meal and sometimes the women would attend more than three meetings in a day. When we found their engagement wavering, we wondered if we were also yet another group trying to engage with them in the city. Spatially our learning community had moved beyond the borders of the university and the classroom; it had moved into their 'everyday' spaces. How they read learning in each of these spaces was different, but what we observed over time was their growth in confidence and ability to question processes related to research ethics, governance and conducting interviews.

Conclusion

University represented different things for each of us. While as academics we are critical of the university as a neoliberal space that perpetuates white supremacy and exploitation of ethnic minorities (Joseph-Salisbury 2018), our peer researchers associated university with freedom and empowerment. The encounter with the university brought an element of hope into their lives. Members of the group reported that being part of the project gave them a purpose and excitement of doing something new and useful and being visible in a space that was beyond their imagination. Comments and evaluations with the group implied that they felt legitimised by the space and our fieldnotes evidence the use of the word 'hope' in many conversations. The graduation ceremony brought this legitimation full circle when other WAST members expressed a desire to 'come to uni' and be trained as community researchers. Marking the end of the training with a graduation ceremony and certificates meant the group had evidence to use for their asylum claims and future job applications. It is a sad irony that asylum applicants must demonstrate forms of good citizenship and societal engagement in the UK when their situation renders them excluded from social structures and community.

In doing this piece of work, as scholars, we realised that our idea of collaborative knowledge production came from a place of privilege. We need to interrogate our deployment of the term critically as the process of conducting peer research meant deployment of invisible emotional labour from our peer ethnographers who worked on their social capital to recruit women whose stories they would be drawing on for analysis. It made us think about how the pursuit of authenticity takes the social capital of the most vulnerable people for granted and how that fits in with peer ethnography as a method. The larger questions for the academy are: can the subject ever be the student? and what would it take for higher education to embrace true communities of learning?

On a final note, the research subject/student/expert positioning brings us to the question of authenticity. The traditional and exclusionary approach of higher education scholarship works to remove authenticity from non-scholars as experts. Authenticity, of course, is dependent on context, such as when members of WAST performed as a choir at a conference on migration scholarship organised by our colleagues, or speaking of trauma to our students learning about precarious lives. In those spaces the group members are legitimated as *authentic asylum seekers or survivors of trauma*. The women's very presence as black women and women of colour and their acts of testimony leave that authenticity in this context unquestioned. Yet, in the Home Office reporting centre, the authenticity of their same narratives is doubted, charged by the courts as something to be proved. Can we say the same about their active roles as campaigners, researchers and expert witnesses? How much harder must they work to become community researchers in their own right, and why does this matter? In the group's own understanding, authenticity is defined by audiences positioning them as the 'experts' and wanting to tap into their lived experiences of forced migration and displacement. But when they were carrying out research and training they kept looking to us as academics for answers as we were the 'authentic academic experts' in that space.

Since we were dealing with failed asylum seekers who had NRPF and who were at the periphery of race and class hierarchy, their reading of race and gender reflected understandings of race and class that they had internalised through their encounters with the asylum system and the NGO world in the city. While they acknowledged Rubina's presence on the project, it was always presumed that there was a hierarchy and group members often joked that she worked for Jenna. It was only during the data analysis sessions, when they saw Rubina in her office, that they realised that she was also staff. For Lorde, regardless of what we do or do not say, we will always be marked as bodies out of place (Puwar 2004). By marking Rubina's body as out of place in the university system, the women were showing us how they saw their own bodies as students within this system. The respect that some of our white colleagues commanded in terms of effectiveness and efficacy was also an extension of the marking of legitimate bodies of knowing and imparters of knowledge.

◆

Rubina Jasani is a Medical Anthropologist and lecturer in Humanitarian and Conflict Response at the University of Manchester. Rubina's areas of interest are anthropology of violence and reconstruction, medical anthropology with a specific focus on social suffering and mental illness, and the study of lived Islam in South Asia and the UK

Jack López is a Medical Anthropologist and assistant professor in Health and Society at the University of Bradford. Jack specialises in sexual, reproductive and gender health matters and the design and ethics of collaborative ethnography. Their broader interests are family life, intimacy, health inequalities and life-course in societies or populations affected by violence. Their research region is principally the UK and Mexico.

Yamusu Nyang, Angie D., Dudu Mango, Rudo Mwoyoweshumba and Shamim Afhsan are project researchers and members of Women Asylum Seekers Together Manchester (WAST). WAST Manchester aims to raise awareness about the issues that force women to seek international protection and aims to empower women asylum seekers.

Notes

1. NRPF is a condition imposed on a person due to their immigration status. Section 115 Immigration and Asylum Act 1999 states that a person will have 'no recourse to public funds' if they are 'subject to immigration control'. See http://www.nrpfnetwork.org.uk/.
2. Biehl's ethnography, *Vita: Life in a Zone of Social Abandonment*, is centred in an unregulated (psychiatric) asylum community in Brazil, a place where families abandon mentally ill, disabled, incurably diseased relatives when they do not have the economic or social resources to care for them.

References

Bhopal, K. 2018. *White Privilege: The Myth of a Post-racial Society*. Bristol: Policy Press.
Biehl, J. 2013. *Vita: Life in a Zone of Social Abandonment*. Berkeley: University of California Press.

Elmusharaf, K., E. Byrne, M. Manandhar, J. Hemmings and D. O'Donovan. 2017. 'Participatory Ethnographic Evaluation and Research: Reflections on the Research Approach Used to Understand the Complexity of Maternal Health Issues in South Sudan', *Qualitative Health Research* 27(9): 1345–58. doi:10.1177/1049732316673975.

hooks, bell. 2003. *Teaching Community: A Pedagogy of Hope*. London: Routledge.

Johnson, A., R. Joseph-Salisbury, B. Kamunge, C. Sharpe and G. Yancy (eds). 2018. *The Fire Now: Anti-Racist Scholarship in Times of Explicit Racial Violence*. London: Zed Books.

Joseph-Salisbury, R. 2018. 'Confronting My Duty as an Academic: We Should All Be Activists', in A. Johnson, R. Joseph-Salisbury, B. Kamunge, C. Sharpe and G. Yancy (eds), *The Fire Now: Anti-Racist Scholarship in Times of Explicit Racial Violence*. London: Zed Books.

Lorde, A. 1984. 'The Master's Tools Will Never Dismantle the Master's House', in *Sister Outsider: Essays and Speeches*, 1st edn. California: Crossing Press, pp. 110–13.

Marrow, J., and T.M. Luhrmann. 2012. 'The Zone of Social Abandonment in Cultural Geography: On the Street in the United States, Inside the Family in India', *Culture, Medicine, and Psychiatry* 36(3): 493–513. doi:10.1007/s11013-012-9266-y.

May. V. 2013. '"Speaking into the Void"? Intersectionality, Critiques and Epistemic Backlash', *Hypatia* 29(1): 95–112.

Price, N., and K. Hawkins. 2002. 'Researching Sexual and Reproductive Behaviour: A Peer Ethnographic Approach', *Social Science & Medicine* 55(8): 1325–36. doi:https://doi.org/10.1016/S0277-9536(01)00277-5.

Puwar. N. 2004. *Space Invaders: Race, Gender and Bodies out of Place*. Oxford: Berg Press.

Walsh, P.W. 2019. 'Migration to the UK: Asylum and Resettled Refugees'. https://migrationobservatory.ox.ac.uk/resources/briefings/migration-to-the-uk-asylum/ (accessed 29 November 2019).

CHAPTER 8
What Happens to a Story?
En/countering Imaginative Humanitarian Ethnography in the Classroom

ERIN GOHEEN GLANVILLE

◆◆◆

This chapter develops a critical pedagogy specific to teaching refugee narratives. It coins the term 'imaginative humanitarian ethnography' to describe a reading practice that closes down the transformative teaching potential of stories. I counter this with a framework developed in conversation with Jo-Ann Archibald's scholarship on 'storywork' and an interview with Sharmarke Dubow (conducted on 10 November 2018). Framing stories as gifts, mapping the relational matrix of reading, and casting readers as listeners can change the way we teach refugee narratives and support ethical encounters in the classroom. Popular claims about the importance of refugee storytelling in its various forms have focused on *what stories can do*. They may effect social change, create empathy, put a face to statistics, bring to light hidden experiences, or establish relations with strangers.[1] What is missed in celebrations of story is the reality that offering another person my story is a choice: to be vulnerable, to gift someone else with hard-earned wisdom and, in the transference of that gift, to make my story vulnerable too. What is missed is the immediate relationality of reading practices. When the listener or receiver of my story is not equally committed to the care and responsibility engendered by the gift, *what happens to the story*? This chapter considers how a critical pedagogy can introduce refugee narratives in the classroom, not as a catalyst for making readers feel responsible for global issues, nor as research data, but rather as an invitation to be responsible to the stories and their tellers.

From 2009 to 2017, I facilitated community education workshops for hundreds of people in Australia, Canada, New Zealand and the United States. The workshops screened multi-media representations of refugee-ed people with the aim of challenging what could loosely be called humanitarian readings of forced displacement narratives. Using different forms of narrative media, produced variously by refugee, diaspora and settler storytellers, to spark discussion with community groups (church sponsorship groups, grassroots organisers, humanitarian workers, undergraduates and graduate students), I encountered patterns of interpreting refugee stories that spanned genres and reading communities. These patterns have coalesced in my thinking to constitute a reading practice I refer to as 'imaginative humanitarian ethnography'. The next two sections unpack this term further, but briefly, I use the term 'imaginative humanitarian ethnography' to describe a way of engaging creative refugee narratives as if reading were a search for hidden knowledge of 'the refugee experience', a search that is motivated by and search results that are understood within humanitarian frames. It is a learning method in which the reader imagines themselves an amateur anthropologist who can 'discover refugee culture' in imaginative texts and turn it into actionable knowledge. Such readings quickly elicit the question, 'what can be done?' and induce emotional statements about privilege, difference and the importance of 'humanising refugees'. In this chapter, 'reading' encompasses the interpretive processes applied to narrative in media and not only literature.

Narratives about refugee lives are often read in the classroom as a form of imaginative humanitarian ethnography rather than as inviting relational responsibility. It may seem routine to consider stories an ethnographic source, but in a variety of educational contexts I have observed a repeated dynamic where the 'data' of a story gets skewed precisely because the story is being read as humanitarian research data. What gets theorised by some students as 'refugees being given a voice', via academic attention, is in fact a particular story being overridden, even silenced, by reading practices that commodify stories. Uncritical reading practices may effectively silence the ability of those narratives to speak on their own terms and to establish relational responsibility. Uncritical pedagogy that allows humanitarian frames to predominate may deaden the potential for diversely positioned participants to contribute knowledge from multiple epistemes and to take the conversation in surprising directions. Often, in community workshops and graduate classrooms alike, I find that the question of what a narrative (and connectedly, a citizen reading and responding to a narrative) can do for and to a person who is seeking refugee protection remains stubbornly central. Even for those who are aware of this problem, it can be hard to imagine an alternative way of reading.

Yet, the stories that students read by people with refugee experience have already been lived or imagined by that person. The story *is* that person's action in the world; it is a gifting. Remembering this, the practice of reading can be understood as a relational event. Readers can ask then about their responsibility to the author and/or community, rather than what readers can do with their knowledge to benefit strangers. For students who are negotiating the question of if/how/when to share their own story of displacement with their class, this approach will be more intuitive. Valuing stories as gifts can lead reading communities to recognise both the way stories are given – as situated knowledge, connected to a community of people, inviting reciprocity – and also the different purposes communities might find in the practice of reading – close listening, an exploration of possibilities, gentle play, aesthetic wonder, and interdependency.

This chapter explores encounters between imaginative humanitarian ethnographic reading practices and refugee narratives and offers an alternative way of envisaging the event of reading. First, I describe the limits of imaginative humanitarian framing, and then I examine the problems with applying ethnographic reading practices to creative refugee narratives. Each section offers an illustrative story about a teachable moment in a university classroom. In the final section, I offer an alternative way of conceptualising stories as gifts along with concrete pedagogical suggestions. Reading stories as gifts has the potential to shape a narrative pedagogy that honours the powerful vulnerability of stories and their communities.

Imaginative Humanitarian Framing

Lyndsey Stonebridge (2017) uses the term 'imaginative humanitarianism' to introduce the historical link between imaginative rights in literature and material rights in culture. Though she does not offer a definition of the term imaginative humanitarianism, she goes on to suggest that 'generous imaginings about others' becomes a replacement for action, recovering 'moral sentiments' through cultural production and asking literature 'to do [what] we cannot' (ibid.). This projection of the humanitarian impulse onto books is present in popular and scholarly readings of refugee fiction and has found its way into some of my earlier research as well. Stonebridge observes that imaginative humanitarianism does not necessarily lead to shared power; empathetic reading does not create material equity. Building on that observation, this chapter notices in imaginative humanitarianism the tendency to ask refugee stories to do both more and less than they can do.

If humanitarian discourse establishes relations of care and empathy among strangers around the globe, then humanitarian communication is the tradition of making those relations legible and public through aesthetic and rhetorical forms. Lilie Chouliaraki (2010: 107) defines humanitarian communication as the 'rhetorical practices of transnational actors that engage with universal ethical claims, such as common humanity or global civil society, to mobilize action on human suffering'. The mandates of humanitarian institutions are integral to understanding the meaning, language and context of humanitarian communication and discourse. Pooja Rangan (2017: 3) describes the institutional mandate shaping humanitarian communication in this way: it 'demands action over thinking, ethics over aesthetics, and immediacy over analysis'. To extrapolate, the humanitarian mandate evaluates any given imaginative narrative by asking, 'will this representation inspire viewers to contribute to humanitarian actions to alleviate the suffering of strangers?' This question presupposes a lack of empathy or action as the problem of global displacement; it recommends consuming books or media and then donating; it finds a solution in the links that are established through cultural production; and it assumes causal relationships among representation and empathy, mediations of suffering and action. Humanitarian communication has been critiqued for emphasising urgent pragmatic action over reflective or deep change, but also for the way it establishes asymmetrical social relationships, for its prioritisation of impact over artistic integrity, and for its tendency to create heightened awareness and one-time donations rather than long-term sustained mobilisation.

Articulating the difficulty with reading and interpreting refugee culture, Marguerite Nguyen and Catherine Fung (2016: 2) point to 'a tension between the ethics and aesthetics of making refugee experience visible' and advocate for 'joining refugee ethics with refugee aesthetics'. Their call for cultural refugee studies is prompted by similar insights to those of critical humanitarianism:

> Refugee aesthetics, whether produced by or about refugees, are bound up in an international discourse of refugee ethics in which refugees are objects of humanitarian concern and require immediate, pragmatic solutions. This frame of reference casts refugees as abject victims and downplays the particularities of refugee situations, including nation-states' accountability and specific refugee histories and poli-

> tics. Put differently, refugees' primary role in this aesthetic is to help establish a refugee ethics, eliciting the care of the international community, which in turn erases Euro-American production of refugees. (Nguyen and Fung 2016: 4)

This way of reading has been shaped by researchers, educators and NGOs alike, who posit imaginative narratives about refugees as an opportunity for citizens to increase empathy for strangers, remember 'the humanity' of refugees, or become global citizens (e.g. Nussbaum 2016; Temple 2017). For the purposes of this chapter, I focus on the impact of popularised humanitarian communication and discourse as I have seen it in the classroom.

I became acutely aware of the frame of humanitarian communication and wary of its power to obscure interpretations of specific stories the first time I taught Nadine Gordimer's 'The Ultimate Safari' (1989) in an introductory English course. Through the narrative voice of a young girl, Gordimer writes about the journey of a group of refugees fleeing Mozambique through Kruger Park. The group survives lions, starvation and Western ecotourists 'on safari', experiencing significant grief along the way, only to arrive in a refugee camp where they become the exotic attraction for humanitarian workers and Western journalists. One learning outcome for the class was opening a critical conversation about how humanitarianism, ecotourism, colonial history and contemporary journalism participate in and rely on a similar discourse entrenching hierarchical global relationships. In our introductory discussion, I asked students for their gut-level response to the story. The first student comment explicitly connected the story to humanitarian frames: 'It was really depressing. This is just like one of those World Vision infomercials – you know, with the little kid who doesn't have shoes and the fly on his face'. The explicitness of this feedback and its misreading of the text opened up a teachable moment. Many other students agreed this had been their reading, and so we spent the rest of that class responding to the frame that had obscured the text, unpacking how the story's form and its use of literary techniques was, in fact, producing a critique of humanitarian communication. By the end of the class, students could see that the detailed description of the children's shoes, the matter-of-fact narrator, the direct characterisation of humanitarian workers as condescending, the fly on the grandmother's face that the granddaughter finds frightening, a plot that ends with fantasising escape from the humanitarian gaze, and repeated images of humans as animals, work together to fashion a strong counter-discourse to humanitarian frames for refugee lives.

Imaginative Humanitarianism as Ethnographic Research

In addition to framing fiction as humanitarian communication, imaginative humanitarianism as a learning method can devolve at times into a popular imitation of ethnographic research. A number of news articles have made a case for literature based on the way fiction allows the reader to stand in the shoes of a refugee-ed person. For example, a *Guardian* article by Gillian Cross (2015) entitled 'Why Fiction Can Help Us Understand the Syrian Refugee Crisis' makes the old but simple point that stories 'help us to understand other people and empathise with them'. The reader of refugee narratives is here cast as a kind of amateur participant observer with humanitarian intentions. Cross's *Guardian* article applies an 'ethnography for empathy' type reading practice to North American refugee narratives without any specificity around political, social and legal realities and without consideration of the way national discourses constrain both the types of narratives being told and published and also the possible range of actions in response to those stories. Tellingly, the distinction between authors with migration experience and authors without it is not addressed in her article or others like it.

James Buzard (2009), who analyses nineteenth-century British novels as auto-ethnography, helps to connect participant observation and imaginative ethnography at a methodological level:

> Inasmuch as cultures have been so closely associated with different territories as to be representable as if they were places themselves ... then a fieldworker's physical traveling, necessary to get to that place on earth where an alien society was to be encountered, became very closely associated and virtually identified with the *mental* journey required to get the fieldworker 'out' of his own customary thought-world and into that of his subjects. (25)

Similarly, champions of refugee narratives have equated the emotional journey of reading a novel or watching a film to a kind of immersion in refugee cultures.

Martyn Hammersley and Paul Atkinson (1983) provide us with an early description of ethnography, in which ethnographic researchers as participant observers of the 'variations in cultural patterns across and within societies' are trying to better describe the subjects of their study and the interpretive lens of the subjects of their study (8). The ethnographer's aim is to create 'detailed descriptions of the concrete experience of life within a particular culture and of the social rules or patterns that constitute it' (8). This kind of description inevitably involves a level of interpretation. Tim Ingold's (2014) helpfully polemical intervention defines ethnography narrowly to avoid commodifying participant observation fieldwork. Arguing that 'ethnographic' is overused as a loose qualifier for research methods, he separates fieldwork (in our case, participant observation) from ethnography, which he defines as 'writing about the people' (385). The collapse of participant observation and ethnography may undermine a researcher's ability to learn *from* people, not learn *about* them because it implies that description and analysis are taking place at the same time as participant observation. 'Participant observation', he declares, 'is absolutely *not* an undercover technique for gathering intelligence on people, on the pretext of learning from them . . . [It is an] ontological commitment' (388). Such 'rigorous . . . inquiry' requires 'long-term and open-ended commitment, generous attentiveness, relational depth, and sensitivity to context' (384). In the classroom, readers may immerse in a creative narrative with the intent of gathering knowledge about refugee culture for class discussion or a term paper. However, Ingold's critique suggests that the elision of immersing and describing may create superficial data points rather than an opportunity for the patient, deep reading that fiction is meant to offer.

My assessment of imaginative humanitarian ethnography addresses both the uncritical use of a participant observer model for reading to learn, and also the very possibility of ethnographies of refugee culture. Several problems with humanitarian ethnography present themselves: (1) There is no discrete, structured refugee culture;[2] (2) People who have sought refuge are culturally heterogenous; (3) The state (alongside NGOs, non-state fascists, citizen lobbies, research institutions and even sometimes corporations) is the primary perpetuator of the idea of 'refugee culture', and arguably no 'refugee' institutions or traditions exist apart from it; (4) People who have sought refuge are geographically dispersed; (5) People often want to shed the refugee label once they achieve permanent resident status, leaving an unrepresentative sample to speak on behalf of a non-discrete, heterogeneous population.

Thus, a central problem with humanitarian ethnography as an approach to refugee stories is the question of culture and how it is delimited. If a course does not grapple with the question of what 'refugee culture' means when exploring refugee culture through imaginative narratives, a learning community may believe it is discovering generalisable data about authentic refugee experiences when in fact it is adding to the bureaucratic, political and humanitarian discourses about refugee experiences. This is in part because the term refugee is inextricably linked to discourse-specific concepts like the nation-state, sovereignty, citizenship, borders, humanitarianism and trauma. To put it differently, people who have sought refuge identify with diverse cultural heritages and tell stories from wide-ranging experiences. But what some readers may think of as 'refugee culture' in a text may in fact be the machinations of citizen or nation-state culture. Reading a refugee narrative as ethnography may erroneously locate refugee subjectivity in the identity of an individual character rather than in the categories of a legal system. The danger of a single story coming to represent a diverse group of individuals is also present. To be clear, my critique of imaginative ethnography is not that stories cannot teach anything about refugee realities. The point is that educators must help students to hedge what can be known through imaginative narratives about displacement. 'What it is like to be a refugee' is the blunt tool students arrive with to interpret stories; a sharper tool is needed.

Imaginative *humanitarian* ethnography is motivated by the belief in universal ethical claims that lead the reader to observe, describe and locate refugee experiences in imaginative texts as a discrete set of cultural patterns. This way of reading believes in the ability of fiction to host participant observers who can then create useful (empathetic) knowledge. Given the predetermination of humanitarian frames, the scholarly potential of this kind of reading remains limited. In the expectation that reading a refugee narrative will provide knowledge of refugee culture through intimate exposure to a character or set of characters, one witnesses the unintended effect of popular defences of literary study: citizens should read refugee stories to unlock the peculiarity of 'refugee tribes'.

As an example, in a recent interdisciplinary graduate seminar course I taught on refugee narratives, the class was discussing Canadian author Lawrence Hill's political thriller *The Illegal* (2015). One student bravely expressed confusion about why they did not like the book and why they could not connect with it. I pressed them on what 'it' stood for, and together we realised that 'it' was the main character, Keita, and that what the student desired was to hear an expression of emotion that reflected the impact of the trauma Keita was experiencing. Without that emotional exposure, the student had a hard time connecting with what they considered to be the experience of forced displacement. As I tried to steer the conversation in the direction of the author's choice of genre rather than the theme of forced displacement, another student continued the line of thinking of the first student: they wondered whether the lack of emotional expression suggested Keita was too traumatised to express his trauma and so to heal. A year later in an undergraduate course where we studied the same book, one student tried to articulate an answer to whose story it was by saying, 'I thought it was Keita's at first, but he's not even there at the end of the novel. So, I'm confused'. Another student said they had felt disappointed by the second half of the book because it 'didn't feel real', specifically, the ending was too neat and the perspective kept changing. Another student's term paper argued that satire was an inappropriate genre for refugee storytelling, given the seriousness of the global 'refugee crisis'. I read the confusion, frustration, disappointment and hesitancy in these moments as thwarted expectations about the consumption of humanitarian stories. Their desires for the text are further complicated by the fact that, while Hill had a family connection to undocumented life, he does not have personal refugee experience.

Countering Imaginative Humanitarian Ethnography

Encountering imaginative humanitarian ethnography, I have turned often to the literary tradition of close reading to help balance ethical and aesthetic concerns.[3] Yet even close readings can produce atomised interpretations that are susceptible to final papers with humanitarian conclusions. Towards what do educators and students of forced migration move when they want to escape humanitarian frames? What alternative reading practices respect the vulnerability of and care for the power of stories about displacement? In the face of globalised neoliberalism, how does one teach stories and employ storytelling so as to fundamentally shift the patterns of consumption and paternalism that undergird encounters between a learner (particularly those without refugee experience) and stories of forced migration?

One of the challenges with reading refugee narratives differently is that imaginative humanitarian ethnography needs to be unearthed and examined before it can be critiqued. The bandwidth required to undo a particular reading practice may mean there is only space to prove the damage and not the regenerative potential found in self-representative media. This chapter might be such an example. In some discussions I have facilitated, we engage in a critical deconstruction of humanitarian communication only to return to the very principles just deconstructed. For example, we may get to the point in a discussion where we recognise the limits of empathy within a humanitarian frame, but then final papers or reflections call for empathy as a solution to the humanitarian frame. As Eve Tuck (Unangax) (2009) has famously observed about what she calls 'damage-centred' research on Indigenous communities, 'the paradox of damage: to refute it, we need to say it out loud' and repeating the damage aloud reiterates and confirms it, sometimes as more primary than the wisdom and hope of communities who experience damage yet carry on (417). Yet 'even when communities are broken and conquered, they are so much more than that – so much more that this incomplete story is an act of aggression' (416). Can the wisdom and hope of a community shape reading practices? Is there a relational way of understanding interpretation that can undo reading practices that feel like an act of aggression?

In the introduction to *Countering Displacements*, my co-authors and I use the term 'counter' to describe the coming together of regeneration and critique:

> To counter a force is both to meet it in strength and also to strategically undermine it, to prepare for a future onslaught and to question injustice in the very moment of displacement . . . More than simply *en*countering displacement, countering encompasses the varying activities of creative and strategic agents. (Coleman et al. 2012: xxx)

Similarly, the work of countering imaginative humanitarian ethnography invites a different conceptualisation of reading that can shift the focus, unearthing what happens to a narrative when it is read and asking what kind of learning practices might respect the narrative's vulnerability. As the introduction to this chapter suggested, one way to counter imaginative humanitarian ethnography is to recast stories as gifts or to consider the exchange of stories as part of the gift economy rather than only the knowledge or information economy. The following section describes stories as gifts that are received by learners, providing a relational description of the event of reading.

Stories as Gifts

In the classroom, explicitly framing refugee stories as gifts is a way of supporting and valuing the participation of students with refugee backgrounds. It also establishes the relational nature of writing and reading stories and, by extension, invites readers to consider their reading a form of relational listening. References to story as gift can be found in Indigenous studies and spiritual traditions (Simpson and Strong 2013; Kuokkanen 2007), in media studies (Dovey 2014; Romele and Severo 2016), in narrative medicine (Spencer 2016; Small 2005), in literary studies (Coleman 2009; McCall 2011), in religious studies (Atkinson 1995; Griesenger and Eaton 2006), and in stories themselves. Different cultural understandings of gift establish specific and varied significances for the conceptualisation of stories as gifts. Rauna Kuokkanen's (Ohcejohka/Utsjoki) (2007) research on storytelling as gift describes the 'logic of the gift' as engendering a relationship 'characterized by reciprocity and by a call for responsibility to the "other"' (2, 23). The kind of recognition that is required by a gift is 'knowledge as well as commitment, action, and reciprocity' (3). Education professor Jo-Ann Archibald's (Stó:lō) (2008) research on the Stó:lō practice of storywork extends the four Rs of ethical Indigenous education – respect, relevance, reciprocity and responsibility (Kirkness and Barnhardt 1981) – to include 'holism, interrelatedness, and synergy' (Archibald 2008: 2). She writes: 'I coined the term [storywork] because I needed a term that signified that our stories and storytelling were to be taken seriously [. . . as] cultural work' (3–4). While Archibald does not explicitly theorise stories as gifts, the language of gift runs through her work as she describes the stories that were 'given' to her by elders during her research. She extends her analysis to stories that have been recorded and written down. Her approach to story as gift highlights the relational nature of narratives and of reading: 'in Stó:lō and Coast Salish cultures the power of storywork to make meaning derives from the synergy between the story, the context in which the story is used, the way that the story is told, and how one listens to the story' (84). Learning from Archibald's research for our discussion of refugee narratives in education, we might surface the relationality existing among the narrative, the context of reading communities, the way texts are written, and the way communities read. The time educators take to participate in local communities and their material struggles enlivens this knowledge.

Yet this chapter has critiqued action-oriented interpretive frames. A brief word of clarification is, therefore, necessary to distinguish between the responsibilities of stories as gifts and the responsibilities of stories as humanitarian communication. More often than not, humanitarian communication is produced by people without refugee experience and urges action on behalf of generalisable 'objects of rescue' (Espiritu 2006). Humanitarian discourse simulates emotional connection between readers and refugee cultures to stimulate a material relationship between readers and humanitarian action. I view this as a separation of the story from the agency of the individual person who has lived it. By way of contrast, stories offered by people with refugee experience and received as gifts among relations remain attached to the persons who lived or tell it. To be responsible to such a gift is to engage in living inquiry: joining a community that is already in action and embedding in relationships with a particular refugee community. Reciprocity and responsibility may look more like supporting, elevating, following and sharing power with those who have navigated the asylum system.

Reading as Listening

Once we acknowledge that the practice of reading takes place within a relational matrix, it makes sense to use the metaphor of conversation to reconceive reading as listening. Given the 'subtle shifts in acoustical agency' implied by 'different senses of the term "listening"', determining what kind of listening a learner aims for is also important (Rice 2015: 100). Working from an oral tradition, Archibald refers to storywork as 'story listening' (2008: 7); she reminds her readers that 'patience and trust are essential for preparing to listen to stories' (8). Her use of the phrase 'listen to' is a significant distinction from the arguably more common instruction in the classroom to 'listen for'. Where 'listening to' may imply receptive, open-ended, relational attention aimed at learning from the storyteller, 'listening for' references the search for particular predetermined knowledge (for example, humanitarian calls to action) in the story.

In my postdoctoral research on refugee stories and dialogue, 'Digital Storytelling as a Method for Refugee Dialogue in Canada' (2017–2019), the importance of 'listening to' emerged as well. I had conducted cross-sector interviews on the ordinary words of asylum discourse, and reading through the transcripts I noticed 'listening' as a keyword. One interviewee, Sharmarke Dubow, who is a former refugee now living in Canada, is an elected city councillor in Victoria, British Columbia. Before our interview, Dubow asked me to tell him my story to make clear my personal intentions, even though he had read my research protocol and we had clarified the research goals. I spoke for a long time and answered all his questions. By 'listening for' something in my story, he subtly switched the agency of the exchange. When he was satisfied that my research intentions had come out of a good story, we began an interview that lasted no longer than my introductory story.

'Stories are listening', he explained. 'We are in a moment that we observe information quickly, and we want sound bites.' Claiming agency at the start of the interview was a brilliant move to protect his own story by first 'listening for' paternalistic patterns of interview listening in me. Describing the significance of listening, Dubow said that listening 'comes out of a good intention, not gaining something . . . it's not [a] transaction. It's curiosity, it's non-judgement, and sometimes you don't gain anything. And you respect that'. Listening to learn needs to be wrested away from abstracted, decontextualised commodity logic and returned to the relationality of gift logic. I offered my gratitude, saying, 'I feel protective of people's stories . . . I always think it's a gift, but I know it's a gift that you can choose to give or not. And I appreciate that you choose to [share your stories with others]'. Dubow's response pushed back slightly: 'It's part of me'. He continued, 'I personally see it as a responsibility [rather than a choice] now that I am Canadian'. In this way Dubow discerns story as indistinguishable from the person whose story it is, and frames storytelling, and by extension story listening, as a relational responsibility without expectation of profit. My task as I edited the video footage was to find a form that might instil an ethic of reciprocity in the viewers/listeners of his words.

Pedagogical Suggestions

How do educators shift the patterns of consumption and paternalism that undergird every encounter between a learner (particularly, but not exclusively, those without refugee experience) and stories of forced migration? How does one teach stories to support learners across difference to remain curious and empowered? Some ideas include: (1) building relationships of trust and mutuality with local communities; (2) inviting guest speakers to comment on the broader culture based on their refugee experiences; (3) getting students into the community through experiential learning appropriate to their level; (4) facilitating rigorous interpretations of each narrative's aesthetic and rhetoric through close readings; (5) assigning refugee authors, theorists and media-makers; (6) studying inequity in international systems and national cultures from the perspective of refugee narratives; (7) assigning materials that benefit displaced communities financially.

Reframing refugee narratives differently from imaginative humanitarian ethnography requires educators to re-evaluate what is most important to learn from a refugee narrative, what is considered common sense about the characters' experiences, what requires explanation, what details can be ignored, and even the book's capabilities and limitations for effecting change in the world. Reframing can occur in all aspects of teaching: assigned reading questions, the course's thematic focus, lecture material and class discussions. The work of reframing refugee narratives may involve redefining the problem or issue as something other than the search for refuge (perhaps something more complex like ethnonationalism, American imperialism, global arms sales, fundamentalism, capitalism, or something else altogether), and it may ask learners to give the authority for answering 'how best to solve the problem' back to those in search of refuge, whether imagined or otherwise. In imaginative narratives, reframing refugee stories could look like asking students to clearly articulate what the problem is *according to the text* and how the *characters* suggest solving that problem, in addition to asking what relationship this may or may not have with *the author's* perspective.

To return to Nguyen and Fung (2016), in social sciences, policy and ethnography, refugees have become 'objects of investigation . . . [but] refugees [are] active participants that use rhetorical and aesthetic means to inform, push against, and redefine the mechanisms that construct them as subjects' (6). In the classroom, resisting simplified interpretations of refugee culture via imaginative ethnography requires an explicit articulation of the object of study as the narrative and not refugee culture (which may result in less discussion of migration themes); it means attending to the ways refugee authors, as co-educators, are interrupting popular cultural narratives or the way refugee theorists are interpreting narratives; and it cautions against the language of authenticity or generalisations about refugee culture as a unitary subject. Positively, it means contextualising each new story within in its own cultural, political, historical and national environment, discovering the particular political vision of each storyteller, and asking the text to offer unexpected knowledge. Concretely, this could take the shape of experiential learning that reminds students of the active role of refugee communities in creating culture and that raises questions about the relationship between cultural production and material gains or losses for refugee communities. Assigning interdisciplinary or cross-cutting scholarship can draw out the relevance of a cultural text and relate it to similar experiences of disenfranchisement, such as that of temporary foreign workers.

Conclusion

What happens to a refugee story in the classroom? A learning process undertaken by students based on their expectations for reading a refugee story. Many students arrive in a classroom already primed to commit humanitarian ethnography against stories. In addition to overriding the lifeworld of the story, this can be an alienating and diminishing experience for students with correlative experiences. Reading refugee stories as imaginative humanitarian ethnography layers the complexity of global politics, onto a personal sense of responsibility to strangers, onto the emotional impact of reading about violence, onto assumptions about human rights and equality, onto a growing knowledge of migration in unmanageable scope. Discussions then about what should be done can turn to despair and short circuit more nuanced analysis. I see the role of the instructor as unmasking and denaturalising this reading process, while simultaneously practising different learning approaches that allow students' readings of narratives to serve as jumping-off points for further relational inquiry.

How to study refugee literature ethically within its relational matrix remains an open question. When developing research methodology, I hold myself accountable to my ancestral story of displacement, to my friendships with people who formerly carried the status of 'refugee', and to refugee claimant communities in my city. In the classroom, my pedagogy resists pragmatic and utilitarian humanitarian readings of cultural texts by highlighting unequal access to the category of 'human', interrogating the language of humanising that often frames refugee storytelling, analysing the social inequity established by commercial representations of refugees, and delaying urgent questions about action by slowly unpacking the aesthetic construction of the text. These pedagogical shifts have proven helpful in resisting a way of reading refugee narratives that joins the frame of humanitarian communication with an ethnographic reading practice. Yet as a settler scholar with a nomadic childhood, an educator in the humanities with a love of story and training in anti-colonial theories and literatures, I still wonder, at an existential level, from what ground I read and teach refugee literature. I make missteps and continue to search for transformative pedagogy and mentors that can help me, as a learner, to be self-aware about the relations engendered in reading.

◆

Erin Goheen Glanville is an instructor in the Coordinated Arts Program at the University of British Columbia, Coast Salish Territory. Dr Glanville's community-engaged research project, Worn Words, develops a cultural refugee studies approach to narrative media-making and pedagogy. She serves on the Executive Committee for UBC's Centre for Migration Studies and on the Board of Directors for Kinbrace Community Society. Glanville is also co-editor of *Countering Displacements: The Creativity and Resilience of Indigenous and Refugee-ed Peoples* (2012). The Worn Words film *Borderstory* (2020) is available online as an educational resource for classrooms and communities: https://vimeo.com/42754559 or www.eringoheenglanville.com.

Notes

1. See, for example, https://enoughproject.org/blog/world-refugee-day-importance-refugee-stories; https://wowlit.org/blog/2016/12/05/sharing-immigrant-and-refugee-stories/; https://greatergood.berkeley.edu/article/item/why_children_need_to_hear_refugee_stories; https://www.msf.org/refugees-around-world-stories-survival-world-refugee-day; https://www.theguardian.com/books/2019/jun/23/refugee-tales-migration-books-ungrateful-refugee-our-city-dina-nayeri-jon-bloomfield-jonathan-portes; https://academic.oup.com/jrs/article-abstract/21/1/117/1513055?redirectedFrom=fulltext.
2. Anthropologist Liisa Malkki's critique in the 1990s of the tendency of refugee research to treat refugee subjects as belonging to a unitary culture is often referenced to make this point.
3. For a practical introduction to close reading, see http://canlitguides.ca/chapter-categories/research-skills/. Or, for a critical history of the close reading method, see Herrnstein Smith (2016).

References

Archibald, J.-A. 2008. *Indigenous Storywork: Educating the Heart, Mind, Body, and Spirit*. University of British Columbia Press.

Atkinson, R. 1995. *The Gift of Stories: Practical and Spiritual Applications of Autobiography, Life Stories, and Personal Mythmaking*. Westport, CT: Bergin & Garvey.

Buzard, J. 2009. 'Part One: Cultures and Autoethnography', in *Disorienting Fiction: The Autoethnographic Work of Nineteenth-Century British Novels*. Princeton, NJ: Princeton University Press, pp. 3–60.

Chouliaraki, L. 2010. 'Post-Humanitarianism: Humanitarian Communication beyond a Politics of Pity', *International Journal of Cultural Studies* 13(2): 107–26.

Coleman, D. 2009. *In Bed with the Word: Reading, Spirituality, and Cultural Politics*. University of Alberta Press.

Coleman, D., et al. 2012. *Countering Displacements: The Resilience and Creativity of Refugee-ed and Indigenous Peoples*. University of Alberta Press.

Cross, G. 2015. 'Why Fiction Can Help Us Understand the Syrian Refugee Crisis', *The Guardian*, 8 September, Author Opinion.

Dovey, J. 2014. 'Documentary Ecosystems: Collaboration and Exploitation', in K. Nash, C. Hight and C. Summerhayes (eds), *New Documentary Ecologies:*

Emerging Platforms, Practices and Discourses. London: Palgrave MacMillan, pp. 11–32.

Espiritu, Y.L. 2006. 'Toward a Critical Refugee Study: The Vietnamese Refugee Subject in US Scholarship', *Journal of Vietnamese Studies* 1(1–2): 410–33.

Fitzpatrick, E. 2018. 'A Story of Becoming: Entanglement, Settler Ghosts, and Postcolonial Counterstories', *Cultural Studies | Critical Methodologies* 18(1): 43–51.

Gordimer, N. 1989. 'The Ultimate Safari', *Granta*, 1 September.

Griesenger, E., and M. Eaton. 2006. *The Gift of Story: Narrating Hope in a Postmodern World*. Texas: Baylor University Press.

Hammersley, M., and P. Atkins. 1983. *Ethnography: Principles in Practice*. Tavistock Publications.

Herrnstein Smith, B. 2016. 'What Was "Close Reading"? A Century of Method in Literary Studies', *Minnesota Review* 87: 55–75.

Hill, L. 2015. *The Illegal*. Harper Collins.

Ingold, T. 2014. 'That's Enough about Ethnography!' *HAU: Journal of Ethnographic Theory* 4(1): 383–95.

Kirkness, V.J., and R. Barnhardt. 1981. 'First Nations and Higher Education: The Four R's – Respect, Relevance, Reciprocity, Responsibility', *Journal of American Indian Education* 30(3): 1–15.

Kuokkanen, R. 2007. *Reshaping the University: Responsibility, Indigenous Epistemes, and the Logic of the Gift*. UBC Press.

McCall, S. 2011. *First Person Plural: Aboriginal Storytelling and the Ethics of Collaborative Authorship*. UBC Press.

Nguyen, M., and C. Fung. 2016. 'Editor's Introduction. Refugee Cultures: Forty Years after the Vietnam War', *MELUS: The Society for the Study of the Multi-Ethnic Literature of the United States* 41(3): 1–7.

Nussbaum, M.C. 2016. *Not for Profit: Why Democracy Needs the Humanities*. Princeton, NJ: Princeton University Press.

Rangan, P. 2017. *Immediations: The Humanitarian Impulse in Documentary (a Camera Obscura Book)*. Durham, NC: Duke University Press.

Rice, T. 2015. 'Listening', in D. Novak and M. Sakakeeny (eds), *Keywords in Sound*. Durham, NC: Duke University Press, pp. 99–111.

Romele, A., and M. Severo. 2016. 'The Economy of the Digital Gift: From Socialism to Sociality Online', *Theory, Culture, and Society* 33(5): 43–63.

Simpson, L., and A. Strong. 2013. *The Gift is in the Making: Anishinaabeg Stories*. Portage and Main Press.

Small, N. 2005. 'The Story as Gift: Researching AIDS in the Welfare Marketplace', in R.S Barbour and G. Huby (eds), *Meddling with Mythology: AIDS and the Social Construction of Knowledge*. London: Routledge.

Smith, L.T. 2012. *Decolonizing Methodologies: Research and Indigenous Peoples*. London: Zed Books.

Spencer, A.C. 2016. 'Stories as Gift: Patient Narratives and the Development of Empathy', *Journal of Genetic Counseling* 25(4).

Stonebridge, L. 2017. 'Does Literature Help or Hinder the Fight for Human Rights', *The New Humanist*, 18 July.

Temple, E. 2017. '15 Works of Contemporary Literature By and About Refugees: Stories and Voices We Need Now and Always', *Lithub.com*, 31 January. https://lithub.com/15-works-of-contemporary-literature-by-and-about-refugees (accessed 5 October 2020).

Tuck, E. 2009. 'Suspending Damage: A Letter to Communities', *Harvard Educational Review* 79(3): 409–28.

CHAPTER 9
Digital Literacy for Refugees in the United Kingdom

ISRAEL PRINCEWILL ESENOWO

━━◆◆◆

With the outbreak of the COVID-19 pandemic and the United Kingdom put into lockdown on 23 March 2020, most higher education institutions in the UK and across the world moved parts or all of their classes online. Over a short period of time, both instructors and students had to adapt to new digital ways of teaching and learning. In this context, debates and controversies concerning digital access in terms of digital literacy as well as material access to a computer and a stable internet connection became key elements of ongoing discussions about inequalities in access to higher education.

Even before the pandemic moved classes online for large segments of the student population, the UK was fast moving towards a highly digitalised society. Indeed, digital literacy is essential in today's modern society and it is recognised in the European Reference Framework as one of the eight key competences for lifelong learning, as included in the recommendations of the European Parliaments and Council (European Commission 2007). The increasing number of online tasks in everyday life makes the use of the internet an integral part of life of many European residents (Costa et al. 2015).

Digital literacy is thus a key feature of social inclusion: it has become a vital proficiency in order to be fully active civil members of the community. Conversely, a lack of familiarity with digital tools and skills has increasingly become a barrier to full and effective participation. While digital exclusion is a broad problem affecting different social groups, displaced learners are confronted with particular forms of digital exclusion, rooted in global and local inequalities in access to and use of digital technology.

To respond to this situation, the University of East London Open Learning Initiative (UEL OLIve) developed a Digital Literacy programme aimed at equipping displaced learners with stronger digital skills. The programme also aimed at breaking down the digital barriers to entering university and developing the skills that students need to be actively involved in the community and support their social inclusion into society.

Based on my experience as an IT instructor at UEL OLIve, this chapter reflects on our digital skills workshops, with a particular focus on the digital barriers faced by displaced learners. It also presents findings from a survey among fifty-two respondents from a diverse community of displaced learners, represented by OLIve students and alumni of OLIve courses (OLIve UEL n.d.). The survey questionnaires aimed to collect data and information for a specific indicator related to awareness and improvement of the digital literacy experience as part of the pre-access programme at the university. Further to this, the chapter explores the pedagogical approach as implemented at UEL OLIve and the challenges faced in the classroom and the solutions put forward.

Barriers to Digital Literacy

Digital literacy has been widely acknowledged as playing a key role in lifelong learning, and the career development of the individual (Chen et al. 2016), while also contributing to greater equality and opportunities for society at large. By participating in bridging knowledge disparities within the community, it contributes to sustainable development. Moreover, digital exclusion is both a cause and a consequence of other inequalities: people and groups already suffering from inequalities are less likely to be digitally literate, while in turn their lack of familiarity with technology and online resources can further reinforce their marginalisation.

While it has been acknowledged as a key component of contemporary societies, the concept and interpretation of digital literacy tend to be all-embracing and often refer to a range of different components such as ICT literacy, information literacy and technological literacy. This chapter broadly refers to digital literacy following UNESCO's definition, which sees it as 'the ability to access, manage, understand, integrate, communicate, evaluate, and create information safely and appropriately through digital technologies for employment, decent jobs and entrepreneurship. It includes competencies that are variously referred to as computer literacy, I.C.T. literacy, information literacy and media literacy' (UNESCO Institute for Statistics 2018).

If we take a more societal-level approach to digital literacy by recognising its contribution to community as a whole, we can also argue that digital literacy can be seen as a public good that favours overall social inclusion and cohesion. The importance of digital literacy is evidenced by the efforts of many national and regional government initiatives, in addition to international organisations, to come up with public policy and the implementation of strategic plans on digital literacy.

Inequality when it comes to digital literacy takes multiple forms in different contexts, yet some broad trends can be identified. The survey among OLIve students and alumni revealed a number of issues relating to digital exclusion and access to higher education, which show some connection between the two processes.

Inadequate Income, Unemployment and Underemployment – 90.4 per cent of respondents are currently experiencing a high level of unemployment and poverty. For those working, there is a probability that they are employed in a low-skilled job, earning less than minimum wage. Livingstone and Helsper (2007) outline four indicators of digital exclusion that are more obviously associated with material deprivation: access, skills, attitudes and types of engagement. This means there is a strong correlation between socio-economic conditions and the experience of digital exclusion.

Immigration Status and No Recourse to Public Funds – The immigration status of displaced learners is a key factor that determines whether an individual will be able to access publicly funded services in terms of welfare benefits like income support, housing benefit, health treatment, education and student finance. Of the displaced learners surveyed, 78.8 per cent indicated that immigration status is a huge challenge and constraint that has a negative impact in terms of digital exclusion. Such constraints hinder displaced learners in developing the digital skills and competency they need in order to be actively involved in the community and further integrate into society.

Lack of Awareness of Institutions and Programmes – Some universities in the UK are already collaborating with migrant community organisations and other stakeholders to address the challenges linked to providing information on opportunities for higher education and digital learning for displaced learners. However, the constraints faced by displaced learners in terms of awareness and lack of information regarding higher education opportunities show that organisations working to support displaced learners need to do more. The survey indicates that 90.4 per cent of respondents would like to have access to information, guidance, advice and support on opportunities related to higher education. Here, a lack of digital literacy works both as a cause and as a consequence of marginalisation in higher education for displaced learners.

Lack of Training and Accessible Facility – The survey questionnaire was inclusive, and it allowed for broader participation in the study by asking key questions about access to, training in, and use of digital technologies. Of those surveyed, 80.8 per cent lack access to training and digital facilities; this is a significant gap and further illustrates the digital exclusion experienced by displaced learners in accessing digital training and facilities.

These survey results allow us to draw a broad picture of the way in which displacement, digital exclusion and lack of access to higher education opportunities intersect and reinforce each other. In the next section, possible solutions and opportunities for change will be outlined.

Responding to Digital Exclusion

The rapid pace of change and the constant deployment of new technologies mean that residents in the UK must develop their skills and competences throughout their lives to actively engage with the community in which they live. People without digital competencies are at risk of becoming excluded from important activities, unable to take full advantage of the opportunities around them, and may also endanger themselves during the usage of digital tools and media (Ala-Mutka 2011).

In order to respond to the need for digital literacy among displaced students, UEL OLIve decided to set up a course addressing this particular issue. As a first step, we had to define what represents the appropriate level of digital literacy required by refugee and asylum-seeking learners. After examining various teaching content on digital literacy and based on findings from the UNESCO Global Framework of Reference on Digital Literacy Skills for Indicator 4.4.2, the Microsoft Digital Literacy Standard Curriculum was selected as a reference for our digital literacy course.

The adoption of the Microsoft Digital Literacy Standard Curriculum was based on the popularity and success of the implementation of the programme and curriculum in eleven countries around the world at the regional, national and international levels. It also provides students with the opportunity to learn digital skills and validate the knowledge and competencies by obtaining a certificate in recognition of their accomplishment.

Our course structure was designed following a pattern that can help learners exploring the use of digital technology in order to support their social inclusion, and to help them grasp the importance of computers in today's world. It focuses in particular on basic understanding of computers and networks, getting to know operating systems, working with applications and using virtual assistants. It also explores common productivity software applications deployed and used in business, education and at home.

The course also explains some of the common threats related to computer use, and how to safeguard networks and manage one's digital footprint. Additionally, it discusses creative skills and ways of establishing an avenue to collaborate with others. A strong focus is put on how best to use technology and digital skills in order to advance students' goals and career aspirations.

The digital literacy course was introduced at the beginning of the academic year 2018-19. One immediate observation was that every student in the class was different: some struggled with learning and some learned very well. In order to ensure that each student in the class was learning and engaged with the curriculum, I quickly understood that there was a need to be flexible in the learning objectives and to adapt methods and objectives based on the learning abilities, backgrounds, ages and ICT skills of each student.

Relatedly, a crucial and challenging step was to customise learning activities to individual interests and to effectively help the students in developing the specific skills they needed for work, study and home-based activities, while utilising the Microsoft Digital Literacy Standard Curriculum and adapting the exercises and activities to complement other e-learning resources.

The digital literacy course is only a first step towards enhancing the learner's ability and gaining an understanding of the opportunities presented by technology. It could also be the foundation that propels the addition of other essential life skills. Having discussed general challenges, in the next section I reflect in more detail on my classroom experience as the digital literacy instructor.

Inside the Digital Literacy Classroom

The OLIve IT students were mostly adult learners diverse in age, cultural background, skill level, education and previous IT experience. Notwithstanding the differences and backgrounds of the students, it was a constant and ongoing effort to reach out to all learners.

The class sessions began with setting up the IT equipment, computers and other resources required to prepare for the class activities. Having observed the students' learning patterns, it was of the utmost importance to take a flexible learning approach to teaching, which took their different learning styles into consideration. The lesson plan for each class session was presented in the form of a PowerPoint presentation, and all class activities involved the use of verbal instruction accompanied by a demonstration on the board and directing the learners to try out the activities by performing a hands-on exercise.

During the class session, as instructor, I found it essential to move around the computer lab to personally observe each student and see that they had accomplished the tasks or activities. In most cases, students who needed more support required longer practice time and additional personal attention in order to complete the tasks.

Guiding and facilitating the learning process and the full participation of all learners in the hands-on exercise and class activities also involved keeping a degree of control over the way the sessions unfolded, not allowing them to stray too far from the particular focus of the class discussion. However, on a few occasions, those learners who responded better to a verbal process tended to dominate the discussion, often distracting other learners from concentrating on the class activities. To minimise this, it was necessary to assign learners to small groups to allow interaction with each other within a smaller unit.

I also introduced quizzes in the teaching sessions in order to aid the learners. This operated as a quick evaluation of the topic covered and as a means to review the learner's knowledge. The use of Kahoot!, a game-based learning platform widely used as educational technology, allowed the learners to collaborate and participate through multiple-choice quizzes. Once Kahoot! was accepted as a learning tool, it proved efficient to increase motivation, concentration and engagement.

In addition to the digital literacy class, we also run an IT study skills support session in order to personalise the learning experience and help the learner to focus on skills of interest. Our aim is to offer the learner a range of IT learning and activities outside of the regular class learning hours. UEL students on placement from the computer science department support this IT session and have provided excellent help to OLIve students through the various activities, assisting them with e-learning resources, and through personalised learning that helps OLIve students to gain more ability in a specific area in a supervised setting. Some aspects of the process produced certain dissatisfaction, such as the constant need to remind learners, often unsuccessfully, to make notes of their log-in details. Such apparently minor issues could accumulate, requiring patience in dealing with requests.

While evaluating the IT class, observations that were made highlighted that each class session and each learner is unique, and that topics of interest and relevance to some learners might not be interesting to others. Some find specific topics more challenging and require additional support to get a thorough grasp of the lessons. One suggested solution was to invite the more advanced learners to help their peers in order to keep the class more actively engaged through collaboration.

In other words, while the aim of the class is to close the digital gap, it was also a constant challenge due to the different skills and interests of the student groups. Allowing for everyone to acquire fundamental skills was sometimes experienced as a frustrating process by quick learners, who felt they were slowed down by others, and this sometimes entailed changing learning schedules and learning plans to allow more time. Finding a creative way to engage learners at different levels in the class proved necessary, and the active involvement of more advanced learners by empowering them to take on a supporting role was one of the efficient ways I found to maintain cohesion in the classroom despite the variety of needs and levels.

Concluding Remarks

Some students learn more quickly than others. However, the privilege and experience of teaching IT to students on the OLIve course has been truly fulfilling. The ability to balance the different needs of the learners and modify teaching methods to reflect students' requirements has been a rewarding and challenging experience. This also evidenced the need to be resilient, creative and patient when working with mature students who sometimes find school environments difficult.

In order to sustain the goal of enhancing the digital experience of the OLIve students and displaced learners in the UK, my experience has led me to believe it is necessary to develop a framework and a standard metric to collect data and determine the full extent of the digital exclusion experienced by the displaced learner community as well as other social groups affected. Refugee and migrant community organisations should collaborate with relevant stakeholders, agencies and government institutions to initiate policy plans and promote digital literacy for displaced learners as a vital step to acquire digital skills for employment, study and participation in society.

The successful experience of adopting the Microsoft Digital Literacy Standard Curriculum at UEL OLIve can serve as a foundation for further ICT courses, which would in turn contribute towards better understanding the centrality of digital literacy in today's world and offering more effective solutions to displaced learners as well as other groups in needs of such support.

◆

Israel Princewill Esenowo, MBCS, is a digital literacy enthusiast and IT instructor who studied for a Joint Degree in Information Technology and Business Information System BSc (Hons) at Middlesex University London. He also holds a Postgraduate Diploma in Business Information Systems Management from Middlesex University. Israel works as an IT instructor for the UEL OLIve weekend programme, a university preparatory course aimed at enhancing access to higher education for displaced students. An experienced PC system engineer, Israel has also planned, prepared and delivered quality lessons in lectures and lab format regarding digital literacy. He is a member of the British Computer Society and active at the BCS since 2010, in addition to being an IEEE Computer Society member.

References

Ala-Mutka, K. 2011. 'Mapping Digital Competence: Towards a Conceptual Understanding'. European Union, Joint Research Centre, Institute for Prospective Technological Studies.

Chen, J.S., J.Y. Wang, F.S. Chen and D.W.S. Tai. 2016. 'Applying Fuzzy Delphi Method to Construct Digital Literacy Competences for Senior High School Students', *Proceedings – 2016 5th I.I.A.I. International Congress on Advanced Applied Informatics (IIAI-AAI)*, Kumamoto, 2016, pp. 277–80.

Costa, F.A., J. Viana, E. Cruz and C. Pereira. 2015. 'Digital Literacy of Adults Education Needs for the Full Exercise of Citizenship', *International Symposium on Computers in Education (S.I.I.E.)*, Setubal, 2015, pp. 92–96.

European Commission. 2007. 'Key Competences for Lifelong Learning', *Official Journal of the European Union*, 1–12.

Livingstone, S., E.J. and Helsper. 2007. 'Gradations in Digital Inclusion: Children, Young People and the Digital Divide', *New Media & Society* 9: 671–96.

OLIve UEL. n.d. *OLIve UEL Digital Literacy Questionnaire*. https://docs.google.com/forms/d/e/1FAIpQLSeVmGBUQjSX2G7aJXQBTKEuxt-WN3JmWFKeCAbilbaypyNgHg/viewform?usp = sf_link (accessed 12 December 2019).

UNESCO Institute for Statistics. 2018. 'A Global Framework of Reference on Digital Literacy Skills for Indicator 4.4.2', Information Paper No. 51. http://uis.unesco.org/sites/default/files/documents/ip51-global-framework-reference-digital-literacy-skills-2018-en.pdf (accessed 15 June 2019).

CHAPTER 10
Insider Views on English Language Pathway Programmes to Australian Universities

VICTORIA WILSON, HOMEIRA BABAEI, MERNA DOLMAI AND SUHAIL SAWA

◆◆◆

This chapter is a collaboration between three university students of refugee background and an Australian teacher-researcher who works with refugee students in Australia. It challenges educational discourses which locate deficits in refugee students rather than in the education systems that underserve them, and discusses the ways in which English as a second language programmes subject refugee background students to paternalistic practices. Such practices – damning students with low expectations, and refusing to recognise their expertise on their own learning – in turn create further barriers, as displaced students must fight for the right to meaningful education.

The idea for this chapter was sparked by an illustrative incident at an international conference on refugees. Two of the refugee-background students (Sawa and Dolmai) had just presented on their educational experiences in Australia, and an audience member (Wilson) commented that their stories correlated with systemic difficulties she had heard from her own students of refugee background. She added that such first-hand accounts were often dismissed or disbelieved by members of her educational community, echoing the arguments regarding mistrust of refugees referred to in the introduction of this volume. At this point, an insider in the educational hierarchy took control of the conversation. This gatekeeper asserted that adult English language students do not understand their learning needs, and it is up to educational providers to tell them which knowledge will serve them best. He concluded that his job mostly involved persuading refugee-background students to lower their ambitions to more obtainable (i.e. unskilled) careers, as their academic goals were unrealistic.

The encounter described above encapsulates the experiences of all the co-authors. All four have had our voices silenced, suppressed and delegitimised, either as students of a refugee background (Babaei, Dolmai and Sawa) or as an educator and ally of refugee students working in the neoliberal higher education sector of Australia (Wilson). Therefore, a primary purpose of this chapter is to legitimise and promote the perspectives of refugee-background adult students regarding their learning experiences and academic capacities. We aim to achieve this by:

- positioning refugee-background students as co-authors, rather than simply as research objects;
- foregrounding the lived experience of the co-authors from refugee backgrounds about their educational experiences in Australia and the systemic barriers they faced; and
- contextualising and validating their perspectives by reference to current research literature.

We begin with first-person accounts of three of the co-authors' transitions to university, or in two of those cases, the transition *back* to university. These accounts challenge three popular distortions about refugee-background students in Australia:

1. that they are a monolithic group who, as a whole, do not have sufficient educational backgrounds for university, and therefore should lower their expectations for tertiary study;
2. that refugees largely seek tertiary education as a means to fulfil familial expectations and boost personal status; and
3. that the capacities of post-school-age refugees to learn English are limited by their own deficits or past misfortunes, rather than by systemic barriers faced by adult English education for refugees and migrants in Australia.

The narratives presented below also emphasise the crucial role that English language plays in the lives of refugee-background students as a means to exercise agency, participate in society, and to build meaningful careers that meet their aspirations and abilities.

Provision of English as a Second Language Education to Refugees in Australia

> Learning language is very important for everybody. It is the key to every locked door, especially for young people who were at university

before they arrived in Australia. English opens the doors to study at university and to find better work opportunities. This is what young motivated people want to do. Learning the language makes you a stable and strong person. No language means you are like a deaf, blind person. (Merna)

If you want to survive, you have to learn English. (Homeira)

Voice, the silencing of voices, and who has the legitimacy to be heard, are both the key drivers and themes of this chapter. In an anglophone country such as Australia, voice is also inextricably linked to access to English. For newcomers, mastery of the English language is the key to education, employability, and to social and cultural capital. It is also required for integration and acceptance within the broader community, without which people of refugee backgrounds 'risk leading isolated, thwarted lives, while social cohesion and public support for migration risks being undermined' (Scanlon Institute for Applied Social Cohesion Research [SIASCR] 2019: 10). To deny meaningful English language education to refugees is to further silence their voices. However, achieving the required level of competency in English is also the largest challenge for students from refugee backgrounds (Harvey et al. 2018).

The Australian government provides free English tuition to post-school-age immigrants and refugees via the Australian Migrant English Program (AMEP). This tuition is delivered by public and private vocational colleges, depending on the state. When AMEP was first established in 1948 – and for decades afterwards – its prime goal was settlement of immigrants and refugees (SIASCR 2019). At its peak, AMEP was considered a worldwide 'exemplar' in English language provision (Moore 2001).

However, with economic rationalism taking over the Australian political landscape in the 1990s, the focus of AMEP changed from settlement to employment (SIASCR 2019). Since 1997, AMEP contracts have been put out to tender, resulting in less stability and coherence, and lower quality as providers compete to provide the most cost-efficient programme (Baker, Due and Rose 2019; SIASCR 2019). Further, in recent years a succession of new business models for AMEP has been introduced, increasing audit and compliance requirements at the expense of pedagogy (Baker, Due and Rose 2019; SIASCR 2019). The result of these combined measures is that AMEP has become increasingly generic, class sizes have increased, less qualified teachers are employed and curriculum standards have been lowered (Michell 2016; SIASCR 2019). In addition, due to attempts to conflate AMEP with vocational training programmes, assessments are no longer tied to English language proficiency, but to an 'inappropriate', invalid and unreliable measurement of employment-focused 'core skills' (Australian Council of TESOL Associations [ACTA] 2018).

Until August 2020, when changes to hours and eligibility were announced, only refugees and immigrants 'with less than functional English' were eligible for the 510 free hours of English classes provided by AMEP (ACTA 2016: 3). This arbitrary number of hours has led to various problems. The specific calculation of 510 hours 'has *no* theoretical, research or administrative validity' and was determined because the '10 on the end sounded really quite scientific. 500 would have looked just a bit too neat' (ACTA 2019: 9). However, data indicates that for students who arrive in Australia with no English, AMEP does not equip them with functional English in 510 hours. In fact, 'a mere seven per cent of migrants and refugees who studied in the AMEP each year achieved functional English as a result, according to the latest available figures, from 2015' (SIASCR 2019: 10).

In August 2020, the Australian government announced that AMEP hours would be uncapped and that the programme would be extended to a vocational level (IELTS 5.5 or equivalent) (Australian Government Department of Home Affairs 2020). However, it is not clear whether these developments will resolve other problems within AMEP. After all, as the relevant government minister admitted, 'currently people only complete about 300 hours of the 510 available' (Tudge 2020: para. 8). This strongly suggests that the quality of the programme, not the number of hours, is its fundamental flaw.

Over the six years that she has been teaching refugee-background students, one of the authors has heard from hundreds of former AMEP students that they were just 'wasting time' while in the programme. They have repeatedly told of being treated like incapable children, not worthy of high expectations. In this respect, AMEP runs the risk of what has been called in the Canadian context 'compassionate repression', that is, treating refugees 'in dehumanizing or patronizing ways as "victims" and "helpless people" who just need "bare life" necessities to survive' (Shakya et al. 2010: 74).

> Unfortunately, studying the language wasn't very helpful for me, because I was placed in a lower language level, when I felt I should have been placed in a higher level. The language school didn't acknowledge my previous education, and made me feel like I wasn't capable. I was disappointed and felt like I was wasting my time. Some of the

teachers were very helpful, but I don't think the English classes prepared me for university life in Australia, so starting uni here has been very hard for me. (Merna)

All of the students were together in one place, all of the different levels, and we had only one teacher. She couldn't teach us because we were a lot for one person. There were 25 to 30 from different levels. The teachers, I think, didn't have any choice because they just tell them to go and teach. But they couldn't control all of the people so sometimes they were just standing and looking at us.

Every morning they just told us to sit in a circle and when we sat, they threw a ball to us and said 'now introduce yourself', every single day. When we started at 8:45, it went until 10:00, because there were so many people. We had to introduce ourselves and we had to wait for others to introduce themselves. Every day. It was really a funny thing because we didn't need to introduce ourselves every single morning. In the afternoon they took us outside and they gave us the ball and they said, 'You can play now. Go and play soccer'. Sometimes they just gave us a pencil and said, 'Draw whatever you want'. We did that maybe twice a week. In the afternoon they gave us 30 minutes and they said 'Read!' but I couldn't read English. I knew the alphabet but that's all. My experience was really terrible. At that time, if I want to be honest, my boyfriend was beside me [after class] and he knew English and he helped me a lot. (Homeira)

Despite dedicated teachers, AMEP fails to deliver. This is due to a system that is focused on compliance at the expense of quality, and an assessment framework that is wholly unsuited to the teaching of English as an additional language (ACTA 2019). Furthermore, 'class sizes and groupings are grossly dysfunctional for teaching English' (ACTA 2019: 7). Coupled with regulatory requirements for constant attendance monitoring and a 'fragmented' curriculum (5) in which 'content is irrelevant' (11), 'continuity and coherence in teaching is impossible' (7). In addition, students are 'continuously admitted to classes' throughout the term (7). As a result, AMEP teachers report that they are left with no alternative but to employ 'the holding pen method of teaching' (7).

Until changes were announced in August 2020, there was an added quandary for the 7 per cent of students who managed to acquire 'functional English' at AMEP or those who entered Australia with higher levels of English. They were considered to have too much English for AMEP, but not enough to enter the workforce or courses in further and higher education. So-called 'functional English is generally regarded as well below the level required in most workplaces and [vocational] courses', but a student with functional English had to leave AMEP (SIASCR 2019: 10).

Compounding the problem, most university-based English language programmes are limited to full fee-paying, international students; while most tertiary preparation programmes for domestic – including refugee-background – students are not specifically designed as English as a second language courses. Only a small number of Australian universities run government-funded English language pathway courses which accept domestic students. Even then, students must first complete their 510 hours of AMEP. At a public university where one of the authors worked, refugees were systematically refused entrance into English language courses because they were seen as a burden on the system compared to full fee-paying international students. Regardless of their English language proficiency, many prospective students, over the course of many years, were constantly told to do their AMEP hours first, and refused an English language placement test.

> I heard a lot of people say, 'You can learn English at university, and after that you can go to university [to do a degree]'. But they did not allow me to study English there. When I wanted to start, I came and applied many times and they said, 'No, you have to go back to [AMEP] and finish your hours'. And then I said, 'OK, I will finish my hours' and then I came back and they said, 'No, your English level is not good for university, and we cannot allow you to come to university'. But I didn't want to go straight to university, I wanted to study English. They said, 'We don't have a course at your level, we only have high level courses'. I later found out that this was not true.
>
> I applied about three or four times and each time they said 'No, you have to finish your hours [at AMEP]'. So I went back but I couldn't learn anything. Then I went back to university but again they told me to go back to [AMEP] and finish my hours. I said, 'OK, I will finish my hours' but when I finished my hours they said, 'No, you have to go back and finish your second lot of hours! Because the government has given you the hours, you have to finish them'. I said, 'No, I don't want to go back there, because I want to study here!' They didn't ask me why I didn't want to go back to [AMEP]. They just said, because the government has given you the hours, you have to finish the hours.
> (Homeira)

Now that AMEP's free hours have been uncapped and are potentially unlimited, university gatekeepers could use this as justification to never provide access to pre-degree English language programmes, as the free hours will never be finished. Regardless, Homeira's experience reflects a number of issues that illustrate the injustices and roadblocks faced by refugee-background students in Australia. First, she was confronted by the seemingly arbitrary changes in the goalposts ('Finish your second lot of hours'). In addition, she spent a significant amount of time and energy fighting for entry to a programme which was ostensibly open access. Both of these further delayed her access to meaningful education. Furthermore, she was stymied by individual administrators and managers who misused their power to arbitrarily deny entry to refugees (see also Cantat, this volume). Finally, the fact that 'they didn't ask me why I didn't want to go back' illustrates again the exclusion and silencing of refugee voices, and the assumption that they cannot be trusted to make adult decisions.

Educational Backgrounds of Refugee Students

> As soon as I arrived in Melbourne Airport, the first sentence that came to my mind was, 'Will I be taking too long to go back to uni?' Thinking about studying is the first thing you will think of once you arrive in Australia.
>
> Many newly arrived young people from refugee backgrounds (especially from Syria and Iraq) were on linear educational pathways prior to arriving in Australia, including commencing or completing tertiary studies, and many had professional careers. So, when we get reconnected as soon as possible to educational pathways, this will help us to adapt faster with all the changes that have happened in our lives. When you have an educational background, and once you get reconnected to the educational pathways, that actually means you have successfully passed most of all challenges as a newly arrived refugee.
>
> And once we reconnect, that will make us feel that we are serving this country, and feel we are a part of it. It will make us feel proud and loved and welcomed, which will contribute to make us feel happier in our new lives in Australia, even feeling like we belong here, and all of these things will give us an additional incentive to serve and defend this country and society. (Suhail)
>
> One challenge many young refugee people face is losing hope to pursue their career aspirations. Making sure that young people are able to pursue their dream careers is very important, especially for young people like me who had started university before in their country. Before I left Iraq, I was studying a Bachelor of Engineering at the University of Mosul, and it was my dream to work as a civil engineer. I came to Australia in 2016 with my whole family. When I came to Australia, I didn't have any networks at all. We all know that having a good net-

work is the key to find good employment opportunities. I would have had a good network through my dad (he is an engineer and used to work in a big company) if I had not left my country. (Merna)

I did twelve years of school in Iran. I finished high school and I was ready to go to university. I really wanted to go. I was born in Iran, but I wasn't Iranian. I was a refugee, and refugees weren't allowed to study at university and to get a good job in Iran. Refugees were nothing there. (Homeira)

Many university graduates and students have been forced into sudden refugee status by events that disrupted their previously stable lives, and now find their qualifications and skills unrecognised after resettlement (Mackay 2019; see also Al Hussein and Mangeni, this volume). This experience is 'frustrating and humiliating' and adds to the difficulties of resettlement, as it 'impacts not only on their income generation and cost of living but is compounded when their parents' and caregivers' previous education is also not recognised. They would like a range of educational and training pathways made more accessible' (Mackay 2019: 41).

For young people in particular, a university education in Australia represents the opportunity to resume their previous trajectory (Stevenson and Baker 2018: 19; see also Al Hussein and Mangeni, this volume). Young refugee-background students often voice frustration that the refugee experience itself has already stolen time from them, delaying their education (Cassity and Gow 2006; Mackay 2019). Thus, a recurring theme among young refugees is a sense of urgency to resume study. Having already lost time due to displacement and discrimination, they are keen to resume the educational tracks that have been disrupted.

Despite having high levels of previous education, refugee-background students are often mischaracterised as holding notions of misplaced snobbery towards vocational colleges in Australia (Beadle 2014; Naidoo et al. 2018). This can be seen as yet another way to silence and delegitimise the voices of refugee students, as it implicitly assumes that they lack the self-knowledge and awareness of educational standards to choose the most suitable path. It also implies that refugee students are an undifferentiated mass, rather than individuals with varying educational backgrounds and skills.

Ultimately, for many refugee-background students, a university education is critical to secure a stable future and fulfilling work, to acquire the 'social and cultural capital' (Naidoo et al. 2018: 160) necessary for successful integration, and to build 'freedom and agency' (26). All of these aspects are also fundamental requirements for recovery from trauma (Harris and Fallot 2001; Silove 2013). In addition, a university education can be vital 'in terms of belonging and beginning to carve a new identity in a host nation' (Naidoo et al. 2018: 90; see also Al Hussein and Mangeni, this volume). Conversely, lack of belonging has been identified as the most significant challenge faced by refugee-background youth in Australia (Mackay 2019). A 'lack of meaningful opportunities can thread together to create a sense of disempowerment, isolation, and mental health issues for refugee young people in communities' (Mackay 2019: 7).

The number of refugee-background students attending university in Australia is largely unknown due to their classification as domestic students (Stevenson and Baker 2018). However, they are believed to be under-represented compared to other equity groups (Terry et al. 2016). As we will argue, this gap reflects neither the ambitions, aptitude nor prior educational experiences of many refugee-background students, but rather systemic barriers to participation.

However, the perceived obstacles to higher education for many former refugees serve to reinforce and orient the actual barriers, as the story of some gets retold as the story of *all*. Widely cited reasons for low rates of participation in higher education for refugees are limited and interrupted education, illiteracy in their first language, and trauma prior to resettlement (Beadle 2014; Molla 2019; Naidoo et al. 2018). Refugees in Australia have also perceived the tendency for others to assume that lack of English constitutes lack of intelligence (Mackay 2019). This deficit narrative has been further simplified in the Australian political discourse, with the then-Immigration Minister, Peter Dutton, claiming in 2016 that refugees were illiterate, innumerate, and both simultaneously unemployable and taking jobs from Australians (Doherty and Davidson 2016).

While some former refugees undoubtedly have experienced severely interrupted education, to categorise the 65.6 million displaced people worldwide as illiterate, damaged and unteachable is highly reductive, and puts the burden of adaptability on refugees (Rajaram, this volume) rather than on institutions. In addition, the formal education levels of refugee-background students in Australia are often underestimated. In reality, only 20 per cent of refugees in Australia arrive without the ability to read and write in their own language (Marshall 2015), although it is unclear whether this statistic accounts for languages that are oral only.

Moreover, while some 'commonalities of experience' exist among refugee-background students (Terry et al. 2016: 33), the significant differences that also exist must be 'accounted for in building their interactions with universities' and other educational providers (34). As with any students, those with more prior experience in education are more likely to succeed in further study (Naidoo et al. 2018: 8). However, even for those who have lived the majority of their lives as refugees or lived for prolonged periods in refugee camps, lack of formal education cannot be assumed. Three-quarters of refugees in Australia have at least a high school education when they enter the country (Australian Survey Research Group 2011). In any case, all refugees bring strengths and transferable skills, such as linguistic ability and intercultural knowledge, which can be a stepping stone to tertiary studies (Harvey et al. 2018; Naidoo et al. 2018; Stevenson and Baker 2018). In addition, refugees 'are, of course, already very competent language learners, as many speak other languages or dialects alongside their mother tongue, and they are highly motivated to learn' (Naidoo et al. 2018: 111).

Furthermore, their very experience of being refugees encapsulates their 'ability to survive adversity' and 'the strengths it has taken to get to where they currently are' (Rafferty et al. 2019: 33). A strengths-based approach does not mean that challenges and barriers are not recognised; rather, it entails building on the attributes and skills that refugees already have, and providing tailored, appropriate support instead of 'one-size-fits-all' approaches (Terry et al. 2016). Although not yet in practice on any large scale, 'the Australian higher education sector now has the ability to identify and engage communities through targeted and culturally-sensitive ways' (Terry et al. 2016: 35) and to respond to the varied specific needs of students from refugee backgrounds. However, the highly disparate educational needs of various refugee cohorts are often not considered in Australia's monolithic and inflexible system.

Conclusion

As discussed above, refugee-background students' voices are silenced when it comes to speaking out on the issue of English language education. Their perspectives on their experiences as adult English language learners in Australia are rarely heard, either in published research or in discussions that affect policy at a local level. The result has been a double silencing of refugee students, by blocking both their metaphorical voices (expression of informed opinion) and literal voices (the capacity to fully express themselves in English).

As an attempt to resist such silencing, this chapter has served two key purposes: to privilege the voices and lived experience of refugee students, and to attempt to subvert the traditional practices and power relations of academic authorship. In the academic milieu, refugees are often positioned as the researched rather than as researchers and writers. As such, their stories are often told by Western academics whose careers benefit as a result (Smith 2012; Stevenson and Baker 2018). Of the four co-authors of this chapter, one is a Western academic born in an anglophone country, using the privilege of linguistic and social capital to access an avenue to which her co-authors may not (yet) have entry. Conversely, the co-authors from refugee backgrounds lend the Western academic an authenticity and insider perspective that she would not otherwise have. There is some discomfort in this. However, it is hoped that by privileging the voices of refugee students and recognising them as co-authors rather than as mere data sources, some of the imbalance is redressed.

The lived-experience-led approach of this chapter reflects the critical research perspective that 'leadership needs to emanate from teachers, students, and community' rather than from only those who currently hold power (Smyth et al. 2014: 113). It has also sought 'to recognize and reposition students as authorities on and authors of their own educational experiences and representations of those experiences' (Cook-Sather 2007: 390). Privileging the voices of those who are usually excluded is 'an expression of individuality in the face of negative social stereotypes' (Campbell 2009: 116), and recognises that students are experts in their own learning and should be treated as such (Smyth 2011: 99). Most importantly, refugee voices are crucial for decision-making processes about issues which directly affect other refugees and in 'identifying where changes can be made to systems' (Rafferty et al. 2019: 26).

For significant change to occur, policy regarding English language education for refugee adults needs to be informed by the experience of refugee-background students themselves. Ultimately, refugee-background students want meaningful education that will open or reopen doors to careers that match their abilities and strengths. For them to have a voice in the community and agency over their lives and futures, they must have access to English education that is truly empowering and equips them to speak about the societies that they are now co-creating.

♦

Victoria Wilson is a PhD candidate at the University of Queensland, Brisbane, researching trauma-informed English language teaching to adults. She also teaches English as an Additional Language to international, refugee and immigrant students at the University of Southern Queensland in the Refugee Welcome Zone of Toowoomba. She has published and presented on trauma-informed English teaching, a research imperative motivated by her experience of teaching in Fukushima, Japan at the time of the 2011 disasters, as well as her student cohort at USQ.

Homeira Babaei is enrolled in a Bachelor of Human Services at the University of Southern Queensland, and a trainee interpreter. A third-generation refugee, she was born in Iran to parents who had also been displaced. She came to Australia in 2017 with her mother and siblings.

Merna Dolmai is a student at RMIT University in Melbourne. Before coming to Australia in 2016 with her family, she was completing a Bachelor of Engineering at the University of Mosul in Iraq. Mosul was under control of Daesh (the Islamic State terrorist group) from 2014 to 2017. It was later recaptured by the Iraqi government in the Battle of Mosul. Merna was a presenter at the 2nd Australian and New Zealand Refugee Trauma Recovery in Resettlement Conference in Brisbane in March 2019.

Suhail Sawa is studying an Advanced Diploma of Building Design at RMIT University in Melbourne. Born in Syria, he was displaced by the ongoing Syrian civil war. Suhail came to Australia in September 2016 and lives with his family in Melbourne, where he works part-time at a pharmacy. Suhail was a presenter at the 2nd Australian and New Zealand Refugee Trauma Recovery in Resettlement Conference in Brisbane in March 2019.

References

Australian Council of TESOL Associations [ACTA]. 2016. Response to Draft Request for Tender for the Adult Migrant English Program (AMEP) 2017–2020. https://tesol.org.au/wp-content/uploads/2019/01/ACTA-submission-on-draft-RFT-for-the-AMEP-final.pdf.

Australian Council of TESOL Associations [ACTA]. 2018. *ACTA Background Paper: Problems in the Adult Migrant English and SEE Programs*. https://tesol.org.au/wp-content/uploads/2019/01/Problems-in-the-AMEP-SEE-Program-25-May-2018-an-ACTA-Background-Paper.pdf.

Australian Council of TESOL Associations [ACTA]. 2019. *Proposals Following the Relocation of the Adult Migrant English Program to the Department of Home Affairs*. https://tesol.org.au/wp-content/uploads/2019/01/626_ACTA_Proposals_following_the_AMEPs_relocation_to_the_Dept_of_Home_Affairs.pdf.

Australian Government Department of Home Affairs. 2020. *Adult Migrant English Program (AMEP) Reform Announcement* [Press release], 28 August. https://tesol.org.au/wp-content/uploads/2020/09/AMEP-Reform-Announcement-General-Communications.pdf.

Australian Survey Research Group. 2011. *Settlement Outcomes of New Arrivals: Report of Findings Study for Department of Immigration and Citizenship.* https://immi.homeaffairs.gov.au/settlement-services-subsite/files/settlement-outcomes-new-arrival.pdf.

Baker, S., C. Due and M. Rose. 2019. 'Transitions from Education to Employment for Culturally and Linguistically Diverse Migrants and Refugees in Settlement Contexts: What Do We Know? '*Studies in Continuing Education*, 1–15. doi:10.1080/0158037x.2019.1683533.

Beadle, S. 2014. *Facilitating the Transition to Employment for Refugee Young People.* https://minerva-access.unimelb.edu.au/handle/11343/45124.

Campbell, J. 2009. 'We Are the Evidence: An Examination of Service User Research Involvement as Voice', in J. Wallcraft, B. Schrank and M. Amering (eds), *Handbook of Service User Involvement in Mental Health Research* [ProQuest Ebook Central version], pp. 72–137. https://ebookcentral-proquest-com.ezproxy.usq.edu.au/lib/usq/detail.action?docID=698284.

Cassity, E., and G. Gow. 2006. *Making Up for Lost Time: Young African Refugees in Western Sydney High Schools.* https://researchdirect.westernsydney.edu.au/islandora/object/uws:11690/datastream/PDF/view.

Cook-Sather, A. 2007. 'Resisting the Impositional Potential of Student Voice Work: Lessons for Liberatory Educational Research from Poststructuralist Feminist Critiques of Critical Pedagogy', *Discourse: Studies in the Cultural Politics of Education* 28(3): 389–403. doi:10.1080/01596300701458962.

Doherty, B., and H. Davidson. 2016. 'Fact Check: Was Peter Dutton Right about "Illiterate" Refugees "Taking Jobs"?', *The Guardian: Australia Edition*, 18 May. https://www.theguardian.com/australia-news/2016/may/18/fact-check-was-peter-dutton-right-about-illiterate-refugees-taking-jobs.

Harris, M., and R.D. Fallot. 2001. 'Envisioning a Trauma-Informed Service System: A Vital Paradigm Shift', *New Directions for Mental Health Services* 2001(89): 3–22. doi:10.1002/yd.23320018903.

Harvey, A., M. Mallman, G. Szalkowicz and A. Moran. 2018. *Raising University Participation of New Migrants in Regional Communities.* https://www.latrobe.edu.au/__data/assets/pdf_file/0004/891463/La-Trobe-New-Migrant-REPORT-Final-May-2018.pdf.

Mackay, K.L. 2019. *Refugee Youth Voice: Postcards to the Premier.* https://www.academia.edu/42150019/Refugee_Youth_Voice_Postcards_to_the_Premier.

Marshall, D. 2015. *Building a New Life in Australia: The Longitudinal Study of Humanitarian Migrants* [Data highlight No. 2/2015]. https://www.refugeehealthnetworkqld.org.au/wp-content/uploads/2018/03/data-highlight-no-2-2015-bnla_pdf.pdf.

Michell, M. 2016. 'Government Plans Downgrading of Adult Migrant English Programs', *The Australian TAFE Teacher* (Spring): 28–29.

Molla, T. 2019. 'Trauma, Racism and Unrealistic Expectations Mean African Refugees Are Less Likely to Get into Australian Unis', *The Conversation*, 27 August. https://theconversation.com/trauma-racism-and-unrealistic-expectations-mean-african-refugees-are-less-likely-to-get-into-australian-unis-121885.

Moore, H. 2001. 'Although It Wasn't Broken, It Certainly Was Fixed: Interventions in the Australian Adult Migrant English Program 1991–1996', in J. Lo Bianco and R. Wikert (eds), *Australian Policy Activism in Language and Literacy*. Melbourne: Language Australia.

Naidoo, L., J. Wilkinson, M. Adoniou and K. Langat. 2018. *Refugee Background Students Transitioning into Higher Education: Navigating Complex Spaces*. Singapore: Springer.

Rafferty, R., N. Ali, M. Galloway, H. Kleinschmidt, K.K. Lwin and M. Rezaun. 2019. *'It Affects Me as a Man': Recognising and Responding to Former Refugee Men's Experiences of Resettlement* [National Centre for Peace and Conflict Studies Policy Paper 2019/1]. https://www.otago.ac.nz/ncpacs/otago715116.pdf.

Scanlon Institute for Applied Social Cohesion Research [SIASCR]. 2019. *Australia's English Problem: How to Renew Our Once Celebrated Adult Migrant English Program*. https://scanloninstitute.org.au/publication/australias-english-problem-how-renew-our-once-celebrated-adult-migrant-english-program.

Shakya, Y.B., S. Guruge, M. Hynie, A. Akbari, M. Malik, S. Htoo, . . . S. Alley. 2010. 'Aspirations for Higher Education among Newcomer Refugee Youth in Toronto: Expectations, Challenges, and Strategies', *Refuge* 27(2): 65–78.

Silove, D. 2013. 'The ADAPT Model: A Conceptual Framework for Mental Health and Psychosocial Programming in Post Conflict Settings', *Intervention* 11(3): 237–48.

Smith, L.T. 2012. *Decolonizing Methodologies: Research and Indigenous Peoples*. London: Zed Books.

Smyth, J. 2011. *Critical Pedagogy for Social Justice*. New York: Continuum International Publishing Group.

Smyth, J., B. Down, P. McInerney and R. Hattam. 2014. *Doing Critical Educational Research: A Conversation with the Research of John Smyth*. New York: Peter Lang Publishing.

Stevenson, J., and S. Baker. 2018. *Refugees in Higher Education: Debate, Discourse and Practice*. Bingley, UK: Emerald Publishing.

Terry, L., R. Naylor, N. Nguyen and A. Rizzo. 2016. *Not There Yet: An Investigation into the Access and Participation of Students from Humanitarian Refugee Backgrounds in the Australian Higher Education System*. https://www.ncsehe.edu.au/wp-content/uploads/2016/08/Not-there-yet-An-Investigation-into-the-Access-and-Participation-of-Students-from-Humanitarian-Refugee-Backgrounds-in-the-Australian-Higher-Education-System-11-Aug-16.pdf.

Tudge, A. 2020. *More Class Hours Available to Help Migrants Learn English* [Press release], 28 August. https://minister.homeaffairs.gov.au/alantudge/Pages/More-class-hours-available-to-help-migrants-learn-English.aspx?s = 03.

CHAPTER 11
Enacting Inclusion and Citizenship through Pedagogical Staff Development

LUISA BUNESCU

The way academics teach is of critical importance for any reform intended to open up universities to displaced students, and more generally to any disadvantaged and under-represented groups of learners. Pedagogical staff development needs to accompany all academic and non-academic support measures meant to enhance access and participation of learners in higher education.

Background of the Initiative

Enhancing pedagogical staff development (i.e. teacher training) in higher education in Europe was one of the main objectives of the European Forum for Enhanced Collaboration in Teaching (EFFECT, 2015–19) project,[1] co-funded by the European Commission, under the Erasmus+ programme. EFFECT was led by the European University Association (EUA), and brought together twelve partners from ten different countries, including national rectors' conferences, higher education institutions, networks and associations active in the field of learning and teaching. Within the EFFECT project, the author of this chapter coordinated the implementation of the pedagogical staff development workshops on inclusion and citizenship skills.

These themes (inclusion and citizenship) were chosen by the project consortium as two of the grand challenges experienced in our societies, and which universities together with other actors should address. Inclusion and equity appear as desiderata in several international, high-level communications. They are reflected in the Agenda 2030 Sustainable Development Goals (SDG), and notably in SDG4 which promotes inclusive, quality and equitable education, with specific reference to vulnerable groups. For more than a decade, national and European agendas, both under the EU and the Bologna Process, have also emphasised equity and inclusion. In 2007, the Council of Europe defined the different missions of higher education as preparation for sustainable employment, *preparation for life as active citizens in democratic societies* (author's italics), personal development, and the development and maintenance, through teaching, learning and research, of a broad, advanced knowledge base (Council of Europe 2007).

And yet higher education in Europe falls short of being truly inclusive and equitable. Students from disadvantaged, under-represented or at-risk groups still find it hard to participate in higher education, especially without targeted support (both academic and non-academic). More recently, financial support (for instance through scholarships, exemption from tuition fees, etc.) has been provided by national authorities and higher education institutions to those in need, but curriculum design, and more importantly the teaching practice, have not changed much. There seems to be a lack of understanding that the way academics teach is of critical importance for any reform intended to enhance inclusion in higher education.

The discourse around inclusion inevitably informs that around citizenship. How do societies, higher education institutions and teaching staff include students from disadvantaged or under-represented groups such as third country nationals, refugees, stateless people and so on within their systems, while empowering them to enact their own acts of citizenship? This was the overarching question that the pedagogical staff development workshops on inclusion and citizenship skills that formed part of the EFFECT project tried to address.

Another important question then arises, namely how well teachers are prepared to consider the societal mission of higher education in learning goals and teaching practice. Interestingly, while the majority of higher education institutions agree on the increasing importance of inclusion and citizenship, they seem not to be priorities for teaching enhancement (European University Association, Trends 2018).[2] Hence, the EFFECT consortium considered it valuable to work on the connection between teaching enhancement and the promotion of values-based higher education (inclusion and citizenship skills).

Reflecting on the Challenges

Even if teaching performance is part of academic staff evaluation, in most European Higher Education Area (EHEA) systems good teaching plays only a small role in teachers' career progression, while research performance remains the most important factor for promotion (Sursock 2015: 80; European Commission/EACEA/Eurydice 2018: 89). The disparity of esteem between research and teaching not only weakens the nexus between the two, but most importantly it drives academic staff to focus more on their research output, rather than paying equal and considerable attention to their teaching activities and pedagogical development. This finding is supported by recent research (Bunescu and Gaebel 2018: 19) confirming that only in a minority (32 per cent) of higher education systems in Europe is participation in teaching enhancement courses considered for career progression. Moreover, even in these systems, financial incentives or rewards for academic staff participating in teaching enhancement are very uncommon. Recognition for teaching enhancement would, therefore, be the first layer of the challenge at stake.

Secondly, even when promoted and implemented, teaching enhancement activities continue to be carried out against a background that lacks consensus on what makes quality teaching in education, how teacher training should be delivered and at what level (individual, departmental, within a specific discipline or interdisciplinary, at the level of the higher education institution or national, etc.). What is perhaps even more challenging is carrying out teaching enhancement activities based on a reflective approach, which has the potential to criticise the tacit understandings that practitioners have developed, and which, at times, prevents them from arriving at new understandings and practice.

Beyond anecdotal evidence, highlighting and measuring the impact of teacher training also remains challenging. This is, of course, not to say that teaching enhancement schemes are not impactful. Quite the contrary. A series of annual reports by Advance HE shows that the introduction of teaching enhancement schemes in UK universities has been having a significant impact on the higher education culture within these institutions, with teachers from the respective institutions stating that pedagogical staff development encouraged them to critically reflect on their practice and helped them to improve their teaching in the longer term (Advance HE 2018: 7).

Undervaluing teaching leaves one wondering about the capacity of our higher education systems to address student diversity and learners' success, which lies not only in funding or legal frameworks, but equally in the capacity of teachers to include all students, and enable, not despite but because of diversity, a richer learning experience.

Promoting inclusion in the classroom means encouraging and facilitating discussions, challenging stereotypes and working with unconscious biases within the learning and teaching process.³ This is particularly evident when working to address inclusion and citizenship in diverse classrooms, where some students tend to be subjected to forms of marginalisation.

Refugee students are a particularly vulnerable group, given their forced displacement and obstacles to accessing and graduating from higher education in the host countries. The needs of students with a refugee background go beyond pragmatic requirements of educational programmes, and involve complex social, cultural, psychological and economic needs. This is why, especially in such cases, pedagogical staff development with a focus on inclusion is of particular relevance.

Inclusion and Citizenship in Higher Education Teaching

The discourse around inclusion and citizenship skills can be framed within the capability approach pioneered by the economist-philosopher Amartya Sen and philosopher Martha Nussbaum, and which, in the past decades, has emerged as a new conceptual framework about development, justice and well-being.

The approach places at its forefront people's capabilities, meaning their genuine opportunities to achieve well-being: 'seeing opportunity in terms of capability allows us to distinguish appropriately between (i) whether a person is actually able to do things she would value *doing*, and (ii) whether she possesses the *means or instruments or permissions* to pursue what she would like to do (her actual ability to do that pursuing may depend on many contingent circumstances)' (Sen 2005: 153).

For Sen, capabilities are available options or alternatives that do not exist only on paper (formally, legally), but are also effectively available to a person. The opportunity to be educated, the ability to travel and study abroad, or to actively take part in the political and civic life of a community could be thought of as capabilities. Importantly, it should be acknowledged that not every person has the same real opportunities. For instance, citizenship rights and benefits are not accessible to all groups in our societies. The right to education and access to social benefits still depend, in many countries, on being a citizen. As Engin Isin puts it, 'in political life, when you are deprived of a nationality status, being just "human" doesn't help' (Pullano 2013).

If we are to transpose Sen's understanding of capabilities to people seeking asylum or to refugees, their capabilities are much more limited than those of country citizens. The United Nations High Commissioner for Refugees (UNHCR) estimates that globally only 1 per cent of refugees have been able to enrol in higher education, compared with a global average of 36 per cent of young people (UNHCR 2018), even though several international conventions (such as the Universal Declaration of Human Rights) stipulate that access to higher education is a human right. In most higher education systems, refugees and asylum seekers are considered as third country nationals (i.e. international students), which automatically qualifies them for much higher, often unaffordable, tuition fees. Thus, although higher education might very well be a formal, legal option for everyone, in reality higher education is not effectively available to specific groups, such as those with refugee status, due to additional and at times invisible obstacles and barriers that such specific groups face. Hence, discussions on access and real opportunities should be the starting point for meaningful conversations around both inclusion and citizenship. Who should be included in higher education, in addition to traditional learners? Who gets to benefit from citizenship rights and to what extent?

Citizenship, understood in its formal, legal sense (the state of being a member of a particular country and having rights because of it), is in fact restrictive, leaving certain groups out: citizens can have rights, but also duties that are denied or only partly extended to other noncitizens residing in a country or to those who are citizens but institutionally marginalised (e.g. Roma populations in certain European countries). Usually, citizenship is a prerequisite for full political rights, such as the right to vote or to hold public office. In its formal, legal interpretation, therefore, citizenship is exclusive, not necessarily being reserved for all residents of a country.

In the context of the EFFECT pedagogical staff development workshops on inclusion and citizenship skills, citizenship was not framed in its formal, legal meaning, but formulated in broader terms and understood as 'participation in civil society, community and/or political life, characterised by mutual respect and non-violence in accordance with human rights and democracy' (Hoskins 2006: 4). This approach to citizenship mirrors Engin Isin's argument that people who are not formal citizens can also 'act out' or enact citizenship: 'Acts of citizenship may be cultivated by or may transgress practices and formal entitlement, as they emerge from the paradox between universal inclusion in the language of rights and cosmopolitanism, on the one hand, and inevitable exclusion in the language of community and particularity on the other' (Isin and Nielsen 2008: 11).

Citizenship thus becomes a dynamic process, where the question 'Who is a citizen?' gets replaced by 'What makes citizens?'. Precisely in this last question lies the bridge between inclusion and citizenship, so that the two concepts have the potential to be brought together.

Inclusion and citizenship were addressed jointly as topics for pedagogical staff development also because neither is currently treated as a priority in terms of teaching enhancement, although several political systems in Europe have been marred by waves of populism and nationalism in the past years, and in particular since the beginning of what is usually labelled as the 'refugee crisis'.

This leaves the question of how well teachers in higher education institutions across Europe are equipped to address grand challenges such as inclusivity and citizenship. Did teachers have the opportunity to follow pedagogical staff development, particularly around such challenges? Did they have the occasion to engage in meaningful conversations on inclusion and citizenship within their institutions? This is vital for providing a learning experience that would enable the development of students as critical thinkers, responsible citizens in a changing world and adults who can address their own and the world's grand challenges.

The Methodology of the Inclusion and Citizenship Skills Workshops

If pedagogical staff development is to achieve psychosocial change among the academic teaching staff, then reflective learning needs to be considered. Reflection is not an end in itself, but rather an important tool which enables teachers to be more intentional and deliberate in their teaching.

However, conservative pedagogical training models, promoting a 'how to' and hands-on training approach, do not sufficiently exploit the potential that critical reflection and personal agency (i.e. the role of teachers as practitioners and individuals) have in the classroom, although both are central in conveying values-based education. This is why the EFFECT consortium undertook an extensive literature review in order to identify a methodology that would encourage critical reflection in pedagogical staff development. The Change Laboratory methodology[4] was chosen, as it offered an opportunity to reconcile formal teacher training and critical reflection, while emphasising personal agency in values-based teaching enhancement.

Change Laboratory intends to reconceptualise activity, by first provoking authentic reactions, responses and disagreements among the participants. Confrontation, authenticity and courage to utter what one really thinks are all elicited from the participants, as 'good teaching requires courage – the courage to expose one's ignorance as well as insight, to invite contradiction as well as consent' (Palmer 1990: 15).

In order to elicit authentic and powerful reactions within the workshops, stimulus material was developed, consisting of original student and teacher testimonials on concrete situations related to inclusion and citizenship in higher education.

> There is no diversity in my programme. I am a final-year PhD candidate and I have never felt culturally or ethnically included. The fact that I am one of two black persons in my programme and that I do not have friends is not my fault. Everything is white and Euro-centric.

Figure 11.1. Example of stimulus material. Image by the author.

A small library of all stimulus material used in the pedagogical staff development workshops on inclusion and citizenship skills was prepared by the project team and is available for public use.[5]

After the disagreement and confrontation surface based on the stimulus material proposed by the workshop facilitator, participants are encouraged to work together to reimagine their teaching activity and identify solutions that would address their practice. As applied in the workshops, the methodology stimulated meaningful conversations and reflection among the participants and brought together different perspectives to a shared challenge.

Implementation of the Workshops

Over 130 academic staff from ten European countries attended the pedagogical staff development workshops on inclusion and citizenship skills organised as part of the EFFECT project. Most of the participants were academic teaching staff, but students, institutional leadership and technical and administrative staff also attended.

Normally, the Change Laboratory methodology presupposes that the same group of participants meets several times over a 9–12-month period, with tasks in between the sessions. The EFFECT team, nevertheless, wanted to test the adaptability of this methodology in different higher education systems around Europe, as well as in a virtual learning environment, so the methodology itself had to be slightly adapted. For the four face-to-face workshops, the implementation team worked each time with a different group of participants, in different national and international contexts. For online workshops, the same pilot group of ten participants followed a series of three webinars following the model of the face-to-face workshops adapted to online delivery.

In the online meetings, the conversations were steered by an experienced facilitator with additional technical support. To make best use of their time online, participants were given home assignments based on issues arising in the sessions, for instance completing a self-assessment questionnaire on unconscious bias[6] or applying the Change Laboratory model to their own teaching practice.

In the face-to-face workshops, participants were split into smaller discussion groups, configured to reflect a diversity of stakeholders around the table: teachers, students, technical, library and support staff as well as institutional leadership. On average, there were about six participants per table. It was thought, and later confirmed, that smaller discussion tables would encourage participants to get more engaged in the conversations, whereas larger tables would lead to the disengagement of some attendees. The discussions, based on stimulus material, were facilitated by well-briefed table scribes, who not only gently steered the conversations, but also captured the main ideas in writing.

A set of open reflective questions built around stimulus material were advanced by the table scribes, to provoke conversations on what teachers face in their own learning and teaching contexts. The following reflective questions were suggested: What are the artefacts, rules and organisational structures at play in your institution and which directly affect your teaching practice? What is your motivation for seeking change? What could be different? What difference will it make? What can you personally do about it? How disruptive are you prepared to be? These questions were mainly designed to challenge the assumptions and status quo by asking participants to reflect both on their individual practice and institutional culture. They were also meant to trigger conversations on how pedagogical reflection can introduce different (refugee) narratives in the classroom and how such narratives can be reframed in all aspects of teaching (reading questions, the courses' thematic focus, lecture materials and class discussions), as Erin Goheen Glanville also describes in her chapter in this volume.

The institutional culture should not be forgotten in such conversations, given the impact that department, discipline colleagues and supervisors have on the outcomes of individual teacher training. In fact, although the role of champions in inclusion and citizenship education was widely acknowledged, it was believed that individual teacher training alone would not be sufficient to change powerful and well-established institutional cultures. Discussions with the teaching staff made it clear that senior encouragement made a difference, not only by creating a sense of obligation, but also by sending a signal that the institutional leadership is committed to the inclusivity agenda.

More detailed information on how the face-to-face and online workshops on inclusion and citizenship skills were implemented can be found in the Appendix to the feasibility study of the EFFECT project.[7]

Lessons Learnt from the Workshops on Inclusion and Citizenship Skills

Since only a few workshops with a relatively small number of participants have been organised, results from this work have to be taken with caution.

The implementation team conducted two rounds of follow-up surveys with the participants of these workshops, one immediately following the event, and the second four to seven months later, the latter mostly in order to inquire about any follow-up activities and impact on teaching practice. The participants credited the workshops for raising awareness and interest in cultural adaptation among the teaching staff, showing more care towards students from under-represented backgrounds, awareness in conveying inclusivity through the academic practice and development of methods and tools to better integrate migrants into local and higher education communities. One workshop table scribe noted: 'The participants appreciated the opportunity to be heard and valued reflection spaces like this one'. Interestingly, a majority of the respondents wrote that they had not attended similar teaching enhancement workshops or initiatives before.

The Change Laboratory methodology was perceived as innovative by the attendees and, in general, the experience of workshops showed that meaningful conversations but also disagreements enable reflections, which allow better understanding of the challenge, before advancing towards solutions. As Schön (1983: 61) wrote: 'Through reflection, he [i.e. the practitioner] can surface and criticize tacit understandings that have grown up around the repetitive experiences of a specialized practice, and can make new sense of the situations of uncertainty or uniqueness which he may allow himself to practice'.

After the pedagogical staff development workshops, some of the participants implemented follow-up initiatives, such as organising workshops for their own students using the Change Laboratory methodology to enhance the inclusion of learners with disabilities or working on developing a boardgame that would help students and teaching staff to improve their cultural understanding. A majority of the participants in the pedagogical staff development workshops said that the discussions raised during the workshops influenced their teaching practice afterwards. They mentioned being more aware of their own unconscious bias or developing more interactive and dynamic activities in the classroom to promote collaboration among students.

One of the lessons learnt is that stimulus material should be carefully prepared, as this is the main element that steers the conversations within the workshops. There should be no reluctance or fear in proposing provocative stimulus material, as the Change Laboratory methodology is intended to be contentious. Moreover, the workshops themselves should provide a safe space for saying what might otherwise remain unspoken. It is likewise important to contextualise the stimulus material, based on the cultural and social issues where the workshop is taking place, but also on the local higher education culture, so that the participants identify themselves with the challenges proposed.

The composition of the smaller breakout/discussion groups should also be carefully considered. There is the risk that a self-selecting group of inclusivity experts will move fast to find solutions to the challenges, rather than systematically unpacking them in order to find novel and sustainable approaches. The discussions were felt to be more meaningful and inclusive with a combination of teachers, students and support staff around the table. A homogenous group (e.g. only teachers) tended to identify solutions outside their scope of influence, rather than recognising their own agency and responsibility in addressing inclusivity and citizenship in the classroom. The implementation team also felt that discussion groups that included attendees from different cultural and disciplinary backgrounds worked better, as peer learning took place in an intercultural and interdisciplinary setting. Participation of institutional leadership did not appear to inhibit the discussions; on the contrary, it enhanced the credibility and importance of the initiative.

The power of these pedagogical staff development workshops rested also on acknowledging that not all students in higher education have the same capabilities (i.e. genuine opportunities), and that, especially in the case of students from under-represented backgrounds, contingent circumstances matter a lot. For higher education institutions and for teachers alike, addressing larger and more diverse student bodies would mean acknowledging that in order to succeed, students have different needs, based on their real and not formal opportunities.

Although access to higher education is a human right, the workshops enabled the participants to reflect critically on what this really presupposes. Invisible barriers, sometimes in the form of unconscious bias from teachers and colleagues, emotional trauma, but also more visible obstacles (e.g. language, financial capacity) were discussed. This transposed into practice Sen's understanding of capabilities which are 'characteristics of individual advantages, [which] fall short of telling us enough about the fairness or equity of the process involved, or about the freedom of citizens to invoke and utilise procedures that are equitable' (Sen 2005: 156).

The initiative to have such pedagogical staff development workshops can also be an impetus for teachers to think more closely about how students can enact citizenship, irrespective of their formal citizenship status. This approach to citizenship leads to an argument in favour of diversity and inclusion, and in broader terms to a humanising agenda that transcends higher education.

Recommendations and Concluding Remarks

Behavioural change requires time and presupposes a reassessment of one's conceptions and attitude. For this to happen, teaching enhancement should have a certain duration and its impact might not become visible immediately. Due to time constraints under the EFFECT project, the Change Laboratory methodology was not implemented in a typical way, in the sense that the implementation team did not work with the same group of participants over a period of nine to twelve months. However, there were early indications of changing attitudes, especially in the online version of the workshops where the same group engaged several times. It is therefore recommended to have a systematic approach to teaching enhancement, rather than one-time and disconnected interventions.

Given their complexity and importance, conveying inclusion and citizenship skills in an academic and pedagogic context should also become a systematic effort at the level of higher education institutions. In this respect, the institutional culture, which is 'not something an organization has, but rather what it is' (Mats Alvesson, cited in Roxa and Martensson 2012: 4), plays a central role. For the institutional culture to change, the effects of pedagogical staff development need to go beyond the individual level, and resonate with departments, disciplines and institutional leadership. All major stakeholders should contribute towards such a shift in the institutional culture.

As mentioned at the beginning of this chapter, teaching as a professional activity, compared to research, is poorly recognised and rewarded in most European higher education systems. This becomes a disincentive for teachers to engage in pedagogical staff development opportunities, and more importantly gives the wrong signal that the personal agency of the teachers is of little importance for student success. Recognition for such teaching enhancement workshops (for example through open badges, career progression) could play an important role in raising the profile of teaching and encouraging more academic staff to enrol for initial and continuous teacher training. Finally, the model of these workshops asks that reflection is harnessed, biases called into question and real commitments to action made.

◆

Luisa Bunescu is a Policy Analyst at the European University Association (EUA) in Brussels (Belgium). Prior to joining EUA, Luisa worked as a Research Assistant in Macroeconomics at the Berlin School of Economics and Law and as Assistant to the Director at the Centre International de Formation Européenne (CIFE) in Nice, France. Her research interests are in the macroeconomics of higher education, as well as in learning and teaching practices to address equity and inclusion in the academic world.

Notes

1. See https://www.eua.eu/101-projects/560-effect.html.
2. In the context of this chapter, I refer to 'teaching enhancement' for any type of formal pedagogical development or training provided to teachers, in various ways and formats, such as initial teacher training and continuous professional development (CPD).
3. This is in line with the tenets of critical pedagogy, as theorised, for instance, by Henry Giroux. According to the latter, critical pedagogy is a moral and political practice that helps to unsettle recurrent assumptions, involving, among other things, a struggle for a more socially just world, and which enables students to focus on the suffering of others (Giroux 2011).
4. The EFFECT project team drew heavily on Bligh and Flood (2015).
5. See Appendix 2, 'The EFFECT Pedagogical Staff Development Workshops: A Repository of Stimulus Material', https://www.eua.eu/downloads/publications/eua%20brochure%202_appendix%202_fin_single%20page.pdf (accessed 9 October 2019).
6. See https://implicit.harvard.edu/implicit/ and https://secure.understandingprejudice.org/iat/.
7. See Appendix 1, 'The EFFECT Pedagogical Staff Development Workshops: Methodology, Assessment, and Lessons Learnt', https://www.eua.eu/down

loads/publications/eua%20brochure%202_appendix%201_fin_single%20page.pdf (accessed 9 October 2019).

References

Advance HE. 2018. *Annual Review of HEA Accredited CPD Schemes 2016–2017.* https://www.heacademy.ac.uk/system/files/downloads/Annual%20Review%20of%20HEA%20accredited%20CPD%20schemes%202016-17.pdf.

Beatty, B.R. 2000. 'The Emotions of Educational Leadership: Breaking the Silence', *International Journal in Education* 3(4): 331–57.

Bligh, B., and M. Flood. 2015. 'The Change Laboratory in Higher Education: Research-Intervention Using Activity Theory', in J. Huisman and M. Tight (eds), *Theory and Method in Higher Education Research*, Vol. 1. http://eprints.lancs.ac.uk/74672/1/Volume_3_Bligh_Flood.pdf.

Bunescu, L., and M. Gaebel. 2018. *National Initiatives in Learning and Teaching in Europe: A Report from the European Forum for Enhanced Collaboration in Teaching (EFFECT) Project.* https://www.eua.eu/resources/publications/799:national-initiatives-in-learning-and-teaching-in-europe.html.

Council of Europe. 2007. *Recommendation CM/Rec(2007)6 of the Committee of Ministers to Member States on the Public Responsibility for Higher Education and Research.* Council of Europe. https://search.coe.int/cm/Pages/result_details.aspx?ObjectId=09000016805d5dae.

European Commission/EACEA/Eurydice. 2018. *The European Higher Education Area in 2018: Bologna Process Implementation Report.* Luxembourg: Publications Office of the European Union.

European University Association, Trends. 2018. *Learning and Teaching in the European Higher Education Area.* Brussels. https://eua.eu/downloads/publications/trends-2018-learning-and-teaching-in-the-european-higher-education-area.pdf.

Giroux, A.H. 2011. *On Critical Pedagogy.* New York: Bloomsbury.

Hoskins, B. 2006. *Draft Framework on Indicators for Active Citizenship.* Ispra: CRELL. http://citeseerx.ist.psu.edu/viewdoc/download?doi=10.1.1.132.1723&rep=rep1&type=pdf.

Isin, E.F., and G.M. Nielsen. 2008. *Acts of Citizenship.* New York: Palgrave Macmillan.

Palmer, P.J. 1990. 'Good Teaching', *Change* 22(1): 10–16.

Pullano, T. 2013. 'Rethinking Citizenship beyond the Nation State. Interview to Engin Isin'. *European Alternatives*, 26 February. https://euroalter.com/2013/rethinking-citizenship-beyond-the-nation-state-interview-to-engin-isin.

Roxa, T., and K. Mårtensson. 2012. 'How Effects from Teacher-Training of Academic Teachers Propagate into the Meso Level and Beyond', in E. Simon and G. Pleschova (eds), *Teacher Development in Higher Education: Existing Programs, Program Impact and Future Trends.* London: Routledge.

Schön, D.A. 1983. *The Reflective Practitioner: How Professionals Think in Action.* New York: Basic Books.

Sen, A. 2005. 'Human Rights and Capabilities', *Journal of Human Development* 6(2): 151–66.
Sursock, A. 2015. *Trends 2015: Learning and Teaching in European Universities*. Brussels. https://eua.eu/downloads/publications/trends%202015%20learning%20and%20teaching%20in%20european%20universities.pdf.
UNHCR. 2018. *The Other One Per Cent – Refugee Students in Higher Education*. DAFI Annual Report 2017.
Wright, C. 2013. 'Authenticity in Teaching and Leadership', *Journal of Accounting and Finance* 13(2). http://www.na-businesspress.com/JAF/WrightC_Web13_2_.pdf.

CHAPTER 12
Focus Pulled to Hungary
Case Study of the OLIve Participatory Video Workshop

KLÁRA TRENCSÉNYI AND JEREMY BRAVERMAN

◆◆◆

This chapter explores the curriculum, methodology and learning outcomes of the OLIve participatory video course to serve as a case study for other educators working with refugees and asylum seekers, and to encourage the use of participatory video tools. It describes the development of participants' visual and creative skills, with the goal of giving authorship to displaced persons over their own visual representations.[1]

In May 2016, during the opening session of the first participatory video course offered within the framework of Central European University (CEU)'s OLIve Weekend Program for students who have experienced displacement, participants were given their first assignment right away: record three shots of something you like, something you hate or something that makes you curious, in the university buildings or outside in the immediate vicinity.

By joining OLIve, its students became part of CEU's highly diverse community from all over the world and were able to escape the intrusive attention of the media and judgemental gaze of passers-by that refugees and asylum seekers often faced in Hungary. During the first day of the participatory video course, when refugees took cameras and tripods to the street in front of St. Stephen's Cathedral, one of the city's most touristic squares, tourists and locals became the focus of the cameras – the subjects of scrutiny – as the refugees viewed them through their lenses. This was precisely one of the main goals of the course tutors: to empower and create space for refugees' own narratives amidst the biased, authorial European media discourse.

When students returned from their first shoot an hour later, full of excitement, they brought back some stunning footage which represented both a symbolic and intimate snapshot of their stay in Hungary. The first crew went to the banks of the Danube and, going beyond the typical touristic images of the bridges and the Buda castle, shot close-up images of the muddy water. As they narrated the images while their film was played to the class, they talked about the river – a different river for the Iranian, Egyptian and Nigerian participants – which nevertheless turned out to be the same river of remembrance, taking them back to their homes through a flood of memories.

Another mixed crew of Ethiopian and Afghan participants shot in reverential silence in the multi-storey library of the university, an ultramodern building with thousands of volumes. The third group of students had a Somali 'news anchor', stopping by the neo-classicist statue of Pallas Athene at the main entrance of CEU, explaining what the university and OLIve meant for him.

Watching the footage of their first shoot – some of them with engaging visuals, others that came to life as students added compelling stories while showing them – reinforced our hypothesis that they had a very strong vision about their host society and the desire to communicate their insights through images. We concluded that our students were ready to turn their cameras from the simple selfies they had been taking during their journeys to Hungary towards observing the world around them. In this way, the reversed gaze of the much discussed 'refugee selfie' (Zimányi 2017; Literat 2017), which had previously been for them a 'mirror with memory' (Frosh 2015), became a mirror of the society in which they live.

The Pilot Project

CEU's OLIve Program – Open Learning Initiative for Refugees and Asylum Seekers – was designed in autumn 2015 and established in 2016 to offer, initially, a Weekend Program and later full-time preparatory courses in various disciplines. The Weekend Program had been running for a semester when the participatory video course was first introduced, adding to OLIve's range of courses in the social sciences, advocacy strategies and English language. The founding tutors of OLIve were Babak Arzani, Iranian editor and activist, Vlad Naumescu, a CEU professor, and documentary filmmaker Klára Trencsényi. The starting point for the workshop was to launch a pilot project to introduce students to the art of filmmaking and empower them to be authors of their own stories, thus offering an alternative to the biased Hungarian media reporting 'about them' through stereotypes and misrepresentation.

According to a range of sources, asylum claims registered in Hungary in 2014 saw a twentyfold increase from previous years, and in the years leading up to that, the Hungarian government had already started to shape the 'migrant image'. In the summer of 2015, they had put up billboards throughout the country to invite Hungarians for a 'national consultation on Immigration and Terrorism'. By September 2015, when thousands of refugees were cordoned off by the Hungarian police in front of Keleti Railway Station for days, not allowed to leave the area or to continue their journeys, most Hungarian media covered the 'migrant spectacle' in a xenophobic way, showing people eating, sleeping and washing in front of the station.

Since the founding of OLIve, Hungarian and Budapest-based foreign media had been intrigued to cover its activities, but after experiencing the media coverage of refugees during the crisis of 2015, OLIve founders and tutors had turned down journalists' requests. As tutors of the participatory video course, we offered refugees the possibility to experience how moving images are designed, captured and put into context through editing, hoping to equip them with the necessary tools to shape their own representation.

Course tutor Arzani had experienced displacement himself, being an Iranian refugee in Hungary, and had already led an art project which took place in 2014 in a refugee camp in Debrecen, Hungary. Naumescu and Trencsényi had been course directors in several documentary development workshops, working with both university students and researchers. As course tutors we all agreed that it was important to offer a rather informal class where students could talk about issues that matter to them using audio-visual tools and create space to bring in their personal experiences as well. When preparing the syllabus for the course, we also agreed that no formal training in film aesthetics and technology would be offered, so as not to impose the conventions of European and American filmmaking on participants. Instead, we gave the participants cameras from the first moment and encouraged them to experiment and try out unconventional ways of 'talking' about themselves and the world around them. The availability of simplified camera functions made this possible even for those participants who had no previous experience operating a camera.

Starting off by taking still photos, then shooting static, tripod-mounted video images, we guided our students slowly towards creating moving images and sequences edited in camera – which meant that students had to shoot all the images one after the other, in the order they wanted them to appear in the final film. After the second session, Arash from Afghanistan expressed his concern that the footage he shot 'did not compare to the visuals seen in Hollywood films'. This opened up a vivid discussion about filmmakers' point of view and the significance of editing in film projects. Course participants realised that despite the original intention of the filmmaker, the edited footage can have multiple meanings, even harshly contrasting the original idea of the cameraperson or going against the nature of the footage itself. This is a great example of how course participants opened up a discussion about filmmaking issues after, and in direct relation to their own experience with the medium.

During every session we sent participants out to complete exercises in small groups. Assignment topics included 'Film a process within the university building' and 'Make a portrayal of a person or an object', among others. They had to prepare in advance for these assignments in the classroom, by planning what they would film and preparing a short storyboard sketch. We also asked them to take turns fulfilling the roles of director, cinematographer and sound engineer, to encourage those who had never tried filming to do the camera work, and to allow the less assertive students to also take on the role of director. In order to involve everyone in the activity, we screened each project and asked other students to comment on the footage. This also helped demonstrate that the same image can have different connotations for people with different backgrounds and perspectives. The tutors' feedback – including explanations of camera angles, framing, camera movement and so on – was offered as part of the discussion, kept on a very practical level, respecting the insight and intentions of the maker of the image.

The active involvement of Babak Arzani also helped the group dynamics. In a lengthy post-course reflection, he said laconically in reference to their shared 'migrant experience': 'I didn't need to explain it to them and they did not need to explain it to me'. It was Arzani's suggestion also to follow OLIve's ethical and psychological guidelines and refrain from asking participants about their journey, their former home or the hardships of leaving it behind. Based on participants' accounts of their daily routines and the difficulties they faced, the workshop seemed to be a place where they could escape for a little while, and genuinely enjoy themselves. And as they felt more and more at ease with the presence of cameras, they also allowed us a glimpse into 'the topics and subjects that culturally and politically interested them', as Arzani put it (for description of the OLIve experience, see Al Hussein and Mangeni, this volume).

'I recall our students proposed to make their final film at the end of the pilot project about homelessness in Hungary', said Arzani when reflecting on his experience during the course in the same conversation. 'I remember vividly how we tried to explain to them that it is the same intrusive gaze if they film the vulnerable homeless people in Budapest, that they normally receive as refugees and asylum seekers from the journalists and videographers that come to film them.' Despite the limited amount of time, we considered it important to discuss ethical issues apart from the technical and visual aspects of filmmaking. In this case, after lengthy discussions, we allowed the students to film and engage with homeless people living on the streets and in the metro stations of Budapest. By shooting sequences of homelessness, intolerance and the growing gap between rich and poor, privileged and underprivileged groups within Hungarian society, they began to use the camera to explore the world around them in new ways and find ways for potential solidarities to emerge.

As the last step in the filmmaking process, we gave students an introduction to the editing process through a general presentation and hands-on training, and after a full day shooting at a place of their choice in Budapest, we encouraged participants to edit their own footage. The level of sensitivity and keen sense of observation enabled them to record some arresting and compelling footage. Some experimented with editing techniques, such as breaking the chronological order of shots, and separating video and audio tracks, and managed to turn the footage into short films reflecting their own narrative. The group that shot about homelessness used one of the filmmakers as a sort of 'news anchor' who appeared in the shots, and made a statement about the way the Hungarian state treats marginalised groups of people (homelessness, like 'illegal migration', is criminalised in Hungary). However, when analysing the shots in the timeline of the editing program, they concluded that the news anchor could be removed as the images spoke for themselves. When another crew had seemingly finished their film, one member suddenly spoke up and asserted that he did not think it was finished. He asked for permission to spend extra hours in the editing room to produce 'his montage' of the rushes. He added his favourite music to the footage (which made the film look like a music video, a common choice of first-time filmmakers, regardless of background), and concluded the film with his own narration, letting his voice and story come through the footage of Budapest.

Through the practice of editing, our students found an answer to one of the key questions explored by the course: how, through montage, can raw footage become an interpretation of reality? Arzani summed up: 'By the end of the course we felt that all of the students would find

Figure 12.1. Stills from participants' films, Budapest, 2016. Open Learning Initiative. Photos by the authors.

future benefits from the experience: few would become filmmakers, but more could use visual tools for their future employment, like one of the Afghan participants, who used to work as a journalist in print media. Moreover, all of our students could get a glimpse into how visual storytelling works, how news coverage works, and get an understanding of how video can choose a point of view'.

The Second Workshop

Building on the experiences of the pilot project, in February 2017 we launched the second edition of the participatory video workshop, making a couple of key changes. First, we brought on board theatre-in-education expert Ádám Bethlenfalvy to include methods of applied drama pedagogy during the sessions. Bethlenfalvy had previously run a theatre course within the framework of OLIve, in which he used various drama pedagogical tools to work with the students' experiences. By doing so, we aimed to offer participants a wide range of methods and creative tools through which they could tell their personal stories. Many participants in the first workshop had expressed an interest in doing this, but mostly due to time limitations were unable to. To facilitate collaboration between all the participants and encourage a deeper personal engagement, Bethlenfalvy conducted icebreakers, warm-up exercises and drama games.

For the second course we received more than thirty applications, including some from participants in the pilot project. Among the students were several female participants, who were taking part in such an activity for the first time. To get a sense of new students' visual imagination and to gather material for the warm-up exercises later on, we asked applicants to submit a photograph taken by them, about them – with the condition that they themselves should not appear in it. We received many interesting pictures, and used these as a criterion for selecting the final twelve participants for the course. It was not the technical level of the pictures but the creative idea behind the task that we took into consideration when making these decisions. This 'homework' was meant to create a distance from the usual selfies and to explore the innovative visual tools that participants might bring along from their own background.

With the help of Bethlenfalvy, we aimed to introduce a new element into our class activities: role play, and playfulness in general. Bethlenfalvy based his approach on the basic principle of drama pedagogy that never asks participants directly 'What happened to you?', but rather 'creates a fictional character, on whom we can project our feelings' – as he explained for the course tutors before the first session.

Another key change we made for the second workshop, based on our previous experience and at the request of students joining the course for the second time, was to offer participants more formalised training in filmmaking techniques. In this respect, we changed our approach, recognising the students' desire to gain a basis for developing filmmaking skills they may use later in their professional lives, and incorporated instruction on such subjects as composition, lighting, basic camera movement and editing. To this end, we involved CEU media education specialist and film instructor Jeremy Braverman, who offered presentations on these subjects, as well as hands-on instruction throughout the process as a full-time participant in the course. Nevertheless, we kept the same structure as during the pilot project: we first encouraged participants to experiment with the cameras prior to receiving formal training, and answered the questions they raised afterwards in the form of analysis of their own footage. In this way, we offered a limited amount of instruction, which we did not frontload but distributed further along the process. For class activities we applied a wide range of participatory video exercises inspired by earlier participatory projects and adapted them to the needs of our course.

For this iteration of the workshop, we encouraged participants to shoot footage at home as well as giving them homework. First, we asked them to bring in five pictures about their current home, and later used these in a photovoice exercise. Seventeen-year-old Shafi from Balochistan made a highly evocative photo essay about the Fót Childcare Centre, where he was hosted along with other under-aged refugee children who arrived in Hungary unaccompanied. Arash from Afghanistan made pictures from the window of his rented room, reflecting an amazing contrast between his balanced inner self and the chaotic world surrounding him. David from Nigeria, who was still staying in a refugee reception camp, took pictures of his life spent in a metal shipping container, which he called home for months.

As a next step, we printed out the images and handed out to each participant the photos of another, without revealing who they belonged to, and asked them to invent the backstory of each picture. By doing so, the storytelling exercise not only triggered participants' imagination and let them travel through various genres – fairy tales, crime stories and docudrama – but it also created an emotional distance from their actual situation. In addition, participants learned through this exercise how objects, people and feelings represented in the picture can be decoded in different ways or recontextualised by outsiders.

As part of the expanded training in cinematic techniques, we introduced a basic editing exercise that we have found extremely effective in demonstrating the potential of film editing to beginning filmmaking students. The exercise was based on the original Kuleshov experiment from the 1920s, in which a shot of a man's face with a neutral expression is intercut with three different images of what he may potentially be considering, allowing the audience to imbue his image with various moods and emotions. After watching it, participants had to shoot three

Figure 12.2. Participants' homework, Budapest, 2017. Open Learning Initiative. Photos by the authors.

images and a close-up of a face, edited by them in the camera – in proper length and order so that we could watch it as a finished work right after shooting. Even though the task was simple – to shoot something that each participant was longing for, fearing or sad about – it was an efficient tool to develop students' visual skills, and reveal their subtle and sensible insights.

Next, we asked participants to prepare short interviews with each other in groups of three. This was a logical next step in fulfilling the main goals of the course: furthering the students' technical skills, while also providing them with a forum to express themselves. Students were required to switch roles to allow all of them to fill the role of the cameraperson, interviewer and subject. Based on our assessment, they seemed to find value in each role – of the interviewee because they felt honoured to be given space and time to talk; of the interviewer because they enjoyed being on the other side of the camera, asking instead of being asked; and of the cameraperson because they were eager to experiment with the technology. Because we did this exercise relatively early on in the course, only a few groups moved beyond the superficial interview format and made a more in-depth piece. In some cases, the interview questions (and answers) remained rather simple, which could also be interpreted as tactfulness towards each other's experiences. In a course extending over several months, we recommend repeating this exercise to illustrate how a longer interview could create mutual confidence, allowing the participants to reveal more of their personal feelings and thoughts, as opposed to the hurried, conventional news reports of the media. But the interviews that 'worked' taught the participants that simple, non-stereotypical questions could launch an intimate, even compelling interview. In one example of this, Majida, a Yemeni woman, was asked about her daily routes in Budapest. She opened up and explained how she was raising her three children mostly alone while her husband was working, and talked about the institutions – nursery, hospital – she encounters in her daily life in Hungary, and the attitudes of those with whom she interacts. When Didar from Afghanistan was asked about his favourite food, we were offered an insight into the life and traditions of Afghans living in Iran and the measures of nostalgia lived through food sharing. While making the interviews and by switching the roles, participants managed to offer reciprocity and handle each other's stories with respect and responsibility, as suggested by Glanville in this volume.

Moving forward from the conventional interview situations, we asked participants to stage a short scene based on a memory of their

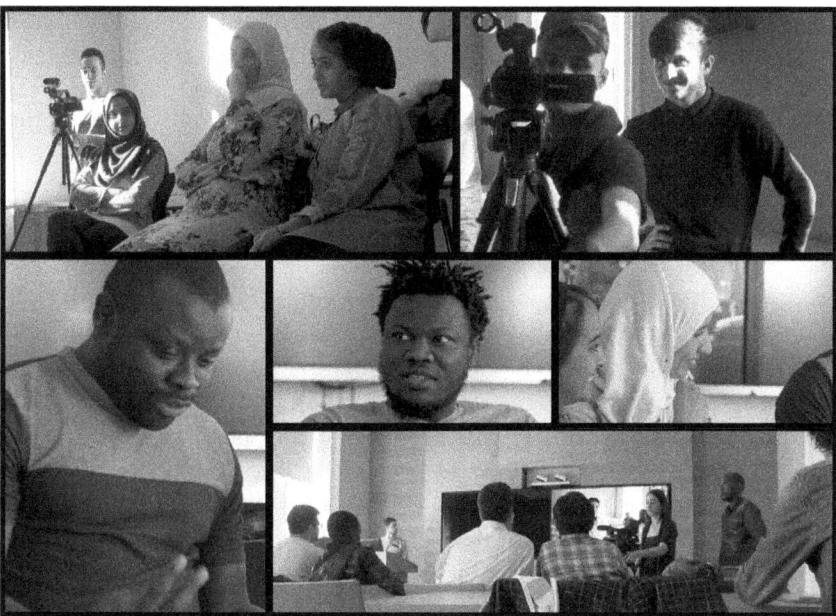

Figure 12.3. Role play and shooting exercise, Budapest, 2017. Open Learning Initiative. Photos by the authors.

original home. We divided the group into two, so one of the students could act out their memories, with others playing roles in their story, while another three students filmed these scenes using one camera each. During this exercise, participants learned to ask questions about small details that developed each story further and to cover these often emotional stories with their cameras in a tactful way.

The drama pedagogical methods and the participatory video exercises had a common denominator in suggesting that we start our classes by 'ventilation', discussing the emotional, social and political issues at the beginning of each session. Towards the end of the workshop, the engaging and often tense exchange of ideas had become even more intense, reflecting the worsening political climate. A few days before our third session, the Hungarian government passed new legislation demanding that asylum seekers be kept in detention during the entire length of their asylum procedure, thus restricting participants' free movement, taking away their financial allowance and food provision. At this point class sessions were completely overtaken by discussions of the situation, with participants sharing plans among themselves for the deepening crisis. This essentially derailed the planned curriculum, yet also created an important safe place for the participants to discuss personal and political issues and find mutual support. However, as a result of this new legislation and numerous prior punitive measures against asylum seekers, OLIve participants started to flee the country.

As we accumulated more and more footage, we quickly realised we had far more than the students could ever fit into the short films we had planned for them to complete. We started considering the possibility of using this in a longer work that would extend beyond the framework of the course, developing a participatory documentary with our students in the roles of co-directors, cinematographers and editors. During the last class, participants discussed the workshop and the film project they had been a part of. Some participants had just been granted refugee status, while others were about to be sent back to closed camps until a court decision was made about their fate. When the session turned to a discussion about what our common film should look like, David from Nigeria presented the idea that 'the true story should be told', and that it 'should be a film about how racism feels'. But Justin from Cameroon reminded him that 'such a film could be dangerous, since the (Hungarian) government is against even the head of the Central European University' (a reference to the university's founder George Soros). So half-jokingly they agreed that our final film should be a comedy or a love story instead.

A week later, the government set the deadline to implement the new legislation regarding closed camps. As a result, within a few days the number of participants in the workshop decreased dramatically. Some had to remain in the refugee camps and could no longer come to filmmaking classes, while others tried to continue their journey towards the West, hoping for more welcoming societies. Soon after, in autumn 2018, further legislation was passed criminalising and penalising all entities 'supporting migrants'. This was interpreted at CEU as a risk for university structures, and led to the suspension of the OLIve programme by the university's administration. OLIve members and students stood in solidarity, remaining committed to the programme and the projects already started: those who left started to send video letters to those who remained in Hungary, and continued filming even after having left Hungary. This showed the cohesion within the group and the impact of the whole programme on some of the refugees' lives, extending far beyond the frames of the course or their presence in Hungary.

Conclusions

Due to the abrupt end of the course, we unfortunately did not have the time or space to get to the final step in our last workshop: the editing session, where participants could have handled their own footage and organised it in a creative, personal way. Another final phase of the participatory action, organising public screenings in the presence of course participants and filmmakers, could not happen since only a few participants remained in Budapest by the time we held our first screening (within the framework of a conference in March 2019).

Some of the participants, when asked to evaluate the course, noted that they expected to 'learn an entire profession' and 'become trained cameramen or directors'. We think that the scope and the possibilities of such a workshop should have been communicated more clearly at the start of the course so as to not create false expectations among the participants. Francis from Cameroon noted, however, that the course 'taught us to work in teams, like in real filmmaking and take account of each other's opinions and input'. Mahak from Afghanistan recalled that there was a 'nice atmosphere' which helped participants 'share many different topics each student had', like 'home' or how students were thinking about their 'new life, about Hungary and the European peoples'. He also underlined that he learned 'how the movies are powerful and depend on the topic, and how we can send messages nicely to people'. Most participants underlined that during the filmmaking activities they felt comfortable talking about their past and present, their home left behind – which was also a crucial issue for the course organisers. Our approach, however, remained very much rooted in that of the ethical starting point of drama pedagogical methodology. As Bethlenfalvy summed up after the course: 'We offered them an opportunity to talk about their hardships, and all the participants treated this chance in a different way. Some opened up, some gave us hints about their experiences'. He added: 'In any case, for us it was important to create this safe space where it is legitimate to talk sincerely about the issues of migration'. He concluded: 'My colleagues and I have been fighting against the old dogma that if somebody brings up a trauma in a drama workshop, it is only a psychologist who can handle it. Traumas are more frequent than ever, so our challenge is to find up-to-date forms to deal with it'.

Another key issue was the participation of women. Bethlenfalvy said: 'During my first OLIve course there were no women participants in the group, and I was really concerned at the beginning when I was planning the exercises for the second one. How close can we go to each other? Can we play the games we usually play in workshops in Hungary – where physical touch is not a taboo?' But during the first sessions we quickly realised that, after getting past their initial timidity, the female participants got really involved during the course and made a more balanced, exciting workshop possible. Their presence, their focus and sometimes their intuition helped the course organisers to handle more delicate situations. At one point, Majida from Yemen, who was among the shyest students at the beginning, decided to share all the footage she had been shooting at home with her children, letting us into her family life and daily struggles. This inspired other participants to open up too.

The tutors set out to offer an emotionally building experience as well as a form of empowerment for all the students. As an active documentary filmmaker familiar with the current trends at documentary film festivals, and the representation of refugees and 'migrants' in major festival hits, Trencsényi also thought that it was high time that refugees' own footage was included in the discourse about the European 'migrant crisis' (Trencsényi and Naumescu 2021). The goal of the course was therefore twofold: to offer a creative skill and activity to the refugees interested in learning the visual language; and secondly, to lay the foundation for a documentary film that would challenge the majority of Hungarian (and European) society's view on refugees. However, tutors and participants all agreed that the course was too short to take any kind of artistic process to its completion. So, just like the short trailer we edited to find further support for the film, the course remained a teaser for the participants as well. Unfortunately, neither the 'love story' that participants proposed making in their last session, nor the in-depth creative documentary that course tutors had in mind were made. The sudden closure of the OLIve programme and funders' fear of supporting the project, despite their belief that it could have a significant impact on European and Hungarian audiences, interrupted our project.

Nevertheless, we believe that the participatory video exercises, short film studies and drama games completed their initial task: empowering the participants to express their thoughts through visuals, and at the same time to be more conscious producers of their own image in the mainstream media. As opposed to the much discussed 'refugee selfie', the participants learned to hold a 'mirror with a memory' to a specific time and space: a print of their experiences while being in Budapest.

Klára Trencsényi is a freelance director and cinematographer committed to creative and social documentaries. Prior to her first feature-length, award-winning documentary, *Train to Adulthood*, she directed two mid-length documentaries (*Corvin Variations*, 2011; *Birds Way*, 2009), and a short documentary (*3Weddings–Elena&Leo*, 2009). Klara has worked in many international productions as director of photography with Dutch, American and Hungarian directors, and won several awards. Since 2020 she is Visiting Professor of Practice at CEU, and she has been a lecturer at the Budapest-based Metropolitan University for four years. Between 2016 and 2018, she acted as tutor on the participatory video course for CEU OLIve. She is a co-founder of DunaDock Creative Documentary Development Forum.

Jeremy Braverman has spent most of his life working in film, both as a filmmaker and educator. He has been teaching filmmaking at university level for the past twenty years, currently as Media & Visual Education Specialist at CEU Vienna, Austria, and prior to that as an Associate Professor and Department Chair in the Department of Cinema Arts at Point Park University in Pittsburgh, USA. As a filmmaker he has directed short films including *Take Care*, *Squared*, and *The Dirt on You*. Recent works include collaborations with faculty on projects that incorporate documentary films.

Note

1. Despite the fact that our course participants have given their consent to include their stories and the visuals they have produced during the sessions, we prefer to use pseudonyms in our chapter to protect their identities.

References

Asadullah, S., and S. Muniz. 2015. *Participatory Video and the Most Significant Change*. Oxford: InsightShare.
Barone, T., and E.W. Eisner. 2012. *Arts Based Research*. London: SAGE Publications.
Frosh, P. 2015. 'The Gestural Image: The Selfie, Photography Theory and Kinesthetic Sociability', *International Journal of Communication* 9.
Kallius, A., D. Monterescu and P.K. Rajaram. 2016. 'Immobilizing Mobility: Border Ethnography, Illiberal Democracy, and the Politics of the "Refugee Crisis" in Hungary', *American Ethnologist* 43(1): 25–37.
Literat, I. 2017. 'Refugee Selfies and the (Self-)Representation of Disenfranchised Social Groups', *Media Fields* 12 (Media and Migration).
Lunch, N., and C. Lunch. 2006. *Insights into Participatory Video: A Handbook for the Field*. Oxford: InsightShare.

Nagy, Z. 2016. 'Repertoires of Contention and New Media: The Case of a Hungarian Anti-Billboard Campaign', *Intersections* 2(4) (Global Migration Crisis and Europe: Whose Crisis Is It?).

Trencsényi, K., and V. Naumescu. 2021. 'Migrant Cine-Eye: Storytelling in Documentary and Particpatory Filmmaking', in K. Nikielska-Sekula and A. Desille (eds), *Visual Methodology in Migration Studies*. Cham: Springer.

Zimányi, E. 2017. 'Digital Transience: Emplacement and Authorship in Refugee Selfies', *Media Fields Journal* 12 (Media and Migration).

PART III
DEBORDERING THE UNIVERSITY

CHAPTER 13
Fuck Prestige

IAN M. COOK

Fuck prestige. Seriously, fuck it. Prestige is the insidious cultural value that has come to define the university. I hate prestige, I hate how academics are so beholden to it, and I especially hate it when displayed by those who profess to be 'critical thinkers'.

Prestige is the great limiter in academia, suffocating free thinking, experimentation and joy like a heavy fog of stupidity. Moreover, as I'll argue in this short angry chapter, programmes and initiatives for learners who have experienced displacement will struggle to become truly transformative within an academe lost within the murky structures of prestige.

This chapter is based on my experiences as a volunteer, teacher, academic coordinator and director within programmes for students who have experienced displacement. This work took place at a locally prestigious international university in Hungary, a country in which the national government has hyperactively worked to create a hostile environment for those termed refugees or asylum seekers, as well as migrants in general (and those groups and individuals they perceive to be helping them).

The argument, which I will elaborate below, goes as follows: academics are needed to run access university education programmes and initiatives, but if they follow the prescriptions within the dominant paradigm of prestige, then they should not work in such initiatives. Or at least they should not if they want or need permanent contracts, promotions or peer recognition for their work. This feeds into and from a demented ranking culture, which has become the almost unquestioned measure of a university or department's worth for certain institutions (especially those who operate within more neoliberal contexts, either nationally or globally). While manifesting itself differently for academics, administrators or students, such quantifiable prestige has universities lost in a haze. Of course, it's possible to carve out small temporary clearings even in the densest of fogs. Using prestige strategically, displaced students can accumulate cultural capital, feel pride in the place they study and expand their horizons of possibility. Furthermore, those who run programmes can also utilise their institution's prestige (or the prestige of universities in general) to create the space needed for such initiatives to exist. However, these openings will remain fundamentally non-transformative as long as they rely on prestige for their continuation.

This argument speaks to this edited volume's interest in whether and how opening up the university for learners who have experienced displacement can be transformative by delineating the prestige structure within which higher education institutions operate. Working within access programmes can be transformative for teachers (Blell et al., this volume), for instance by developing collaborative methods that recognise different forms of expertise (Jasani et al., this volume), but teaching in general remains poorly recognised and rewarded (Bunescu, this volume) and is rarely bestowed with prestige. Learning within such programmes can also be transformative for individual students (Al Hussein and Mangeni, this volume), but when universities seek to build prestige through the promotion of outstanding students they can privilege those with pre-existing 'suitable' characteristics, such as language skills (Burke, this volume; Wilson et al., this volume) and thus contribute to the university serving as a site for the reproduction of racialised, gendered and classed social relations (Cantat, this volume).

Prestige, in and of itself, would not be so bad. It is, after all, the feeling of admiration or respect that a thing or a person receives because of what they have done. The issue is the structures it feeds from and helps create, and the way these prestige structures reinforce hierarchical relationships. For prestige is relational, it is dependent on the non-prestige of others: it requires the lack of prestige and even subservience of others for it to be durable over time.

The Prestige Structure

The original meaning of the word prestige is the conjuror's trick. And while it has come to denote something quite different in the social sciences and society at large, it is helpful to keep its etymology in mind. Or to put it more bluntly, I believe that academic prestige is a trick, a slight of hand that makes the audience believe one thing when another quite different thing has taken place. However, revealing the conjuror's secret will not stop academics and universities believing that their prestige is worthy, because we (as staff or students) are both the conjuror and the audience at once, pulling grant-shaped rabbits out of our hats and papers for 'prestigious' journals from up our sleeves, clapping our peers as they chop themselves in half.

But how does this trick work? Ortner and Whitehead theorise prestige's structuring possibilities from a symbolic anthropology perspective in their introduction to *Sexual Meanings* (1981), which I will detail at length, adding examples from academic life to make my argument.

A person or group's prestige position – or their social value – results from social evaluation. The mechanism through which people or groups are placed in a certain position (and how these processes are reproduced) is what they call the 'prestige structure'. Sources of prestige might include the command over material resources (winning grants, scholarships, negotiating a high salary), political might (becoming a student representative, university senate member, school or department chair) or personal skill (being a great scholar). However, simply being related or affiliated with others who are wealthy, mighty and skilful can also be a source of prestige (having famous academic parents, having a 'big name' as a supervisor). Prestige is enacted when these sources are used effectively, something possibly enhanced by displaying concern for the social good. Prestige is not, of course, a fixed entity, with historical reputation also playing a part in upholding, sometimes in a rigid fashion, social positioning (a degree from a fancy university can be referenced forever).

Further to this, there are two channels through which prestige can be bestowed by evaluators: ascriptive channels (based on given attributes – e.g. being from an academic family, having the class *habitus* of an academic) and achievement channels (based on what you have done – gaining entry to a university programme, publishing a paper in a top-ranked journal).

Prestige structures interact with the political economy, but are emergent and partially autonomous structures that cannot be simply mapped onto or replaced by relations of production (i.e. social class does not equal social standing in the prestige economy). Prestige is about more than simple economic domination. Rather, prestige structures are a 'screen' between other structures – political, material and so on (it is possible to have the prestige of graduating from a certain university, or having won prizes or published in the 'top' journals and still be basically unemployable).

Prestige, however, would not function unless people believed in it, enacted it and worked to maintain it: it needs an ideological underpinning. As Ortner and Whitehead (1981: 14) argue, prestige structures are always supported by, indeed they appear as direct expressions of, definite beliefs and symbolic associations that make sensible and compelling the ordering of human relations into patterns of deference and condescension, respect and disregard, and in many cases command and obedience. These beliefs and symbolic associations may be looked at as legitimating ideology. A system of social value differentiation, founded on whatever material base, is fragile and incomplete without such an ideology.

As such, it needs students, staff and wider society to buy into the prestige structure. People need not to believe that aspects of prestige in academia are well functioning all of the time to keep it running. For example, people can critique how the whiteness of European academia reveals it is not a true meritocracy, while still believing that, in general, prestige should be bestowed. For example, academics can observe how bad their workplaces are for gender or ethnic equity, especially when it comes to pay, but may also earnestly assert that those who have a big wage or fancy chair have them due to their excellence and hard work. The problem, according to this line of argument, is that biases are polluting the fair distribution of prestige (and its material rewards). This is an argument that the system needs tweaking, not demolishing. However, as you might have gathered from the title of this chapter, I strongly disagree. Take for example the way it makes individuals behave within it, to which I now turn.

Homo Prestigicus

University education programmes for students who have experienced displacement need to be organised and run with the central involvement of academic staff, who provide pedagogical and disciplinary-specific experience and expertise. However, doing such work is not 'prestigious' within the currently dominant forms of evaluation. Of course, prestige is not the only motivating factor among academics (at least I hope not). Blackmore and Kandiko (2011) suggest that academics are motivated by (i) an intrinsic interest in academic work; (ii) material/financial benefits; and (iii) prestige rewards. They draw on the work of Bourdieu (1986, 1988), specifically his famous argument that there are different forms of capital – social capital, cultural capital and economic capital. Using this base, they argue that within the 'prestige economy' in academia, a 'system of valuing and exchange of a range of forms of capital' (Blackmore and Kandiko 2011: 404–5), academic communities (i.e.

professional bodies or one's department peers) evaluate other scholars, allowing them to accrue social, cultural and economic capital.

However, I would argue that over the past decade or more, two distinct yet entwined processes have created disjunctures between academics' intrinsic love of their work, the financial rewards offered in academia and any prestige gained. These disjunctures highlight the increased difficulties of transferring the benefits between different forms of capital (e.g. between cultural and economic). This ultimately makes running programmes for displaced learners more difficult.

The first disjuncture-causing process is the extreme tightening of the academic job market, that is, a large floating academic labour reserve army, and budget cuts that threaten previously secure academics. Those on fixed term or insecure contracts have little to no loyalty to departments or their universities in the long term, increasing the need for prestige to be acknowledged outside the sphere of their immediate peers. The most immediate way to realise this, most people agree, is through getting published in high-ranking journals. For those without permanent contracts, this is, in effect, an effort to convert the cultural capital gained by publishing in such journals into the economic capital promised with a permanent contract (while for tenure track academics, something similar takes place when they are up for promotion). However, there is no easy conversion between different forms of capital. Bourdieu (1986) argued that the different processes needed to accumulate different forms of capital have different temporalities. For example, for a first-generation academic, the economic capital accrued when she becomes a university professor will not automictically result in a higher degree of social capital for her, but it might for her children (for a fascinating discussion of this 'subtle economy of time', see Slama 2017). The current academic job market promises a conversion from cultural to economic capital. Except for those born with silver spoons in their mouths (of which there are of course more than a few in academia), this means not 'wasting' time engaging in potentially life-changing initiatives for displaced learners, but rather (re)using their research data for (another) journal article.

The second tendency creating a harmful disjuncture between prestige and other motivations in academia is the rise of university rankings. This rise is part of an 'audit culture' that goes beyond universities, creating new forms of global governmentality though rankings, international measurements and risk management (Shore and Wright 2015). Some of the consequences of this audit culture especially relevant for academia include the reshaping of institutions as they enter into ever-growing systems that monitor, rank and measure them; a shift away from professional judgement and towards measurable criteria; and the creation of disengaged, cynical employees who develop gaming strategies to 'beat' the system (ibid.). Rankings are absurd, zero-sum games that say nothing meaningful about the quality of a university and yet they are uncritically embraced by not only management, but often also scholars (Brankovic 2021). In universities, these tendencies have been augmented through the rise of digital technologies that can easily measure and compare the output of individuals (Hall 2013), helping further elevate a marketised production over learning and scholarship (Fernback 2018). There has been an erosion of trust, a rise of paperwork (and its attendant army of consultants), an increase of competition and an increased need to create fabrications about deliverables (Shore and Wright 2015). Because measurement not only counts but also creates standards (Beer 2016), it would be a trap to argue for the inclusion of 'refugee education programmes' in matrices of measurement. This would ultimately hand over power to output-obsessed management, rather than allow initiatives to grow, develop and experiment based on students' needs. Of course, it might be argued that one of the things students need is a prestigious university.

The University and Its Prestige

When Michael Ignatieff, the President and Rector of the university where I work, came to say some words at a programme for displaced learners, he made, to my mind, two quite problematic points. Firstly, he compared his own biography with those students gathered before him. He came from a refugee family, he told them, referencing the moment when his aristocratic Russian family was forced to flee the Bolshevik Revolution. Look what he had become, in spite of this intergenerational setback, was the message. As far as I know, none of the students gathered there from mostly Middle Eastern and African countries were members of the aristocracy. Secondly, and possibly related in his thinking, he spoke about how programmes like the one he was speaking before might be able to help exceptional individuals flourish, and that such would-be scholars could climb up the ladder in their new societies.

Of course, he is not the first liberal elite to imagine a super refugee hero action figure emerging from the rubble of trauma, to imagine a university finding an uncut gem and polishing it so it can shine as an example of the wonders of Western higher education, and to imagine the prestige that might be bestowed upon a university for the valiant work they did in uncovering her. It is through such heroic acts of education, after all, that universities hope prestige can be harvested by the programmes they fund. Producing exceptional refugee trajectories fits into the prestige structures of the university, not by bumping up the institution in the official rankings, but in the more blurry world of reputation building and good news stories, beloved by communications officers.

While potentially empowering particularly 'gifted' students, the elite-refugee-learner-trajectory model undermines the access and success of those from marginalised groups more generally, as it runs the risk of reproducing the non-transformative, highly individualised forms of academic practice that ultimately create closures. It benefits those with pre-existing language skills and pre-existing educational experience comparable to that found in 'the West' (while normalising a certain ideal of 'the West' with which the 'refugee learner' must play an impossible game of catch-up). Furthermore, it is to the detriment of those who, for reasons of gender, ethnicity or class, might have been unable to access or flourish within higher education settings back home.

A university's given prestige can, however, be a big draw for students. And this, of course, is completely understandable. It is from a position of privilege (and possibly stupidity if anyone reads this the next time I need to apply for a job) that I am able to say, 'fuck prestige'. Students tell me that being able to say they are attending university gives them kudos in their workplaces, especially with their bosses. Aside from whatever important benefits being at the university brings in terms of learning and community, the prestige of a higher education institution also allows 'refugees', to a certain degree, to cover their legal label with an educational one – to say I'm not a refugee, I'm a student.

To be clear, I am not stating that individual students who are looking for ways to remake their lives should not use prestige instrumentally, should not feel pride in having gained entry into a prestigious university, and should not boast about it to their family members back home (if they so wish). Nor am I saying that those of us who help run initiatives for displaced learners do not need to play with and on the prestige of our universities (and the idea of 'the university' more generally) to open doors for people in the short term. We often are forced to reappropriate the rewards of prestige structure creatively to further knowledge and advance pedagogy.

However, with the above outlined prestige structure and the interplay of different forms of capital in mind, I am arguing that these actions, in the long term, help maintain the prestige structure, suffer from the same struggles around converting different forms of capital and thus, ultimately, are fundamentally non-transformative. If the work of access programmes is only about expanding the privilege of the institution, then it keeps the structures of privilege production in place, it only expands prestige's filtering mechanism.

As such, because the prestige structure (and lack of money) disincentivises scholars from working within initiatives for displaced learners, and because the prestige structure creates trajectories for 'exceptional' students while closing doors for those arriving without the requisite background, we have little choice but to say that prestige should really fuck the fuck off.

Can We Fuck with the Prestige Structure Please?

In the long term, if we were to imagine a fairer system of higher education we might want to tackle questions around access to and evaluation of the sources of prestige (especially in terms of the material and political sources of prestige); we might further want to shed light on good and bad practices around how people use these sources of prestige in a university setting; and we should certainly call out ascribed prestige and critique how achieved prestige is distributed within academia's prestige structure. Transparency, equity and justice are desperately needed.

One of the difficulties in calling for prestige to get fucked is that – as students, scholars, staff, library users and potential future students – we are all invested in it. The interplay between political-economic structures and the ideology that underpins prestige seems impenetrable, because we are all involved (critically, hypocritically) in its reproduction. Maybe the best example of this is the accumulated prestige of European Commission grants where the Principal Investigator (PI) receives the accolades, while the work of postdocs, students or precarious research assistants is only known if the PI chooses to highlight it. These secondary workers should work hard and keep quiet about any inequalities or injustices, as one day soon their chance will also come to win a large grant that will change their career (especially as universities increasingly value the winning of grants, due to changing funding models). However, labouring under this illusion enables the development of structures that are good for the reproduction of prestige-capital but not for the advancement of those 'others' (and may lead to abuse). In short, one academic raises their prestige, in part, through the invisibilised labour of others.

This is because what one achieves has to be recognised by others as achievement for the prestige structure to work, and consequently one has to strive to retain the structures of evaluation that have bestowed prestige upon us. It is why people don't ask you, 'What did you publish?', but 'Where did you publish?'. It is why people don't ask you, 'What are you working on?', but 'Where are you working?'. It is why people don't ask you, 'What was your PhD about?', but 'Who was on your PhD committee?'. Of course, a reader might think, 'this author is very bitter because he has failed to gain enough academic prestige by publishing in such and such journal or winning such and such grant, and his supervisor is some loser nobody'. But this is why prestige is so fucking insidious, because I can either ignore the point and hope you take my argument on its merits or point you towards the prestigious things/people I may or may not have done or may or may not have been associated with.

The unbreachable walls of academia's prestige structure present a special irony for precarious scholars. Whereas investing time to accumulate social and cultural capital should yield results in the long term – or so prevalent discourses in society suggest – a quick glance at the current academic job market reveals that for most people who gained a PhD and wish to stay in academia, the opposite is true. The prestige achieved through the accumulation of degrees from fancy universities, journal publications and grant awards does not pay off for those who remain on the inside. Though the cultural capital gained through university degrees is still convertible outside the university (into economic and potentially, over time, social capital), the seemingly unassailable prestige of the university within society is also coming under attack, especially from the right. So why join in the prestige game? Why not quit? If you will excuse an academic insider joke, you have nothing to lose but your H-Index ranking! (Of course precarious scholars are not encouraged to quit, the underlings are required to uphold the structure, it needs subservient workers to keep it running.)

Quitting the prestige game offers a certain sort of freedom. Yes, of course, it offers the 'freedom' of impending unemployment or underemployment. But it also offers scholarly freedom, the freedom to do intrinsically good work – such as working within programmes for displaced learners, to write book chapters with 'fuck' in the title and (funds permitting) to research and publish what interests us as scholars (be they students or full professors). It is liberating because when we work with prestige in mind, we work to fill in pre-existing categories. We see the structures, and we fill them in. It is a closed academic practice; an ontology defined by its end goal before it has begun. Opening up the university, teaching and learning with displaced learners, could and should be about an open-ended learning experience.

Finally, if individuals, groups and institutions that enjoy high prestige are respected or admired, and we accept that the prestige structure in academia is both broken and a suffocating force, then one possible solution would be to stop respecting or admiring people, groups and institutions based on their ranking within the prestige structure. We should actively push against mechanisms that uphold these structures of rank; critique groups and individuals when they defer to the power of prestige; and ultimately forge, together, a system of higher education based on a dominant cultural value that yes, of course, rewards great work and scholarship, but does so in a way that does not close off the transformative potential of the university.

◆

Ian M. Cook (Central European University, Budapest) is an anthropologist who works on urban change, environmental (in)justice, podcasting and opening up the university.

References

Beer, D. 2016. *Metric Power*. London: Palgrave Macmillan. http://dx.doi.org/10.1057/978-1-137-55649-3.

Blackmore, P., and C.B. Kandiko. 2011. 'Motivation in Academic Life: A Prestige Economy', *Research in Post-Compulsory Education* 16(4): 399–411. https://doi.org/10.1080/13596748.2011.626971.

Bourdieu, P. 1986. *Distinction: A Social Critique of the Judgement of Taste*. London: Routledge.

Bourdieu, P. 1988. *Homo Academicus*. Cambridge, UK: Polity Press.

Brankovic, J. 2021. 'The Absurdity of University Rankings', *LSE Impact Blog*, 22 March. https://blogs.lse.ac.uk/impactofsocialsciences/2021/03/22/the-absurdity-of-university-rankings/.

Fernback, J. 2018. 'Academic/Digital Work: ICTs, Knowledge Capital, and the Question of Educational Quality', *TripleC: Communication, Capitalism & Critique. Open Access Journal for a Global Sustainable Information Society* 16(1): 143–58. https://doi.org/10.31269/triplec.v16i1.878.

Hall, R. 2013. 'Educational Technology and the Enclosure of Academic Labour inside Public Higher Education', *Journal for Critical Education Policy Studies (JCEPS)* 11(3).

Ortner, S.B., and H. Whitehead. 1981. 'Introduction: Accounting for Sexual Meanings', in S.B. Ortner and H. Whitehead (eds), *Sexual Meanings, the Cultural Construction of Gender and Sexuality*. Cambridge: Cambridge University Press.

Shore, C., and S. Wright. 2015. 'Governing by Numbers: Audit Culture, Rankings and the New World Order', *Social Anthropology* 23(1): 22–28. https://doi.org/10.1111/1469-8676.12098.

Slama, M. 2017. 'A Subtle Economy of Time: Social Media and the Transformation of Indonesia's Islamic Preacher Economy', *Economic Anthropology* 4(1): 94–106. https://doi.org/10.1002/sea2.12075.

CHAPTER 14
Reimagining Language in Higher Education
Engaging with the Linguistic Experiences of Students with Refugee and Asylum Seeker Backgrounds

RACHEL BURKE

University initiatives to facilitate more equitable entry to higher education for people with refugee and asylum seeker backgrounds provide much-needed alternative pathways to enrolment. Yet there is an urgent need for institutions to critically engage with students' linguistic experiences as they progress through university studies. Language and academic literacy requirements are among the chief barriers to success for many students with refugee and asylum seeker backgrounds (see Hirano 2014; Naidoo 2015; Fagan et al. 2018; Hartley et al. 2019). Linguistic challenges, which are frequently exacerbated by past experiences of disrupted education due to war and/or poverty, may significantly impact learners' academic progress and social inclusion, undermining the transformative potential of widening participation initiatives for both the individual student and the university. Critically reflecting on the linguistic experiences of learners with refugee and asylum seeker backgrounds provides an important opportunity to challenge assumptions about the universality of the literate practices privileged in higher education, reconceptualise institutional approaches to language support, and explore the need to better recognise and engage with students' diverse linguistic repertoires.

While higher education staff and student populations continue to diversify in terms of language background, the literate practices valued in the academy remain comparatively static (Ivanic 1998; Lillis 2001; Wingate 2006). Further, there is a prevailing expectation in higher education that students from traditionally under-represented backgrounds[1] will adopt dominant language forms, frequently with limited opportunities to be apprenticed into such textual practices, and with minimal scope for enriching tertiary institutions through the incorporation of alternative linguistic repertoires (Delpit 1988; Morrice 2013; Daddow 2016).

Dominant language forms, such as discipline-specific expectations regarding the navigation and production of text, and engagement with academic discourses and literacies, reflect – and construct – particular epistemological paradigms and ideological traditions (Unsworth 1999; Schleppegrell and de Oliveira 2006). Yet these powerful forms of 'linguistic capital' (Bourdieu 1991) are often treated unproblematically in higher education, with an assumption of universality that belies the linguistic diversity of student (and staff) populations. Such attitudes help perpetuate established patterns of educational marginalisation by denying certain learner groups access to the textual practices valued within the academy (Delpit 1988; Lillis 2001; Daddow 2016).

In this sense, the experiences of many students with refugee and asylum seeker backgrounds are indicative of the broader, systemic exclusion of populations with linguistic repertoires that differ from the literate practices foregrounded in higher education (Morrice 2013). Lillis (2001: 39) notes how language practices in education can 'privilege the discursive routines of particular social groups whilst dismissing those of people who, culturally and communally, have access to and engage in a range of other practices'.

Here, I suggest that genuinely engaging with the linguistic repertoires – including strengths and needs – of students with refugee and asylum seeker backgrounds offers an important opportunity to transform 'mainstream'[2] instructional practices in higher education. This requires students and staff to collectively explore discipline-specific literacies practices, problematise the cultural and epistemological perspectives embedded within powerful text types, and engage with alternative 'discursive routines' (Lillis 2001: 39). Such approaches may provide opportunities for sharing linguistic repertoires, creating space for all students to incorporate socio-cultural practices and values that may have been traditionally under-represented or disregarded in higher education institutions. For instance, in the Australian university context, important work is being undertaken to foreground the need for educational institutions to better recognise and value Aboriginal and Torres Strait Islander students' rich and varied linguistic practices and knowledges (see Koramannil 2016; Wilks et al. 2020).[3]

This chapter originates in my own struggles as a scholar-practitioner working with students in so-called 'mainstream' higher education to ensure their access to powerful forms of discipline-specific language, while also seeking to value and learn from their linguistic repertoires. The chapter is not intended to provide an exhaustive account of existing literature focused on the linguistic experiences of students with refugee and asylum seeker backgrounds,[4] but is a reflective exploration of selected themes emanating from my experiences and identified in research undertaken at the nexus of widening participation, applied linguistics and higher education. I seek to investigate possibilities for honouring refugee and asylum seeker background students' linguistic strengths and needs, and consider ways in which institutional structures and teaching approaches may better facilitate such engagement. The hope is that this chapter will contribute to larger conversations regarding the need to transform linguistic practices within higher education, disrupt deficit framing of students with refugee/asylum seeker experiences, and genuinely commit to linguistically rich, productive and generative learning spaces.

Importantly, I acknowledge that, as a first language speaker of English – one of the dominant means of communication in higher education but certainly not the original or only language of teaching and learning in the place[5] in which I often live and work – I write from a privileged position. I also acknowledge that the issues of language and power discussed in this chapter are complex, deeply personal and highly contested. I recognise that, regardless of attempts to maintain reflexivity, my engagement with the research and practices in my field is filtered through my own cultural and linguistic experiences, ideologies and limitations. Finally, while I use the terms 'students with refugee and asylum seeker experiences' and learners from 'traditionally under-represented backgrounds', I acknowledge the rich diversity characterising these populations.

Higher Education, Language and Learner Outcomes

Language is central to most teaching, learning and epistemological engagement in higher education. Core knowledge and concepts are usually (although not always) communicated linguistically, and an inability to demonstrate cognitive engagement and understanding by using expected academic literacies and language generally has a significant impact on learner outcomes (Harris and Marlowe 2011; Lea and Street 1998; Lillis and Scott 2007; Daddow 2016). Many students from traditionally under-represented backgrounds gain access to higher education through targeted entry programmes, only to struggle with the language required for engagement with academic content, classroom participation and assessment when they transition into 'mainstream' contexts (Jacobs 2005; Gray and Irwin 2013; Hirano 2014; Naidoo et al. 2015).

While academic literacy practices are often unconsciously adopted as 'common sensical' or 'natural' by discipline insiders, they represent particular forms of 'linguistic capital' (Bourdieu 1991) that are privileged in the academy but not necessarily obvious or familiar to all students. Yet this important aspect of widening participation in higher education is often overlooked in institutional policy regarding equity initiatives (Briguglio and Watson 2014; Klinger and Murray 2012; McWilliams and Allan 2014; Percy 2014; Burke 2020).

All students can struggle with the academic literacy requirements of higher education; however, learners from traditionally under-represented populations, whose literate practices of home and community may contrast significantly with those of the academy, tend to be most disadvantaged within the linguistic hierarchy of the tertiary institution (Morrice 2013; Rai and Lillis 2013; Daddow 2016). Such students are more likely to be unfamiliar with discipline-specific literacies, to be disadvantaged by a lack of institutional support for apprenticing learners into these textual practices, and to experience the 'rendering invisible' (Morrice 2018) or 'misrecognition' (Fraser 1998) of their linguistic repertoires and identities. As Morrice (2013: 654) observes regarding systemic exclusion in higher education, 'there are commonalities in the experiences of refugees and other non-traditional students'.

For learners continuing to develop proficiency in the language(s) of instruction in higher education, those with diverse first language(s) and literacies backgrounds, and/or those experiencing the ongoing impacts of forced migration, the task of gaining expertise in the linguistic forms required for tertiary learning may involve particular challenges. Yet the relative paucity of research specifically examining the complex linguistic transitions required of students with refugee and asylum seeker backgrounds in higher education, particularly as they move beyond intensive language instruction and university preparatory courses to engage with the various text types and discursive practices of discipline area studies in mainstream higher education, may reflect and perpetuate their institutional invisibility.

Further, within the limited corpus of research that specifically examines the linguistic experiences of students with refugee and asylum seeker backgrounds in tertiary education, minimal attention is given to students' linguistic strengths. This emphasis on student needs may reflect the urgency of advocating for sector-wide recognition of the many barriers to higher education confronting people with refugee and asylum seeker backgrounds. However, this foregrounding of students' needs may also unintentionally contribute to the deficit framing of the population, impeding attempts to harness students' linguistic strengths as the basis for ongoing learning and enrichment of institutional practices.

The Complex Linguistic Repertoires of Students with Refugee and Asylum Seeker Backgrounds: Moving beyond Deficit Framing

Many students with histories of forced migration have complex and rich linguistic repertoires, speak a number of languages and dialects, and are experienced at code switching (Delpit 1988) according to communicative context (Baker et al. 2018). However, these linguistic capacities can be disregarded or 'misrecognised' (Fraser 1998) in Australian higher education institutions, where the traditional emphasis on English, print literacy (reading and writing), and a limited set of textual practices reflecting the communicative norms of particular social groups, can leave minimal opportunity for valuing and incorporating alternative ways with language. Lack of awareness regarding the wide-ranging linguistic practices students undertake outside of university may be compounded by enduring conceptualisations of learners with refugee/asylum seeker experiences in deficit terms. Foregrounding student needs (however well-intentioned) and failing to appreciate alternative linguistic strengths, such as highly developed oral language repertoires, can perpetuate the construction of learners as 'lacking', and shifts focus away from the need for institutions to develop responsive and tailored instructional approaches that recognise a diverse range of linguistic resources.

Students with a history of disrupted education who have not had the opportunity to learn the written script of their first language(s) are described in the research literature as 'non-literate'; while those who have acquired partial knowledge of print literacy in their first language(s) are described as being 'semi-literate' in these codes (Burgoyne and Hull 2007; Burt, Peyton and Adams 2003). However, other students with a history of displacement may come from 'preliterate backgrounds', in which their first language(s) do not have a written form, and this will obviously impact their experiences learning print literacy in the language of instruction at university. For example, language specialist staff participating in the first nationwide study of barriers to higher education for people seeking asylum in Australia expressed particular concern for students learning to engage with print literacy practices for the first time as they simultaneously learn English and discipline content knowledge (Hartley et al. 2018). Such learners are required to develop new understandings of written systems for representing and constructing meaning, from concepts of sound/symbol relationships and grammatical forms through to knowledge of complex schematic structures and linguistic features of academic texts. Accordingly, refugee/asylum seeker background learners' experiences with language are as diverse as the population itself, with students' literate resources and practices informed by past educational experiences, individual circumstances, socio-cultural values and communicative traditions (Fozdar and Hartley 2012; Watkins, Razee and Richters 2012; Hatoss and Huijser 2010; Brooker and Lawrence 2012; Nicholas and Williams 2003).

However, there is very little praxis-driven support for tertiary educators seeking to better understand different orientations to language/literacies, and how these diverse practices can be incorporated in mainstream learning contexts. For instance, students who are pre-, non- or semi-literate in their first language(s) are likely to have highly developed oral language repertoires which represent important foundations for learning, but may require additional assistance with subject-specialist terminology and the conventions and structures of written text (Burgoyne and Hull 2007; Burt, Peyton and Adams 2003). Yet the limited research regarding adults who are pre-, non- and semi-literate in their first language(s) is mostly focused on the earliest stages of print literacy learning in the second language(s), meaning there is an urgent need to explore such students' later experiences in the specific context of academic literacies instruction in higher education.

Vásquez's (2007) investigation of one refugee background learner's experiences attending a university Intensive English Program (IEP) in the United States provides a nuanced and holistic account of the student's highly developed oracy and communicative competence in spoken English, which contrasted with her written English repertoires. O'Rourke (2011), writing in Aotearoa/New Zealand, similarly notes that students with refugee and asylum seeker backgrounds frequently have strong oracy skills and less developed academic writing resources. In Vásquez's (2007) study, the student's strong oral language proficiency allowed her to pass the Intensive English Program (IEP) but was insufficient for success in mainstream university studies. Such research illustrates the importance of ensuring refugee and asylum seeker background students' highly developed oracy skills do not result in underestimation of their written academic literacy needs, and that preparatory courses align with the language required for success in mainstream studies. Vásquez's (2007) study also highlights the need for staff in preparatory courses and discipline instruction to have opportunities to exchange knowledge regarding learners' linguistic histories and resources to assist with successful student transitions into mainstream courses.

While some students with refugee and asylum seeker backgrounds have highly developed oracy in their first and/or additional language(s), other learners articulate a sense of shame, embarrassment, and feelings of infantilisation and isolation due to perceived deficiencies in their spoken language (Kanno and Varghese 2010; Fagan et al. 2018; Sontag 2018). These learners report that self-consciousness regarding pronunciation and communicative competence in the language of instruction at university prevents them from making social connections with peers and attending or verbally participating in class (Fagan et al. 2018). Frequently, students indicate that staff attribute such silence in class to a lack of knowledge or motivation rather than the impact of language anxiety or unfamiliarity with culturally specific discursive practices such as classroom debates, critical reflections or presentations.

Researchers have also noted the tendency for refugee and asylum seeker background students to assume disproportionate responsibility when facing linguistic challenges at university, perceiving such difficulties to stem from their own personal deficiencies rather than resulting from educational exclusion and/or institutional/structural barriers (Kanno and Varghese 2010; Turner and Fozdar 2010; O'Rourke 2011). Kanno and Varghese (2010: 322) refer to such attitudes as evidence of students 'acquiescing to the university's institutional culture that frames the lack of native-level English proficiency as a deficit'. As Morrice (2018: 8) has suggested, 'Forms of knowledge, qualifications, experiences and ways of learning which cannot be accommodated are rendered incomprehensible and invisible. . .'. For learners from traditionally under-represented backgrounds who may struggle to participate in expected communicative practices, 'their diversity is not recognised as an asset and they are denied a role of active contributor and potential transformer' within tertiary institutions (Morrice 2018: 8).

The educational experiences of refugee/asylum seeker background learners – whether those from oracy-focused cultures who may experience challenges with print literacy or those with greater competence in reading or writing but less confidence with oral language – therefore reveal the need for educators to be aware of the various factors that may shape students' communicative practices and individual linguistic strengths and needs. This necessitates professional development for all teaching staff, and ongoing consultation and collaboration with learners to explore ways in which linguistic strengths can provide bridges to developing expertise in less familiar textual practices.

Linguistic Diversity and Notions of 'Integration'

A key theme in studies that examine refugee and asylum seeker background learners' linguistic experiences in higher education is the significant time required to navigate academic texts in an additional language/dialect. While the linguistic processes vary according to student proficiency levels, many learners describe complex and time-consuming practices involving careful translation between two or more languages, in order to engage with course content and academic reading (Fagan et al. 2018). Navigating subject-specific vocabulary and specialist terms, as well as unfamiliarity with practices of critical reading and the use of sources in academic writing, are identified as particularly time consuming. For many students with experiences of displacement, ongoing and discipline-specific language tuition is inaccessible due to financial constraints.

Issues of language become particularly fraught in contexts where learners' grades are at stake (Hirano 2014). In their investigation of student experiences at a university in the United States, Kanno and Varghese (2010) found examinations were particularly inequitable for students with refugee and asylum seeker backgrounds, with the time required to understand the language in order to engage with the content rendering discipline-specific examinations indirect tests of English. This important equity issue relates to broader discussions regarding the consequences of standardised testing, which have been shown to disadvantage already marginalised groups via the problematic rationale that 'equality' of assessment practices results in equitable outcomes (Volante 2008). For students with experiences of displacement and trauma, time-limited, high-stakes examinations add an extra layer of stress to assessment in an additional language, and can be detrimental to mental health and learning outcomes.

Academic staff in Harris and Marlowe's (2011) exploration of the educational experiences of students from refugee backgrounds attending a South Australian university also identified the significant additional time staff dedicated to engaging with meaning in learners' written assignments. With the university system for staff remuneration allocating a set amount of time for the assessment of each student's work regardless of language background, and the absence of clear guidelines concerning the relative weight that should be ascribed to grammatical accuracy in the allocation of overall grades, academic staff reported feeling overwhelmed and pressured. The responsibility to correctly interpret the intended meaning expressed in student assignments in order to fairly assess conceptual engagement and degree of understanding, rather than language proficiency, was a source of significant stress for staff, many of whom had little to no training in language/literacies education.

Questions regarding institutional practices for assessing language are timely and significant in the linguistically diversified academy, with one student participant in Harris and Marlowe's (2011) study explaining: 'We're not saying give us a pass because "poor us" – I mean when I [show I can] apply the law, why mark me down for punctuation?' (190). Harris and Marlowe (2011: 192) state that acknowledgement of students' differing linguistic and literacies backgrounds 'does not mean that principles of academic integrity or rigorous curricula should be abandoned. Rather, it highlights the necessity to critically engage these concepts in contemporary and comparative contexts'.

Assessment-related practices regarding academic integrity have also been identified as posing significant challenges to students with refugee and asylum seeker experiences. In their study of learners attending Australian higher education institutions, Fagan et al. (2018) documented student struggles with highly culture-specific notions regarding plagiarism, institutional expectations concerning the synthesising of source materials into writing, and the purposes and use of plagiarism detection software (Fagan et al. 2018).

Digital literacy requirements have also been shown to create challenges for students who have not had the opportunity to develop functional and/or critical technological repertoires (Sontag 2018; Baker et al. 2018). Institutional assumptions of digital literacy are particularly problematic and exclusionary given the current push to digitise learning spaces across higher education, especially in the context of remote delivery due to COVID-19 (see Princewill Esenowo, this volume). Fagan et al. (2018) discovered refugee and asylum seeker background learners in Australia were frequently unable to arrange learning assistance sessions, book study spaces and access online sources due to a lack of digital literacy skills.

In addition, confusion regarding institutional expectations surrounding due dates, task requirements and acceptable circumstances for applying for extensions can further hinder progress for many students from refugee and asylum seeker backgrounds (Fagan et al. 2018). Institutional failure to explicitly communicate these fundamental and culturally specific expectations can prevent students from accessing learning support. The resulting lack of assistance can increase learner isolation, ultimately contributing to attrition, and further perpetuating deficit framing of linguistically diverse populations. In fact, institutional processes that do not take into account the unique circumstances and literacies resources of many learners from refugee/asylum seeker backgrounds have been shown to create structural barriers to inclusion that begin with students' first interactions with universities. Challenges locating information about scholarship opportunities and university entry pathways are particularly common for learners with refugee and asylum seeker backgrounds (Hartley et al. 2018). Aside from lack of access to the internet, many students also experience confusion regarding admissions processes that incorporate repurposed documentation originally used for international student enrolments and therefore intended for learners with different circumstances (Hartley et al. 2018). Many students identify the importance of the language support provided by community advocates as key to their navigation of university admissions processes.

Again, such experiences with the opacity of institutional expectations are often encountered by a range of populations within higher education. While students with histories of forced migration are likely to experience specific challenges resulting from significant interruptions to education due to the social, cultural and health implications of seeking refuge, other student populations, including those with First Nations backgrounds, learners from particular socio-economic status groups or geographic locations, those with Culturally and Linguistically Diverse (CALD) backgrounds, and students with specific learning or health needs and abilities, are also among those more likely to experience challenges with language-related expectations in higher education. While the specific issues faced by many learners within these populations may vary according to background, the central issue of exclusion and the 'rendering invisible' of 'experiences, knowledges and practices' through the processes of higher education is common (Morrice 2018: 2).

Both the linguistic and academic literacies challenges experienced by many higher education students with refugee and asylum seeker backgrounds, and the ubiquity of deficit framing of such learners, need to be considered in relation to overarching concepts of 'integration' at both the institutional and societal level. Expectations regarding the universality of dominant language forms, and minimal scope for students to contribute diverse language/literacies repertoires, reflect understandings of 'integration' as a unidirectional adjustment on the part of the 'newcomer' and rarely on behalf of the 'host'.

Greater acknowledgement of the diverse linguistic practices students bring to higher education would allow for what Morrice (2018: 2) describes as a move 'away from dominant epistemological canons which disqualify and make invisible the knowledge and skills of some learners, towards acknowledgement of the incompleteness of all knowledges'. Further, Morrice (2018: 8) suggests: 'It is only through deconstructing this hegemonic mono-culture of knowledge and recognising that other knowledges have been delegitimized and rendered invisible that global cognitive justice, and consequently global social justice, can be achieved'. Such understandings of integration as a 'two-way' process call for more dynamic conceptualisations of the role of language within higher education, and genuine engagement with the culturally situated nature of discipline literacies and institutional processes.

Possibilities for Collaborative Approaches to Linguistic Support

Despite the increasingly diverse linguistic landscape of higher education, in some contexts there has been comparatively limited institutional attention to the role of academics in scaffolding learner engagement with academic literacies across the disciplines. Rather, universities have responded to increasing linguistic diversification by providing language assistance within bridging and enabling programmes and/or learning centres. Bridging and enabling programmes provide important pathways to tertiary enrolment and offer tailored linguistic and cultural support to students as they commence studies (see Baker and Irwin 2016). Learning centres provide essential language assistance to students after they transition into mainstream studies. However, frequently the latter are physically located away from the teaching undertaken in the faculties, with some scholar-practitioners arguing that this may perpetuate the idea that language and literacies support is the sole responsibility of learning centre staff and that linguistic diversity does not impact discipline instruction (see Wingate 2018; McWilliams and Allan 2014).

This model of language support may also impede collaboration between language specialists and discipline experts, restricting opportunities for knowledge exchange and shared approaches to supporting students through the linguistic transitions they undertake throughout their degree. There is a strong body of literature advocating for greater integration of language and academic literacies support across higher education (see McWilliams and Allan 2014; Daddow 2016; Wingate

2006, 2018). Collaborative approaches to language support also emphasise the deeply social nature of language learning, and the importance of strong networks for students with experiences of displacement and trauma. The significance of this social support to student engagement with language/literacies learning in higher education is illustrated powerfully in research conducted by Baker et al. (2018), who investigated student uptake of institutional support services in a regional Australian university. While the students described the advisors working in the central learning support services as 'helpful, professional and expert', they expressed a preference for assistance from familiar contacts, including friends or peers, who were not necessarily expert, or from staff members who acted as trusted brokers, described by the researchers as 'warm' sources of support (Baker et al. 2018: 10), drawing on notions of 'hot, warm, and cold information' (Ball and Vincent 1998; Slack et al. 2014).

These trusted brokers were individuals known for having previously assisted students, their friends or wider communities, and the connections were forged outside of the staff members' institutional roles (Baker et al. 2018). The staff took on responsibility for assisting students to navigate the academic literacy and language requirements of their studies in addition to their recognised workload. While preferences for familiar brokers to assist with language needs reflect patterns seen in the support-seeking behaviours of students from a range of traditionally under-represented backgrounds, the students in Baker et al.'s (2018) study link this preference to the unique circumstances of having sought refuge and 'the sense of trust that the participants attached to engaging with persons who are involved in the wider social and personal lives of refugees at the university and in the local community more broadly. . .' (11). Baker et al. (2018) suggest that their study shows the importance of decentralising language assistance and involving 'warm' support people from across the university – trusted brokers who are engaged with the refugee background community more broadly.

Ongoing collaboration between language specialists and discipline experts is essential to the task of providing responsive and tailored linguistic support for learners with refugee and asylum seeker backgrounds. Many academics working in discipline content instruction articulate a desire to provide embedded language assistance to students, but lack the experience or knowledge to do so effectively (Harris and Marlowe 2011; Burke 2020). The context-dependent nature of literate practices means targeted student support not only requires specialist knowledge of language and literacies learning, but epistemological expertise in the subject matter of the discipline. This necessitates staff collaboration across various university departments, and the foregrounding of student experiences in planning, trialling and evaluating strategies for responsive, inclusive and effective practice.

Important work with translanguaging, or the use of multiple linguistic resources to maximise learner outcomes, is continuing in a range of educational contexts (Garcia and Wei 2014; Mendenhall and Bartlett 2018). García (2009: 140) describes translanguaging as the process of 'accessing different linguistic features or various modes of what are described as autonomous languages, in order to maximize communicative potential'. Drawing on the work of scholars such as Grosjean (1982), proponents of translanguaging argue that 'a bilingual is not two monolinguals in one but a linguistically unique language user whose languages reflect the differential experience a bilingual may have with each language' (McSwan 2017: 171). Accordingly, translanguaging approaches recognise and value the full range of students' linguistic repertoires, and conceive of diverse languages and literacies practices as complementary (Garcia and Kleyn 2018).

The implementation of translanguaging approaches requires careful planning and professional development. Further, application of translanguaging principles may vary according to discipline, student and staff linguistic identities, learning preferences and instructional modes. However, there is a central emphasis on explicitly discussing the text types and communicative practices featured in course content, while creating opportunities for learners to share and utilise the full range of their linguistic knowledge, skills and repertoires. Teaching staff are not required to be proficient in the learners' languages and literate practices but can encourage students to reflect on similarities and differences between these practices and those foregrounded in the academy. Further, teaching staff can suggest that students may want to explore ways of applying their existing linguistic expertise to the learning they are undertaking at university. For example, some students develop dual language resources such as course glossaries or vocabulary journals in which subject-specialist terms can be translated into a variety of languages (Fagan et al. 2018). Similarly, some students find it helpful to undertake particular parts of a task, such as brainstorming, planning or note taking, in multiple languages and/or dialects, or to discuss or describe core concepts from different cultural perspectives or through varied text types.

Other ways of building on students' linguistic strengths involve harnessing individual areas of expertise to develop new repertoires. For example, students with highly developed oracy skills often prefer to begin written output with verbal language activities that activate background knowledge and clarify textual expectations, gradually incorporating forms of print literacy to build towards the final output (Burke 2020). One example of this approach was described by a participant in my small-scale study of academic supports for linguistically diverse learning in a regional Australian university, and involves students verbally explaining a theoretical framework or key concept to their peers, while members of the group record the main points on mini whiteboards, which they collectively turn into formal writing after discussing and refining their ideas (Burke 2020). This peer construction of written output allows for shared navigation of the features and expectations of the text type, and reiterative crafting of the final product, with verbal language providing a strong foundation and overarching medium for negotiating content and process throughout.

Explicit engagement with language, including deconstructing academic text types, modelling assessment task requirements and deconstructing assignment exemplars, also provides important linguistic scaffolding (Burke 2020). These learning supports need to be organically woven into discipline area instruction, as discussing both the course content and the discipline-specific ways in which this content is communicated and assessed helps students engage with text types and discursive practices in context (Daddow 2016). These learning supports can also present opportunities for critical conversations regarding issues of language and power, including the relative status of different linguistic codes (Delpit and Kilgour Dowdy 2002) or dialects, and may support students to consider their own linguistic identities in relation to their participation in higher education, their field of study and more broadly.

Conclusion: Reimagining Language in Higher Education

Central to discussions regarding equitable university participation for students with refugee and asylum seeker backgrounds is the need to collectively re-examine our understandings of language in higher education. Each researcher cited in this chapter calls for issues of language to be brought in from the periphery of higher education, to be central to the mission statements and actions of universities, and to explicitly and consciously become 'everyone's business', rather than remaining the sole responsibility of learning centres or language specialists.

Attention to the role of language as a powerful mediator of learning in higher education requires us to recognise that the discursive practices particular to each field of study are often products of the Global North; powerful forms of 'linguistic capital' (Bourdieu 1991) that reflect disciplinary histories, boundaries and ideological traditions. To assume universality of these textual practices is to disregard the linguistic diversity of the student population, and deny learners, particularly those from under-represented backgrounds, access to powerful textual practices and core epistemological perspectives. This, in turn, perpetuates already entrenched patterns of educational disadvantage.

Tailored, embedded and ongoing language support informed by student experiences – such as those foregrounded in research discussed in this chapter – must be central to widening participation efforts. Presently siloed structures of the university – in which language experts and discipline specialists rarely have the opportunity to collaborate – need to be reconsidered in order to effect institution-wide change and facilitate the explicit scaffolding of student language development within content area instruction. Indeed, much of the task of reconceptualising the role of language support in higher education requires close and critical scrutinising of the underlying structures of contemporary tertiary institutions. Research reveals the extent to which students with refugee and asylum seeker backgrounds currently rely on language support provided by staff who offer this assistance in addition to their official workload. Ensuring all learners have access to language support that assists them to mobilise their existing linguistic repertoires requires purpose-driven professional development and adequate staff compensation as part of institutional equity and diversity policies. Importantly, all staff – including the growing numbers of casually employed academics who undertake the bulk of teaching – must have access to these institutional supports. Of course, investing in professional development resources and compensating staff for the associated workload raises inevitable questions of funding.

Finally, institutional responsibility to ensure all students have access to disciplinary language does not preclude concurrent acknowledgement and valuing of students' linguistic repertoires. Creating spaces for refugee and asylum seeker background learner enrichment of institutional language practices allows us to collectively imagine more linguistically diverse, globally representative classroom cultures. Exploring how these spaces may function across degrees, faculties and institutions necessitates ongoing research and consultation with students from refugee and asylum seeker backgrounds – including those who successfully complete tertiary education, those who withdraw from studies, and those who wish to enrol – as well as staff and communities.

Reimagining higher education to better reflect the diverse linguistic repertoires of the student population is a complicated, wide-ranging and long-term exercise, subject to different views and experiences. However, this work is fundamental to approaching integration as a process characterised by reciprocity, and central to the task of transforming tertiary education. Redressing deeply engrained and entrenched power relations within higher education requires explicit acknowledgement that each of us is positioned in more or less powerful ways in the academy by virtue of the 'linguistic capital' (Bourdieu 1991) we bring. In valuing and supporting the linguistic experiences of students with refugee and asylum seeker backgrounds, tertiary institutions have an important opportunity to collectively imagine and enact more linguistically rich, productive and generative spaces of higher education.

◆

Rachel Burke is an Applied Linguist at the University of Newcastle, Australia. Her research and advocacy focus on linguistically and culturally diverse contexts, with emphasis on strengths-based approaches to tertiary education for learners from traditionally under-represented backgrounds, including students with migrant, refugee and asylum seeker experiences.

Notes

1. I use the term 'traditionally under-represented backgrounds' to refer to populations who have been historically excluded from higher education and whose linguistic repertoires may differ from those literacy practices still privileged in the academy today. I acknowledge that such terms should be problematised.
2. In this chapter, the term 'mainstream' is used to refer to educational contexts in which there is no official provision of additional support in the language(s) of instruction.
3. The continent that is now known as Australia is characterised by rich and enduring linguistic diversity, established over many thousands of years. At least 250 languages and many more dialects were estimated to have been in use among First Nations peoples in 1788 (Biddle and Swee 2012). The languages and literate practices of the world's oldest continuous living cultures endure, despite the events of the colonial and postcolonial period, such as the forced separation of children from their families and communities. Numerous community-led programmes continue to preserve and promote Aboriginal and Torres Strait Islander languages and literacies (Malcolm 2018; Wigglesworth and Simpson 2018).
4. The research accessed here is largely located within the Global North, illustrating both the limitations of my own linguistic expertise as well as the Western-centric nature of the field.

5. I acknowledge and respect the traditional Custodians of the Land on which I live and work, the Pambalong Clan of the Awabakal people, and I pay my respects to Elders past, present and future. I also acknowledge and respect the rich and enduring linguistic practices and knowledges of the Awabakal people and of all First Nations peoples.

References

Baker, S., and E. Irwin. 2016. 'Core or Periphery? The Positioning of Language and Literacies in Enabling Programs in Australia', *The Australian Educational Researcher* 43(4): 487–503.

Baker, S., G. Ramsay, E. Irwin and L. Miles. 2018. '"Hot", "Cold" and "Warm" Supports: Towards Theorising Where Refugee Students Go for Assistance at University', *Teaching in Higher Education* 23(1): 1–16.

Ball, S., and C. Vincent. 1998. '"I Heard it on the Grapevine": "Hot" Knowledge and School Choice', *British Journal of Sociology of Education* 19(3): 377–400.

Biddle, N., and H. Swee. 2012. 'The Relationship between Wellbeing and Indigenous Land, Language and Culture in Australia', *Australian Geographer* 43(3): 215–32.

Bourdieu, P. 1991. *Language and Symbolic Power*. Cambridge: Polity Press.

Briguglio, C., and S. Watson. 2014. 'Embedding English Language across the Curriculum in Higher Education: A Continuum of Development Support', *Australian Journal of Language and Literacy* 37(1): 67–74.

Brooker, A., and J. Lawrence. 2012. 'Educational and Cultural Challenges of Bicultural Adult Immigrant and Refugee Students in Australia', *Australian Journal of Adult Learning* 52(1): 66–88.

Burgoyne, U., and O. Hull. 2007. *Classroom Management Strategies to Address the Needs of Sudanese Refugee Learners: Advice to Teachers – Support Document*. Report by the National Centre for Vocational Education Research. https://eric.ed.gov/?id=ED499674.

Burke, R. 2020. 'Widening Participation and Linguistic Engagement in Australian Higher Education: Exploring Academics' Perceptions and Practices', *International Journal of Teaching and Learning in Higher Education* 32(2): 201–213.

Burt, M., J.K. Peyton and R. Adams. 2003. *Reading and Adult English Language Learners: A Review of the Research*. Washington, DC: Center for Applied Linguistics.

Daddow, A. 2016. 'Curricula and Pedagogic Potentials When Educating Diverse Students in Higher Education: Students' Funds of Knowledge as a Bridge to Disciplinary Learning', *Teaching In Higher Education* 21(7): 741–58.

Delpit, L. 1988. 'The Silenced Dialogue: Power and Pedagogy in Educating Other People's Children', *Harvard Educational Review* 58(3): 280–99.

Delpit, L., and J. Kilgour Dowdy. 2002. *The Skin That We Speak: Thoughts on Language and Culture in the Classroom*. New York: New Press.

Fagan, S., S. Baker, E. Irwin, J. Dantas, S. Gower, S. Singh, M. Taiwo and A.M. Ross. 2018. *(Re)Claiming Social Capital: Improving Language and Cultural Pathways for *Students from Refugee Backgrounds into Australian Higher Education*. Report for the Australian Government Office for Learning and Teaching. https://ltr.edu.au/resources/ID15-4758_Fagan_FinalReport_2018.pdf.

Fozdar, F., and L. Hartley. 2012. *Refugees in Western Australia: Settlement and Integration*. Perth: Metropolitan Migrant Resource Centre.

Fraser, N. 1998. 'From Redistribution to Recognition? Dilemmas of Justice in a "Post-socialist" Age', in C. Willett (ed.), *Theorizing Multiculturalism: A Guide to the Current Debate*. Malden, MA: Wiley, pp. 19–49.

García, O. 2009. 'Education, Multilingualism and Translanguaging in the 21st Century', in A. Mohanty, M. Panda, R. Phillipson and T. Skutnabb-Kangas (eds), *Social Justice through Multilingual Education: Globalising the Local*. New Delhi: Orient Blackswan, pp. 128–45.

Garcia, O., and T. Kleyn. 2018. *Translanguaging with Multilingual Students: Learning from Classroom Moments*. New York: Routledge.

García, O., and L. Wei. 2014. *Translanguaging: Language, Bilingualism and Education*. London: Palgrave Macmillan.

Gray, K., and E. Irwin. 2013. *Pathways to Social Inclusion: The Participation of Refugee Students in Higher Education*. In Proceedings of the National Association of Enabling Educators of Australia Conference; Flexibility: Pathways to Participation, Melbourne, Australia, 27–29 November.

Grosjean, F. 1982. *Life with Two Languages: An Introduction to Bilingualism*. Cambridge: Harvard University Press.

Harris, V., and J. Marlowe. 2011. 'Hard Yards and High Hopes: The Educational Challenges of African Refugee University Students in Australia', *International Journal of Teaching and Learning in Higher Education* 239(3): 186–96.

Hartley, L., S. Baker, C. Fleay, and R. Burke. 2019. '"My Study is the Purpose of Continuing My Life": The Experience of Accessing University for People Seeking Asylum in Australia', *Australian Universities' Review* 61(2): 4–13.

Hartley, L., C, Fleay, S. Baker, and R. Burke. 2018. *People Seeking Asylum in Australia: Access and Support in Higher Education*. Perth: National Centre for Student Equity in Higher Education (NCSEHE), Curtin University.

Hatoss, A., and H. Huijser. 2010. 'Gendered Barriers to Educational Opportunities: Resettlement of Sudanese Refugees in Australia', *Gender and Education* 22(2): 147–60.

Hirano, E. 2014. 'Refugees in First-Year College: Academic Writing Challenges and Resources', *Journal of Second Language Writing* 23: 37–52.

Ivanic, R. 1998. *Writing and Identity: The Discoursal Construction of Identity in Academic Writing*. Amsterdam: John Benjamins.

Jacobs, C. 2005. 'On Being an Insider on the Outside: New Spaces for Integrating Academic Literacies', *Teaching in Higher Education* 10(4): 475–87.

Kanno, Y., and M.M. Varghese. 2010. 'Immigrant and Refugee ESL Students' Challenges to Accessing Four-Year College Education: From Language Policy to Educational Policy', *Journal of Language, Identity, and Education* 9: 310–28.

Klinger, C.M., and N. Murray. 2012. 'Tensions in Higher Education: Widening Participation, Student Diversity and the Challenge of Academic Language/Literacy', *Widening Participation and Lifelong Learning* 14(1): 27–44.

Koramannil, G. 2016. 'Looking for the Invisible: The Case of EALD Indigenous Students in Higher Education', *Journal of Academic Language & Learning* 10(1): 87–100.

Lea, M., and B.V. Street. 1998. 'Student Writing in Higher Education: An Academic Literacies Approach', *Studies in Higher Education* 23(2): 157–72.

Lillis, T.M. 2001. *Student Writing: Access, Regulation, Desire*. London: Routledge.

Lillis, T., and M. Scott. 2007. 'Defining Academic Literacies Research: Issues of Epistemology, Ideology and Strategy', *Journal of Applied Linguistics* 4(1): 5–32.

Malcolm, I.G. 2018. *Australian Aboriginal English: Change and Continuity in an Adopted Language*. Boston: de Gruyter.

McSwan, J. 2017. 'A Multilingual Perspective on Translanguaging', *American Educational Research Journal* 54(1): 167–201.

McWilliams, R., and Q. Allan. 2014. 'Embedding Academic Literacy Skills: Towards a Best Practice Model', *Journal of University Teaching & Learning Practice* 11(3).

Mendenhall, M., and L. Bartlett. 2018. 'Academic and Extracurricular Support for Refugee Students in the US: Lessons Learned', *Theory into Practice* 57: 109–18.

Morrice, L. 2013. 'Refugees in Higher Education: Boundaries of Belonging and Recognition, Stigma, and Exclusion', *International Journal of Lifelong Education* 32(5): 652–68.

Morrice, L. 2018. 'Abyssal Lines and Cartographies of Exclusion in Migration and Education: Towards a Reimagining', *International Journal of Lifelong Education* 38(1): 20–33.

Naidoo, L. 2015. 'Educating Refugee-Background Students in Australian Schools and Universities', *Intercultural Education* 26(3): 210–17.

Naidoo, L., J. Wilkinson, K. Langat, M. Adoniou, R. Cuneen and D. Bolger. 2015. *Case Study Report: Supporting School-University Pathways for Refugee Students' Access and Participation in Tertiary Education*. Sydney: University of Western Sydney.

Nicholas, H., and A. Williams. 2003. 'Oracy Is More than the Absence of Literacy: Changing Learner Groups in ESL Classrooms in Highly Literate Societies', in G. Wigglesworth (ed.), *The Kaleidoscope of Adult Second Language Learning: Learner, Teacher and Researcher Perspectives*. Sydney: National Centre for English Language Teaching and Research, Macquarie University, pp. 29–52.

O'Rourke, D. 2011. 'Closing Pathways: Refugee-Background Students and Tertiary Education', *Kotuitui: New Zealand Journal of Social Sciences Online* 6(1–2): 26–36.

Percy, A. 2014. 'Re-integrating Academic Development and Academic Language and Learning: A Call to Reason', *Higher Education Research and Development* 33(6): 1194–207.

Rai, L., and T. Lillis. 2013. '"Getting It Write" in Social Work: Exploring the Value of Writing in Academia to Writing for Professional Practice', *Teaching in Higher Education* 18(4): 352–64.

Schleppegrell, M., and L. de Oliveira. 2006. 'An Integrated Language and Content Approach for History Teachers', *Journal of English for Academic Purposes* 5(4): 254–68.

Slack, K., J. Mangan, A. Hughes, and P. Davies. 2014. '"Hot", "Cold" and "Warm" Information and Higher Education Decision Making', *British Journal of Sociology of Education* 35(2): 204–23.

Sontag, K. 2018. 'Highly Skilled Asylum Seekers: Case Studies of Refugee Students at a Swiss University', *Migration Letters* 15(4): 533–44.

Turner, M., and F. Fozdar. 2010. 'Negotiating "Community" in Educational Settings: Adult South Sudanese Students in Australia', *Journal of Intercultural Studies* 31: 363–82.

Unsworth, L. 1999. 'Developing Critical Understanding of the Specialised Language of School Science and History Texts: A Functional Grammatical Perspective', *Journal of Adolescent and Adult Literacy* 42(7): 508–21.

Vásquez, C. 2007. 'Comments from the Classroom: A Case Study of a Generation-1.5 Student in a University IEP and beyond', *Canadian Modern Language Review* 63(3): 345–70.

Volante, L. 2008. 'Equity in Multicultural Student Assessment', *The Journal of Educational Thought (JET) / Revue De La Pensée Éducative* 42(1): 11–26.

Watkins, P.G., H. Razee, and J. Richters. 2012. '"I'm Telling You . . . The Language Barrier Is the Most, the Biggest Challenge": Barriers to Education among Karen Refugee Women in Australia', *Australian Journal of Education* 56(2): 126–41.

Wigglesworth, G., and J. Simpson. 2018. 'Going to School in a Different World', in G. Wigglesworth, J. Simpson and J. Vaughan (eds), *Language Practices of Indigenous Children and Youth*. Palgrave Studies in Minority Languages and Communities. London: Palgrave Macmillan.

Wilks, J., A. Dwyer, S. Wooltorton and J. Guenther. 2020. '"We Got a Different Way of Learning": A Message to the Sector from Aboriginal Students Living and Studying in Remote Communities', *Australian Universities' Review* 62(2): 25–38.

Wingate, U. 2006. 'Doing Away with "Study Skills"', *Teaching in Higher Education* 11(4): 457–69.

Wingate, U. 2018. 'Academic Literacy across the Curriculum: Towards a Collaborative Instructional Approach', *Language Teaching* 51(3): 349–64.

CHAPTER 15
Our Voice

KUTAIBA AL HUSSEIN AND AKILEO MANGENI

━━━◆◆◆

There is no doubt that education is an important element in human development and it should be accessible for everyone, and Europe is a place that on the surface offers equal access to higher education for students who are eligible and seeking to enhance their skills. However, there is a common practice among universities that tends to ignore the fact that refugees face different life challenges, such as coming from different educational backgrounds without any preparation to study abroad, cultural differences, emotional and psychological challenges and different languages of prior instruction, among others. This impacts the lives of refugees and how they integrate academically. Taking note of all these systemic disadvantages, universities should be considerate when addressing displaced students, and they should provide a safe space for refugees for their academic advancement.

Another important note when thinking of higher education is that the institutions of higher learning should take into consideration that some students cannot make contact with their former schools regarding their educational certificates, something that is greatly challenging for them when building their case during application processes. Therefore, higher education institutions should specifically consider refugee programme courses as well as creating or providing opportunities for eligible refugees willing to go back to school to enhance their careers and personal development.

This chapter will highlight the different life challenges and experiences that a number of refugees face in accessing higher education based on the authors' experiences in Hungary as refugees and former students of the Open Learning Initiative (OLIve), and further as students within Master's degrees in Public Administration and International Business Law at the Central European University (CEU). It will further shed light on the possible steps that could be taken to promote refugee access to higher education, such as understanding refugees' needs for higher education, financial obstacles and the role of universities as part of society in easing the social inclusion of refugees. However, we further believe that the challenges and issues included in this chapter are not exclusive to Hungary, but might apply to any other European country as well as Australia (see Wilson et al., this volume).

Why Focus on Higher Education and How Difficult Is It to Be Part of the Process?

Arriving in Europe (Hungary in this context) after enduring a horrific past and all the immigration procedures, our basic first step was to find a job and to make a living, just like anyone else. However, to find a decent job or a job that could pay enough to cover our living expenses was very hard, as we arrived in Budapest as persons with refugee status, with all the negative stereotypes associated with the migration crisis of 2015. Similarly, to be able to compete in the job market, we needed either appropriate skills and outstanding work experience or an educational equivalency to justify our eligibility. In so many cases, it has been very difficult for refugees to gain employment using college certificates acquired from their home countries, for reasons such as issues around credibility and document verification.

Faced with the tremendous sets of skills required in the labour market, in all honesty we were unable to adjust and fill in the gaps in our applications as refugees with no work experience in Europe, especially with the high demand for professional qualifications and high level of competition from other applicants. Going back to school was our only option to attain at least a certificate to increase our chances in the labour market. Studying at CEU gave us the opportunity to learn about recent events and gain basic information that helped us to enhance our knowledge and to draw a general picture of the system in Hungary and how it works. So, based on our own personal experiences, we believe that providing opportunities to access higher education is a core element in helping refugees to integrate into a new society and to give them the confidence and ability to compete in the labour market.

Being a refugee and 'uneducated' at the same time is quite challenging, as most receiving societies are more or less closed and unwilling to accept refugees in higher education systems. Even if a refugee has qualifications from their home country, these qualifications are not considered in most cases in the host countries due to reasons such as language of instruction, the grading system, duration of study programmes and so on. This makes it difficult for refugees to rely on their previous qualifications to continue their education trajectory.

Nevertheless, we made the decision to continue our studies. In the beginning, it was very difficult to know how to start searching for universities. Even non-governmental organisations could not help us, stating that it was impossible to find a scholarship in Hungary. We tried contacting some universities with questions as to whether there could be scholarship programmes available for refugees, but we received no responses other than application links, with no further information or comments.

Eventually, the Open Learning Initiative Program (OLIve-WP)[1] was introduced at Central European University, Budapest in 2016, offering weekend courses in academic subjects, English, advocacy and other training to refugees. After successful progress with the weekend programme in 2017, a more comprehensive and intensive University Preparatory Program (OLIve UP)[2] was launched, a programme basically tailored to prepare students with refugee status for MA programmes. Through OLIve-UP, we finally got scholarships and studied for our Master's degrees at the CEU.

Despite this, we had a tough experience with the administration process when applying to CEU. The application is tailored in a way that tries to be fair to all applicants. However, there was a lack of consideration for the needs of applicants like us who have refugee status and who, in most cases, are not financially or academically prepared for the application, and may not have their certificates at hand due to numerous circumstances back home. The application process was complicated, and the requirements were suited to applicants with a 'normal situation'; it was apparently not for us.

For instance, the application process can include requirements such as letters of recommendation from previous universities and proof of previous qualifications, but for safety reasons it is often impossible for refugees to communicate with their previous university. Similarly, many refugees fled their countries of origin without completing university programmes or without copies of their academic papers, and because of the uncertain communication with their previous professors and universities, obtaining copies of diplomas can be extremely difficult. The fees involved and the financial vulnerability of refugee students is another factor: there is often a lack of financial support to cover expenses such as the language exam, the application fee and translation expenses.

Our situation was made worse by the Hungarian government's decision to exclude refugees from applying for a Stipendium Hungaricum Scholarship,[3] a scholarship programme for foreign students that is funded by the Hungarian government and is considered to be the main platform for non-Hungarians to obtain scholarships at Hungarian universities.

We believe that Helen Keller (1903/2003: 10) perfectly described our situation at that time:

> Have you ever been at sea in a dense fog, when it seemed as if a tangible white darkness shut you in and the great ship, tense and anxious, groped her way toward the shore with plummet and sounding-line, and you waited with beating heart for something to happen? I was like that ship before my education began, only I was without a compass or sounding-line, and no way of knowing how near the harbor was. 'Light! Give me light!' was the wordless cry of my soul, and the light of love shone on me in that very hour.

The OLIve programme arrived at the right time in a desperate situation.

Key Takeaway

The first time we applied to the OLIve-WP, we did not have high expectations of the programme. It was new, and we never thought we would qualify for a chance at a scholarship. When the OLIve-UP introduced us to CEU, however, we felt we finally had a foot in the door to obtain a scholarship and complete our Master's at CEU, which we then successfully accomplished.

The OLIve programmes did not merely involve sitting in lecture rooms, reading articles or making notes, but provided us with a safe space in which to share ideas, comfort and confidence, other learning experiences and the ability to establish meaningful relationships with colleagues. From our perspective, we can tell you without doubt that higher education, besides its functions in information sharing, builds sustainable relationships within and outside the academic community and, more importantly, helps students to create better opportunities for their future and facilitates career building. It helped us start our new lives and become more accepted by the host society.

As well as the opportunity to step into a classroom again, the programmes offered us life-changing opportunities to build our professional careers and networks by interacting with many different professions and disciplines. From our personal point of view, the opportunities we gained from CEU changed our lives for the better in many different ways. For example, it opened opportunities to network through different career services offered by the university. Most people see refugees as a threat to them, their families and relatives, but with the CEU community we were like family. In some European societies where refugee candidates have the ability to go to school, such people are looked at differently. This notion that refugees are a threat to society generates undue emotional challenges which have negatively impacted our lives in Hungary. These challenges sometimes result from excessive pressure to integrate in order to prove that we pose no threat.

Apart from the positive aspects, the OLIve programmes also came with a number of problems. One issue was that the intensity of the workload during the OLIve-UP preparatory programme was not comprehensive enough to prepare us for the MA programmes. Upon entering our MA programmes, we faced workload-related challenges that made us feel completely unprepared, such as the large amount of reading we had to do, academic writing-related challenges and numerous assignments for which we never felt prepared.

It is also worth mentioning that the OLIve programmes' selection criteria and limited opportunities, coupled with limited financial support, have also been a key obstacle for refugees who are interested in entering the university. Similarly, it is also important to acknowledge that the scholarship programme was not part of the university application system, but a result of an informal arrangement between the OLIve programme and the provost. Nevertheless, we interacted with several students with refugee status who had different ambitions and career paths, who couldn't make it to the university due to limited scholarships or lack of availability of courses/programmes that interested them.

Many host countries lack education programmes for refugees provided by receiving governments as part of the integration process. Even student loans, which are managed in Hungary by Diákhitel,[4] were not an option for us because of the complicated process, high interest fee and the uncertainty that we would be able to pay back the loan. This excludes many refugees from education-related opportunities that could change their lives or even catalyse the integration process. In this case, institutions of higher learning should acknowledge the need for education if they wish to take action that can add meaning to someone's future. Similarly, despite the set standards for entry requirements, many refugees have faced difficulties that have limited their ability to complete BA programmes and some have lost their certificates before arriving in their host countries. Case-by-case assessments could allow many refugees to change their lives by joining universities.

Our Conclusion

In conclusion, we would like to raise our voice and say that universities should take the opportunity to do more than 'integrate' refugees into societies, regardless of government policies. We believe that our experience is a good example and real proof that universities can change the life trajectory of a significant number of refugees, who are in a similar situation to us but have not had the same chances. Although our path was bitter, we are now tasting the sweetness of its fruit, even in a country like Hungary, which is largely anti-refugee. We can now introduce ourselves as refugees with no hesitation, as we have decent jobs and adequate skills and knowledge that forces others to respect us. Thus, we have the courage to step forward and integrate into society in a comfortable way.

What we want to say here is that, first of all, higher education institutions must consider the establishment of a programme similar to OLIve-UP in order to assess and prepare potential students before entering universities. And also to facilitate the administration process for both students and universities, as this may mitigate the gaps between them and give potential students a chance to be considered in the context of their special situation.

Universities should also pay attention to the fact that they can play a significant role in helping refugees to integrate into society. On the other hand, acceptance of refugee students can also enhance the diversity of university environments by including students with distinct experiences, backgrounds and cultures. In regard to integration, universities can help challenge perceptions about refugees by treating people not merely as represented by their legal status, but rather as students who want to learn. Challenging such negative perceptions could, thus, help students build their confidence and develop various skills through various disciplines in order to address life challenges within different societies.

◆

Kutaiba Al Hussein is a legal and business advisor at an international law firm and a volunteer at Central European University's Open Learning initiative (OLIve-WP) in Budapest. He earned his Master's degree in Legal Studies from Central European University through OLIve University Preparatory Programme (OLIve-UP) as a refugee from Syria.

Akileo Mangeni has been part of the OLIve community since 2016. In 2019 he finished an MA in Public Administration at the School of Public Policy at Central European University, Budapest. Currently, he works as a finance consultant for the Food and Agriculture Organization of the United Nations. He is passionate about human rights and inclusion programmes for minority groups.

Notes

1. 'OLIve Weekend Program (OLIve-WP) | Central European University', https://www.ceu.edu/project/olive-weekend-program-olive-wp (accessed 30 June 2020). Also see https://www.refugeeeducationinitiatives.org/.
2. OLIve University Preparatory Program, Refugee Education Initiatives, https://www.refugeeeducationinitiatives.org/olive-up (accessed 9 May 2020).
3. https://stipendiumhungaricum.hu/uploads/2020/11/BA_MA_OTM_Call_for_Applications_2021_2022.pdf & https://stipendiumhungaricum.hu/apply/ (accessed 1 October 2021).
4. Diákhitel – Főoldal, https://www.diakhitel.hu/en (accessed 9 May 2020).

References

Keller, H. 1903/2003. *Story of My Life*. Project Gutenberg e-book produced by C. Rainfield.

CHAPTER 16

'Where Are the Refugees?'
The Paradox of Asylum in Everyday Institutional Life in the Modern Academy and the Space-Time Banalities of Exception

KOLAR APARNA, OLIVIER THOMAS KRAMSCH AND OUMAR KANDE

> Exiles stand outside the law and their fate thus depends exclusively on the disposition of the colonial rulers. We are therefore never troubled by the need to refer to laws or other general regulations. Justice . . . does not apply to us.
> —Sultan Sjahrir, *Out of Exile*, 1949

> The reflection to which we are subject is known by all: it is the phenomenon of clandestine immigration.
> —Oumar Kande, 2019[1]

Where are the refugees? A spectre is haunting (university life in) Europe: the refugee, the migrant, the exile. Cutting-edge object of contemporary desire in what has become a flourishing migration-research-industrial-complex, she is at once sought after for valuable 'experience', while her body is denied entry onto university premises for lack of legal papers. Yet the bodily absence of refugees at university generates its own crisis of legitimacy and authority. In our hyper-reflexive times, the strange presence-absence of the 'missing refugee' on conference panels and in scientific fora produces a *malaise* that is summed up by the ever-more insistent query: *'Where are the refugees?'* The 'where' in the question points to an underlying anxiety within the scholarly community as to the proper 'place' of refugees in the research process, and marks the fissure whereby refugees are both desired and denied entry at university. Additionally, the place of refugees, we aver, cannot be analytically separated from the 'time' of the university, one which evacuates 'different' bodies both at the very upper and lower tiers of the campus power structure, for different reasons, as shall be elaborated. By way of three short vignettes, we seek to illuminate the contradictory dynamics of this space-time fissure, while considering the practical as well as theoretical stakes involved in its reproduction.

In doing so, we adopt an assertively auto-ethnographic approach, each speaking from our experience as thinking, exilic subjects active in university reform movements and refugee-support in locations extending from Nijmegen/Kleve (The Netherlands/Germany) to Bolzano (Italy) to the fraught political moment the editors of this volume are experiencing in their struggle to maintain academic freedoms in an increasingly authoritarian Hungary (Cantat et al., this volume). Within the framework of an informal initiative co-founded by two of the authors under the rubric 'Asylum University', we have found ways to question, if not fully challenge, the political-economic inequalities shaping academic knowledge production at our university. These criteria are largely driven by friendships that are dedicated to formalising (through access to classroom, partial remuneration, co-authorship, co-teaching) and legitimising the work done by comrades outside academic status and contracts. A large part of the texts that make up this chapter was typed over WhatsApp, since the luxury of laptops and/or full-time contracts were not a condition available to all the authors.

However, in co-producing this narrative, we establish a continuum of affective solidarity between migrants and refugees, and precarious and marginalised university staff. Affective solidarity emerges from experiences of discomfort that serve as a productive basis from which to seek solidarity rather than solidarity based on assumptions of how the Other feels or from shared identity (Hemmings 2012). Although the experiences of precarious academic staff speak from a far more privileged vantage point (see Cook, this volume), each experiences the sharp end of exclusionary practices. It is perhaps from this perspective of evacuation and containment that throughout our narrative we are shadowed by the prison writings of Soetan Sjahrir – the first prime minister of Indonesia, but also an Indonesian student activist in the Netherlands, and key intellectual of mid-twentieth-century decolonisation (1949). Sjahrir's meditations on space, time, knowledge and struggle are apposite for our project of thinking the place of refugees and marginalised staff in the transformation of universities today because they speak uncannily to the reigning atmosphere of contemporary university life in Europe.

'Where Are the Refugees in Bolzano/Nijmegen?'

> It is not that I have the conviction that all this knowledge will be necessary in practice, but rather that I have an increasingly strong feeling that the world is presently governed by words. To me, all this fashionable glib wisdom that currently provides the keynote of power is only quasi knowledge and pseudo knowledge conscripted into the service of politics and propaganda. It is, moreover, not difficult to find in this new and modern wisdom platitudes and long outdated axioms. As an end result of mass production and of over standardization, the spiritual level of the facile slogan has been glorified to meet the needs of the new wisdom of emotionalism, of antirationalism, of fanatical irrationalism, and of conscious emphasis on race, blood, and state. (Sjahrir 1949: 12–13)

At a session with students training to become high school teachers in Bolzano, one of the authors, along with a colleague, has been invited to share our research processes of producing a public tool – an audio-guide – to have conversations on 'hospitality, citizenship and borders' in Bolzano. We share some processes of a collective condition of impotence, ones that are experienced unequally at different levels between the actors subjected to bureaucracies of asylum procedures. This is because not everyone involved in the asylum procedure is subjected to the same kinds of legal consequences of a negative decision (such as deportation under forced conditions for those 'seeking asylum'). For instance, the conversations we had with people involved in manufacturing the 'biography' of a potential 'asylum-seeker' (i.e. the biography-writer/volunteer, the person providing the story needing (asylum) citizenship papers, the lawyer and the person interviewing) and what such procedures *do* to one's sense of being human. However, when the floor was open for questions, the teacher leading the group asked, 'But, where are the refugees?'

This question is not new to us anymore, since it constantly seems to be a concern of people to *see* 'real' refugees whenever the topic of borders and asylum citizenship is discussed in the EU, especially after 2015. While it is legitimate to demand accountability and responsibility of research processes that talk *about* actors and often speak on behalf of actors who are themselves often absent, this question came from another place. A place that wanted to hear the stories of refugees from the 'horse's mouth'. My colleague and I were not 'real' refugees. While one of our main collaborators for the same project was a 'refugee' (legally), he was first and foremost a 'geographer' for us, and he was not present with us that day because of other engagements.

This, however, raises many important issues relevant for our discussion on 'opening up the university'. This question, 'Where are the refugees?', has been so besieging in our work over the last years that it has come to represent the paradoxes and hypocrisies of modern academic life in Western Europe. As an institution and as employees of a geography department in the Netherlands, we and our colleagues work on topics of borders, citizenship and migration, producing relations with students that are often involved in doing fieldwork with actors in the 'terrain of asylum'. This terrain inevitably involves students contacting asylum-seekers, volunteers, organisations active in refugee support and other policy-related organisations. The irony of relying on actors who are invisible to the state (and therefore also invisible in the eyes of the university) as passive members of knowledge production while actively being 'sought after' by students and researchers became evident in a conversation I (Kolar Aparna) recently had with a university officer responsible for student diversity and inclusion.

Among other tasks, this officer was appointed recently to initiate a programmed transition year (*schakeljaar*) for refugees. This '*schakeljaar*' is meant to allow people with a 'refugee background' (those already possessing legal documents) to study at bachelor level, provided they have some bridging skills. The said officer contacted me through a colleague to find out more about our informal initiative to enable access to courses for refugees. She told me that she would like to map the needs of the people, rather than depart from the projects conceived by volunteers for initiatives and reforms on refugee education at our university. She said that she senses a huge gap between the 'desires' of the volunteers[2] and the needs of people with 'refugee' status living in Nijmegen and around. I told her about my recent meeting with the coordinator of the night shelter[3] in Nijmegen who put forward the idea of submitting a proposal to facilitate specific forms of access to the main educational institutions in Nijmegen based on the needs of people waiting for their asylum documents, along with some other local organisations. She said that she was enthusiastic to meet him. However, I also noticed her hold her enthusiasm back immediately. She asked, 'But does the night shelter involve people "out of procedure"? This can be tricky because then I have to be accountable to people in the university who might find this problematic. This would be illegal. I would have to check what the implications are if we involve people who are "out of procedure"'. She and I got into a deeper discussion after she raised this concern. Is it appropriate for us as an institution to send students to conduct research in the night shelter or other local support organisations, constantly relying on the stories of the people living there to produce theses and articles and other forms of 'scientific production', and at the same time deny access to the same people contributing to this knowledge?

On the one hand, institutions such as universities are complicit in denying access to education and, therefore, to tools of representing their own stories to people whose stories are analysed and *about* whom much is written. And at the same time, the question of 'Where are the refugees?' continues to drive conversations on asylum citizenship in academic discussions, as revealed previously. This desire to see the Other at arm's length while operating within institutions that deny relations of knowledge production on an equal footing produces a partial inclusion (i.e. we want to see you and hear you as different and therefore cannot accept you as Us (those who study you)), what Edward Said has called 'Orientalism' – Orientalist exception, that is normalised in the everyday institutional life of the modern academy. Joining the broader call to acknowledge the 'Eurocentric epistemologies and pedagogies that ignore imperial colonial histories and patriarchal occlusions' in the modern, Western academy (see Cantat et al., this volume), in what follows, we delineate the contours of an alternative space-time future for university life that harbours the potential to break through the misery of the present.

What Time Is the University?

> I notice that I have unconsciously become accustomed to thinking as little as possible within a context of time. In fact, I sometimes have trouble in remembering whether a visitor has been here the same day or several weeks ago. This is due probably to the fact that so little has happened and that the various periods of time are so empty and void, as it were, that you can hardly distinguish between them. . . .
>
> I think furthermore that there is still another cause of this lack of realization or appreciation of time: the fact that my term of imprisonment has not been fixed. . . .
>
> . . . For me, time has a meaning only in so far as it tells me that I have now been in prison so long, or in connection with the few happenings, and consequently the less often they take place, the less notion I have of time. My interest is wholly fixed on what happened; that is, on the event itself.

> I have thus learned that time is tied to the thinking subject and is more or less dependent on him; and that it is merely a thought-form [*denk-vorm*], which has no existence apart from the thinker. . . . (Sjahrir 1949: 10–11)

> More interesting – in my focus – is the historical question: How does the spirit of the time have its own influence into the debates in universities about any political topic? (Jurgen Hasse, personal communication, November 2019)

The spatiality of the university today is mediated unevenly by temporality and historicity. Indeed, what 'time' is the contemporary Dutch university? As Sjahrir makes clear that time loses meaning in the context of his own confinement, for those labouring on the lower echelons of the university's institutional ladder, time is also differentially experienced depending on one's status, (im)permanence of contract and *taaklast* load ('assigned duties', a spreadsheet prominently showing which hours are assigned for various duties: teaching, thesis supervision, administrative duties, research). Each task is implicitly assigned a value, with a gradient moving upwards starting from the lowest esteemed, teaching – bachelor-level at the very bottom – up through MA-level courses, then on to higher and higher valued activities: research, and, ultimately, managerial coordination, preferably involving projects involving large sums of externally secured funding. Staff involved in lower-level functions are made to feel as if they are 'stuck' in time, merely involved in the department's core, reproductive, largely invisible functions. Not by accident, such staff are mostly junior, and female. On the other hand, staff working at the upper levels of the value chain are made to feel at the 'cutting edge' of departmental and faculty happenings. They are invited to 'high level' meetings with deans and vice-deans. In short, they are *seen*, and thus partake in the real 'historical' time of the university. Lower-level staff do not enter this rarefied temporal tier, but they are aware of it via the ghostly exchange of unseen higher echelons, whose emails they occasionally intercept via group-wide lists. Privilege and power are thereby attributed to those who are so busy they simply 'have no time'. Not by accident, such staff are largely senior, and male. This is the time of the relatively privileged faculty with permanent contracts.

Staff on part-time or short-term contracts feel time as fragmented, precarious, dependent on the will of others, in short, vulnerable. This is particularly experienced at the level of PhD students. Those considered as 'internal PhDs' are granted all the privileges of full staff, offered office space and opportunities to develop themselves professionally by acquiring valuable teaching experience. So-called 'external PhDs' – usually funded under the auspices of foreign ministries and governments – are not afforded such privileges. A large majority of such students often hail from 'the Global South', in our case mostly Indonesia and China. The 'time' of Indonesian and Chinese PhD students is that of impermanent migrancy, labouring in a class that is subaltern to that of their peers. Their 'visibility' is arbitrary, at the whim of a supervisor who may call them to account at any moment. Despite the fact that the border between being an 'internal' or 'external' PhD gets played out as simply what one gives value to rather than constituting a fixed hierarchy, it is precisely the invisibility of external PhD students that enables prejudices and stereotypes of 'intelligent versus subaltern bodies' to get mapped onto everyday interactions. 'I feel this border every day', says a colleague to one of the authors (Kolar Aparna) at the coffee corner.[4]

Monthly staff meetings constitute the spectacular 'event' during which both temporalities at university collide. A collision occurred during one such staff meeting when all the PhDs in our department organised a discussion with their supervisors to demand better working conditions.[5] During this meeting a number of issues came to the fore. Referring to the unwritten rules of supervisory relations and the ambiguities of what was expected of her while being overworked, a fellow PhD student from China confessed, 'I feel afraid'. It took considerable courage for her to make herself vulnerable in such a way, especially in front of members of the department present during this meeting. At the same time, this confrontation also exposed the less spoken about high-tension atmosphere of our work environment that is often suppressed because of the dominance of so-called informality at all levels of workspace interactions among staff. Another major concern raised was that migrant PhDs felt 'left on their own' in dealing with issues such as housing, as well as administrative barriers to moving to the Netherlands with family. This led to a defence by some staff in charge of supervising PhDs, who argued for separating supervision processes from other administrative functions. Such a response not only ignored the emotional labour of living in a foreign country (which may spill over to producing a PhD thesis), but also silenced the voices that had dared to speak for the first time in such a pan-departmental setting.

As we write, the racialised contexts of finding housing in Nijmegen and Bolzano (from where the authors speak and write) collide into each other as well. In Nijmegen, a fellow PhD from Mexico has been asked to leave his room on very short notice with the excuse that the owner needs the house for family reasons. Our colleague has heard this excuse before from previous landowners, while he has witnessed new Dutch-speaking tenants moving into the same houses from which he has been chased out. 'I think I will just move into one of our office rooms in the Faculty building if I don't find a place soon! How am I expected to work under these conditions?', he remarks, while working on reviewer comments for an article submission deadline.

This condition of a colleague connects to one of the authors leading a (non-white) refugee/asylum-seeker-led committee in Bolzano fighting for the rights (legal help, housing, work, education, among others) of both newly arriving asylum-seekers and long-staying migrant communities without Italian citizenship in Bolzano.

> Finding gold in Tambacounda (Senegal) is easier than finding a house for rent in Bolzano. Yet this city of one hundred thousand inhabitants is among the Italian cities that offer a better quality of life. The 'population' lives in good conditions. Foreigners are the people who suffer more for this lack of housing, especially those from sub-Saharan Africa. The difficulty is explained away by some homeowners as a lack of confidence and fear that 'There is no guarantee and we are afraid that our houses will be destroyed'. To have a house here, you need months or even years. The waiting time is very long. A lot of people live in unacceptable situations. There are plenty of people working on an indefinite contract and making quite decent money at the end of the month but they cannot find a rental. There are more than sixty people sleeping on the streets in the winter cold, and others in their cars. This number is only increasing. The mayor of Bolzano thinks he can solve this problem by building several houses. (Kande, diary notes, October 2019)

We argue that what is at stake is more than the physical availability of housing, and has a more deep-rooted basis in who is seen as deserving of living in Europe. If indeed, as Sjahrir suggests, time is but a 'thought-form' (*denk-vorm*), with 'no existence apart from the thinker' – hence conferring a fully embodied dimension to the experience of time – how can precarious and 'exilic' bodies and/or staff produce counter-temporalities that bring them more fully into the 'lived time' of the city/university? Better yet, how can a temporality be crafted that reconfigures the time of the city/university as we know it? Reconnecting to older, late twentieth-century debates in our field, we might hazard to say that what may be required is the production of a new kind of *space*, one which assertively foregrounds difference as a central axis of being-in-the-world (Soja 1989; Jameson 2005; Aparna et al. 2020).[6]

Rather than having the staff meeting 'event' around a conference table with pre-structured agenda marking a 'timeless time' of managerial 'efficiency', the semi-autonomous 'flash mob' tactics of a reading group devoted to postcolonial themes, operating from an on-campus bookstore lounge. In lieu of a fixed office space, a roving, nomadic *praxis* hovering just below the threshold of visibility, emerging in and out of classrooms, hallways, cafeterias, google-group lists, off-campus venues and WhatsApp chatrooms. When bodies do meet under these ephemeral conditions, 'face-time' takes on a nearly incandescent power, as one face, smiling at another says: 'I am here with you and not elsewhere'. This face-time takes on a whole other dimension in light of the current exilic conditions of the coronavirus pandemic during which we rework our text. We have just rounded off (in early March 2020) a Zoom-run classroom session connecting students in Nijmegen and Glasgow on the theme of 'encampment' under conditions of the university strikes in the UK and the coronavirus pandemic. Italy was at the time blocked and one of the authors who was supposed to travel to Nijmegen Zoomed-in from Bolzano. The rest of the authors facilitated discussions in Nijmegen with a colleague and an anti-deportation activist from Berlin/Istanbul/Lesvos. Precisely because of these mostly empty classroom sites of strikes and virus, the stories shared in the semi-virtual classroom produced an unprecedented intimacy in revealing the anxieties, fragilities, prejudices and hierarchical violence of our times. A condition in which being elsewhere became the norm without planning for it to be this way.

Moreover, rather than perceiving the act of writing as an act meant merely to fulfil a task load/*taaklast*, performed solely by academic staff, and as this chapter performatively reveals, writing for us emerges as a process of making space for forms of expressions and exchange that otherwise do not exist at university – a space for shared conversations beyond legal statuses of citizenship. For us, writing, then, is largely driven by shared existential conditions and spontaneous exchanges which in turn trigger questions otherwise impossible to be raised within the sanitised spaces of classrooms and research hotspots that follow from 'strategic' visions. Writing becomes a way of cutting through the hopelessness of asylum procedures. This is something one of the authors has been going through during the time of writing this chapter, and has moved from being in (legal) waiting to gaining (temporary, legal refuge). Additionally, the exclusionary temporalities of 'the city' can be questioned by claiming academic space, while claiming legitimacy for one's thinking body and thinking from one's gut (Jones

2006). At the same time, this allows for bringing the body fully back into discussions that are otherwise driven by assumptions of academic staff as mere 'floating brains'. This is the affective solidarity that is also built in the course of writing this piece, in which all the authors start from their experiences of discomfort and from there search for shared intellectual grounds.

Clandestinely Secreted Ink

> I have ... kept myself occupied with other things: with my family, with everything that I had to leave behind, and above all, and recently, with study. I can now see the whole field that I must still study, and it is very large. (Sjahrir 1949: 12)

Around 1960, Africa experienced a wave of decolonisation.[7] This era of independence led to a process of reconstruction for several independent African countries, accompanied by political, financial and economic instability, followed by an impoverishment of natural resources. All of these internal factors resulted in numerous young people leaving their regions of birth to gain a living and satisfy the needs of their parents by reaching the European continent, through the phenomenon called clandestine immigration.

And be aware that we cannot speak of this topic without addressing the factors lying at the origins of this phenomenon. Be aware that in the text that lies before you I (Oumar Kande) shall be in the position of bringing light to bear on all questions relating to immigration. For I am African. Yes! I come from West Africa. I take pride in this assertion of being African, for numerous are those Europeans, when speaking of Africa, who [only] think of poverty. And yet, Africa overflows with an enormity of natural and human resources.

But in our day, the greatest concern of the African continent is that it is emptying itself out of its youth due to wars, poverty and bad governance. Myriad are those young people who leave this continent in search of gain, so as to satisfy their needs and to acquire better living conditions. Indeed, in African society, when one does not find gainful employment or does not take part in pecuniary activities, one is often confronted with oppressions or even ridicule. This is what gives young people the propulsive desire to undertake journeys to reach what they believe to be El Dorado. [My] conversations with young migrants from the University of Bolzano (Free University of Bozen) are a perfect illustration thereof. In what follows I tell the story of a comrade who has successfully undertaken such a journey, and then go on to tell my own.

Let us start with the case of Michael Treasure, a student of economics and a refugee from Nigeria, born in 1992 in Lagos. She began her elementary school studies in her native city. But unfortunately, she was not able to complete her secondary school cycle due to problems of insecurity and persecution that forced her in 2015 to flee her country and find refuge in Italy. Thanks to the project 'Unitedbz', she could attend university two years after her arrival, an opportunity to continue her studies and realise her dreams. She found a job in a restaurant in order to pay her small bills, eat, buy books and documents. . . Despite the early challenges and difficulties with the Italian language, she has not abandoned her pursuits for one second. Today, she remains very optimistic on the chances of her success. Her dream is to become an expert in accounting.

I, Oumar Kande, arrived in Italy in March 2015. For a long time now, I have worked in an asylum reception centre. In 2017, I studied economics and management at the University of Bolzano. It was an opportunity for me to attend courses at this university. In my classes there were students of African origin and those from Europe. Some were nice and others not. But at any rate this experience has given me the opportunity to practise the Italian language and to learn German, which is useful in this region (South Tyrol).

And yet, I also must remember a racist episode experienced by an African student at the entrance of the university, where a security guard offended the young man by telling him to go out in the rain so that at least he could wash himself due to his bad odour. How sad this is! And now, the last message the ink of my pen will secrete: the world would be better off if Blacks and Whites agree to share the earth in harmony, cohesion and peace.

We Are Here

Homogenising practices in academia through exclusion – be it in the indirect signals within supervisory processes towards migrant PhDs or blatant racism against black bodies seen as 'smelly', and the increasing desire to quantify knowledge production – continue to dominate the affective space of the university today. However, the repulsive desire to undertake exilic journeys, the hidden sensorialities of informal face-to-face collective meetings of reading groups, the urgent need to claim intellectual thinking to overcome the dreadfulness of imposed 'wasted times' of the waiting part of asylum procedures, all have and are and will be producing their own novel space. Seen from such spaces, the present is always past-future (Cusicanqui 2012). The optimism-yet-sharpness of voices of those yet to gain access to university entangle contrastingly with the pessimism-yet-hopefulness of those working to actively transform the university. 'Where are the refugees?' *We are here.*

――――――――――◆――――――――――

Kolar Aparna is a mother of a four-year-old.

Olivier Thomas Kramsch is professor of geography and border studies within the Department of Human Geography, Radboud Universiteit, and a core member of the Nijmegen Centre for Border Research.

Oumar Kande is a cultural mediator and leading member of a self-represented refugee committee in Bolzano.

Notes

1. Original: La réflexion, à laquelle nous sommes soumis, est connue de tous : c'est le phénomène de l'immigration clandestine.
2. Volunteers who conceived this project as an outcome of the efforts that emerged spontaneously with the coming and disassembling of the largest refugee camp close to our campus recently (between September 2015 and April 2016).
3. The night shelter is reserved especially for people waiting for their asylum documents.
4. This quotation stems from the conversation of one of the authors with a doctoral student.
5. This collective action itself came as a response to the case of a fellow PhD who was abruptly informed that her contract would be terminated, in a manner that was under unsafe conditions in a public space where she fainted and did not have access to support of peers or friends. This action had implications for her residency in the Netherlands, given that she would be forced to return to her home country outside the EU against her will.
6. Sultan Sjahrir's prison meditations on 'time' and the 'event' may help to qualify in important ways the supposedly European origins of the so-called 'ontological distortion' at the heart of the late twentieth-century and early twenty-first-century 'spatial turn' in the social sciences, whereby temporal categories have been seen to predominate at the expense of spatial ones for much of the modern period (see Soja 1989). This calls for a much more global appreciation of the role intellectuals in the so-called peripheries of the modern world-system have played in the generation of cutting-edge socio-spatial theory than has until now been acknowledged, a project in which two of the authors are currently engaged.

7. Note: All text that follows in this section is translated by the authors from the original French.

References

Aparna, K., O. Kande, J. Schapendonk and O. Kramsch. 2020. '"Europe Is No Longer Europe": Montaging Borderlands of Help for a Radical Politics of Place', *Nordic Journal of Migration Research* 10(4): 10–25.

Cusicanqui, S.R. 2012. '*Ch'ixinakax utxiwa*: A Reflection on the Practices and Discourses of Decolonization', *South Atlantic Quarterly* 111(1): 95–109.

Harney, S. and F. Moten. 2013. 'The University and the Undercommons', in *The Undercommons: Fugitive Planning and Black Study*. Wivenhoe: Minor Compositions, pp. 22–43.

Hemmings, C. 2012. 'Affective Solidarity: Feminist Reflexivity and Political Transformation', *Feminist Theory* 13(2): 147–61.

Jameson, F. 2005. *Archaeologies of the Future: The Desire Called Utopia and Other Science Fictions*. London: Verso.

Jones, B.G. (ed.). 2006. *Decolonizing International Relations*. Rowman & Littlefield.

Sjahrir, S. 1949. *Out of Exile*. J. Day Company.

Soja, E.W. 1989. *Postmodern Geographies: The Reassertion of Space in Critical Social Theory*. London: Verso.

CHAPTER 17
The Importance of the Locality in Opening Universities to Refugee Students

ESTER GALLO, BARBARA POGGIO AND PAOLA BODIO

◆◆◆

Refugees in the Locality

This chapter highlights the importance of analysing the inclusion/exclusion of refugee students within the university in relation to the shifting socio-economic and political dynamics of the locality. It discusses how a focus on the territorial embeddedness of higher education communities contributes to our understanding of the internal and external borders of universities.

In recent years, the importance of the locality for immigration management is increasingly acknowledged within migration and multi-level governance (MLG) studies. Cities, in particular, are recognised as active agents in addressing the challenges related to diversity accommodation and in developing policies that can influence state-based models of governance (Hepburn and Zapata-Barrero 2014; Zapata-Barrero, Caponio and Scholten 2017). While nation-states remain central in policy-making processes (Caponio 2018), reception policies, legal recognition and cultural diversity management are partially devolved to sub-national levels (Adam and Torrekens 2015; Scholten and Penninx 2016). A focus on how different municipalities engage with migration and refugee flows holds relevance in order to overcome a dominant focus on global cities, and to delve into the 'specificities of localisation' (Glick-Schiller and Çağlar 2009: 196): it allows us to unravel the peculiarity of the history and present socio-cultural embeddedness of immigration in the local fabric of different cities. Recent work on urban migration policies and sanctuary cities shows how the locality is 'not inherently more inclusionary or progressive with respect to the nation state' (Garcia and Jørgensen 2019: 201). The tensions emerging from a phenomenon increasingly perceived as problematic among local polities can lead cities to enact restrictive and exclusionary policies (Ambrosini 2012; Gallo 2016; Gattinara 2016). Yet municipalities also need to counterbalance the state's orientation or inertia with local pragmatism and inclusiveness, by developing collaborations with the local civil society networks and non-governmental organisations (Bauder 2016; Hoekstra, Kohlbacher and Rauhunt 2018).

While MLG literature does not problematise the 'integration' paradigm overall, it questions the cohesion of the national 'whole' against which the incorporation of immigrants/refugees is usually measured (Schinkel 2018): it problematises the organicist representations of receiving states as integrated bodies, highlighting how inclusion becomes a contested subject between different territorial levels and social actors. Differential access to socio-economic and cultural capital emerges in local contexts of prolonged displacement, where inclusion largely remains a 'forbidden solution' (Long 2014: 476). While it is at local level that refugees try to negotiate possibilities, this process is often 'between and beneath the law' – with the locality becoming a space where refugees are 'trapped in a prolonged state of limbo' (Long 2014: 481; Fielden 2008). Overall, within migration studies, the role of the locality in the development of tertiary education policies for displaced people has received limited attention. Interesting insights come from pioneer work within higher education literature. The latter highlights, on the one hand, how refugee access to higher education (HE) in many European and North American contexts is fostered through strict collaboration between municipal/regional governments, universities and civil society organisations (Streitwieser et al. 2019; Baker et al. 2018; Ferede 2010). On the other, it also stresses how these initiatives have remained largely invisible within and beyond local higher education communities as well as the local society (Crea 2016).

Drawing from the programme 'Refugee and Asylum Seekers at the University' (RASU) at the University of Trento (north-eastern Italy), this chapter reflects on the importance of the locality in opening universities to students with a refugee background. The 'locality' refers here to the context of a particular historical and political relationship between the provincial government, the university and the city. A multi-level analysis of educational policies for refugees is beyond the scope of this contribution. However, it is important to look at receiving HE communities alongside the specific web of relations in which they are historically located, and at how their connections with the locality may influence regional and national policy orientations. Universities do not operate in a vacuum but have been integral to the history, socio-economic development and cultural outlook of local urban environments in many European contexts. This holds relevance for the analysis of the relationship between refugees and HE communities. The opening of universities to displaced students constitutes a process that goes beyond the physical and intangible borders of academic institutions to reflect their broader embeddedness. The RASU programme aimed to bring HE communities closer to refugees' lived realities, and to strengthen the collaboration between the university, the Autonomous Province of Trento (PAT) and local civil society. It faced challenges emerging from within the higher education communities as well as tensions with the provincial and national governments, illustrating the importance of analysing the opening and potential closure of universities to refugees not only in relation to changing academic culture but also to shifts in local and national politics.

The Italian Multi-Level Government System, Refugees and Higher Education

The Italian state includes fourteen regions, four 'special statute' regions, and the two autonomous provinces of Trento and Bolzano. Federal reforms (1971, 2001) devolved legislative and administrative powers, including on social policy matters, to sub-national governments.[1] On immigration, multi-level government alternates between devolved and centralist turns. Although the Italian state formally has exclusive jurisdiction over immigration,[2] issues of reception, legal recognition and 'public security' were transferred to sub-national levels throughout the 2000s up until 2017.

The 2002 National Asylum Program, subsequently renamed the 'Protection system for asylum seekers and refugees as well as for migrants with humanitarian status' (SPRAR), demonstrates the growing multi-level approach to refugee policies. SPRAR was originally subscribed to by the Interior Ministry, the United Nations High Commissioner for Refugees (UNHCR) and the National Association of Italian Municipalities, and by 2014 it also included the Regional Coordinating Groups on Asylum. It reflects a decentralised multi-level governance model: vertical coordination of the Interior Ministry and UNHCR is integrated with the horizontal activation of sub-national authorities in collaboration with local public institutions, NGOs and private actors (Giannetto, Ponzo and Roman 2019). However, particularly after the 2015 'refugee crisis', the system increasingly operated with an emergency approach and was often unable to ensure a balanced regional/municipal redistribution of asylum seekers (Kuschminder 2019).

The effects of the 2008 economic crash, the moral panic generated by the perceived 'mass influx' of refugees, and political concerns over the loss of electoral consensus combined to determine a more centralist turn in 2017. The Minister of the Interior in the centre-left Gentiloni government, Marco Minniti, promoted policies designed to increase repatriations, reduce inflows through agreements with origin/transit countries, centralise economic and administrative control of the Italian reception system, and prioritise international protection holders over asylum seekers in accessing SPRAR. The 2017 bid scheme harmonised SPRAR across regions but limited sub-national actors' involvement in decision-making (Giannetto, Ponzo and Roman 2019). Space for multi-level consultation was further diminished during the populist coalition government of the Five Star Movement (M5S) and the Lega Party in 2018, exemplified by Law 132/2018. This excluded 'humanitarian protection' holders from reception services, suppressed inclusion/support services for asylum seekers, and reduced refugees' income per capita from 35 euros to 19–26 euros.

To our knowledge, there are no previous studies on refugee inclusion in Italian HE, and statistics are currently unavailable. However, looking at different programmes as described on university and government websites,[3] it seems that since 2016 universities have initiated processes of 'opening' to refugees in response to two factors: first, the realisation that students with a refugee background were already present in the university, but had largely been invisible;[4] and second, the pressing expectations of both internal members and local polities in promoting more inclusive educational policies. Fostering collaboration with sub-national governments and SPRAR was key for universities entering into dialogue with refugees wishing to enter or resume higher education. With limited public investment in HE, private foundations and enterprises have been important in terms of establishing fellowships, while civil society associations have provided students with linguistic and psychological support. Since 2016, however, a national programme of 100 yearly fellowships has been launched by the Interior Ministry and the National Conference of Italian Rectors (CRUI). The recruitment basin varies considerably, ranging from the municipal to the national level (through the SPRAR network) and, more recently, to the international level by way of humanitarian corridors. The process of opening universities to refugees involves the locality in terms of both economic and organisational support as well as pedagogical initiatives. Overall, it is highly probable that local university initiatives for refugee students have inspired – and impacted on – national policy developments. At the same time, as we will show in the context of Trento, centralist turns may deeply affect the premises and feasibility of HE programmes for refugees gradually developed in sub-national territories.

The University of Trento: Between Autonomy and Dependence

The University of Trento is unexceptional with respect to the national trends outlined above. However, its location within an autonomous province and status as the only HE institution in the city offers insight into the limits and potentials of its embeddedness within the locality. In line with the national context, the university's spatial organisation reflects a 'diffuse campus' model (Di Lorenzo and Stefani 2015), and academic, cultural and social activities are considered part of the urban tradition. Established in 1962, it has increasingly attracted students from outside the province (around 56 per cent), although its recruitment basin remains relatively confined to the north-eastern regions. In 2019, it had 16,531 students, with 847 foreign citizens mainly from South Asia, Central Asia and West Africa.

The university is part of the Italian state university system but enjoys a special autonomy under Legislative Decree no. 142/2011, which followed the 2009/42 'Milano Agreement'. The latter assigned to the Autonomous Province of Trento (PAT) the responsibility for financial programming and funding of the multiyear strategic plan, which takes into account four macro-areas: course provision, research orientations, recruitment and career development, and knowledge transfer on the socio-economic situation (University of Trento 2012). The statute emphasises the importance of the university's role as an agentive partner of the local political and civil society, and its commitment to economic and socio-cultural development. While this change encouraged a synergistic collaboration between the university and the province, it also increased the former's (economic and political) dependence on the local government in marked contrast to other regional contexts.

The 2008 economic crisis has visibly affected access to HE in Italy. At national level, the European University Association notes a 9 per cent decrease in registered students between 2008 and 2017 (EUA 2018), whereas the National Institute of Statistics reports a 13.2 per cent fall in registration, particularly in the south (ISTAT 2019). This data reinforces a longstanding national trend. An average of 15 per cent of those aged between twenty-five and sixty-four hold a university degree in Italy, compared with 28 per cent in Europe. Between 2012 and 2017, Trento reportedly lost between two thousand and three thousand students, while registering a mild increase of 0.6 per cent in 2017 (ISPAT 2018) and maintaining an overall percentage of graduates slightly higher than the national average (22 per cent to 19 per cent). As in other Italian universities, access to the university is also regulated by an annual quota and entrance exam.

Opening the University to Refugees

In 2019, immigrants accounted for 8.8 per cent of the total population in Trento, with immigration flows having increased constantly since the 1980s. Trento joined the national protection system for asylum seekers and refugees in 2006, and since 2014 the province has agreed to accept 0.89 per cent of forced migrants in Italy. In 2019 there were around 1,600 asylum seekers, mostly from Central Africa and South Asia, with nearly 1,100 in the SPRAR system (CARITAS 2019). Although the numbers between 2015 and 2019 have remained low (relative to the national average), the presence of refugees was viewed locally as an emergency situation requiring intervention (Ambrosini, Boccagni and Piovesan 2016).

The 2016 Memorandum of Understanding between the University of Trento and the PAT initiated a four-year plan of refugee-oriented initiatives. Importantly, this responded not only to the commitment of internal members but also to the PAT's expectations towards the university in terms of its contribution to managing the perceived 'refugee crisis'. The Memorandum stressed the growing refugee quota assigned to the province by the 2014 State-Regions agreement. The 'relation of reciprocity' between the PAT and the university required the latter to run educational programmes aimed at valorising refugee skills, and to train the broader student community in migration-related issues in order to acquire necessary labour market entry skills.

The locality has been involved in two main ways. First, it provides the university with legal and organisational support through local associations and migration offices as well as information about possible difficulties or requests involving displaced students. Second, the university is committed to developing pedagogical initiatives raising awareness of forced migration beyond its traditional audiences by supporting students who undertake internships within the SPRAR system and local NGOs and associations. Pedagogical initiatives also arise from student association activities, such as the 'SuXr – University Students for Refugees' programme, an interdisciplinary evening course attended by students involved in local organisations.

Established as a pilot programme, 'Refugee and Asylum Seekers at the University' involves Year 5 students who, until 2018, could be both international protection holders and asylum seekers within the province's SPRAR system. RASU circumvented the national regulation that formally required students to obtain international protection status in order to register for a university degree, although students must still obtain this (or another form of residence permit) before their course ends in order to graduate. Orientation includes intensive Italian and IT classes, a course on the Italian migration/refugee system, subject-oriented classes and individual tutoring. An annual quota is reserved for students with a refugee background, subject to their passing an entry exam. Students have four attempts to pass the entry exam within one year or they have to leave the programme. The programme includes university tax exemption, free accommodation, a daily meals card, transport card and university sports card. Students may also work between 150 and 400 part-time hours (yearly) within the university.

Between 2016 and 2020, the programme involved nineteen students in total (fifteen men and four women) aged between twenty-one and thirty-four, with most coming from West African and South Asian states. Only seven students remained in the programme in 2020. Of these, two students hold refugee status, one subsidiary protection status and four humanitarian protection status. The high drop-out rate reflects several issues including economic precarity, difficulties in balancing study and family life, and institutional failures involving the provision of educational support.

Internal Challenges

The Memorandum of Understanding between the Trento Province and the university was implemented in a context of limited exchange between similar initiatives in Italy. Trento's experience was marked by a 'learning by doing' approach, with many predicaments affecting the actual openness of the university to refugees. We focus here on three interrelated aspects: the balance between humanitarian and academic approaches; difficult transitions from reception centres to the university community; and the tensions between 'special attention' and invisibility as experienced by refugee students.

Between Humanitarian and Academic Approaches

RASU faced the problem of balancing considerations of academic assessment with those relating to students' backgrounds. Oversimplifying access to the university for students with a refugee background, for instance, would have risked tensions within the broader student community, as well as scepticism – or paternalism – among teaching staff. This problem became clear in relation to the conditions students had to meet to remain in the programme. The yearly credit target proved to be too high, particularly in the STEM disciplines, where the tutoring support offered to close the gap between students' educational backgrounds and the departmental average was probably inadequate. The time constraints of the programme, combined with students' own academic anxieties, and uncertainties around their legal status, led to frequent drop-outs.

Internal regulations generated a higher drop-out rate among the first two student cohorts (2016–2018). This was partly because these students entered the university sooner after arriving in Italy, with lower language skills and limited knowledge of the university system. Further, institutional inexperience in dealing with the specific requirements of refugees affected the degree and quality of support provided. Although drop-outs persist in the more recent cohorts, these have benefited to some extent from the prior experiences and lessons at the individual and institutional level.

Transition from Reception Centres to the University Community

The move from the 'centre to the classes' is far from smooth. This was partly due to students' limited familiarity with Italian university culture, although some of them had experiences of higher education in the original and transit countries. Partly, entering the university transforms students' relationships with other refugees at the reception centre and produces uncertainty around their renewed identities. Some students reported that their decision to enrol for a degree was not always understood by their peers, who were more concerned with finding employment and supporting their families. They were not always encouraged by reception centre workers, who sometimes underlined that employment might be found more easily in domestic or care work. Nor did they always feel guided within the university. Students' insecurities in dealing with paperwork and training were increased by limited knowledge of the Memorandum within the university, inefficient communication between offices, or difficulties in identifying an appropriate tutor. Teachers' responses have also differed widely: while some empathised with students and actively supported their inclusion in departmental life, others remained relatively detached.

For refugee students, the move into university residences further increased the sense of uprooting and the difficulty of establishing new relationships. Rarely able to count on family support or other forms of income, they also faced additional economic pressures. While some found part-time jobs, economic reasons, alongside feelings of guilt for being 'unproductive', pushed some students to leave the programme.

Exceptionality and Invisibility

The visibility of refugee students as an exceptional category within the university community emerged as a key issue in our experience (on the issue of visibility, see also Aparna, Kramsch and Kande, this volume). While entering university often requires specific administrative, academic and psychological support (Ramsay and Baker 2019), we also need to consider refugee students' concerns regarding potentially paternalistic attitudes from their teachers and supervisors, and their wishes not to be evaluated on 'special' terms. Students often expressed the desire to hide their histories from peers and to establish relations free of charitable or suspicious attitudes. However, this combined with the equally widespread request for spaces within the community where they could feel at ease in communicating anxieties about their education and futures. This tension between the search for ordinary student life and the desire to share experiences of forced mobility requires the university to implement strategies aimed at transforming the overall image of refugees within the local community.

Opening in Times of Crisis

The Memorandum was implemented in a period of prolonged economic crisis, with declining university access mirroring wider growing inequalities. The initiatives locally developed by the PAT and the university triggered tensions with the state, as they were deemed to contravene specific national interests, and critiques of RASU have increased since 2016 at multiple government levels. Members of both the national parliament and the provincial government raised formal questions about the programme. It was argued that, in attending specifically to refugee-related issues, the university had failed to take into account other forms of marginalisation or disadvantage.[5]

These critiques called for the university to extend similar inclusion initiatives to other sections of the locality and the country more broadly.[6] With respect to the SuXr programme, for instance, the awarding of extracurricular credits to students who volunteered with refugees was questioned. The lack of similar programmes to support elderly or disabled people was highlighted, with the university accused of 'indifference to the increasing malaise and instability of the national society'.[7] The university's response to these criticisms stressed that both RASU and SuXr developed on the bases of international convention, its constitutional commitment, and its special status within the province. It also stressed that a system of scholarship traditionally supports disadvantaged students, with other extracurricular programmes existing to support disabled students.

Changes in national and provincial politics further highlighted the limits of a dependent relationship between the PAT and the university. Up until 2018, the centre-left coalition in the provincial government partially ensured the continuity and legitimacy of the RASU programme. However, the 'reciprocal relation' between the two parties changed after the radical-right Lega Party won national and provincial elections in March and October 2018. In the same year, the national Law 132 cancelled the humanitarian protection status, rendering it non-renewable and meaning it could not be converted into a study permit. While the effects for refugee students at national level are still unclear, University of Trento students holding humanitarian protection status can no longer be enrolled in RASU.

At provincial level, the impact of the immigration policies developed since 2018 overlaps with the end of the Memorandum in 2020. In the last eighteen months, CINFORMI and several reception structures have radically reduced or transformed their mandates. These changes raise concerns for the university around the sustainability of the projects and the continuation of collaborations, as the relationship with political and civil society is increasingly fraught. This demands the development of a more outward-looking approach from the university. In-depth dialogue and collaboration at inter-regional and national levels is needed in order to foster economic, organisational and pedagogical initiatives to sustain the programme in the long term. Currently, the university is exploring collaborations with UNHCR in order to reach out to refugee students in Italy or through international university corridors.

Conclusions: The Meanings of Openness

The locality is a context of waiting and agentiveness for refugees, where juridical and socio-economic uncertainties combine with aims of retrieving educational projects. Drawing from the recent experience of Trento, this chapter has discussed the meanings of 'opening up the university to refugees', taking into consideration the particular relationship between higher education (HE) communities, the provincial government and the city, and with regard to broader national orientations. The aim was to contribute to a bourgeoning literature on the local turn in migration/refugee studies – within and beyond an MLG perspective – by delving into the relatively little-studied dimension of the tertiary educational experiences and prospects of displaced people within the university community and the city. The present discussion cannot be generalised, and further analysis is certainly required in order to map the specificities and continuities of localising HE strategies for refugees across different cities, regions and in regard to shifting national policies. However, we can say that refugee policies in Italy, including those related to HE, have been open to the inclusion of sub-national actors and initiatives to a substantial degree. National fellowship schemes have been developed in parallel with – and partly influenced by – university programmes developed at sub-national levels. The Italian case thus seems to confirm wider trends in the key role of sub-national governments and local civil society networks in fostering university programmes for refugees (Streitwieser et al. 2019). Yet we must also note that consultations with lower government levels and non-public actors in Italy are not constitutionally binding, and ultimate decisions remain highly centralised in the hands of the national government and Interior Ministry. As such, national-level changes can deeply influence local initiatives and plans, enhancing and inhibiting sub-national programmes.

In Trento, the opening of the university to refugees was primarily a response to local transformations and perceptions. It reflected a distinct relationship between the university and the PAT, which called upon the university's commitment to provide services to the wider community. Several challenges have emerged from the relative 'novelty' of the initiatives and the difficulty of balancing approaches centred on the 'special' needs of refugee students with the need to meet the criteria of selection, competitiveness and performance that increasingly characterise academic culture in Italy. While the system values the swift completion of credits, this contradicts the complexities students face in transitioning from refugee situations to membership of an HE community – as the high drop-out rate illustrates. Internal regulations combine with economic problems and prolonged legal uncertainties to cause student outflows.

Other challenges result from a lack of cross-regional dialogue and national coordination (Ramsay and Baker 2019) on common challenges and good practices (see Di Stefano and Cassani, this volume). Without diminishing local initiatives' importance in responding to specific territorial concerns, the risk of a monadic approach to refugee students and higher education should be considered. So far there has been limited national political and academic debate about refugees' access to HE. Many universities tend to approach the presence of displaced students in the educational community and the city through a short-term 'everlasting emergency' approach, which side-lines the longer-term presence of students with refugee backgrounds in Italian universities and limits discussion of the pedagogical possibilities of a more inclusive university. The 'Manifesto for an Inclusive University' promoted by UNHCR-Italy (UNHCR 2019) is a first important step in this direction, although it is too early to predict its potential national and sub-national impacts.

Changing local and national political scenarios – partly induced by radical right parties' prolonged influence on migration politics, policies and discourses – contribute to further weakening the legitimacy of inclusive educational policies and the openness of universities to refugees and asylum seekers. Trento's experience shows how the relationship between the university and the provincial government, together with national political shifts, may easily translate into closure. It raises broader questions about the autonomy of the university, and demonstrates the need to implement national-level policies that can configure and sustain local initiatives in future. The language and content of national and provincial parliamentary interrogations outlined above oppose refugees to a more 'legitimate' community of university learners and beneficiaries. It creates a hierarchy between deserving national subjects and 'external' bodies deemed to be seizing educational opportunities from nationals. These critiques disregard the multi-level legal frameworks (local, national and international) requiring host societies to work towards refugee inclusion, as well as the initiatives developed by universities towards other disadvantaged groups.

At the same time, however, the challenges of widening educational access in a context where university study has traditionally been a privilege of the few, and where prolonged economic crisis has led, in turn, to public higher education cuts, cannot be easily dismissed (cf. Loher et al. 2019). Future implementation of expansive national policies in HE aimed, among other things, at 'opening' universities to traditional and newly marginalised groups would reduce the risks of making refugee students the scapegoats of a more general malaise. As such, future analyses of the meanings, outcomes and challenges related to 'opening up universities to refugees' will need to address the growing inequalities and marginalisation – across class, ethnicity, nationality, gender and religious differences – that characterise European universities and societies more broadly.

◆

Ester Gallo is Associate Professor in Anthropology at the Department of Sociology and Social Research, University of Trento. Her research interests cut across migration, religion, gender, colonial history and memory, forced migration and higher education. She is University Delegate for Academic and International Solidarity and the co-coordinator of the national network *Scholars at Risk – Italy*.

Barbara Poggio is Professor in Sociology at the Department of Sociology and Social Research, University of Trento. She is responsible for the University Programme of 'Equity and Diversity' which aims at monitoring gender, ethno-religious and class discrimination within the university and to develop more inclusive policies. Since 2016 she coordinates with Paola Bodio the project 'Asylum Seekers and Refugees in the University'. Her research interests include gender inequality, sociology of organisations and labour precarity.

Paola Bodio works as administrative staff in the Diversity Management Department of the University of Trento, which aims at the implementation of inclusive policies with respect to gender, class, racial and ethnic diversity. With Barbara Poggio, she coordinates the project 'Asylum Seekers and Refugees in the University'.

Notes

1. In Trento, issues otherwise devolved by the state to regional or municipal governments usually become competencies of the provincial government.
2. Title V, Art. 117, Comma 3 of the Italian Constitution.
3. For an overview from the Italian government website: http://www.integrazionemigranti.gov.it/Attualita/Approfondimenti/Pagine/Borse-di-studio-per-beneficiari-di-protezione-internazionale.aspx (accessed: 13 March 2020).
4. This crucial aspect addresses the ambivalent construction and categorisation of students as 'refugees', and requires further reflection.

5. Inquiry no. 047 made by senator De Bertoldi (FdI) on 16 October 2018 to the Ministry of Education, University and Research.
6. Inquiry made by provincial councillor Fugatti (Lega) to the Provincial Autonomous Province on 30 November 2016.
7. Inquiry no. 047 made by senator De Bertoldi (FdI) on 16 October 2018 to the Ministry of Education, University and Research.

References

Adam, I., and C. Torrekens. 2015 'Different Regional Approaches to Cultural Diversity', *Fédéralisme Régionalisme* 15: 1–18.

Ambrosini, M. 2012. '"We Are Against a Multi-Ethnic Society": Policies of Exclusion at the Urban Level in Italy', *Ethnic and Racial Studies* 36(19): 136–55.

Ambrosini, M., P. Boccagni and S. Piovesan. 2016. *L'immigrazione in Trentino - 2015*. Trento: CINFORMI.

Baker, S., S. Ramsay, E. Irwin and L. Miles. 2018. 'Hot, Cold and Warm Support', *Teaching in Higher Education* 23(1): 1–16.

Bauder, H. 2016. 'Sanctuary Cities: Policies and Practices in International Perspective', *International Migration* 55(2): 174–87.

Caponio, T. 2018. 'Immigrant Integration beyond National Policies?', *JEMS* 44(12): 2053–69.

CARITAS. 2019. *Migration Statistics Dossier – Italy*. Rome: IDOS Publications.

CINFORMI. 2019. *Statistics 2019*. https://www.cinformi.it/ (accessed 31 May 2020).

Crea, T.M. 2016. 'Refugee Higher Education: Contextual Challenges and Implications for Program Design, Delivery, and Accompaniment', *International Journal of Educational Development* 46: 12–22.

Di Lorenzo, P., and E. Stefani. 2015. *Università e città*. Rome: Fondazione CRUI.

EUA (European University Association). 2019. *Public Funding Observatory - Country Sheet*. https://eua.eu/101-projects/586-public-funding-observatory.html (accessed 25 May 2020).

Ferede, M.K. 2010. 'Structural Factors Associated with Higher Education Access for First Generation Refugees in Canada', *Refuge: Canada Journal on Refugees* 27(2): 79–88.

Fielden, A. 2008 'Local Integration: An Under-Reported Solution to Protracted Refugee Situations', UNHCR Working Paper no. 158 (New Issues in Refugee Research).

Gallo, E. 2016. 'Introduction', in E. Gallo (ed.), *Migration and Religion in Europe*. New York: Routledge, pp. 15–42.

Garcia, Ó., and M.B. Jørgensen. 2019. 'Solidarity Cities and Cosmopolitanism from Below: Barcelona as a Refugee City', *Social Inclusion* 7(29): 198–207.

Gattinara, P.T. 2016. *The Politics of Migration in Italy*. London: Routledge.

Giannetto, L., I. Ponzo and E. Roman. 2019. 'National Report on the Governance of the Asylum Reception System in Italy', CEASEVAL RESEARCH Paper no. 21. http://ceaseval.eu/publications/WP3_Italy.pdf.

Glick-Schiller, N., and A. Çağlar. 2009. 'Towards a Comparative Theory of Locality in Migration Studies: Migrant Incorporation and City Scale', *Journal of Ethnic and Migration Studies* 35(29): 177–202.

Hepburn, E., and R. Zapata-Barrero. 2014. 'Immigration Policies in Multi-Level States', in E. Hepburn and R. Zapata-Barrero (eds), *The Politics of Immigration in Multi-Level States*. New York: Palgrave MacMillan, pp. 3–17.

Hoekstra, M., J. Kohlbacher and D. Rauhunt. 2018. 'Migration Governance in Three European Cities: New Local Paradigm?', in T. Lacroix and A. Desille (eds), *International Migration and Local Governance: A Global Perspective*. Basingstoke: Palgrave MacMillan, pp. 17–37.

Kuschminder, K. 2019. 'The Multi-Level Governance of Asylum in Italy', *Journal of Refugee Studies*. https://academic.oup.com/jrs/advance-article-abstract/doi/10.1093/jrs/fey074/5316011.

ISPAT (Trento Autonomous Province Annual Statistics). 2018. 'Report 2018'. Trento: PAT Publication. http://www.statweb.provincia.tn.it/.

ISTAT (Italian National Institute of Statistics). '2019 Annual Report'. https://www.istat.it/it/archivio/230897.

Loher, D., S. Strasser, D. Monterescu, E. Dabağci, E. Gallo, et al. 2019. 'On Politics and Precarity in the Academia' – Forum, *Social Anthropology* 27 (S2, December): 97–117.

Long, K. 2014. 'Rethinking Durable Solutions', in E. Fiddian-Qasmiyeh, G. Loescher and N. Sigona (eds), *The Oxford Handbook of Refugee and Forced Migration Studies*. Oxford: Oxford University Press, pp. 475–87.

Ramsay, G., and S. Baker. 2019. 'Higher Education and Students from Refugee Backgrounds', *Refugee Survey Quarterly* 38: 55–82.

Schinkel, W. 2018. 'Against "Immigrant Integration"', *Comparative Migration Studies* 6(31). https://doi.org/10.1186/s40878-018-0095-1.

Scholten P., and R. Penninx. 2016. 'The Multilevel Governance of Migration and Integration', in B. Garcés-Mascareñas and R. Penninx (eds), *Integration Processes and Policies in Europe*. Springer: Cham.

Streitwieser, B., B. Loo, M. Ohorodnik and J. Jeong. 2019. 'Access for Refugees into Higher Education', *Journal of Studies in International Education* 23(4): 473–96.

UNHCR. 2019. 'Manifesto dell 'Università Inclusiva' (Manifesto for an Inclusive University). https://www.unhcr.it/wp-content/uploads/2019/11/Manifesto-dellUniversita-inclusiva_UNHCR.pdf.

University of Trento. 2012. Statute. https://www.unitn.it/norme-regolamenti/186/lo-statuto.

Zapata-Barrero, R., T. Caponio and P. Scholten. 2017. 'Theorizing the "Local Turn" in a Multi-Level Governance Framework of Analysis', *International Review of Administrative Science* 83(2): 241–46.

CHAPTER 18
Strategies against Everyday Bordering in Universities
The Open Learning Initiatives

AURA LOUNASMAA, ERICA MASSERANO, MICHELLE HAREWOOD AND JESSICA ODDY

―――――――――――――――――――――――――――――◆◆◆

In 2012, as Home Secretary of the UK, Theresa May announced her plan to create 'a hostile environment' in the UK in order to deter further migration and encourage voluntary departures (Kirkup 2012). The consequences of this have been far-reaching and involved a shift in responsibility to institutions, including universities, to check and report on the immigration status of people affiliated with them. Yuval-Davis, Wemyss and Cassidy (2017, 2019) call the effects of these latter policies 'everyday bordering'. In some cases, this leads to discriminating against anyone who may be deemed a 'risk' – anyone who may look or sound 'foreign' (Nava 2015). These policies of everyday bordering also create further barriers for forced migrants to access higher education.

This chapter will discuss the way in which processes of bordering are imported into the space of the university in the United Kingdom, how this affects displaced students, and how these processes may be resisted and challenged (for a breakdown of the history and structure of the neoliberal and neocolonial university in the UK, see Ivancheva, this volume). We discuss these issues in reference to the Open Learning Initiative, a pre-sessional programme for forced migrant students, offered by the University of East London, Central European University, Bard College Berlin, the University of Vienna and the Aristotle University of Thessaloniki since 2017. It will also argue that political positioning is necessary and inevitable in projects such as this, even if the main focus is on education.

UK Higher Education and the 'Hostile Environment'

Migration of all types, including forced, has always been a deep, integral part of European culture and society. A total of 0.6 per cent of current UK citizens, or an estimated 361,000 people, were once refugees. While a third of them have lived in the UK for fifteen years or more, there are also many newer arrivals. At least 35,099 people submitted an application for asylum to the UK Home Office in 2020 (UK Government 2020). Fifty per cent of asylum seekers wait more than six months, and many for several years, for the initial decision about their legal status to be granted, during which time they are prevented from working (Bulman 2019). Starting or continuing university education during this time of limbo is an attractive option for many, but one that comes with multiple barriers.

Asylum seekers usually have the right to study, but there are different temporary humanitarian protection visas providing limited or no access to public funds, which means that those who have received asylum may still be effectively prevented from accessing education (Article 26 Network and Coram Children's Legal Centre 2016). Those who have been granted temporary protection statuses usually only have the right to study for the duration of their temporary leave, which may not cover the duration of their studies. Asylum seekers are often charged international fees and have no access to public funds to cover these. Some universities have opted to charge them Home Fees, which are significantly lower, but still out of reach for most asylum seekers. Only those who have been granted refugee leave to remain have the right to study and access to public funds, including student finance. Even if on paper the support appears to be there, it isn't always the case. While seventy-five universities in the UK are providing scholarships for asylum seekers and refugees, due to poor planning and lack of understanding of the barriers forced migrants face in accessing universities, a proportion of these scholarships remain vacant every year (Murray 2017).

Those asylum seekers and refugees who do succeed in accessing universities often struggle to understand the requirements of the system and are faced with the structural racism and inequalities endemic in the hierarchical education sector (Ivancheva, Lynch and Keating 2019). A student with an asylum seeker background states:

> Although some opportunities are available (including generous scholarships for asylum seekers), information about services, funding opportunities, policies and practices regarding higher education is difficult to access. Some of us have been offered places in universities

and invited to come and enrol, only to be told on arrival that we cannot start as our status does not permit access to student finance. (Lounasmaa and Esenowo, with OLIve students 2019: 42)

Those who succeed are seen as extraordinary individuals, who persevere and succeed due to individual talents. The 'ordinary' refugee has no chance of success in a system so severely stacked against them.

In addition to lack of clarity around the right to study, lack of access to funding and structurally high tuition fees, other barriers for entry experienced by forced migrant students are lack of information about opportunities; language requirements, often to be proven exclusively through expensive certificates such as International English Language Testing System (IELTS); hostile culture and environment in HE institutions; lack of recognition of previous learning; lack of support for meeting application requirements and to develop necessary skills; lack of psychosocial support for those dealing with trauma and more (Lounasmaa and Esenowo, with OLIve students 2019). Some of these barriers are unique to their situation as refugees and asylum seekers, while others are shared with other populations in the UK.

Some of the barriers that are unique to legal status are a direct result of implementation by Theresa May as Home Secretary of her 'hostile environment' policies from 2012 onwards. Deportation was made easier to carry out before appeals were heard (UK Parliament 2013); vans with anti-immigration messages drove the streets (UK Home Office 2013); checks on thousands of elderly former migrants, especially from Caribbean countries, resulted in Commonwealth citizens who had spent their lives in the UK being deported, in many cases illegally (Agerholm 2018). Moreover, this period saw the implementation of the Immigration Acts of 2014 and 2016 (UK Home Office) which have shifted the responsibility for checking immigration status to landlords, healthcare professionals, employers and educational institutions. Moreover, universities have become border institutions. They are required to check the eligibility of each student to study in the UK throughout their programmes, and face fines and risk losing their licence to support international students' visa applications in the future if found in breach of the current policies. In 2012, London Metropolitan University received a ban on sponsoring international student visas for failing to comply with immigration policies (Meikle 2012). While asylum seekers do not require study visas and hence do not fall into this category, a failed asylum claim or a study ban once a student has already enrolled could put a university at risk of non-compliance.

In 2017, the Home Office began issuing study bans as part of the bail conditions for asylum seekers without providing adequate rationale and guidelines. Many individuals have been able to challenge these conditions, but this requires a legal inquiry and the assistance of an immigration lawyer. While all universities have compliance teams to manage student visa issues, not all have expertise in forced migration, and hence many forced migrant students are turned away from universities even after they have managed to secure a place on a programme. Some seventy-five universities now offer scholarships for asylum seeker students,[1] but the same universities may struggle to support the scholarship holders when it comes to defending their right to study. The hostile environment and how it transcends university is reflected upon by another OLIve student:

> ever-changing policies make it even harder to know our rights regarding education and mean that many educational institutions are reluctant to support us. In 2017 some of us were banned from studying by a randomly applied immigration bail condition. Although the decisions were later overturned, this took several months, further increasing the gap since we last studied and further damaging our confidence. (Lounasmaa and Esenowo, with OLIve students 2019: 42)

Borders, Bordering and Barriers

Yuval-Davis, Wemyss and Cassidy (2017, 2019) define the effects of these policies as 'everyday bordering'. They argue that the policies have shifted state borders away from airports and ports to citizens' private lives, workplaces and service-providing institutions. Instead of trained immigration officers, private landlords, school administrators, hospital receptionists and employers are now charged with understanding and applying immigration legislation. Misinterpreting or wrongly applying current legislation can incur personal fines of up to £10,000 or loss of an institutional licence to operate. Those without access to legal expertise often err on the side of caution and refuse to serve or recruit anyone whose status they are in doubt of. This distinguishes the UK from other countries such as Italy where students from a refugee and asylum seeker background may access higher education through unofficial channels and be already more present within it, though invisibilised (see Gallo et al., this volume). In some cases, this leads to discrimination against anyone who may be deemed a risk – anyone who may look or sound 'foreign' (Nava 2015). Together, these practices form a 'performance of borders', which means that 'borders are invoked and materially enforced in new ways' (Gilmartin, Wood and O'Callaghan 2018: 11). Of course, these performances and policies affect migrants differently based on ethnicity, gender, religion and class (Yuval-Davis 2011). This is also true in UK universities, which are effectively weaponised for purposes of border control (Candappa 2019).

These barriers, related to the legal immigration status of individuals, do not exist independently of Britain's colonial history and the racial politics that stem from it, and hence, as El-Enany states, 'cannot be corrected through the doling out of legal status to a select few' (2020: 222). When we look at the British educational system, it is impossible to separate it from its imperialist past and the continued shadows it casts. Many early funders of UK universities were implicated in the slave trade and supported apartheid policies. Students and staff in UK universities have been campaigning for removal of such emblems from campuses for several years, with the most notable example being Oxford University's refusal to remove a statue of Cecil Rhodes despite the global reach of the Rhodes Must Fall campaign, which began in Cape Town in 2015. The statue was finally removed in 2020 and Oriel College, where it was placed, has called a further inquiry into how to support Black and minority ethnic students and staff (Mohdin, Adams and Quinn 2020).

Another aspect relevant to the barriers that forced migrants face in higher education is their perceived ethnicity. The most common nationalities of asylum seekers in the UK are of Middle Eastern and African states (Walsh 2019), meaning they are more often than not people of colour. Black and minority students are proven to be at a disadvantage in the UK educational system. This culminates in the UK's 25.3 per cent degree attainment gap, meaning that upon completing a degree, 25.3 per cent more white students than Black and minority ethnic students are awarded the two higher grades; many jobs require those grades for entry (Advance HE n.d.). Reasons for this gap range from straight racism and bias to educational approaches being too homogenous to lack of acknowledgement and encouragement (Stevenson 2018). Unsurprisingly, then, professors who are Black or minority ethnic are 0.6 per cent of the total, with only twenty-five Black British female professors in the whole of the UK (Advanced HE 2017). Attainment gaps start at primary school levels and increase at secondary and tertiary level education, placing Black and minority ethnic students at a disadvantage (Smith 2017; Strand 2011). Research and praxis have centred on supporting access to primary and secondary education (Skjerven and Chao Jr. 2018). While ensuring all children have access to this is vital, it has meant that those wishing to advance to university level studies are often left behind.

In short, Black and minority ethnic students, even when they are not asylum seekers, begin their educational journey in a system which has a history of racism, continue it in an environment which at best does not cater to them and at worst is directly against them, and when they complete their degrees, they do not stay in it. Since they are Black and minority ethnic, it is reasonable to think that the same biases and barriers are experienced by the majority of asylum seekers as well, and if anything, are compounded by stereotypes related to their legal status.

Finally, UK universities and their relationship with students, staff and applicants cannot be separated from the intense marketisation the sector has undergone in the last twenty years, as discussed by Ivancheva in this volume. Since the introduction of student fees in 1998, students have increasingly been treated as paying customers and education as a marketable product. Priority in recruitment is given to fee-paying students. University rankings, or 'prestige' as Cook calls it (in this volume), measure graduate employability and other metrics, where white, middle-class students are likely to perform well due to their existing social and cultural capital, hence making them more attractive applicants for universities. Barriers such as high tuition fees also affect access to universities for many UK working-class applicants and applicants who have grown up in social care. To alleviate this widening access gap, initiatives such as Widening Participation have been introduced in a bid to increase support for applicants and students who do not fit this profile, but often these initiatives are harnessed for further marketing purposes rather than designed with long-term change in mind (Lounasmaa 2020). This neoliberalisation of the sector, together with the systemic racism discussed above, creates the myriad barriers displaced students face in accessing university education.

Evidently, even after accessing higher education, forced migrant students, Black and minority ethnic students and working-class students (which may or may not be one and the same) face ongoing discrimination and lack of adequate support to successfully navigate the university system. It is in this context that the Open Learning Initiative (OLIve) at the University of East London, a study programme targeted at forced migrants who wish to enter or re-enter higher education, was born and operates.

Refugee Education Initiatives and Open Learning Initiatives

The University of East London (UEL) is a former polytechnic which gained university status in 1992. In the UK, such universities are known as 'post-1992' or 'new' universities, in opposition to older, more established institutions. Approximately 70 per cent of UEL students are from ethnic minorities; more than 40 per cent of UEL students are from poorer socio-economic backgrounds, and many are the first in their family to go to university (University of East London 2020). All UEL campuses are in the borough of Newham, which has the highest incidence of poverty in London as well as very high rates of child poverty, homelessness and low pay (Trust for London 2020). The university has also been caught in disputes about how it deals with its links to colonialism and the slave trade, as the statue of John Cass, a key culprit in the establishment of the Atlantic slave trade, was only removed from UEL's Cass School of Education and Communities building in May 2020 after the Black Lives Matter protests questioned his legacy as a philanthropist. More recently, the university has moved to make a number of social sciences professors, including trade union activists and one of Britain's leading Black professors working on the intersections of race and capitalism, Gargi Bhattacharyya, redundant. UEL is therefore a prime example of an educational institution where students from forced migrant backgrounds and home students will be facing intersectionally linked challenges.

UEL has been home to Refugee Studies programmes since 1998. The programmes have always employed a refugee-centred approach, working in close collaboration with practitioner and policy organisations. Consequently, in 2015 UEL started teaching a short university course in the Calais 'Jungle', the largest unofficial refugee camp in Northern France. The course, Life Stories, was loosely based in social sciences, with a learner-centred focus. Learners compared their own life stories and personal experiences to those of public figures such as Malala Yousafzai, Nelson Mandela, Malcolm X and others. This supported them in making sense of the political, social, psychosocial and cultural context in which they now found themselves (Squire and Zaman 2020).

In 2016, a team of academics at the Central European University (CEU) in Budapest, Hungary, put together a proposal to start education programmes for displaced students across Europe, called Open Learning Initiative (OLIve). These programmes recognised the role of quality education in protecting refugees and promote sustainable solutions to the challenges they face in their adopted environments (UNHCR 2015). Hence, in response to the rising number of refugees arriving in Europe at the time, it aimed to extend access to university education. This would be achieved through offering pre-sessional courses to refugee learners aspiring to study in Budapest, Vienna and London in 2016–18 and Vienna, London, Berlin, Budapest and Thessaloniki in 2018–20. Many universities in Europe extended their offers at the same time; the University of Lille offered forty fully funded places for refugee students who were made homeless when the 'Jungle' refugee camp in Calais was dismantled; the Article 26 scholarship network offered funding for asylum seeker students across the UK; numerous universities began offering language tuition through voluntary student schemes, summer schools and extending existing student services to refugee learners. However, it is worth noting that these universities' responses also coincided with a rise in right-wing political discourse, tougher immigration control and new bordering regimes throughout Europe (Inglehart and Norris 2016).

The main purpose of the programme is to foster social and economic inclusion of refugees and their integration into higher education through responding to existing barriers. Entry into higher education is achieved through assessing and validating previous learning and promoting inclusive learning practices. Additionally, the project aims at providing refugees with tools for durable social integration. This is facilitated through language learning, advocacy training and creative pedagogies which aim to build learners' confidence. A further objective is to disseminate and scale up good practice beyond the immediate consortium.

UEL started their own OLIve programme in 2017. As discussed previously, in the UK those with refugee status have the right to study and to access student loans. The rate of refugees accessing higher education is believed to remain low, but as refugees are identified in the systems as Home (UK) students, the number of refugees in universities is difficult to ascertain (Stevenson and Baker 2018). Those with refugee status may still struggle to access relevant information about the higher education system. They may also lack vital skills and knowledge required to choose programmes and institutions, apply and succeed in their studies. While waiting for a decision on their legal status, most asylum seekers have the right to study and, based on our experience working with OLIve students and applicants, many seek opportunities to gain different skills during the waiting period. However, they can only rely on scarce scholarship programmes that offer payment of the high international tuition fees most universities charge asylum seekers, and possibly a maintenance grant. Because of this, UEL included students at various stages of their asylum applications in the OLIve Weekend Programme, one of the aims of which is to point students towards scholarship schemes and assist with applications.

UEL offers foundation programmes in many subject areas; the OLIve UP programme was designed to be linked to a specific one. Instead of designing a separate programme, refugee learners were given tuition fee waivers to attend alongside other students who required an intensive foundation course: school leavers, care leavers, international students, mature students, students with additional learning needs and those who have struggled in previous educational institutions. This was a cost-effective way to deliver the programme and has also been found to offer supportive and suitable skills training and immersion into UK academic culture. One of the students noted while on the programme: 'This is the only place where I don't feel like an asylum seeker'.

UEL OLIve has two intakes a year. Each cohort differs from the next, with individual experiences and differing group dynamics. It is important to be able to respond to these differences in an effective way. Thus, the learning experience is reliant on the quality of the team, their experience and attitudes (Musa and Kurawa 2018). However, it also relies on the production of a reciprocal relationship, one in which the voice of the learner is promoted and utilised (Freire 1970). In this way, the programme becomes flexible but robust, and is able to adapt to the needs of each group. Within this framework, evaluations provide part of the required communication. Feedback is therefore solicited throughout the course in an attempt to respond to needs in real time. Although individual experiences are varied, learners highlight common themes regarding challenges in accessing their required level of education. OLIve students have cited issues with various agencies whose role it is to support them. Concerns include receiving misinformation or a lack of information and support, leading to despondency and self-doubt. Students consistently question whether the immigration system is set up to 'waste time' or 'hold us back in our education'.

This was discussed during a conference planning meeting with three students of the Winter 2020 OLIve Weekend Programme: Pearlgin Lindiwe Goba, Landiswa Jessica Phantsi and Fridoon Pouyaa. The students were part of the OLIve conference group and had all expressed interest in presenting their own words in academic and non-academic contexts, instead of having their words presented by others. Goba commented: 'I come from an English-speaking country. Why do I have to start by doing entry level English, functional skills? I'm sure they do that just so that you waste time and then give up'. Moreover, she had experienced that 'whenever I say I want to do a degree in prosthetics I am asked why and told I won't be able to do that'. Phantsi explains: 'We are always being told to do health and social care like that is all they think we are capable of doing. Several women I know keep being told to do this. Whereas many have simply said "I gave up"'. In this way, the 2019–20 cohort likened accessing higher education to 'a game of snakes and ladders', with a feeling of going in a cycle back to where they started. They highlight the impact of this on their self-esteem and mental health. According to them, they live in limbo and a state of contradiction. They express wishes to contribute to their own independence and the society in which they now find themselves. However, they feel blocked from doing so and in turn feel stereotyped as being lazy freeloaders, even to the point of asking: 'Why do they hate us so much? What have we done?' (For an analysis of exclusion in education from the perspective of learners from a refugee background, see Jasani et al., this volume).

The role of the project therefore becomes to empower, protect and encourage students (UNHCR 2020). The meeting itself came after these students presented their creative work at a UEL conference on borders, and was meant to discuss their participation in a Refugee Education Initiatives (REIs) conference in Budapest where they would present on refugee education, which would have been long-distance due to the movement restrictions they are subject to and ultimately was postponed due to COVID-19. These instances both addressed the question of including OLIve students into the wider context of the university, and showed some of the barriers they encountered. Thus, OLIve also becomes a response to bordering practices and a way of developing methodologies which adapt to and challenge existing limitations. The only way to provide real access to the 'ordinary' refugees to access universities at anywhere near the national average level of those achieving higher education is to reconsider universities and the higher education sector itself.

Politics of Education

There are multiple human rights arguments to support better access to higher education for refugees (United Nations 1948, art. 26; Stevenson and Baker 2018). There are also clear economic arguments, and arguments based on the Sustainable Development Goals (SDGs), to support access to higher education for refugees (UNHCR 2016). Yet a project such as OLIve cannot remain outside of the current political events and discourses. Further thinking is required regarding the type of education needed to equip learners to survive this new climate and ultimately to thrive.

The University of East London's work in the Calais 'Jungle', teaching a university course and enrolling students from an unofficial refugee camp outside of Britain, doubled as an act of political defiance in the face of the hostile environment (Hall, Lounasmaa and Squire 2019). With only thirty-seven enrolled students, the course received national recognition and the Guardian University Award for widening participation in 2017. But in order to build further political resistance, it is not enough to merely continue to teach the skills to access a broken system. In March 2019, OLIve partners gathered in Budapest with other radical educators and students of diverse backgrounds to think about what the role of universities is in our current societies and how learning and pedagogy can contribute to a politics of resistance. Recurrent themes in the discussions were validating students' experiences, moving towards more inclusive and participatory practices and finding ways to resist the neoliberal tendencies to marketise education.

The Open Learning Initiative has aimed to do this by including refugee support organisations and refugee-led organisations into the planning, delivery and student support in all countries it operates in. By offering creative content alongside academic skills and topics, the programmes aim to bring a life story approach to learning and to show learners the importance of their own experiences and knowledge in the learning process. A diverse team of instructors putting the validation of student feedback and voice at the forefront follows a Freirean approach to dialogic learning, where students are invited to critique the systems that they are part of, including the systems that are providing them access and support (this is only one of many approaches used across OLIve and other refugee education initiatives to bring to the forefront the role of experts by experience; see Jasani et al., this volume, for methodological reflections on research by a group of learners). For example, post-course evaluations highlighted limitations of the programme, including lack of funds for travel. Yet overwhelmingly, students' feedback did not contradict the expectation of gratefulness which they may have felt was placed upon them (Nayeri 2019). Throughout OLIve, we believe only an open and honest conversation truly valuing students' needs can provide the radical platform for change that can help students to continue resisting the politics of hostility. This resonates with the positions of critical pedagogical theorists such as Giroux (2004), Freire (1970) and McLaren, Macrine and Hill (2010), who argue that transformative 'sites of learning' must build on the histories and struggles of excluded and marginalised groups. Such sites can serve as powerful lenses focusing on the unequal distribution of power, potentially leading to political, economic and educational impacts (Boronski and Hassan 2015: 76; for the importance of locality in the establishment of sites of learning, see Gallo et al., this volume).

While it is important to provide forced migrant students with key skills, critical pedagogies and creative practices in which the students are involved with their own learning in active ways and reflect upon their life story, identity, positionality and experience rather than only focusing on skill-building have proven particularly fruitful. Decoloniality and antiracism also become powerful and indispensable tools with which all OLIve teaching must reckon to build methodologies and curricula which support students to empower themselves. Therefore, the consortium and access programmes necessarily must keep challenging the nature of teaching and the role of universities more widely.

UEL's cross-border Calais 'Jungle' university-accredited course and the multiple universities across Europe offering OLIve programmes provide examples of critical sites of learning challenging 'bordering'. They contribute to a wider call that has gained traction in recent years around decolonising the 'ivory tower' of academia through opening traditionally privileged sites of knowledge production towards a 'plurality of perspectives, ontologies, epistemologies and methodologies in which scholarly enquiry and political praxis take place' (Bhambra, Gebreil and Nişancıoğlu 2018: 2). Aparna and Kramsch (2018: 98) argue that dialogue around decolonisation of universities must engage with concepts of debordering, presenting the 'asylum university lens' as an example and framework to resituate the university as a space that joins social activism, knowledge production and academia in mutually reinforcing and productive ways. Borne out by an initiative in the Netherlands to open universities to asylum seekers and refugees, they posit that by making spaces on and off campuses, connecting multiple border localities, creating social networks between and across groups and bringing together actors who are 'proactively responsive to transformative moments in the geopolitical landscape of our borderlands', universities can provide a space to resist and counteract powerful bordering forces (104).

Conclusion

The OLIve programmes have faced many challenges since they began in 2016. While some of these have been institutional, the main challenges have been political. The aim of the project was initially to provide access to higher education and thus enhance the social inclusion of refugees into European societies. The barriers encountered by forced migrant students who face structural oppression within the context of the neoliberal university are no doubt significant all over Europe. In the United Kingdom, some of these barriers, such as exorbitant fees and lack of financial support, are shared with students who have citizen status and are holders of marginalised identities, such as working-class, Black and ethnic minority students. These are topics that OLIve at UEL attempts to address through practical support to access financial and academic resources and spaces. While the barriers remain daunting and hard to defy, in some of these spaces, solidarity can arise and the students can be empowered to come forth with their grievances and try new practices that build towards inclusion.

The current issues in refugee education, however, are exacerbated by rising right-wing resistance to migration. The OLIve programmes continue to provide access courses in five countries despite rising animosity towards refugees and those who act in solidarity with them. These aims are in themselves political, and an act of resistance in an environment growing ever more hostile all over Europe. The conditions under which OLIve operates in the United Kingdom may not be uniquely challenging, but they are uniquely marked by Brexit. Ultimately, anti-migrant sentiments and policies have led Britain to a political standstill where leaving the European Union is seen as the only way to progress past the current political division and climate of hostility, not only against migrants but indeed between disagreeing Brits. Brexit has made the future of European collaboration uncertain and made the REIs consortium cautious about the inclusion of British partners in further projects. Restrictions on movement already impact OLIve students' opportunities in higher education as well as their private lives. When it comes to the future of freedom of movement, it is clear that those people whose rights are most precarious, such as OLIve students, stand to lose the most.

As universities struggle to comply with new anti-immigrant legislation, they simultaneously continue to operate as humanitarian institutions. The same university may be policing the immigration status of its students and staff and providing support for those caught in the immigration system. This complexity can help projects like OLIve strive in the short term, but in order to support the sustainable inclusion of refugees in Europe, a more thorough overhaul of our universities is needed.

Aura Lounasmaa is a lecturer in social sciences at the University of East London, and the director of its Erasmus+ funded Open Learning Initiative (OLIve). OLIve started at UEL in 2017 and since then has been introducing forced migrant students to the UK higher education system. Dr Lounasmaa also worked on the award-winning Life Stories course in the Calais unofficial refugee camp 'the Jungle' and co-edited a book by students of the course. Her PhD is in women's studies, and her research currently focuses on ethics and decoloniality in education and refugee studies. She is a research fellow at the Centre for Narrative Research.

Erica Masserano is a PhD researcher at the University of East London and member of the Centre for Cultural Studies and Centre for Narrative Research. Her research is based on life writing by marginalised Londoners and its relationship to their experience of place and identity, in collaboration with CityLife. Erica is a creative writing tutor on the OLIve course. She has been working as an editor and translator in journalism and multimedia for fifteen years.

Michelle Harewood is a PhD researcher at the University of East London, at the Centre for Narrative Research. Her research focuses on the experiences of migrant communities and their use of creative and cultural resources in an international development and human rights context. Michelle works as an academic tutor on the OLIve course. She has fifteen years of experience working globally in the fields of international development and human rights with non-governmental organisations.

Jessica Oddy is a PhD researcher at the University of East London, at the Centre for Refugees, Migration and Belonging. Her research focuses on displaced adolescents' experiences of education in humanitarian and resettlement contexts. Jessica works as an academic tutor on the OLIve course; she is a qualified teacher with ten years of experience.

Note

1. For a full list of universities offering Sanctuary scholarships in the UK, see https://star-network.org.uk/access-to-university/scholarships/ (accessed 21 September 2021).

References

Advance HE. n.d. 'Degree Attainment Gaps'. https://www.advance-he.ac.uk/guidance/equality-diversity-and-inclusion/student-recruitment-retention-and-attainment/degree-attainment-gaps (accessed 2 July 2020).

Advance HE. 2017 'Equality in Higher Education: Statistical Report 2017'. https://www.advance-he.ac.uk/knowledge-hub/equality-higher-education-statistical-report-2017 (accessed 2 July 2020).

Agerholm, H. 2018. 'Windrush Generation: Home Office "Set Them Up to Fail", Say MPs', *The Independent*, 3 July. https://www.independent.co.uk/news/uk/home-news/windrush-home-office-set-them-up-fail-mps-affairs-select-committee-a8428041.html (accessed 7 May 2020).

Aparna, K., and O. Kramsch. 2018. 'Asylum University: Re-situating Knowledge-Exchange along Cross-Border Positionalities', in G.K. Bhambra, K. Nişancıoğlu and D. Gebrial (eds), *Decolonizing the University: Context and Practice*. London: Pluto.

Article 26 Network and Coram Children's Legal Centre. 2016. 'Who Needs to Comply?', Article 26, Helena Kennedy Foundation. http://article26.hkf.org.uk/_/uploads/506/who_needs_to_comply_pilot_sept_2016.pdf (accessed 1 May 2020).

Bhambra, G.K., D. Gebreil and K. Nişancıoğlu. 2018. *Decolonising the University*. London: Pluto.

Boronski, T., and N. Hassan. 2015. *Sociology of Education*. London: Sage.

Bulman, A. 2019. 'Asylum Waiting Times at Record High as Thousands "Left in Limbo"', *The Independent*, 22 August. https://www.independent.co.uk/news/uk/home-news/asylum-seekers-waiting-times-home-office-immigration-a9075256.html (accessed 5 May 2020).

Candappa, M. 2019. 'Border Politics, the "Hostile Environment" for Migration, and Education in the UK', *Hungarian Educational Research Journal* 9(3). https://akjournals.com/view/journals/063/9/3/article-p414.xml (accessed 5 May 2020).

Cantat, C., E. Sevinin, E. Maczynska and T. Birey (eds). *Challenging the Political across Borders: Migrants' and Solidarity Struggles*. Budapest: Central European University. https://cps.ceu.edu/publications/books/challenging-political-across-borders-migrants-and-solidarity-struggles (accessed 17 September 2019).

Council of Europe. n.d. 'European Qualifications Passport for Refugees'. https://www.coe.int/en/web/education/recognition-of-refugees-qualifications (accessed 5 May 2020).

El-Enany, N. 2020. *Bordering Britain: Law, Race and Empire*. Manchester: Manchester University Press.

Freire, P. 1970. *Pedagogy of the Oppressed*. New York: Seabury.

Gilmartin, M., P.B. Wood and C. O'Callaghan. 2018. *Borders, Mobility and Belonging in the Era of Brexit and Trump*. Bristol: Policy.

Giroux, H.A. 2004. 'Cultural Studies, Public Pedagogy, and the Responsibility of Intellectuals', *Communication and Critical/Cultural studies* 1(1): 59–79.

Hall, T., A. Lounasmaa and C. Squire. 2019. 'From Margin to Centre? Practicing New Forms of European Politics in the Calais "Jungle"', in C. Cantat, E. Sevinin, E. Maczynska and T. Birey (eds), *Challenging the Political across Borders: Migrants' and Solidarity Struggles*. Budapest: Central European University. https://cps.ceu.edu/publications/books/challenging-political-across-borders-migrants-and-solidarity-struggles (accessed 17 September 2019).

Inglehart, R., and P. Norris. 2016. 'Trump, Brexit, and the Rise of Populism: Economic Have-Nots and Cultural Backlash', Harvard Kennedy School, Faculty Research Working Paper Series.

Ivancheva, M., K. Lynch and K. Keating. 2019. 'Precarity, Gender and Care in the Neoliberal Academy', *Gender, Work and Organization* 24(4): 448–62.

Kirkup, J. 2012. 'Theresa May Interview: We're Going to Give Illegal Migrants a Really Hostile Reception', *Daily Telegraph*, 25 May. https://www.telegraph.co.uk/news/uknews/immigration/9291483/Theresa-May-interview-Were-going-to-give-illegal-migrants-a-really-hostile-reception.html (accessed 8 May 2020).

Lounasmaa, A. 2020. 'Refugees in Neoliberal Universities', in G. Crimmins (ed.), *Strategies for Supporting Inclusion and Diversity in the Academy: Higher Education, Aspiration and Inequality*. London: Palgrave Macmillan.

Lounasmaa, A., and I. Esenowo, with OLIve students. 2019. '"Education Is Key to Life": The Importance of Education from the Perspective of Displaced Learners', *Forced Migration Review* 60: 40–43. https://www.fmreview.org/sites/fmr/files/FMRdownloads/en/education-displacement/FMR60_English_Education_2019_web_0.pdf (accessed 17 September 2019).

McLaren, P., S. Macrine and D. Hill (eds). 2010. *Revolutionizing Pedagogy: Educating for Social Justice within and beyond Global Neo-liberalism*. London: Palgrave Macmillan.

Meikle, J. 2012. 'London Metropolitan University Visa Licence Revoked: Q&A', *The Guardian*, 8 August. https://www.theguardian.com/education/2012/aug/30/london-metropolitan-university-visa-revoked (accessed 17 September 2019).

Mohdin, A., R. Adams and B. Quinn. 2020. 'Oxford College Backs Removal of Cecil Rhodes Statue', *The Guardian*, 17 June. https://www.theguardian.com/education/2020/jun/17/end-of-the-rhodes-cecil-oxford-college-ditches-controversial-statue (accessed 27 June 2020).

Murray, R. 2017. 'Reject the Exclusion of Forced Migrants from Higher Education', *OpenDemocracy*, 17 May. https://www.opendemocracy.net/en/reject-exclusion-of-forced-migrants-from-higher-education/ (accessed 17 September 2019).

Musa, A., and G. Kurawa. 2018. 'The Role of Education in the Resettlement of Internally Displaced Persons in Nigeria: An Exploratory Discourse on the Plight of the Devastated Communities in the Northeast of Nigeria', in E. Sengupta and P. Blessinger (eds), *Strategies, Policies and Directions for Refugee Education*. Bingley: Emerald.

Nava, O. 2015. *Everyday Borders* [video file]. https://vimeo.com/126315982 (accessed 5 May 2020).

Nayeri, D. 2019. *The Ungrateful Refugee*. Edinburgh: Canongate.

Sengupta, E., and P. Blessinger. 2018. *Strategies, Policies, and Directions for Refugee Education*. Bingley: Emerald.

Skjerven, S., and R. Choa, Jr. 2018. 'Refugee Education: International Perspectives from Higher Education and Non-Governmental Organisations (NGOs)', in E. Sengupta and P. Blessinger (eds), *Strategies, Policies and Directions for Refugee Education* (Innovations in Higher Education Teaching and Learning, vol. 13). Bingley: Emerald Publishing.

Smith, S. 2017. 'Exploring the Black and Minority Ethnic (BME) Student Attainment Gap: What Did It Tell Us? Actions to Address Home BME Undergraduate Students' Degree Attainment', *Journal of Perspectives in Applied Academic Practice* 5(1): 48–57.

Squire, C., and T. Zaman. 2020. 'The "Jungle" Is Here, the Jungle is Outside: University for All in the Calais Refugee Camp', in J. Bhabha, W. Giles and F. Mahomed (eds), *A Better Future: The Role of Higher Education for Displaced and Marginalized People*. Cambridge: Cambridge University Press.

Stevenson, J. 2018. 'Why Is There Still an Attainment Gap? Findings from Research and Practice', Keynote at Warwick University Education Conference, 15 May. https://warwick.ac.uk/services/od/academic-development/conference_2018/edconfkey/jacqueline_stevenson_keynote_why_is_there_still_an_attainment_gap_15_may_2018.pdf (accessed 2 July 2020).

Stevenson, J., and S. Baker. 2018. *Refugees in Higher Education: Debate, Discourse and Practice*. Bingley: Emerald.

Strand, S. 2011. 'The Limits of Social Class in Explaining Ethnic Gaps in Educational Attainment', *British Educational Research Journal* 37(2): 197–229.

Trust for London. 2020. 'London's Poverty Profile'. https://www.trustforlondon.org.uk/data/ (accessed 2 July 2020).

UK Government. 2020. 'National Statistics: How Many People Do We Grant Asylum Protection To?', https://www.gov.uk/government/publications/immigration-statistics-year-ending-march-2020/how-many-people-do-we-grant-asylum-or-protection-to (accessed 2 July 2020).

UK Home Office. 2013. 'Operation Vaken Evaluation Report'. https://assets.publishing.service.gov.uk/government/uploads/system/uploads/attachment_data/file/254411/Operation_Vaken_Evaluation_Report.pdf (accessed 7 May 2020).

UK Home Office. 2014. 'Immigration Act'. http://www.legislation.gov.uk/ukpga/2014/22/contents/enacted (accessed 7 May 2020).

UK Home Office. 2016. 'Immigration Act'. https://www.legislation.gov.uk/ukpga/2016/19/contents (accessed 21 September 2021).

UK Parliament. 2013. 'Oral Answers to Questions'. https://publications.parliament.uk/pa/cm201314/cmhansrd/cm131022/debtext/131022-0001.htm (accessed 21 September 2021).

UN. 1948. 'Universal Declaration of Human Rights'. https://www.ohchr.org/EN/UDHR/Documents/UDHR_Translations/eng.pdf (accessed 7 May 2020).

UNHCR. 2015. *Education and Protection*. Brief 1. https://www.unhcr.org/560be0dd6.pdf (accessed 9 May 2020).

UNHCR. 2016. *Missing Out: Refugee Education in Crisis*. https://www.unhcr.org/57d9d01d0 (accessed 7 May 2020).

UNHCR. 2020. 'Education'. https://www.unhcr.org/uk/education.html (accessed 9 May 2020).

University of East London. 2020. 'Key Facts and Figures'. https://issuu.com/universityofeastlondon/docs/annual_review_2020 (accessed 21 September 2021).

Walsh, P.W. 2019. *Asylum and Refugee Resettlement in the UK*, The Migration Observatory, 11 May. https://migrationobservatory.ox.ac.uk/resources/briefings/migration-to-the-uk-asylum/ (accessed 2 July 2020).

Yuval-Davis, N. 2011. *The Politics of Belonging: Intersectional Contestations*. London: Sage.
Yuval-Davis, N., G. Wemyss and K. Cassidy. 2017. 'Everyday Bordering, Belonging and the Reorientation of British Immigration', *Sociology*, 22 May.
Yuval-Davis, N., G. Wemyss and K. Cassidy. 2019. *Bordering*. Oxford: Polity Press.

AFTERWORD
Privilege, Plurality, Paradox, Prefiguration
The Challenges of 'Opening Up'

JOHN CLARKE

Reading this wonderful collection has been a demanding and thought-provoking experience. In this brief reflection, I share some of those thoughts and reflect on what's at stake in 'opening up the university'. These thoughts are organised around four themes: the university as a privileged site; the university as a plural and complex institutional formation; the paradoxical position of displaced people; and what I will call the puzzles of prefiguration. These four themes emerge at points where the themes, analyses and arguments presented here bump into my own concerns and orientations, particularly those concerned with questions of nations, states and welfare, the contested formations of citizenship and, not least, the making – and breaking – of publics. The processes and politics of displacement cut across all of these and unsettle them, most obviously by revealing their national – and nationalising – assumptions.

Each of those areas tends towards the nation as their, often unspoken, condition of possibility, and each has increasingly become the focus of nationalist and nativist politics in the last decade, particularly (though not only) across the Global North. Such politics, as many contributions here make clear, have had consequences for universities and for their attempts to engage in offering education for displaced persons as refugees, migrants, asylum seekers and more. In this piece, I follow the editors in referring to 'displaced people' rather than the various juridical and quasi-juridical categories of asylum seekers, migrants and refugees. While those categories certainly have consequences (if not necessarily those originally intended), they tend to split and conceal the common dynamics of displacement: people being brought into motion by a variety of conditions (economic, political, social, military, climatological – and often more than one). Given that these conditions are unlikely to reduce or disappear in the near future, perhaps this is the time to move beyond the short termism of what Gallo, Poggio and Bodio (this volume) call the 'everlasting emergency' and start to remake the university and its borders. Given the focus of this book, let me begin with the entangled relationship between the university and privilege.

The University as a Privileged Site

The University is, as Cook's chapter argues, a setting for the production and exploitation of a certain form of privilege – prestige. It is able to function in that way because it has long been a site of social privilege, as is made clear in Cantat's chapter on access to the university. This institutionalisation of social privilege has worked in several ways, beginning with the relatively strong institutional boundaries between the university and the wider society, grounded in the claim to produce and distribute valued knowledge. Those boundaries have manifested themselves in various ways, most obviously in the claim for 'academic freedom' in the pursuit of knowledge (Ivancheva, this volume), but also in the longer history of the university as a (largely) self-governing community – a community of scholars. This institutional separation delivers what the French Marxist philosopher Louis Althusser once called 'relative autonomy' (1969). Althusser was, of course, referring to the 'relative autonomy' of the other instances of a social formation (the 'superstructures') from the economic base as a way of dealing with questions of determination. But the term might also be used as a way of thinking about the 'relative autonomy' of the university from the wider social formation and, indeed, the demands of the (nation-) state. I think it's useful because the concept quickly takes us to more empirical questions about the degree of relative autonomy (just how relative is this autonomy?) and its conditions and limits. But for this approach to make sense, there is another move to be made – a shift from talking about The University (as a singular and abstract concept) to universities in the plural, while recognising the symbolic prestige and privilege that the idea of The University brings with it. The idea(l) of the University has been materialised in different forms in different places and times and is subjected to different forces in those contexts. Several of the chapters in this book, as well as the editors' introduction, make this context-specific institutional formation of universities clear. Here I want to draw attention to the contradictory implications of the relative autonomy of universities. It makes them a space of possibility, innovation and experiment – both in general terms and in the specific form of experimenting with education for displaced people. As the chapters by Aparna et al. and Lounasmaa et al., as well as the OLIve initiative that created the springboard for these conversations, make clear, universities offer spaces for creative innovation and contain people who are willing to engage in – and fight for – those innovations and for the resources necessary to make them happen. I will come back to some of the (changing) contingency of those possibilities later, but it is important to celebrate even the cramped, confined and straitened spaces of innovation that universities have held open. Universities are not alone: civil society organisations of many kinds have also worked with displaced people to help with their transitions and to resist their marginalisation and exclusion, but universities offer one variety of privileged space that, contingently, makes possible routes to access weaker forms of privilege and prestige, not least in certification and routes to further study. In this dynamic, it is worth thinking beyond the binary distinction between inclusion and exclusion and injecting a third term: the varieties of subordinated inclusion that states and social formations make available (see also the idea of 'differential inclusion' developed by Mezzadra and Neilson [2013] and its use by Segrave [2019]). Sometimes, these positions are referred to as being 'second-class citizens'; at others, they are marked by a more marginal and liminal presence: tolerated but not accepted (temporary residents, migrant workers and so on), present but disdained or despised for not being 'really' British/Italian/French/European.

Nonetheless, the relative autonomy of universities needs to be understood as a changing condition, such that when we talk of 'opening up the university' we have to recognise the ways in which universities have been – and are being – reshaped in ways intended to constrain and discipline aspects of that relative autonomy. At the core of these changes has been a growing desire to 'instrumentalise' the university, to find ways of making its privilege add value to a range of economic, political and social projects. From the creation of a global higher education market to the systems of 'workload management' for individual academics, a whole variety of reforms have been put into play as ways of 'modernising' the university (discussed more extensively in Clarke 2010). We might include the systems of comparison, competition and ranking that now produce – and valorise – university reputations nationally and internationally. Then there are the expectations that universities will be producers of 'useful' knowledge, rather than knowledge in general: such useful knowledge should be developed in the service of economic advantage and the greater success of The Nation plc. Indeed, the globalisation of higher education coincides precisely with the drive to nationalise universities, articulating them to national systems of control (e.g. research and teaching evaluations, new financing systems and calls for 'accountability'); to imagined national futures (building a 'knowledge society' and so on) and to nation-building projects. Meanwhile, universities are expected to produce 'subjects of value' as employable material and, as Rajaram's chapter reminds us, as properly socialised 'active' (rather than activist) citizens both within nations and in the European Union space. It is certainly true that the forces and demands bearing on universities vary from place to place. Hungary's view of both what can be taught and what sorts of institutions may award degrees is not the same as England's installation of the mindset and tools of the New Public Management (or new managerialism) across the world of higher education. But both reflect the desires of governments to constrain the autonomy of universities and to subject them to nationalising forms of discipline. The drive towards instrumentalisation (and the narrowed concept of value that underpins this drive) coincides painfully with the rise of nationalist politics in the Global North (and elsewhere, for example in the effects of Hindu nationalism on Indian universities or in Safta-Zecheria's discussion of the attack on universities in Turkey in this volume). As the Central European University (CEU) found, this shift towards nationalism and nativism takes a dim view of universities spending scarce resources on 'outsiders' of different kinds (with the exception of value-bearing 'international students', of course).

As a result, the idea of the University as a privileged space operates in increasing tension with the current imperatives that seek to both constrain and instrumentalise the production and distribution of knowledge. That tension is experienced across the range of activities that universities engage in, especially in times of fiscal austerity, and comes to bear particularly on those activities of low symbolic and material value, most visibly in education for displaced people. Nonetheless, those activities may, at times, intersect with different imperatives that universities are, sometimes and contradictorily, expected to acknowledge and address, notably in the pressures to 'widen access' in the pursuit of a more equitable society, or at least (more instrumentally) in creating a critical mass to be counted as a 'knowledge society'. But it is precisely this sense of contradictory pressures that points to the complex institutional formation of universities.

The Plurality of the University: What Needs to 'Open Up'?

The image of 'opening up' the university is a compelling one (especially for someone who spent most of his working life at the UK's Open University). But that same experience makes me attentive to the puzzles and problems of opening, as well as their importance. The Open University's open-ness largely rested on a passive liberal understanding of being open to anyone who might want to study. This sense of openness overcame some blockages (entry requirements, evaluation interviews and the criteria – visible and invisible – that tend to govern entry to university education). But it had little to say about less obvious dynamics of culture, of hidden (as well as visible) curricula, the economic and emotional costs of studying at a distance and more. Later, widening participation programmes struggled with some of these, driven by concerns about classed and racialised imbalances of application and retention. 'Access' to university education covers many different types and practices of inclusion and exclusion, from formalised entry requirements that assume membership of a common – national – culture to the more literal sense of entering the physical space of the university. As a critical story in Aparna et al.'s chapter here reminds us, universities are spaces of privileged access, regulated by security systems and security personnel. My nominally 'Open' university implemented a system of entry to its buildings, governed by swipe cards, and I remember the collective embarrassment that accompanied our hosting of a conference of the Oecumene[1] (Citizenship After Orientalism) project. All visitors had to move between sessions, refreshments and even toilets accompanied by a person with an OU card to ensure they could get access to what was to happen next. Sites of privileges protect their privileges in multiple ways, as projects to widen access or participation have recurrently discovered (see also Cantat, this volume).

As the editors have made clear, one key part of the challenge of 'opening up' the university involves the structures and systems of knowledge itself. Epistemologically exclusive, offering a world of knowledge framed and structured by a Western, colonial and patriarchal conception of what is to be known and what it means to know, the university produces and circulates a strangely ossified and commodified version of knowledge to which its Others are expected to be grateful to be allowed 'access'. Without ever needing to say so, the knowledges framed in this way carry with them a hierarchy of bodies and ways of knowing that remains profoundly differentiating and disempowering. Challenging these ways of knowing and the curricula in which they are enacted in the name of 'decolonising the university' (Bhambra, Gebreil and Nişancıoğlu 2018) has become an important and recurring site of conflict both for the excluded and for the rising nationalist right (committed to defending the national or European way of knowing as history's natural end point). This privileged institutionalisation of knowledge extends to both the practices of knowledge creation (and the celebration of the heroic lone scholar) and to the disciplinary – and disciplining – ordering of the world into relatively closed academic compartments. As the chapters by Blell et al. and Jasani et al. in this volume have indicated, such knowledge framings tend to exclude both other ways of knowing and other desires for knowledge that do not fit with this ordering.

These framings of knowledge and the canonical systems that they deliver merge almost imperceptibly into questions of pedagogy. Pedagogy remains largely framed by questions of transmission: the processes by which those who know things transmit what they know to those who do not know, but desire access to the knowledge. The architecture, apparatuses and technologies of teaching remain inextricably linked to this model of educating people – and the lecture remains the model device for transmission (whether in person or online). A colleague in a university moving to online teaching as a response to Covid-19 told me that the 'support' for his move to online teaching included a virtual backdrop that would make it look as though he was speaking in a lecture theatre. This dominant conception of pedagogy has been challenged, not least by those working in marginal and innovative settings with what are sometimes called 'non-conventional students' (including the 'disadvantaged' and displaced persons). Diverse pedagogic innovations have tried to displace the 'transmission' model of learning, offering more collaborative, exploratory and dialogic relationships and practices, often challenging the finished or over-solidified conceptions of knowledge that underpin the transmission line. Nevertheless, student-centred learning, student-driven learning and collaborative learning practices remain emergent alternatives, rather than the dominant educational processes.

These, however, are the visible dimensions of the university as a social institution. There are also the less visible elements of the arrangement of people, places and power that bear upon the challenge of opening. Some of these, as Rachel Burke's chapter demonstrates, involve questions of language (the formal languages of university conduct and the languages of sociality) which tend to reproduce normative national (and indeed international) assumptions about how universities work, and on whom. Language conditions 'access' in many ways, enabling or denying entry and engagement. Then there are the ways in which universities act as organisations: as the editors make clear in their introduction, universities function as rule-bound bureaucracies, as more or less adaptive organisational cultures, and as systems of habits and expectations. Bureaucratic rules and categories govern entry to the university and progress within it: they announce roles, norms and the expectations that universities have of 'the student' (usually a singular and monocultural figure). Those expectations are translated into practice within departments, units and teams who may bend or flex them in unpredictable ways (sometimes in a spirit of generosity, at other times in excluding and oppressive ways). All bureaucratic organisations (which certainly includes universities, however much they may try to imagine themselves otherwise) also create the spaces and possibilities of what Lipsky (1982) called 'street level bureaucrats' decision-making. Academic and administrative staff in universities may think themselves above street level, but they operate in the messy decision-making spaces created by university regulations and managerial imperatives. As Humphris's study (2019) of Romanian migrants to the UK has shown, critical decisions (about forms of welfare and citizenship) are increasingly negotiated in the interactions between migrants and front-line workers, and are significantly shaped by the moral, political and social judgements of those workers. In the process, relationships of both conflict and collusion, desire and dependency are surprisingly central to apparently 'rational' bureaucratic order.

These issues lead in two rather different directions. On one side, they underscore the complexities of 'opening up the university' because the university is not a coherent and singular entity that requires only one type of can opener. On the other, the diversity of sites for possible contestation also multiplies the potential alliances that might be formed in pursuing the challenge of opening universities. Existing struggles – to decolonise the university; to challenge oppressive and discriminatory behaviours; to change standpoints; to challenge academic and student precarity, debt and more – create potential intersections and possible allies committed to transforming the university in progressive ways and to resisting the pressures that seek to enclose them.

The Paradoxical Place of Displaced People

As Aparna et al. (this volume) suggest, displaced people occupy a paradoxical place in the value regime of universities, being both desired and despised. As research subjects, their stories may be of value (see also Glanville, this volume, on the humanitarian ethnographic gaze). By virtue of occupying liminal positions in the inter-state system of nationalised identities, migrants, refugees and others can speak to the effects and experiences of displacement. In contrast, they are of little or no value to the educational calculus of universities. They are not fee-bearing 'national' students who add value to departmental and university budgets. Nor are they the 'super' fee-bearing international students so avidly desired and recruited by universities of the Global North (as manifested in the proliferation of recruiting shop fronts opened by European and North American universities in southern and eastern states). Displaced people, in this calculus, are precisely the wrong sort of international: they incur economic, organisational and social costs rather than being 'subjects of value'.

Nevertheless, they may sometimes carry value with them. For example, they may enable universities to add reputational value (see Cantat, this volume). Those universities offering educational provision for displaced people may discover symbolic value in being able to present themselves as liberal, humanitarian and internationalist. Such symbolic value may add lustre to their reputation among current or potential students, although as CEU discovered it may also attract the attention of nationalist and nationalising governments. In such circumstances, providing education for displaced people can bring economic, symbolic and political costs. Either way, the paradoxes of displaced people as students remind us of the profoundly national framing of (educational) citizenship. Discussions of access to education (of all sorts) typically take the nation as the framing scale and spatiality, occasionally interrupted by regional innovations (as in the EU's commitment to cross-national possibilities of study and the promotion of European values). This is the long history of citizenship as an identity formed and lodged in the nation-state, rather than an effect of recent nationalist political movements. But such movements have recurrently framed welfare questions (including access to education) in terms of the costs to 'our people' who are imagined as being deprived of their birth right by 'in-comers' who have earned no 'entitlements'.

This paradoxical status means that projects providing education to displaced persons have a potentially contradictory relationship with other educational innovations aimed at 'widening access'. They share many political, philosophical and pedagogical orientations, given that they are working – literally and metaphorically – on the borders of university institutions. They stretch the conception of 'the student' by seeking to enrol 'non-traditional' demographics from the 'under-represented' or 'hard to reach' groups and often share a conception of 'opening up the university' in diverse ways. Many of the pedagogical initiatives derive from shared understandings of the failings and limitations of mainstream educational policies and practices – and the name of Freire occurs regularly across such initiatives.[2] However, the drive to widen access in the UK has remained largely framed by the national conception of citizenship and rights of access. While such projects certainly aim to broaden access for marginalised or excluded groups, these are typically groups within the nation, rather than in the liminal space at the nation's edge: for example, drives to get women into subjects dominated by men (e.g. Women into Science and Engineering); the construction of non-standard entry routes to those lacking formal qualifications (such as adding a preparatory year in adjunct institutions); or the attempt to enrol increased numbers of working-class or minority students to elite universities. Even if the 'target' groups for widening access projects do not match the imagined and preferred national citizen, especially being members of minoritised ethnic groups (for example, what official discourse in the UK now refers to through the uncomfortable acronym of BAME communities – Black, Asian and Minority Ethnic), they are nonetheless citizens who are deemed worthy of being promoted from second-class to first-class citizens in educational terms. Of course, these are not stable differentiations, as the pursuit of 'hostile environments' by successive UK governments over the last decade has demonstrated (Gentleman 2019). In those policies, settled Black and Asian people with UK citizenship were nonetheless pursued, harassed and even deported under the assumption that they were not 'legitimate' rights-bearing citizen-subjects. Such bordering practices create shifting categorisations of membership.

In these atmospheres of intensified hostility and suspicion, displaced people become the focus of governmental scrutiny and concern, to the extent that organisations (whether universities or civil society groups) find themselves exposed to extra scrutiny and run the risk of making those with whom they work visible in new ways. In the UK, the combination of the 'hostile environment' and the Prevent scheme (aimed at identifying potential radicals en route to terrorism) have applied extra demands on universities to monitor both the status and the attitudes of 'suspicious' people. This enrolment of universities into what Yuval-Davis, Wemyss and Cassidy (2017, 2019) have called 'everyday bordering' (away from the nominal borders) exemplifies the drive towards abjection – the constant suspicion of and threat towards the person deemed to be 'out of place'.

The Puzzles of Prefiguration

As Cantat (this volume) demonstrates, experiments in education for displaced people take place in the margins of universities. Indeed, the margins are the usual space for experimentation and innovation – a location that has some benefits, such as weaker systems of scrutiny, management and regulation to offset against the many downsides of marginality (ranging from chronic underfunding to precarious status, for both projects and those who work on them). Marginal spaces, both in universities and the wider social formations in which they are embedded, are seed beds for future-oriented projects, including what some feminist scholars have called 'prefigurative' practices. In these comments, I borrow from the work of legal scholar Davina Cooper (2017, 2020; and Cooper, Dhawan and Newman 2019) who has explored questions of everyday utopias, the dynamics of reimagining social and political arrangements and ways in which prefigurative practices may create the possibilities of institutional and social transformation. One specific focus of Cooper's interest is a form of prefiguration oriented around the principle of acting 'as if' the desired conditions already prevailed:

> Unlike prefigurative registers which explicitly foreground the relationship between means and ends, here the effectiveness of what is done (or the worldmaking it is part of) may depend on obscuring its 'as if' character. Yet, the 'as if' is important. When overtly aligned with play, it allows actions to happen – crowd-sourcing a people's constitution, for example – that might otherwise struggle for lack of official propriety and formal legitimacy. More generally, acting 'as if' gives political action a boost. This is partly because innovative, utopian or provocative actions happen despite lacking the institutional conditions they seem to require. But it is also because actions reimagine their conditions of possibility, and act as if they were already there. Prefigurative action entails a significant reimagining of the environment in which action is set so that a social, scientific, ethical and political 'otherwise' justifies, validates, normalizes and holds up the actions undertaken. (2020: 896–97)

Education for displaced people can, of course, sometimes be a functional translation of existing educational forms and pedagogical practices to a new target audience – the migrant, the refugee, the asylum seeker. More often, however, it tends to be prefigurative in one or more ways. It may treat displaced people as if they are already citizens (whether citizens as bearers of rights or members of an egalitarian political community). It may be prefigurative in terms of pedagogy and the relationships through which knowledges are created and shared, breaking hierarchical norms and forms. It may also, as the editors of this collection indicate, be prefigurative of new institutional forms and relationships of the university in wider terms, creating different conceptions of the 'academic community', its internal ordering and relationship to its wider social and political conditions. Enacting new ways of being and being with (or accompaniment; see Watkins 2019, for example), new forms of conduct, new pedagogic practices, new epistemologies and practices of knowledge production and sharing, even new institutional and architectural forms of 'The University' that challenge extant conceptions of the Ivory Tower, the Knowledge Factory, or massified and instrumentalised education: all of these might prefigure the wider transformations at stake in 'opening up the university'.

As Cooper and others recognise clearly, prefigurative practices carry no guarantee that they will deliver the desired outcomes (much like every other form of political investment, perhaps). Such risks are integral to prefigurative politics and are similarly embedded in the dilemmas of working at the margins of institutionalised systems. Cooper describes institutions in terms that I recognise, pointing especially to their contradictory character as structures of domination and possibility, and as both contingent and contestable:

> Adopting an expansive account of institutions, to take in more than rules (including the tacit 'rules of the game'), I approach institutions as durable, patterned processes and formations, tying together rules, procedures, norms, systems, knowledges, temporalities, spaces, things, moralities and people in ways that are meaningful, forceful and with effects. This does not mean institutions are stable or monolithic ... They evolve and change; are plural, heterogeneous, and contradictory; and can be counter-cultural and hybrid as work on critical institutionalism also explores ... Yet, despite their variation and contingency, institutions remain important to the extent that patterns, routines and processes – established and recognised by dominant forces, and giving rise to unequal effects – exist. Indeed, it is this very existence which stimulates and provides a target for critical (as well as more hopeful) political engagement. (2020: 894)

Although not the focus of Cooper's analysis, it is important, as I suggested above, that institutions have margins: less tightly governed spaces in which both innovation and 'leakages' between inside and outside can take place (the idea of a 'leaky' institutional system or nexus borrows from Enzensberger 1970). The margins form a space of possibility but also encompass characteristic dilemmas for those seeking to build on experiments to create transformative possibilities. In some respects, these centre on questions of scale – and the implications of 'scaling up' innovative projects or, to borrow a different framing, the demands of 'mainstreaming'.

Such transitions are typically framed by the pessimistic concept of incorporation: radical projects have their radicalism defused, they become assimilated into dominant ways of thinking and being; or they are at risk of being 'bought off' and 'bought in' (the financial imagery is not accidental). Drawing on a study of how feminist activists negotiated 'spaces of power', moving between activism and government, Newman (2012) has suggested that this view of incorporation or co-option misunderstands the shifting and dynamic nature of power and opposition. While recognising that 'neoliberal inclined governments tend to seize on such interventions and bend them to their own purposes', Newman nonetheless argues that:

> Rather than a singular narrative, of a post-political world heralded by the triumph of neoliberalism, this points to the need (political as well as theoretical) to understand the simultaneous dynamics of retreat and proliferation, creativity and constraint, activism and incorporation. (2013: 528)

Borrowing from a different conceptual vocabulary, I am tempted to argue that our inherited concepts of incorporation and co-option are strikingly undialectical. They treat political outcomes as fixed in one decisive moment in which domination is once again secured rather than as part of an ongoing 'war of position' (Gramsci 1971). Gramsci's idea of a war of position addressed the constant – and shifting – struggle for cultural domination and hegemony in which the state and the apparatuses of civil society (including, of course, educational institutions) formed the terrain of conflict. (This idea is interestingly explored in a study by Peter Mayo [2005] of an adult education project in Malta.) A more dialectical understanding of these processes would consider the ways in which dominant ideas – and resources – may be borrowed, bent and redeployed for alternative purposes, framed by an understanding that the meanings of ideas and practices are never permanently fixed but are always contingently open to contestation.

Despite their current structures of domination, marginalisation and exclusion, the three domains that the editors introduced at the beginning of this volume – the university, the wider social formation and the state – are also contradictory and contested fields. Displaced people are the products of those fraught dynamics and, from time to time, become the object of efforts to 'include' them into other places (as well as the more visible efforts to exclude them). Such inclusion is, needless to say, not unconditional: it is hedged around by doubts, disciplinary practices and systemic marginalisation. But it is these spaces of possibility – however confined and contradictory – that this book has explored in a commitment to understanding the ways in which both displacement and education for displaced people matters. At their core, such innovations point us towards the twin project of 'democratic education' and 'education for democracy'.

◆

John Clarke is an Emeritus Professor of Social Policy at the UK's Open University. He currently holds a Leverhulme Emeritus Fellowship concerned with work on the turbulent times marked by the rise of nationalist, populist and authoritarian politics. Recent publications include *Making Policy Move: Towards a Politics of Translation and Assemblage* (with Dave Bainton, Noémi Lendvai and Paul Stubbs; Policy Press, 2015) and *Critical Dialogues: Thinking Together in Turbulent Times*, based on a series of conversations with people who have helped him to think (Policy Press, 2019).

Notes

1. http://www.oecumene.eu.
2. Paulo Freire's work has remained a constant source of inspiration for educationalists across many settings (not just universities). His commitment to – and modelling of – anti-oppressive practice remains a key reference point not only for education but for workers across a range of public services, including social work (see, e.g., Freire 1996).

References

Althusser, L. 1969. 'Contradiction and Overdetermination', in *For Marx*, trans. Ben Brewster. New York: Random House, pp. 87–128.
Bhambra, G.K., D. Gebreil and K. Nişancıoğlu. 2018. *Decolonising the University*. London: Pluto Press.
Clarke, J. 2010. '"So Many Strategies, So Little Time. . .": Making Universities Modern', *Learning and Teaching* [LATISS] 3(3): 91–116.

Cooper, D. 2017. 'Prefiguring the State', *Antipode* 49(2): 335–56.
Cooper, D. 2020. 'Towards an Adventurous Institutional Politics: The Prefigurative "as if" and the Reposing of What's Real', *The Sociological Review* 68(5): 893–916.
Cooper, D., N. Dhawan and J. Newman (eds). 2019. *Reimagining the State: Theoretical Challenges and Transformative Possibilities*. London: Routledge.
Enzensberger, H.M. 1970. 'Constituents of a Theory of the Media', *New Left Review* 64: 13–36.
Freire, P. 1996. *Pedagogy of the Oppressed*, rev. edn. New York: Continuum.
Gentleman, A. 2019. *The Windrush Betrayal: Exposing the Hostile Environment*. London: Guardian Faber Publishing.
Gramsci, A. 1971. *Selections from the Prison Notebooks*. London: Lawrence and Wishart.
Humphris, R. 2019. *Home-Land: Romanian Roma, Domestic Spaces and the State*. Bristol: Bristol University Press.
Lipsky, M. 1982. *Street-Level Bureaucracy: Dilemmas of the Individual in Public Services*. New York: Russell Sage Foundation.
Mayo, P. 2005. '"In and against the State": Gramsci, War of Position, and Adult Education', *Journal for Critical Education Policy Studies* 3(2): 65–90. http://www.jceps.com/wp-content/uploads/PDFs/03-2-03.pdf (accessed 11 October 2020).
Mezzadra, S. and B. Neilson. 2013. *Border as Method: Or, the Multiplication of Labor*. Durham, NC: Duke University Press.
Newman, J. 2012. *Working the Spaces of Power: Activism, Neoliberalism and Gendered Labour*. London: Bloomsbury Academic.
Newman, J. 2013. 'Performing New Worlds? Policy, Politics and Creative Labour in Hard Times', *Policy & Politics* 41(4): 515–32.
Segrave, M. 2019. 'Theorizing Sites and Strategies of Differential Inclusion: Unlawful Migrant Workers in Australia', *Theoretical Criminology* 23(2): 194–210.
Watkins, M. 2019. *Mutual Accompaniment and the Creation of the Commons*. New Haven, CT: Yale University Press.
Yuval-Davis, N., G. Wemyss and K. Cassidy. 2017. 'Everyday Bordering, Belonging and the Reorientation of British Immigration', *Sociology* 52(2): 228–44.
Yuval-Davis, N., G. Wemyss and K. Cassidy. 2019. *Bordering*. Oxford: Polity Press.

Index

academia
　competition within, 97
　and nationalism, 6
　prestige in, 209, 212. *See also* prestige
　working conditions in, 82
academic freedom, 78, 82, 83-84, 85, 294
　and casualisation, 57-58
　and Cordoba Reform, 63
　and digitalisation, 57-58
　history of concept, 52-54
　and il/liberal regimes, 51-52, 54, 63-4
　and marketisation, 56-59
　and no platforming, 54
　and open access, 59
　and progressive reform, 60-1
　and research/teaching evaluation, 58
　and state/market divide, 54, 63-4
　and student debt/fees, 57-58
academics
　criminalisation of, 78, 80, 83
　displacement of, 79, 80
　labour, 103, 213
　precarisation of, 78, 79, 81, 83
　reserve army of, 82
　at risk, 85
　solidarity with and between, 78, 84-86
　transnational labour market, 80, 82
　transnational mobility of, 78
　transnational support networks and, 82, 85
access programmes at universities, 91, 106
　foundation programme, 112, 113
　institutionalisation of, 103-106
　taster courses, 118-120
access to university, 91-95, 97, 106, 300-301
　equity and access to, 95, 98-99, 296
　merit and access to, 92, 97, 99
　social hierarchies and, 89, 97, 98
　women and, 92-93, 96
activism, 125
　research as, 127
antiracism, 286
Asylum Procedures Directive (APD), 39-40
Australia, 164-175
Australian Migrant English Program (AMEP), 166-175

Birkbeck College, 120
Bolzano, 248
　everyday bordering, 253, 277-279, 281-287, 301-2
borders, 14, 32-33, 35-41, 43, 46-47, 145, 249. *See also under* universities
bordering, 33, 47, 275, 301
Bristol, UK, 111-122
Bristol, University of, 111-122
Bristol Refugee Rights, 113

capability approach, 181
capital
　forms of, 212-213
　linguistic, 221, 223, 234, 235
Central European University (CEU), 4, 22, 102-103, 192, 202, 242, 244, 296, 300
change laboratory methodology, 183, 184, 186, 187, 188
citizenship, 41-48, 94, 178-179, 181-186, 188, 249-251, 297, 300, 301, 303
　active citizen, 31-32, 34-35, 42-43
code switching, 224
colonialism, 1, 15, 38, 40, 55, 64, 93-95, 142, 235, 247, 251, 279, 297

community education, 138–139
contestation, 300
culture
  consumer culture, 146, 150
  cultural refugee studies, 141
  refugee cultures, 141, 144–245, 151
curriculum design, 111–122

decolonial, 12, 60, 85, 104, 286
decolonising the university, 12, 286, 298
desegregation, 98
digital
  barrier, 157
  exclusion, 156–159, 162
  literacy, 156–163, 228; social inclusion and, 156–158, 160
  skills, 157, 160
Dutton, Peter, 172

early-career researchers, 79, 80
English language teaching, 164–174
ethnography, 143
  autoethnography, 248
  'imaginative humanitarian ethnography', 139, 140–141, 144–146
  peer ethnography, 127, 135
  problems with reading refugee story as ethnography, 144; countering it, 146–147, 150–151, 152
European Forum for Enhanced Collaboration in Teaching (EFFECT), 178, 179, 182, 183, 184, 186, 188
European values, 32–33, 35–37, 42–44, 46–47

film
  documentary film, 198, 202, 204
  participatory video workshop, 192–206
Freire, Paolo, 12–13, 125, 285, 301, 305
Frontex, 35, 38–40, 48

Gordimer, Nadine, 142

habitus, 211
higher education policy, 41–47

hooks, bell, 98, 125
hostile environment. *See under* United Kingdom
humanitarianism, 105, 139, 141, 142, 145–146
Hungary, 22, 47, 78–79, 84–85, 241–242, 244–245, 248, 296

inclusion, 295, 297, 301
  subordinated inclusion, 295
incorporation, 304
innovation, 295, 304
integration (of migrants and refugees), 2, 31–33, 35–37, 41–47, 166, 171–2, 227, 229, 230, 235, 244–245, 261
intersectional, 3, 4, 11–13, 20, 89, 96, 101, 103, 104, 106, 112, 127, 281
Iran, 171, 175
Iraq, 170, 175

Kleve, 248
knowledge production, 5, 10, 18, 37, 62, 78, 83, 94, 106, 248, 250–251, 257, 286, 296, 303
  collectively meaningful, 79, 84–86
  co-production, 116–117, 126, 134–135
  democratic, 85–86
knowledge society, 296
knowledge structures and systems, 297

language, 298–9
  language support, 220, 229, 230, 231, 234
liminal positions, 300, 301
literacy
  academic literacy(ies), 220, 222, 223, 225, 229, 230, 231
  literate, 220, 221, 223, 225, 231, 232, 235
  non-literate, 224
  pre-literate, 224
  print literacy, 224, 225, 226, 233
  semi-literate, 224, 225
  See also oracy
locality, 261, 263–64
Lorde, Audre, 125, 135

managerialism, 296
Manchester, UK, 127
marginalisation, 305
margins, 303–4
marketisation of higher education
  of research, 56–57
  of teaching, 57–58
  of service, 59
media representation, 194, 196, 204
mistrust (of refugees), 164
multi-level governance, 261–263, 268–269

nation, 7, 36, 95, 106, 145, 260, 293–294, 296, 300, 301
nation-state. *See* nation
nationalising, 293
Nationalist, 34, 293, 294, 296, 298, 300
Nijmegen, 248
Nussbaum, Martha, 181

Open Learning Initiative (OLIve), 4, 16, 21, 90, 102–103, 157–159, 161–163, 192–206, 240–246, 277–278, 280–287, 295
Open University, 120
oracy, 225, 226, 233
  oral language, 224, 225, 226
Orientalism, 81

paradox, 299–300
pedagogy, 298
  alternative pedagogies, 82
  assessment practices, 223, 227, 228, 233
  critical pedagogy, 138, 150–152, 189
  drama pedagogy, 197, 201, 203, 204
  inclusion and, 178–186, 188
  language support, 220, 229, 230, 231, 234
  learning support(s), 229, 231, 233
  participatory video workshop, 192–206
  staff development and, 178–184, 186–189
positionality, 89, 96, 101, 103, 104, 106
postcolonial, 11, 13, 54, 235, 255
plurality, 297

prefiguration, 302–3
prestige, 105, 209, 211, 295
  prestige economy, 212–213
  prestige structure, 211, 216–218
privilege, 294, 297
privileged site, 294
public university models
  Anglo-American research-intensive, 53
  Bolivarian University of Venezuela, 60–62
  Humboldtian, 52
  Latin American, 53, 61
  Napoleonian, 53
  neoliberal, 56–59
  UK mass university, 55
  Venezuelan Autonomous University, 61–62

racism, 31, 94, 202, 257, 279–280
  institutional, 118, 276
  See also antiracism
reading communities, 140, 147, 152
refugee, concept of, 1–2
refugee students, 2
  and access to university, 23, 46, 69, 70, 72–74, 170–173, 240–246
  and emotional and psychological challenges, 243, 244
  visibility of, 266, 268
  women, 127
Refugee Women of Bristol, 113
relative autonomy, 294
reputation, 295

Scholars at Risk, 81
self-advocacy, 125
Sen, Amartya, 181
Sjahrir, Soetan, 248
social hierarchies, 89, 97, 98
solidarity academies, 82–83
Spivak, Gayatri Chakravorty, 111
story
  as gift, 140, 147–149, 150
  Jo-Ann Archibald's 'storywork', 138, 148
  as listening, 149–150
  as relational responsibility, 140, 150

street level bureaucrats, 299
student movements, 61–62
subjects of value, 300
symbolic anthropology, 211–212
Syria, 170, 175

teaching
  enhancement, 179, 180, 183, 186, 188
  unconscious bias in, 185, 187, 188
  See also pedagogy
third mission, 74, 75
translanguaging, 232
Turkey, 78–86
  petition crisis in, 79–82

unconscious bias, 185, 187, 188
United Kingdom, 52, 55–59
  hostile environment, 275–278, 285, 301
universities
  access to (see access programmes)
  audit culture, 213–214
  autonomy of, 264–265
  borders of, 5–7
  embeddedness in society, 262, 264, 270–271
  ideologies and, 91, 93
  inclusion in, 91–95
  marketisation (see marketisation of higher education)
  massification of, 96
  nationalisation of, 6–7, 95–96
  nation-state and, 95, 99
  neoliberalism and, 86
  opening up, 2–5, 10, 14–15, 24–25, 90–91, 93, 95–96, 98–100, 104–105, 126, 210, 218, 262–263, 270–272, 286, 297, 301
  rankings of, 213–214
  religion and, 91
  state sovereignty and, 91, 95, 99
  See also public university models

Venezuela, 52, 60–62
voice, 166, 170, 171, 173, 174, 240–246
vulnerabilised groups, 79, 83, 85
vulnerability, 81

war of position, 304